Consumer Insurance Law

Disclosure, Representations and Basis of the Contract Clauses

Consumer Insurance Law

Disclosure, Representations and Basis of the Contract Clauses

General Editor

Peter J Tyldesley
Lecturer in Insurance Law
University of Manchester

Bloomsbury Professional

Bloomsbury Professional Ltd, Maxwelton House, 41–43 Boltro Road, Haywards Heath, West Sussex, RH16 1BJ

With thanks to Susan Tyldesley, Saira Paruk of Quadrant Chambers, Raif Howe, Laura Giachardi of 1 Gray's Inn Square and Theodore Rifat for commenting on an initial draft of this work.

A CIP Catalogue record for this book is available from the British Library.

ISBN: 978 1 84766 918 6

Typeset by Kerrypress Ltd, Luton, Beds

Printed and bound in Great Britain by CPI Group (UK) Ltd, Croydon, CR0 4YY

Foreword

There is an assumption that significant reforms require complex legislation and lengthy debate. Having spent many hours on the line by line scrutiny of the Financial Services Act 2013, I know that this can be the case. But I also know that far-reaching reforms can also be achieved in the blink of a parliamentary eye. This was certainly the case for the Consumer Insurance (Disclosure and Representations) Act which glided effortlessly through Parliament.

It is a testament to the work of the Law Commissions and all those who collaborated on the bill that such a long-needed and far-reaching reform could be achieved without controversy and with so much agreement.

This is a tribute to the painstaking way in which the Law Commissions built a consensus not just on the need for reform but also for the reforms themselves.

It has long been recognised that the law around disclosure of information to insurers needed change. Laws dating back over a century, designed for commercial insurance contracts, were the legal basis for rules of disclosure by consumers. Some claims were being turned down on the grounds that policyholders had not disclosed all information even if it was not relevant to the actual claim made. Whilst custom in the insurance market had evolved, policyholders were in fact relying on the goodwill of insurers to honour claims when incomplete information had been provided when the policy was taken out. It was time for the law to catch up with custom and practice. The process led by the Law Commissions and assisted by lawyers, academics, consumer groups and the industry culminated in the Consumer Insurance (Disclosure and Representations) Act.

I believe the Act strengthens consumer protection and safeguards the credibility of the insurance sector. Denying claims on the basis of legislation that was past its sell-by date undermined confidence in insurance to the detriment of consumers and insurers alike.

I was pleased to be able to play my part in putting these measures into law, but I know that credit for this legislation rightly belongs to others, many of whom have contributed to this book, and it is to them that policyholders should be grateful.

Mark Hoban MP
Minister for Employment and former Financial Secretary to the Treasury

Contents

Table of cases

Table of Statutes

AUSTRALIA

FRANCE

Table of Statutory Instruments

Chapter 1 The Current Law

John Birds

John Birds is Emeritus Professor, School of Law, University of Manchester and Honorary Professor, School of Law, University of Sheffield. He was previously Professor of Commercial Law at both institutions (in Sheffield from 1989 to 2006 and in Manchester from 2006 to 2012). He is the author of Birds' Modern Insurance Law (9th edition, Sweet and Maxwell, forthcoming 2013), an editor of MacGillivray on Insurance Law (12th edition, Sweet & Maxwell, 2012), general editor of the Encyclopedia of Insurance Law (Sweet & Maxwell) and co-editor of The Principles of European Insurance Contract Law (Selier, 2009). This chapter is based on the equivalent accounts in Modern Insurance Law.

Introduction

1.1 The Consumer Insurance (Disclosure and Representations) Act 2012 is expected to be brought into force in April 2013. It will introduce new legal rules on disclosure, representations and basis of the contract clauses for consumer insurance contracts. This chapter sets out the current law in these three areas.

The Act will not be retrospective. Knowledge of the current law is therefore required not simply for an understanding of the reasoning behind the reforms but also because it will continue to apply to many existing consumer contracts. Most general insurance contracts such as motor and household policies are renewed on an annual basis. They will therefore be subject to the new law no later than one year after the commencement date of the Act. In contrast, long-term contracts such as life insurance policies which are effected before the commencement date will remain subject to the current law for their full terms. This could be a period of many years.

It should also be borne in mind that the current law is not strictly applied in practice because of the impact of rules issued by the Financial Services Authority, guidance from the Financial Ombudsman Service and self-regulatory codes. These measures are discussed in Chapters 3 and 4.

The principle of utmost good faith

1.2 As one of the most important features of insurance law is the principle of utmost good faith that imports a duty of disclosure, this account will start with consideration of that before looking at misrepresentation and the basis of the contract clause. The reforms discussed in this book are concerned with what happens before an insurance contract is concluded or renewed rather than during its term, so we shall consider only briefly the extent to which there is a continuing duty of disclosure on an insured. The general issue of the mutuality of the principle of utmost good faith is similarly outside the scope of this book, but the extent to which it might restrict the remedy that an insurer would otherwise have must be considered here.

Utmost good faith and non-disclosure

1.3 The contract of insurance is the primary illustration[1] of a class of contracts traditionally described as *uberrimae fidei*, that is, of the utmost good faith. Section 17 of the Marine Insurance Act 1906, which in this respect, as in some others, is said to represent the law applicable to all insurance contracts, puts it as follows:

> 'A contract of marine insurance is a contract based upon the utmost good faith, and, if the utmost good faith be not observed by either party, the contract may be avoided by the other party.'

As already indicated, whether or not this duty to observe the utmost good faith has a continuing effect is not in general discussed in this chapter. Nor is it necessary to discuss what the addition of 'utmost' to 'good faith' means, as, for present purpose, the result of s 17 (as far as the potential insured is concerned and as further spelt out in s 18, which is cited below) is that the potential parties to an insurance contract are bound to volunteer to each other information that is material before the contract is concluded, regardless of whether or not they are asked for that information. However, it should be noted that some of the modern cases refer simply to an obligation, whether on the insured or the insurer, to act in good faith, which perhaps imports more than making full disclosure as discussed below. Further it is not necessary here to discuss the obligation on the insurer to disclose material facts pursuant to the general principle of s 17.[2]

1.4 Section 18(1) provides as follows:

---

1 The others are said to be family arrangements and contracts to take shares in public companies, the disclosure obligations in the latter case being imposed largely by statute.

2 That there is such a duty, albeit limited in scope and attracting only the remedy of avoidance for breach, was confirmed in *Banque Financière de la Cité v Westgate Insurance Ltd* [1991] 2 AC 249.

> 'Subject to the provisions of this section, the assured must disclose to the insurer, before the contract is concluded, every material circumstance which is known to the assured, and the assured is deemed to know every circumstance which, in the ordinary course of business, ought to be known by him. If the assured fails to make such disclosure, the insurer may avoid the contract.'

In line with this and other relevant subsections in s 18, the basic effect of the duty of disclosure can be summarised as requiring an applicant for insurance to disclose to the insurer, prior to the conclusion of the contract, but only up to this date, all material facts within his knowledge that the latter does not or is not deemed to know. A failure to disclose, however innocent, entitles the insurer to avoid the contract *ab initio*, although in some consumer cases the Insurance Conduct of Business Sourcebook made by the Financial Services Authority will require the payment of a claim.[3] If avoided by the insurer, the contract is deemed never to have existed.[4] The insurer must avoid within a reasonable time of becoming aware of the non-disclosure and avoidance is effective as soon as the insurer's election to avoid is communicated to the insured,[5] although the right to avoid may be lost by affirmation.[6] The duty arises whenever a fresh contract is concluded and, most importantly, this includes upon a renewal of any contract except that of life insurance.[7] This basic description requires further elucidation, and its various aspects are examined in the next parts of this chapter.

Rationale

1.5 The duty of disclosure is of some antiquity, being first laid down in 1766 in the leading case of *Carter v Boehm*.[8] Here Lord Mansfield said:[9]

> 'Insurance is a contract upon speculation. The special facts, upon which the contingent chance is to be computed, lie most commonly in the knowledge of the insured only: the under-writer trusts to his representation, and proceeds upon the confidence that he does not keep back

---

3 ICOBS 8.1.1. and 8.2.2.

4 This is not straightforward in some circumstances. For example, *Mackender v Feldia AG* [1967] 2 QB 590 appears to have decided to the contrary, and there is an argument that avoidance means the parties being restored substantially to the position that they would have been in if no contract had been made: see *Brit Syndicates v Italaudit SpA* [2006] Lloyd's Rep IR 483 and the discussion in *MacGillivray on Insurance Law* (12th ed), para 17–030.

5 *Brotherton v Aseguradora Colseguros SA* [2003] EWCA Civ 705, [2003] Lloyd's Rep IR 758.

6 Whether the court can refuse the remedy of avoidance on other grounds is discussed below.

7 See *Lambert v Co-operative Insurance Society* [1975] 1 Lloyd's Rep 465.

8 (1766) 3 Burr 1905. Note that in *Banque Financiere de la Cite v Westgate Insurance Co Ltd* [1990] 1 QB 665, affirmed [1991] 2 AC 249, it was held that the duty of disclosure is equitable in origin, and this view was repeated *in Pan Atlantic Insurance Co v Pine Top Insurance Co* [1995] 1 AC 501, which is considered later. This is perhaps curious given that Lord Mansfield was Chief Justice of the King's Bench and well-known for applying principles of the law merchant to the common law. See generally the excellent analysis by Bennett [1999] LMCLQ 165.

9 (1766) 3 Burr 1905 at 1909.

> any circumstance in his knowledge, to mislead the under-writer into a belief that the circumstance does not exist, and to induce him to estimate the risque as if it did not exist.'

The insurance was of a fort in Sumatra by the Governor of what was then a British colony. The material fact was that the fort was likely to be attacked by the French. It was held that the underwriters in London should have known that as well as the insured; indeed it was said that they were more likely to know. On that basis, the insurer's defence failed on the facts.

1.6 There can be no doubt that the contract of insurance is a special one in the terms that Lord Mansfield expressed, but a number of comments can be made about his formulation of the duty of disclosure. First, it is by no means certain that he was intending to lay down as broad a doctrine as subsequent cases have established,[10] although this has been an academic question for many years. Second, it is also noteworthy that Lord Mansfield regarded his principle of good faith as he called it as applying to all contracts.[11] He could hardly have been referring to the broad duty of disclosure as it is known today. Thirdly, *Carter v Boehm* involved a contract entered into at a time when communications were poor and insurers were not equipped with means easily to discover all the information they needed to know by asking questions of the proposer. More modern circumstances suggest that the justification for an all-ranging duty of disclosure is not so apparent today, and indeed this has been accepted by insurers themselves in respect of consumer insurances,[12] by law reform bodies, the Financial Services Authority and the Financial Ombudsman Service, commentators and indeed by the highest courts.[13] The impact of these various moves is considered in subsequent chapters and has indeed partially materialised in the Consumer Insurance (Disclosure and Representations) Act 2012.

There are also indications in modern cases dealing with business insurance that the courts are to some extent formulating a rather stricter test as the basis for establishing a non-disclosure. As the Law Commissions have pointed out:[14] 'It is now common for the courts to describe the policyholder's duty in terms of making a fair presentation of the risk'. This, they argue, 'is a more

---

10 See Hasson, 'The doctrine of uberrima fides in insurance law: a critical evaluation' (1969) 32 MLR 615. Note that the United States courts developed a much narrower duty of disclosure from the same source, at least in non-marine insurance; see for example, *Vance on Insurance* (3rd ed) at 370ff; *Sebring v Fidelity Phoenix Insurance Co* 225 NY 382 (1931).

11 See (1766) 3 Burr at 1910. The extent to which a principle of good faith is generally applicable in contract law is still a contentious one.

12 When they agreed to the now defunct Statements of Insurance Practice.

13 See the House of Lords' restatement of the test of materiality in *Pan Atlantic Insurance Co v Pine Top Insurance Co*, above, which is considered later.

14 'Insurance Contract Law: the Business Insured's Duty of Disclosure and the Law of Warranties', LCCP 204, SLSDP 155, June 2012 at 5.12 and 5.13.

limited concept than 'every material circumstance', citing the following dictum of Clarke J in *Garnat Trading & Shipping (Singapore) Pte Ltd v Baominh Insurance Corporation*:[15]

> 'A minute disclosure of every material circumstance is not required. The assured complies with the duty if he discloses sufficient information to call the attention of the underwriter to the relevant facts and matters in such a way that, if the latter desires further information, he can ask for it. A fair and accurate presentation of a summary of the material facts is sufficient if it would enable a prudent underwriter to form a proper judgment, either on the presentation alone, or by asking questions if he was sufficiently put upon enquiry and wanted to know further details, whether to accept the proposal and, if so, on what terms.'

While one can agree that this approach is a fairer one than some earlier decisions would perhaps indicate, it does seem little more than applying the doctrine of waiver, which is considered later.

Facts and opinions

1.7 The duty to disclose is concerned with the disclosure of facts and not opinions. A misstated opinion is actionable only if not given in good faith.[16] However, the distinction between questions of fact and questions of opinion is not always an easy one to make. This point can be illustrated particularly by the example of proposals for life insurance, where applicants may very well not know highly material facts regarding their health, because they are not experts, or if they do know something, may very well fail to appreciate its significance. In *Joel v Law Union & Crown Insurance Co*,[17] a statement as to the health of the proposer, made by her, was regarded as a statement of opinion. This makes sense, as the proposer who is not a medical expert or told specifically by such an expert of facts as to his health cannot be expected to give more than an opinion. However, in *Godfrey v Britannic Assurance Co Ltd*,[18] which raised a similar issue, a proposer who failed to disclose a visit to a specialist was held to be guilty of non-disclosure of a material fact, even though he did not know that there was anything seriously wrong with him. Thus, although a mere statement as to health without more is a statement of opinion, at least where the proposer does not know any relevant facts, if a proposer for life insurance has consulted a doctor in more than an ordinary way, the fact of consultation will almost certainly be a material fact requiring to be disclosed.

---

15 [2012] EWHC 2578 (Comm), [2011] 1 Lloyd's Rep 589.

16 *Anderson v Pacific Fire & Marine Insurance Co* (1872) LR 7 CP 65, and see the later discussion, in the context of misrepresentation, of *Economides v Commercial Union Assurance plc* [1997] 3 All ER 636.

17 [1908] 2 KB 863. See also *Life Association of Scotland v Forster* [1873] 1 Macph 351.

18 [1963] 2 Lloyd's Rep 515.

Knowledge of the proposer

1.8 The question of the knowledge of the proposer for insurance raises three further questions: first, their knowledge of the duty to disclose, secondly, whether their opinion as to materiality is relevant, and thirdly, what knowledge of the material facts on their part is required. As to the first point, it is clear that whether or not the proposer knows that they are under a duty to disclose is totally irrelevant. Innocent non-disclosure is as actionable as negligent non-disclosure or fraudulent concealment. The vast majority of the decided cases referred to in this chapter are to this effect. Similarly, the proposer's opinion as to the materiality of non-disclosed facts is irrelevant even though they may well have acted in good faith. As has been pointed out, it is the law that a man may act in perfect good faith within the ordinary meaning of the phrase, yet still be held not to have acted in the utmost good faith in the legal sense.[19]

Constructive knowledge

1.9 The question that then arises is whether or not proposers are bound to disclose only those material facts that they actually know or whether their 'knowledge' includes facts that they ought to know. Clearly they are not bound to disclose what they do not know in either sense, and some cases, particularly in the life insurance field, have long assumed that only actual knowledge imposes a duty.[20] The issue was clearly raised and decided as far as consumer insurances are concerned,[21] in *Economides v Commercial Union Assurance plc*.[22] The facts of this case, where the primary issue was misrepresentation rather than non-disclosure are described in more detail later.[23] For the present the issue was whether the non-disclosure of the true value of the contents of the insured's flat, which was some one-third more than their sum insured, entitled the insurers to avoid the contract.

Although it was accepted that the non-disclosed fact was both material and had induced the insurers to enter into the contract,[24] the insured argued that he was not guilty of non-disclosure because he did not know the truth; this was accepted on the facts. The view that the insured is bound to disclose

---

19 See eg McNair J in *Roselodge Ltd v Castle* [1966] 2 Lloyd's Rep 113 at 129. This distinction between 'good faith' and 'utmost good faith' seems to have been overlooked in some more recent authorities, but it is consistent with what Lord Mansfield said in *Carter v Boehm*, as cited earlier, even if he did not add the 'utmost', and is certainly implicit in s 18 of the Marine Insurance Act.

20 This is not altogether surprising given the difficulties faced by the average proposer with regard to knowledge of his state of health (see the comments above). See also *Simner v New India Assurance Co* [1995] LRLR 240.

21 The position in business insurance is different because of the wording of s 18(1); see the discussion and authorities cited in *MacGillivray on Insurance Law*, para 17–013.

22 [1997] 3 All ER 636.

23 See **1.42**.

24 As to these requirements, see below.

only what is known to him, in the ordinary sense of that word, had been put previously by Fletcher Moulton LJ in *Joel v Law Union and Crown Insurance Co*,[25] to which reference has already been made, where one of the issues was whether the proposer was bound to disclose the fact that she had suffered from acute depression, it being accepted that, despite having consulted a doctor, she was unaware of the fact. It was held not and the Court of Appeal made it clear that that there is no duty to disclose what the proposer does not know. 'The duty is a duty to disclose, and you cannot disclose what you do not know. The obligation to disclose, therefore, necessarily depends on the knowledge you possess.'[26] In *Economides v Commercial Union Assurance plc*, the Court of Appeal adopted Fletcher Moulton LJ's view and stated that this was the position at common law before the codification in the Marine Insurance Act.[27] The insured was required to be honest, which on the facts he was, and, provided that he did not wilfully close his eyes to knowledge, then he was under no obligation to make further inquiries, of any sort, in order to discharge his duty of disclosure.[28]

1.10 It is not entirely settled whether, in consumer insurances, the knowledge of the proposer's agent, acquired in the course of his duties, is the knowledge of the proposer. There is a dictum in *ERC Frankona Reinsurance v American National Insurance Co*[29] that implies not, as it would be inconsistent with the decision in *Economides*. This seems correct in principle.[30]

What need not be disclosed

1.11 Facts which are material need not nonetheless be disclosed to the insurer if (i) they diminish the risk; (ii) they are facts which the insurer knows or is presumed to know or are matters of common knowledge; or (iii) they are facts of which the insurer waives disclosure. Many of the points under heads (i) and (ii) are self-explanatory. *Carter v Boehm* itself was a case where the insurers could not rely upon the non-disclosure because, as we have seen, the material facts were a matter of common knowledge. Another good example is the dangers of asbestos, of which insurers have been held deemed to know.[31]

---

25 [1908] 2 KB 863.
26 *Ibid*, at 884.
27 [1997] 3 All ER 636 at 648 per Simon Brown LJ, quoting *Blackburn Law & Co v Vigors* (1887) 12 App Cas 531 at 543, per Lord MacNaughten. Before *Economides* It had been cases involving life insurance policies where actual knowledge only had been required.
28 [1997] 3 All ER at 648 (Simon Brown LJ) and 653 (Peter Gibson LJ).
29 [2006] Lloyd's Rep IR 157 at [120].
30 It is clearly otherwise in business insurances, save in cases of co-insurance and where an agent is acting in fraud of his principal.
31 *Canadian Indemnity Co v Canadian Johns-Manville Co* (1990) 72 DLR (4th) 478, Canadian Supreme Court.

Knowledge of the agent of the insurer

1.12 An insurer will be deemed to have the knowledge that his agent has if that knowledge was acquired by the agent acting in the scope of his authority, actual or ostensible. It is essential that the agent is in law the agent of the insurer. Imputing an agent's knowledge to his principal may be of great importance in the context of the duty of disclosure. For example, in *Ayrey v British Legal & United Provident Assurance Co*,[32] the district manager of the insurer knew the fact that the insured, who effected a life policy and was by occupation and on the proposal form described as a fisherman, was also a member of the Royal Navy Reserve. It was held that this knowledge was imputed to the insurer who could not therefore rely upon its non-disclosure by the insured. In *Blackley v National Mutual Life Association of Australasia*[33] the agent knew before the contract was concluded that the life insured had a brain tumour that had just been operated upon. Again this knowledge was imputed to the insurer.[34] It should be noted, though, that the fact that the agent could have known of the material fact, for example, by a proper medical examination, is not enough. Similarly, the fact that the insurers have the means of knowledge, for example, the name of the doctor of a proposer for life insurance, does not relieve the insured of his duty of disclosure.

It should also be noted that the position regarding imputation of an agent's knowledge will probably be different where the proposer warrants the accuracy of an incorrect statement even when the agent knows the true position. This question is discussed below.[35]

Waiver

1.13 Waiver of the duty of disclosure raises a number of points. First are those that arise from the fact that in many cases insurance is effected following the completion by the proposer of a proposal form on which a great deal of information is solicited. It is clear that the fact that many questions are expressly asked does not relieve the proposer of his duty to disclose facts outside the scope of the questions,[36] and indeed the questions may also show that the insurers regard certain matters as material,[37] but in some cases the form of questions asked may reduce the scope of the duty of disclosure. Similarly, if the proposer leaves a blank to a question which is

32 [1918] 1 KB 136.

33 [1972] NZLR 1038. The judgments in the New Zealand Court of Appeal contain a very comprehensive review of the principles governing the imputation of an agent's knowledge to his principal.

34 See also *Woolcott v Excess Insurance Co* [1978] 1 Lloyd's Rep 533.

35 See **1.54–1.56**.

36 *Glicksman v Lancashire & General Assurance Co* [1927] AC 139; *Schoolman v Hall* [1951] 1 Lloyd's Rep 139.

37 *Hazel v Whitlam* [2004] EWCA Civ 1600, [2005] Lloyd's Rep IR 168. See also *McNealy v Pennine Insurance Co Ltd* [1978] 2 Lloyd's Rep 18.

accepted without inquiry by the insurer, this will normally be taken as a waiver by the insurer of any duty of disclosure in respect of the matters covered by the question.[38] This would not be the case, however, if in the circumstances, the blank space implies a negative answer to the question. If this is so, and a negative answer is incorrect, the insurers will be entitled to avoid the contract.[39]

Waiver as a result of the form of questions asked will usually arise where an express question asks for some details of certain facts or types of facts.[40] Disclosure of other details will be waived if it is felt that a reasonable man reading the proposal form would consider that the insurer did not seek the other details.[41] For example, a question asking the proposer for details of previous losses he has suffered within a five-year period would waive disclosure of losses outside that period even though such losses might well be material facts according to the usual test. Similarly, a question asking about the claims history of the proposer in relation to the type of insurance for which he is applying might well be regarded as waiving any duty of disclosure of losses or claims in respect of other types of insurance that in some circumstances might be regarded as material facts.[42]

There has been some discussion in modern cases about whether the insurer is in fact obliged to ask questions before an argument based on waiver can be made. This issue is discussed by Law Commissions in their June 2012 Consultation Paper.[43] They refer in particular to the judgment of Rix LJ in *WISE (Underwriting Agency) Ltd v Grupo Nacional Provincial SA*.[44] He links the issue with that of fair presentation of the risk, and suggests that the duty of good faith on an insurer may require it to ask questions. While the possibility of development along these lines must be recognised, it does seem clear that there is as yet no actual decision in support of this view.[45]

Where a question asked on a proposal form is ambiguous, a fair and reasonable construction must be placed upon it and it will be construed *contra*

---

38 *Roberts v Avon Insurance Co* [1956] 2 Lloyd's Rep 240.

39 *Ibid*. Properly, though, the grounds for avoidance will be misrepresentation or breach of warranty.

40 *McCormick v National Motor Accident Insurance Union Ltd* (1934) 49 LILR 361, 363, per Scrutton LJ; *Schoolman v Hall*, above, at 143, per Asquith LJ.

41 See *Doheny v New India Assurance Co Ltd* [2004] EWCA Civ 1705, [2005] Lloyd's Rep IR 251, especially at [14] to [20] and [37]. Even though the view expressed here was obiter, it is clearly authoritative. Longmore LJ was also at pains to stress that the principle was not confined to consumer insurance situations.

42 In *Hair v Prudential Assurance Co Ltd* [1983] 2 Lloyd's Rep 667 it was held that the effect of a general warning on a proposal form of the need for disclosure, of the sort then required by the Statements of Insurance Practice, was to waive the proposer's need to do any more than answer the questions put to him. However, this seems to be going too far (see [1984] JBL 163).

43 'Insurance Contract Law: the Business Insured's Duty of Disclosure and the Law of Warranties', LCCP 204, SLSDP 155, especially 5.38ff.

44 [2004] EWCA 962. They also cite Lord Mansfield's views in *Carter v Boehm* (1766) 3 Burr 1905.

45 Rix LJ's judgment in the WISE case was a dissenting one. The majority judgments of Longmore and Peter Gibson LJJ proceeded along more conventional lines. It may be that the Law Commissions will make formal recommendations to encompass this view when they issue their final Report in 2013.

proferentem when the proposal form is incorporated into the contract. If, for example, the answer of the proposer is true according to a construction that a reasonable man might have put on the question, the insurers cannot rely upon its inaccuracy.

The test of materiality

1.14 Much of the criticism of the wide-ranging nature of the duty of disclosure has been directed at the central question of the test for determining materiality. A fact is material for the purposes of both non-disclosure and misrepresentation if it is one that would influence the judgment of a reasonable or prudent insurer in deciding whether or not to accept the risk or what premium to charge.[46] This test was conclusively adopted for non-marine insurance purposes in *Lambert v Co-operative Insurance Society*,[47] the Court of Appeal holding that its statutory formulation in these terms in section 18 of the Marine Insurance Act 1906[48] was a codification of the common law applicable to all insurance contracts. Despite some indications to the contrary, it is thought that in respect of a pure non-disclosure[49] the view of the particular insurer is not relevant if a fact is not objectively material.[50]

1.15 However, the words of section 18 – 'influence the judgment' – are capable of at least two interpretations. One view is that the non-disclosed fact must have had a decisive influence on the judgment of the prudent or reasonable insurer. Another is that all that is required is that the prudent insurer would have wished to know about the fact when reaching his decision. Surprisingly, perhaps, until relatively recently no case had adopted a definitive view on this matter. The first occasion when it was properly raised and decided was in *Container Transport International Inc v Oceanus Mutual Underwriting Association (Bermuda) Ltd*.[51] Here it was held that, for the purposes of section 18, the requirement that a fact must be one which 'would influence the judgment' of a prudent insurer did not mean that an

---

46 Or, possibly, whether to impose particular terms in the contract such as an exclusion or an excess. This may well be within the ambit of the present test; the Law Commission (Report No 104, para 4.48) thought so and that, in any event, it should expressly be brought within it.

47 [1975] 2 Lloyd's Rep 485. See Merkin (1976) 39 MLR 478. Some earlier non-marine cases, eg *Joel v Law Union* [1908] 2 KB 863, suggested a test depending on the opinion of the reasonable insured. The Court of Appeal in *Lambert* did not like having to reach their decision and thought that the law should be changed. See also *Kelsall v Allstate Insurance Co Ltd*, The Times, March 20, 1987, where the test was accepted, but was modified by an express provision in the contract, 'no known adverse facts', which had the effect of requiring the insured to disclose only facts known by him, as a reasonable man, to be adverse.

48 See also s 151(9) of the Road Traffic Act 1988 which lays down the same test for certain motor insurance purposes.

49 As opposed to answering specific questions.

50 See the discussion in MacGillivray, para 17–039.

51 [1984] 1 Lloyd's Rep 467. See also *Highlands Insurance Co v Continental Insurance Co* [1987] 1 Lloyd's Rep 109, where the judge felt bound to follow the decision in a non-marine misrepresentation case, though clearly with some misgivings.

insurer must have acted differently if he had known the fact, but merely that he would have wanted to know of the fact when making his decision; 'judgment' was construed as meaning 'the formation of an opinion,' not the final decision. It was arguable, however, that the decision was based on a misreading of earlier authorities,[52] and it certainly imposes a particularly heavy burden on the insured.

In *Pan Atlantic Insurance Co v Pine Top Insurance Co Ltd*,[53] the House of Lords had the opportunity to rule authoritatively on the question, and, by a bare majority of 3 to 2, they decided to follow the *CTI* ruling.[54] Although this could be regarded as unfortunate, and the dissenting opinion of Lord Lloyd in favour of the decisive influence test seems to read as persuasively as the leading majority judgment of Lord Mustill, the question is clearly now settled.[55] However, in order to mitigate what their Lordships recognised was the potential harshness of this aspect of the law, they introduced a separate requirement of inducement into the test of materiality. We will consider this separately shortly.

Evidence of materiality

1.16 Because the test of materiality depends initially on the opinion of a reasonable insurer, the courts have long been prepared to accept the opinion of other insurers as evidence of whether or not particular facts are material.[56] In some cases, such opinions appear to have been accepted very readily, but some of the more modern decisions emphasise that they are in no way binding on the court, which must decide the issue as a question of fact. For example, in *Roselodge Ltd v Castle*,[57] an insurer's evidence to the effect that it

---

52 See the excellent article by Brooke, 'Materiality in Insurance Contracts' [1985] LMCLQ 437 analysing all the earlier cases, especially the Privy Council case of *Mutual Life Insurance Co of New York v Ontario Metal Products Co Ltd* [1925] AC 344. This case concerned the construction of a Canadian statute which required, in respect of life insurance, not just that a misrepresentation be material but also that it induced the actual insurer to enter into the contract (cf s 151(9) of the Road Traffic Act 1988, which contains the same requirement). As Brooke points out, the Privy Council was careful to distinguish these two points and was clearly of opinion as regards the first that a non-disclosed or misrepresentation fact must actually have influenced a reasonable insurer to decline the risk or to have stipulated for a higher premium in order to be material; see Lord Salveson at 351. See also the judgment of Lloyd J at first instance in the *CTI* case [1982] 2 Lloyd's Rep 178. The *CTI* case was not followed in some other common law jurisdictions: see eg *Barclay Holdings (Australia) Pty Ltd v British National Insurance Co Ltd* (1987) 8 NSWLR 514; Ying [1990] JBL 97. For a general review, see Clarke 'Failure to disclose and failure to legislate: is it material?' [1988] JBL 206, 298.

53 [1994] 3 All ER 581.

54 Note that the Court of Appeal in *Pan Atlantic* ([1993] 1 Lloyd's Rep 443) had adopted a 'middle way', requiring proof that a prudent insurer would have treated the fact as increasing the risk, even though ultimately he might not have rejected the risk or charged a higher premium.

55 It is thought, though, that the adoption of the decisive influence test would have produced a fairer result; for a detailed critique, see Birds and Hird (1996) 59 MLR 285.

56 See eg *Babatsikos v Car Owners' Mutual Insurance Co* [1970] 2 Lloyd's Rep 314, for a general survey, but compare the comment of Lord Mansfield in *Carter v Boehm* (1766) 3 Burr 1905 at 1918. For a general criticism, see Hasson (1969) 32 MLR 615. See also Evans (1984) 12 Australian Bus L Rev 4.

57 [1966] 2 Lloyd's Rep 113 at 132.

would be material to an application for insurance many years later that the proposer was caught stealing apples at the age of 12 was ridiculed by McNair J. Similarly, the judgment of Forbes J in *Reynolds v Phoenix Assurance Co*[58] is instructive. He rejected the arguments that if an insurer is telling the truth and he is held to be a reasonable insurer, the court must accept his evidence as conclusive. The evidence is expert evidence that assists the court but never binds it. This is particularly so, of course, where there is conflicting evidence from different insurers. It may be crucial also in determining the issue of inducement to which we now turn.

Inducement

1.17 As we have seen, in *Pan Atlantic v Pine Top* the House of Lords introduced a new additional requirement into the law of non-disclosure, clearly being influenced by the need to temper the harshness of the general test for materiality. This additional requirement is that the non-disclosed fact, material in the opinion of the prudent insurer, must also have induced the actual insurer to enter into the contract.[59] This was effected by reasoning first that the inducement requirement for misrepresentation in general contract law must also be held apply to misrepresentation in insurance law.[60] Then, it was held simply that the same requirement should also apply to non-disclosure, even though, as we have seen earlier, conceptually, misrepresentation and non-disclosure are quite different creatures, certainly when they are 'innocent'.[61] While at first sight it is somewhat difficult to see how anyone can be induced by something of which they were unaware, it is better expressed as the requirement that the non-disclosure was an effective cause of the insurer entering into the contract, although it does not to have been the sole cause.[62] It would clearly be going too far to require what might be one non-disclosed fact to be the sole cause of the insurers' decision, where there will normally be a whole range of facts that go towards this.

---

58 [1978] 2 Lloyd's Rep 440 at 457–459.

59 In effect this is a causation requirement which had been hinted at earlier in *Berger v Pollock* [1973] 2 Lloyd's Rep 442. For certain motor insurance purposes, statute imports a requirement of inducement, and it has always been possible for a policy to provide for it.

60 Notwithstanding the fact that s 20 of the Marine Insurance Act 1906, which codified misrepresentation in marine insurance, does not contain the requirement. It was held that inducement comes from the development of the equitable jurisdiction to permit rescission of a contract, and that this was impliedly included in the codification.

61 Again, the fact that the 1906 Act (s 18 in this instance) does not require inducement was regarded as no obstacle. In the words of Lord Mustill, 'If this requires the making of new law, so be it' ([1994] 3 All ER at 617). Perhaps a more fundamental issue is whether the 'equitable' notion of inducement should have a place in a largely common law based doctrine. It is certainly arguable that this is what the duty of disclosure is, stemming as it clearly did from the common law jurisdiction of Lord Mansfield. Having said that, however, there is no doubt that the requirement is now firmly entrenched.

62 *St Paul Fire & Marine Insurance Co (UK) Ltd v McDonnell Dowell Constructors Ltd* [1995] 2 Lloyd's Rep 116; see Hird [1995] JBL 608; *Assicurazioni Generali SpA v Arab Insurance Group* [2002] EWCA Civ 1642, [2003] 1 WLR 577 at [59], [87].

1.18 From *Pan Atlantic* itself, it was perhaps somewhat unclear as to what exactly what the force of the inducement requirement was. In the judgment of the House of Lords there were clear dicta that there is a presumption of inducement,[63] albeit a factual presumption and not a legal presumption, and this was followed by the subsequent Court of Appeal decision in *St Paul Fire & Marine Insurance Co (UK) Ltd v McDonnell Dowell Constructors Ltd*.[64] This particular point will be considered further shortly. More recently it has been clarified that the insurer must show that had he known the non-disclosed fact, he would not have concluded the contract on the same terms or at all, because if he would have made the same contract, the non-disclosure cannot have made any difference.[65] One way of doing this is to show that disclosure of the relevant fact would have led the insurer to ask further questions which, if answered correctly, would have led him to impose different terms.[66] A robust attitude to this issue was revealed in the Court of Appeal decision in *Drake Insurance plc v Provident Insurance plc*,[67] a decision that merits more detailed consideration.

In 1996, K caused a road accident when driving her husband's (S) car. K and S had separate insurance covering K's liability. K's own policy, issued by Drake, covered her whilst she was driving any vehicle with the owner's consent. S's policy covered K as a named driver. Drake settled the claim brought against K by the injured third party and then sought a 50 per cent contribution from Provident. Provident denied liability on two grounds but the one relevant here was an alleged pre-contractual non-disclosure by S of a speeding conviction incurred by K, which, they argued, was both material and induced them to enter into the contract. It was common ground that the non-disclosure was objectively material, so Provident's case turned on the question of inducement. Provident's underwriting policy worked on a mechanical system of points, allocated according to particular risks. If a proposer had 16 points or fewer, then a normal premium was charged. Over 16 points attracted an increase in premium of 25 per cent. An accident that was the fault of an insured attracted 15 points and a speeding conviction 10 points, so one of each automatically attracted the 25 per cent increase in premium. K had been involved in an earlier accident, which S had disclosed to Provident in February 1995 as K's fault, but by itself this did not affect the premium as it attracted only 15 points. However, on renewal in February

---

63 See Lord Mustill [1994] 3 All ER at 610 and 617, although Lord Lloyd strongly disagreed, saying that this was 'a heresy long since exploded' (p 637).

64 See footnote 62 above.

65 See especially *Assicurazioni Generali SpA v Arab Insurance Group*, above.

66 *International Management Group v Simmonds* [2004] 2 Lloyd's Rep IR 247. In another case it was held that a liability insurer had been induced by the non-disclosure of a claim for $5 million that had been made against the insured because the premium would have been raised, even if the precise amount of the increase could not be shown: *New Hampshire Insurance Co v Oil Refineries Ltd* [2003] Lloyd's Rep IR 386.

67 [2003] EWCA Civ 1834, [2004] Lloyd's Rep IR 277. The case also raised important issues of the insurer's duty of utmost good faith.

1996, S failed to disclose that when the accident was investigated, K was found not to be at fault. Crucially, he also failed to disclose that K was convicted of speeding in 1995. Had both these facts been disclosed on renewal, the points tally would have been only 10, so a normal premium would again have been charged. As neither was disclosed, the tally was 25, so an increased premium was charged at renewal.

The Court of Appeal held that Provident had no right to avoid the policy, as it had not been induced to enter the contract by reason of the non-disclosure of the speeding conviction. Had it been disclosed on renewal, Provident would have sought to charge a higher premium which S would have queried and the mistake regarding K's accident would have come to light at this time. Inducement must be proved by the insurer. Provident therefore had to prove that the mistake would not have come to light had the speeding conviction been disclosed, which clearly it could not do. Whilst this approach is extremely advantageous for an insured, it has been pointed out that this comes perilously close to allowing the court to underwrite the policy itself.[68]

As far as the presumption point is concerned, if a fact is obviously material,[69] the court may be justified in inferring that the insurers were induced even where they do not give evidence and thus to this extent they can benefit from the presumption of inducement.[70] This will normally be the situation when other insurers' evidence as to materiality has been accepted.[71]

Examples of material facts

1.19 While the test to be applied to determine whether or not a non-disclosed fact is material is a question of law, the actual determination of the issue in any particular case involves the resolution of a question of fact.[72] As such, it is generally a question solely for the trial judge or arbitrator and not subject to appeal, and, strictly, no decision is actually binding in a later case under the doctrine of precedent.[73] However, there are some categories of facts that are obviously material and others which have arisen so often in decided cases that they would normally be so regarded. It is appropriate, therefore, to describe and illustrate some of these categories. It must be

---

68 R Merkin, Insurance Law Monthly, (2004) Vol. 16 No 2.

69 See below for examples of facts that have normally been regarded as material.

70 See *St Paul Fire & Marine Insurance Co (UK) Ltd v McDonnell Dowell Constructors Ltd* and *Assicurazioni Generali SpA v Arab Insurance Group*, above.

71 See, for example, *Marc Rich & Co AG v Portman* [1996] 1 Lloyd's Rep 430, *Aneco Reinsurance Underwriting Ltd v Johnson & Higgins* [1998] 1 Lloyd's Rep 565, *Insurance Corporation of the Channel Islands v Royal Hotel Ltd* [1998] Lloyd's Rep IR 151, *International Management Group v Simmonds*, above and *Toomey v Banco Vitalicio Espana* [2004] Lloyd's Rep IR 354. In some of the cases the court has accepted such evidence where the insurers have not done everything possible to enable it to hear the actual underwriter involved, an approach that has been criticised by Yeo [2004] 10 JIML 84

72 Eg *Glicksman v Lancashire & General Assurance Co* [1927] AC 139.

73 For a recent example of an unsuccessful appeal on the question of materiality and inducement, see *Laker Vent Engineering Ltd v Templeton Insurance Ltd* [2009] EWCA Civ 62.

remembered, as we have seen, that in any given case the actual insurer must also have been induced by the non-disclosure of such a fact, although as regards most of these 'traditional' material facts, this is unlikely to be a difficult requirement to satisfy, regardless of where the burden of proof lies.

Material facts relate in general either to the physical hazard, that is the property, life or liability insured, or to the moral hazard. Facts relating to the physical hazard are those that are generally obviously material. In property insurance, they would include, for example, the nature, construction or use of an insured building, or whether it is particularly exposed to risk; in life insurance, they would include health or a high risk occupation or hobby, excessive consumption of alcohol,[74] or the results of any health tests known to the insured;[75] in liability insurance, they would include a bad accident record and loss record.[76] The modern cases rarely concern such issues, not least because they are invariably the subject of questions on a proposal form when the answers may be warranted and materiality is irrelevant.

Impact of the Equality Act 2010

1.20 The 2010 Act seeks to provide protection from discrimination on grounds of nine characteristics: age, disability, gender reassignment, marriage and civil partnership, pregnancy and maternity, race, religion or belief, sex and sexual orientation. It replaces earlier legislation including the Sex Discrimination Act 1975 and the Race Relations Act 1976.

Discrimination in insurance would include, for example, declining to offer cover, charging a higher premium or applying exclusions based on one or more of these protected characteristics. Potentially the bar on discrimination means that matters which an insurer might otherwise regard as material can no longer be relied upon.

However, Part 5 of Schedule 3 to the 2010 Act contains a number of exemptions relating to insurance. Group policies arranged by employers are entirely exempt since they are not rated on the characteristics of individual employees. For individual policies, discrimination relating to disability and

---

[74] *Mundi v Lincoln Assurance Co* [2005] EWHC 2678 (Ch), [2006] Lloyd's Rep IR 353.

[75] For example for HIV, or even genetic, tests. While there can be no doubt that such facts are material as a matter of strict law, whether or not the insurance industry should always be entitled morally to know of them is another matter and one which has been much discussed in recent years. See Davey, 'Future imperfect: human genetics and insurance' [2000] JBL 587. At present there is a Concordat and Moratorium on Genetics and Insurance, under which the ABI and government have agreed essentially that there is no requirement to disclose the results of genetic testing except in very limited circumstances approved by the Genetics and Insurance Committee. For a detailed examination, see Wilkinson, 'Gene rummy', unpublished PhD thesis, University of Manchester, 2009; see also Wilkinson, 'Unjustified discrimination: is the moratorium on the use of genetic test results by insurers a contradiction in terms?', available at http://www.springerlink.com/openurl.asp?genre=article&id=doi:10.1007/s10728-009-0137-9.

[76] See *New Hampshire Insurance Co v Oil Refineries Ltd* [2003] Lloyd's Rep IR 386.

age[77] is exempt where it is reasonable and based on information relevant to the risk to be insured. Originally discrimination on grounds of sex, gender reassignment, pregnancy and maternity was allowed where it was reasonable and implemented by reference to actuarial or other data. However the impact of the decision of the European Court of Justice in the *Test-Achats* case[78] on 1 March 2011 is that such discrimination has been prohibited as from 21 December 2012.[79]

Moral hazard

1.21 Facts as to the moral hazard of the proposer were traditionally less likely to be solicited by express questions, although in practice now such questions are likely to be asked in consumer insurances.[80] Moral hazard cases can perhaps be regarded as falling into three categories: (i) those relating to the insurance history of the applicant; (ii) those relating to his nationality or origins; and (iii) those relating to criminal convictions or dishonesty.

The insurance history of the proposer includes both previous refusals to insure by other insurers as well as his claims history. In *Glicksman v Lancashire & General Assurance Co*,[81] G and his partner applied for burglary insurance. It was held that the fact that G had when trading on his own previously been refused insurance was material, regardless of the reasons for the previous refusal and of the fact that there was on the proposal form a question which elicited such information in a way which could have been interpreted as applying to a previous proposal made by the applicants together. The House of Lords, in deciding the case, was full of regrets, but really there was nothing their Lordships could do. The materiality of the fact was a question of fact, which had been conclusively decided by the arbitrator. It should be noted that, in vivid contrast, in marine insurance a previous refusal to insure is not material.[82]

1.22 Whether or not a previous refusal to insure in respect of a type of insurance other than that for which the proposer is applying is material is not so clear. In *Ewer v National Employers' Mutual & General Insurance Association*[83] Mackinnon J clearly rejected such a wide proposition, but in *Locker & Wolf Ltd v Western Australian Insurance Co*[84] a previous refusal of motor

---

[77] The Equality Act 2010 (Age Exceptions) Order 2012

[78] Case C-236/09 *Association belge des Consommateurs Test-Achats ASBL and Others v Conseil des ministres.*

[79] The Equality Act 2010 (Amendment) Regulations 2012

[80] The former Statements of Practice used to require this. There certainly seem to be proposal forms in existence that do not solicit all material facts other than by general question, although it appears to be the practice now to ask for details of criminal convictions.

[81] [1927] AC 139. See also *London Assurance v Mansel* (1879) 11 Ch D 363 for an example in life assurance and *Stowers v GA Bonus plc* [2003] Lloyd's Rep IR 402 regarding the refusal of a renewal.

[82] Glicksman in the Court of Appeal, [1925] 2 KB 593 at 608.

[83] [1937] 2 All ER 193 at 202–203.

[84] [1936] 1 KB 408.

insurance was held material to a proposal for fire insurance, quite apart from the fact that there was a general question on the proposal form. It would appear that such a previous refusal may be material when it relates in a general way to the integrity of the proposer.[85] A mere refusal would therefore not be material, but a refusal based on the insurance history of the proposer, for example, as to his claims experience, might well be.[86]

1.23 Previous losses of the sort against which the proposer is seeking insurance are clearly material,[87] although in practice these will be solicited by express questions and the answers warranted, and, quite possibly, any duty to disclose outside the scope of the question waived. Many of the other facts relating to the moral hazard of the proposer are affected by legislation. Although the nationality of the proposer was held to be material in *Horne v Poland*,[88] the decision cannot stand in the light of the Equality Act 2010, which as has been noted prohibits discrimination by insurers, among others, on the ground of race.[89] Similarly, discrimination against an applicant on the grounds of sex is prohibited by the 2010 Act.

Criminal history and dishonesty

1.24 Perhaps the most important fact affecting the moral hazard of the proposer, apart from insurance history, is any criminal history. Certainly a majority of the modern cases appear to have been concerned with this question and the fact that the insured is facing serious criminal charges may be as material as an actual conviction.[90] This too may be affected by legislation, in this instance the Rehabilitation of Offenders Act 1974. A number of cases involving mostly the insurance of valuables establish that criminal convictions for offences of dishonesty are normally material, including those that relate to 'a dim and distant past,' 12 years[91] and, possibly, 20 years[92] prior to the insurance application. In *Roselodge Ltd v Castle*,[93] though, a conviction for bribery was held not material to the insurance of diamonds, though a smuggling conviction was material. It appears also, logically enough, that the mere commission of an offence may be material, even if the proposer is acquitted by a jury, provided, of course, that the insurer can prove to the satisfaction of the civil court that the proposer did

---

85 *Ibid* at 414, per Slesser LJ.

86 But what if the insurers were told of the claims experience, but not of the refusal based on it?

87 Eg *Arterial Caravans Ltd v Yorkshire Insurance Co* [1973] 1 Lloyd's Rep 169.

88 [1922] 2 KB 364. But see the comment of McNair J in *Roselodge Ltd v Castle* [1966] 2 Lloyd's Rep 113 at 130.

89 Section 29 (replacing s 20 of the Race Relations Act 1976).

90 See *North Star Shipping Ltd v Sphere Drake Insurance plc* [2006] EWCA Civ 378, [2006] Lloyd's Rep IR 519, distinguished in *Norwich Union Insurance Ltd v Meisels* [2006] EWHC 2811, [2007] Lloyd's Rep IR 69.

91 *Schoolman v Hall* [1951] 1 Lloyd's Rep 139.

92 *Regina Fur v Bossom* [1957] 2 Lloyd's Rep 466.

93 [1966] 2 Lloyd's Rep 113.

commit the offence.[94] A wrongful conviction should also be disclosed.[95] Although judicial opinion has been divided as to whether a proposer must disclose the fact of arrest where he was innocent,[96] the prevailing view is that allegations of serious criminal conduct and serious criminal charges should be disclosed.[97] In *Lambert v Co-operative Insurance Society*[98] it was the convictions of the proposer's husband that were material facts. Although the result of this case has been criticised,[99] the offences were of dishonesty, and the insurance was an all-risks one on jewellery, including some which was owned by the proposer's husband. In *Drake Insurance plc v Provident Insurance plc*[100] it was common ground that a speeding conviction was material in motor insurance, and in *Joseph Fielding Properties (Blackpool) Ltd v Aviva Insurance Ltd*[101] it was held that a failure to disclose a material conviction to a previous insurer was itself a material fact that should have been disclosed to a subsequent insurer.[102]

1.25 *Woolcott v Sun Alliance & London Insurance*[103] appears to be a more extreme example because here there was no obvious connection between the non-disclosed conviction and the sort of insurance applied for. The claimant proposed for fire insurance on his house through the building society to which at the same time he was making a mortgage application.[104] He failed to disclose the fact that he had been convicted of robbery some 12 years previously. It was held that the insurers could avoid the policy.[105] The learned judge appears to have accepted, without demur, the evidence called for the insurers that the fact related to Woolcott's moral hazard. With respect, it is not at all obvious why a convicted robber should be more risky in relation to the insurance of a building than anyone else, even though it must be accepted that Woolcott's conviction was serious. In contrast, in *Reynolds v Phoenix Assurance Co*,[106] after perhaps a more thorough review of the law, Forbes J held that a conviction for receiving was not a material fact in relation to fire insurance. Admittedly the matter was comparatively trivial

---

94 *March Cabaret Club & Casino Ltd v London Assurance* [1975] 1 Lloyd's Rep 169.

95 *Ibid.*

96 *Ibid,* at 177. The opposite was held in *Reynolds v Phoenix Assurance Co Ltd* [1978] 2 Lloyd's Rep 440 at 460.

97 See especially *Brotherton v Aseguradora Colseguros SA* [2003] EWCA Civ 705, [2003] Lloyd's Rep IR 758; *North Star Shipping Ltd v Sphere Drake Insurance plc* [2006] EWCA Civ 378, [2006] Lloyd's Rep IR 519.

98 [1975] 2 Lloyd's Rep 465.

99 Merkin (1976) 39 MLR 478.

100 [2003] EWCA Civ 1834, [2004] Lloyd's Rep IR 277.

101 [2010] EWHC 2192 (QB), [2011] Lloyd's Rep IR 238.

102 This was so even though the conviction was spent under the Rehabilitation of Offenders Act 1974 at the time of the proposal to the subsequent insurer; it had not been at the time of the proposal to the previous insurer.

103 [1978] 1 All ER 1253.

104 There was no proposal form; the insurance application was simply the answer to one question on the mortgage application form.

105 But the building society that was also insured was able to recover as the policy was not a joint one.

106 [1978] 2 Lloyd's Rep 440.

and the insured was merely fined. It was held that the matter depended basically on the extent of the dishonesty and the age of the conviction. As the learned judge admitted, hard and fast rules cannot be laid down about this sort of case. This must be correct, even though it makes the application of the law somewhat uncertain, and the insured in the unenviable position of having to find evidence to challenge that of the insurers. One interesting comment in the judgment in *Reynolds* relates to the lack of experience among the experts called of actual disclosures by proposers of their previous convictions. Forbes J[107] understandably found this surprising in view of the large numbers of crimes dishonestly committed every year and the almost universal adoption of some form of insurance for buildings. Clearly he did not believe some of the more extreme evidence as to materiality put forward in that case.[108]

It seems, in summary, that any conviction relevant to the insurance sought will be regarded as material unless it is both trivial and old. An irrelevant conviction, that is one not directly germane to the risk, will affect the moral hazard of the proposer certainly when it is serious, presumably meaning punished by imprisonment or a substantial fine. An ancient trivial offence would not be material. It is less certain whether a recent unconnected trivial offence would be material. In the decided cases of relevance, the offences were all quite old.

Spent convictions

1.26 However, regardless of the above, an applicant for insurance is never bound to disclose a conviction which has become spent under the terms of the Rehabilitation of Offenders Act 1974.[109] There are different periods laid down for rehabilitation depending on the seriousness of the sentence imposed. Most importantly, a conviction resulting in a sentence of two and a half years' imprisonment or more can never become spent. Otherwise, convictions with custodial sentences of between six months and two and a half years become spent after ten years and those of less than six months after seven years. In respect of other sentences, the period is five years, except in relation to absolute discharges (six months) and conditional discharges and probation (one year).

There is one provision though, in section 7(3) of the 1974 Act, which gives the court a discretion to admit evidence as to spent convictions if the court is satisfied that 'justice cannot be done in the case except by admitting it.' The issue arose in earlier proceedings in *Reynolds v Phoenix Assurance Co*[110] because the offence already referred to came to light only after the case

107 *Ibid,* at 460.
108 Today, this would clearly also affect the question of inducement.
109 Section 4(3)(a).
110 [1978] 2 Lloyd's Rep 22.

commenced and the insurers sought to amend their pleadings to allege its non-disclosure. The Act did not apply when the insured applied for the insurance in 1972, but it did when the matter came to trial. The Court of Appeal held that the pleadings should be amended on the ground that no prejudice would be caused to the insured. Whether or not the evidence of the conviction should be admitted was then a matter for the trial judge. Forbes J subsequently held that the evidence should be admitted, although this did not matter in the result as he held that the conviction was not material, as we have already seen.

It is unfortunate that in the *Reynolds* litigation the courts did not really decide the effect of section 7(3) on the duty of disclosure. They may have been influenced by the fact that the alleged non-disclosure took place before the 1974 Act existed. It can hardly be said to be just to admit evidence of spent convictions in relation to insurance effected after 1974 when, since that time, the proposer has been under no duty to disclose them.

Dishonesty

1.27 Proven dishonesty, even in the absence of a criminal conviction, may be a material fact. In *Insurance Corporation of the Channel Islands v Royal Hotel Ltd*[111] a director of the insured, who was also its company secretary, had prepared false invoices in order to give the insured's bankers a more favourable impression of its profitability. Although these had not been used by the time of the insurance proposal, and no criminal offence had actually been committed, it was held that this kind of dishonesty was material. This seems unobjectionable and is in line with the authorities already mentioned regarding allegations of criminality.

Non-disclosure and misrepresentation in co-insurance

1.28 Some interesting questions arise regarding non-disclosure and misrepresentation in co-insurance situations. Co-insurance, or composite insurance, arises when more than one party insures separate interests under the same policy, for example a mortgagor and mortgagee insuring their different interests in the same property, or the various parties involved in a construction project.

The question is whether, when one co-insured is guilty of a material non-disclosure or misrepresentation, the insurers are entitled to avoid the policy only against that co-insured, or against all those insured under the policy. If the policy is one single contract, then the insurers would argue that

---

111 [1998] Lloyd's Rep IR 151. See also *Gate v Sun Alliance Insurance Ltd* [1995] LRLR 385 and *Markel International Insurance Co v La Republica Cia Argentina de Seguros* [2004] EWHC 1826 (Comm), [2005] Lloyd's Rep IR 90.

they ought to be allowed to avoid against all the parties because they have been misled as to the overall risk, and, in principle, avoidance against one co-insured ought to be possible only if, on its true construction, the policy contains separate contracts.[112]

1.29 However, in *Woolcott v Sun Alliance & London Assurance*,[113] which concerned a single contract, the insurers were allowed to avoid against a mortgagor, despite the fact that they had indemnified the mortgagee in respect of its separate interest. It might have been argued that the insurers had waived the right to avoid the whole contract by paying the mortgagee, but this point was not raised. In *New Hampshire Insurance Company v MGN Ltd*[114] the Court of Appeal similarly held that the insurers were not entitled to avoid against an innocent co-insured, where the various parties insured were the different members of a group of companies. The court relied on the House of Lords' decision in *P Samuel & Co Ltd v Dumas*.[115] This latter case concerned a claim brought by shipbrokers, the named assured on a marine hull policy, for the benefit of both the owners and the mortgagees of the insured ship. The vessel was scuttled by the owners without the knowledge of the mortgagees. The insurers argued that the policy was joint, but the House of Lords held that it was a composite policy, and, as such, the innocent co-insured could recover, despite the fraud of the owner. In the *New Hampshire* case Staughton LJ raised the crucial issue of whether the contract was single, or whether there were several contracts. He said:

> 'Technically, one ought to enquire whether … there was one contract or as many contracts as there were companies insured. And, if the former, can a contract be avoided for non disclosure as against one or some of the insured but not against others?'[116]

However, he felt that the court was relieved from having to tackle the issue because the principle established in *Samuel v Dumas* regarding wilful misconduct by a co-insured should equally apply to a non-disclosure. It is, however, clear from his remarks that he thought there were several separate contracts in this case. The decision is probably correct, at least in terms of justice; it cannot be fair to allow an insurer to avoid the whole policy when only one single co-insured out of many has failed to disclose facts relevant to the risk. However, it does not adequately deal with the problem that Staughton LJ himself recognised, that of whether there is in fact one single contract or several contracts.

---

112 Where a composite policy is a single contract, albeit that the insurer can undertake distinct obligations to the separate parties, then it is difficult to see how the insurer can avoid only against one party – see *Federation Insurance v Wasson* (1987) CLR 303.

113 [1978] 1 All ER 1253.

114 [1997] LRLR 24.

115 [1924] AC 431 (HL).

116 [1997] LRLR 24 at 57–58.

1.30 The issue was considered again in *Arab Bank plc v Zurich Insurance Co.*[117] Here, the clients of a company that ran an estate agency recovered judgments in respect of negligent valuations by the managing director of the company, which they sought to recover from the latter's insurers under the Third Party (Rights against Insurers) Act 1930. There was no question that the managing director, who was a co-insured under the policy, had failed to disclose the material fact that he had been involved in making fraudulent valuations. Rix J held that the insurers were not entitled to avoid the policy as against the company. It was common ground that the professional indemnity policy in question insured separate interests and was specifically worded to ensure that the dishonesty of one co-insured would not deny recovery by the others if they were not complicit in the deceit. This, together with provisions in the policy concerning subrogation and a general condition spelling out the penalties for innocent non-disclosure, provided a basis for the judge to hold that the insurers were liable to the innocent company.[118] However, he went on to say that in fact the policy in question involved a bundle of separate contracts between the insurers and the various co-insureds, and that the dishonesty of one did not allow total avoidance against all. He said that this ought to be the 'prima facia' position under all composite policies, without meticulous examination of the terms. With respect, this seems too wide. It was not necessary for Rix J to tackle this issue; because of the particular contract in this case, he had ample ammunition to deny avoidance on its own terms. Whether there is one contract or several is crucial if this issue is to be resolved in accordance with legal principle; to say that as a matter of course all such insurances consist not of a single contract but of several contracts cannot be satisfactory.

1.31 It would appear, however, that this view was given at least tacit approval by the Court of Appeal in *FNCB Ltd v Barnet Devanney (Harrow) Ltd.*[119] This case concerned the placing of composite insurance by the defendant broker on behalf of the claimant bank and its mortgagor. The mortgagor was found to have made a material non-disclosure and the insurer avoided the policy. The bank's claim was settled for less than the outstanding amount of the mortgage and it sought to recover the shortfall from the broker. The bank argued that the broker was in breach of duty in failing to ensure that a mortgagee protection clause was inserted into the policy. It was common practice at the time the insurance was effected in 1987 to insert such a clause, preserving an innocent mortgagee's rights under the policy in the event that the mortgagor could not effectively make a claim. The court at first instance refused to find the broker negligent, relying on the *New*

---

[117] [1999] 1 Lloyd's Rep 262. For a detailed examination of this decision, see Birds [1999] JBL 151.

[118] The insurers further argued that the managing director's knowledge of the fraud ought to be imputed to the company, but this argument was also rejected. The fraud of an agent is never imputed to his principal. It could be argued that even the policy provisions relied on by Rix J were not really support for his conclusion; see Birds, above.

[119] [1999] Lloyd's Rep IR 459.

Hampshire decision as having established that a mortgage protection clause was unnecessary, because the bank was protected from avoidance in any event. On appeal, the Court of Appeal found for the bank, saying that the *New Hampshire* decision could not apply to insurance contracts effected in 1987. The court did not, however, cast any doubt on the principle that all composite insurances are now to be regarded as containing separate contracts. While it could be argued that this is too important a principle to be dealt with in such a cursory fashion, it must be regarded as settled,[120] although it will often be subject to the proper construction of the terms of the policy.[121]

Excluding the duty of disclosure and remedies for breach

1.32 It is clear that the law, except in cases of fraud, will uphold clauses that exclude the remedies for misrepresentation or exclude or limit the duty of disclosure or the remedies for breach. It is not uncommon for a policy to do so in situations of co-insurance, such as those considered above. Another very important context is where insurance is taken out by a bank as security for a loan, for example in order to finance the making of a film (known as film finance insurance). This was the type of insurance in issue in *HIH Casualty & General Insurance Ltd v Chase Manhattan Bank*,[122] where the contract in question contained what was described as a 'truth of statement' clause, which provided, among other things, that the insured would not have any duty or obligation to make any representation, warranty or disclosure of any nature, express or implied (such duty and obligation being expressly waived by the insurers) and that any non-disclosure by the insured or by others would not be a ground for avoidance of the insurers' obligations. Neither the principle of utmost good faith nor public policy invalidated such a provision, except where there was fraudulent concealment by the insured.[123]

Losing the right of avoidance by affirmation

1.33 The insurers will waive the right to avoid for non-disclosure or misrepresentation if they elect to continue with the contract and so affirm it.

---

120 It might also be argued that the courts have allowed arguments based on commercial convenience to overcome properly thought-out principle in the situations where insurers seek to exercise subrogation rights against a co-insured.

121 For a recent example of such a situation, see the House of Lords' decision in *Brit Syndicates Ltd v Italaudit SpA* [2008] UKHL 18, [2008] Lloyd's Rep IR 601.

122 [2003] UKHL 6, [2003] Lloyd's Rep IR 230.

123 As indicated earlier, the House of Lords left open the question of whether a clause could be effective in the event of fraud by an agent to insure.

Relatively recent case law[124] has clarified the requirements in this respect. The insurers must have actual, not constructive, knowledge of the non-disclosed fact and know that they have the right to avoid. They have a reasonable time for decision and there must be an unequivocal communication to the insured[125] by words or conduct that they have made an informed choice to affirm. An unequivocal communication depends on how a reasonable person in the position of the insured would interpret the insurer's word or conduct. Delay by itself is not sufficient but will count if the insured is prejudiced by it or it is explicable only on the basis that the insurers are affirming the contract. Otherwise any kind of conduct by the insurers that leads the insured reasonably to believe that the insurers intend to continue to insure him is sufficient. This can include failing to avoid and return the premium while refusing to pay a claim, making an interim payment, accepting a premium and giving instructions to the insured concerning the subject matter of the insurance.

The continuing duty of utmost good faith

1.34 Hitherto in this chapter we have examined the principle of utmost good faith, which was first expressed by Lord Mansfield in *Carter v Boehm*[126] and is codified in section 17 of the Marine Insurance Act 1906, in the context of its imposing a pre-contractual duty of disclosure on the insured. Our concern at this stage is the extent to which the principle has a continuing effect. Although referred to very occasionally in earlier case-law, it is really only in the last 30 years or so that this has become an important issue.

Section 17 provides that the remedy for breach of the principle is avoidance of the contract, which would normally mean from the beginning (ab initio), because the parties are put back into the position they were in before the contract was entered into. The contract is treated as though it never existed and any previously paid claims must be refunded. Although this is a natural consequence of avoidance for a pre-contractual misrepresentation or non-disclosure,[127] it is far harder to justify for a breach of utmost good faith during the life of the contract. In line with breach of a fundamental term, the contract should be avoided only from the date of the breach, but this is hardly consistent with the wording of section 17. This has led to much debate about the exact ambit of the section. One argument is that because the only remedy is avoidance ab initio, section 17 can never have been

---

124 *Insurance Corporation of the Channel Islands v Royal Hotel Ltd* [1998] 1 Lloyd's Rep IR 151; *Spriggs v Wessington Court School Ltd* [2004] EWHC 1432 (QB), [2005] Lloyd's Rep IR 474. See also *Scottish Coal Co Ltd v Royal & Sun Alliance plc* [2008] EWHC 880 (Comm), [2008] Lloyd's Rep IR 718.

125 Communication to the third party in the case of liability insurance is not enough: *Spriggs v Wessington Court School Ltd*, above.

126 127 (1766) 3 Burr 1905.

127 Which in any event is spelt out in sections 18 and 20.

intended to impose any duty of utmost good faith on either party beyond a pre-contractual one and that the word 'utmost' in this context relates to that pre-contractual duty, with the section acting merely as a preamble to the later specific sections on non-disclosure and misrepresentation.[128] On the other hand it can be argued that, if section 17 is no more than a preamble to sections 18 to 20, it is superfluous and unnecessary and therefore it must be assumed that it was intended to impose a wider, continuing duty. It is clear as a matter of current law that the section does have a continuing effect,[129] but the exact nature of this continuing duty of utmost good faith is unquestionably currently one of the most academically challenging issues in insurance law. The most important application of section 17 as far as the insured is concerned will be either where an express term to supply information is breached or where the insured makes a fraudulent claim. The case law has gone some way to dealing with the issues, but in doing so, has raised some as yet unanswered questions.

1.35 What is not in doubt is that the basic duty to disclose material facts is cast upon the proposer or insured only before the contract or a renewal is concluded. At common law, there is no general duty to disclose material facts which occur during the period of insurance, although of course the duty will arise again upon renewal. The authority for this is the old case of *Pim v Reid*,[130] where the insured changed his trade and caused a large amount of highly inflammable material to be brought on to the insured premises. It was held that his non-disclosure of this fact to the insurer was not actionable. This basic common law position has more recently been confirmed by the Court of Appeal in *Kausar v Eagle Star Insurance Co Ltd*,[131] although specific 'increase in risk' clauses often arise as express terms of the contract.

In the leading case of *Manifest Shipping Co Ltd v Uni Polaris Shipping Co Ltd (The Star Sea)*,[132] Lord Hobhouse confirmed that 'utmost good faith is a principle of fair dealing which does not come to an end when the contract

---

[128] As there is no corresponding pre-contractual duty of disclosure in general contract law, it is thought that utmost was intended to mean this, in the sense of something over and above any duty of good faith which might be applicable to all contractual dealings. 'Utmost' is a rather clumsy translation of the Latin 'uberrima', in the phrase that was often used at one time. What is notable is that many judges in the modern cases analysed below simply refer to good faith. The real answer may then be that there is a duty of utmost good faith before a contract is concluded (or renewed), with a particular consequence of a duty of disclosure, whereas there is a duty of good faith during the contract, a breach of which may have various consequences but does not lead to avoidance ab initio. The case law does not though appear to proceed upon this basis, with the terms utmost good faith and good faith often being used interchangeably.

[129] See *The Star Sea*, discussed below.

[130] (1843) 6 M&G 1.

[131] [1997] CLC 129.

[132] [2001] UKHL 1; [2001] 2 WLR 170.

has been made',[133] although he did say that the 'content of the obligation to observe good faith has a different application and content in different situations'. He confirmed the basic common law principle stated above and said expressly of the duty in sections 18 to 20 of the Marine Insurance Act: '[i]t is not necessary to disclose facts occurring, or discovered, since the original risk was accepted material to the acceptance and rating of that risk. Logic would suggest that such new information might be valuable to the underwriter … But it need not be disclosed.'[134]

The nature of the duty of disclosure would appear therefore to fluctuate depending on the stages of the contract. Because, however, the precise nature and content of the post-contractual duty post was not spelt out further, this has given rise subsequently to difficulties, most notably as to when the remedy of avoidance ab initio will be available. The decision in *The Star Sea* was closely followed by two Court of Appeal decisions – *K/S Merc-Scandia XXXXII v Certain Lloyd's Underwriters (The Mercandian Continent)*[135] and *Agapitos v Agnew (The Aegeon)*.[136] These three decisions, taken together, cast doubt on the right to avoid the contract ab initio for breach of a post contractual duty of utmost good faith and in the light of them it would be wise for insurers to consider their position by focusing on their contractual remedies.

The Star Sea decided as such only that any post contractual duty of good faith comes to an end once litigation proceedings had commenced. From the decision in *The Mercandian Continent*, it seems safe to assume that the section 17 duty is confined to cases where there is an express contractual obligation to provide information. If this is breached in so serious a way that the breach would entitle the insurer to repudiate the contract, then, assuming the breach is fraudulent, the insurer will be granted the remedy of avoidance ab initio. This will be an alternative to treating the contract as terminated from the date of the breach. However, to avail himself of this more draconian remedy, the insurer will have to prove that the fraud is 'material', in the sense that it caused him significant prejudice.

The Aegeon applied the principle confirmed by the House of Lords in *The Star Sea* that any post contractual duty stops on commencement of litigation, which is governed by the rules of the court. Mance LJ went so far as to say that an attempt to continue the post contractual duty by express terms would be frowned upon because of public policy issues. He also drew a distinction between what he called 'material fraud' such as the conduct in *The*

---

133 Although the House did confirm that it came to an end once litigation proceedings has commenced – para 75. *The Star Sea* was a marine insurance case, but it was common ground that the principle of utmost good faith in this context is applicable to all contracts of insurance – para 47 per Lord Hobhouse; Lords Hoffmann and Steyn agreed.

134 [2001] UKHL 1; [2001] 2 WLR 170 para 48.

135 [2001] EWCA Civ 1275, [2001] Lloyd's Rep IR 802.

136 [2002] EWCA Civ 247, [2002] Lloyd's Rep IR 573.

Mercandian Continent and the use of 'fraudulent devices' to advance a fraudulent claim, which was the conduct complained about in *The Aegeon*. He said that section 17 should not apply where the breach of utmost good faith alleged is the latter. His Lordship made clear that in his opinion a fraudulent claim signals 'forfeiture of all benefit under the policy' because of public policy principles,[137] and that this is not at all the same thing as the remedy of avoidance of the contract ab initio laid down in section 17.[138]

Fraud

1.36 This topic can be disposed of quickly; more detailed discussion can be found elsewhere.[139] A proposer is guilty of fraudulent misrepresentation if he knowingly makes a statement that is false, without belief in its truth or recklessly as to whether it is true or false.[140] He is guilty of fraudulent non-disclosure if he wilfully conceals from the insurer any material fact that he knows the insurer would wish to be aware of. In addition to the right to avoid a contract entered into by an insured who has been fraudulent, the insurer may also have the right to claim damages in the tort of deceit, and can in addition retain any premium paid.[141] A clause purporting to protect an insured from the consequences of his fraud is unenforceable on public policy grounds.[142]

Misrepresentation

1.37 An insurer can avoid an insurance contract if he was induced to enter into it by a misrepresentation of fact made by the proposer that was false in a material particular, whether the proposer acted negligently or quite innocently, although the Insurance Conduct of Business Sourcebook may require an insurer to pay a claim in a case of innocent misrepresentation.[143] The onus of proof as regards inducement, described as 'always difficult for an insurer or reinsurer to discharge,'[144] is on the insurer and the right to avoid differs little

---

[137] Also the usual wording used in policies for the remedy for a fraudulent claim.

[138] *The Aegeon* [2002] EWCA Civ 247, para 45.

[139] See eg *MacGillivray on Insurance Law*, Ch 16.

[140] *Derry v Peek* (1889) 14 App Cas 337.

[141] See *Chapman and others, assignees of Kennet v Fraser* B R Trin 33 Geo 111. It was unclear whether an insurer could, in fact, retain the premium after fraud; the point is assumed finally settled here. Lord Mansfield had always held to the view that only if the fraud was 'particularly gross' could the insurer keep the premium; see eg *Tyler v Horne* reported in Park (1800) at 219. The question came to be expressly decided in Chapman, and the court held that on any fraud the insurer was able to keep the premium. Whether this amounts to unjust enrichment is another matter.

[142] *HIH Casualty & General Ins Ltd v Chase Manhattan Bank* [2003] UKHL 6, [2003] Lloyd's Rep IR 230. The House of Lords here left open the question as to whether a clause could protect the insured in the event of dishonest misrepresentation or non-disclosure by his agent to insure.

[143] See Chapter 3.

[144] See Longmore J in *Sirius International Insurance Corp v Oriental Insurance Corp* [1999] Lloyd's Rep IR 343 at 354. The same is true of non-disclosure.

from that attaching generally in the law of contract.[145] Historically, misrepresentation in the strict sense has not been of particular importance in the insurance context. This is partly because the extreme width of the duty to disclose material facts, as described below,· has meant that often non-disclosure has subsumed questions of misrepresentation. Cases have frequently failed to distinguish between the two defences taken by an insurer and indeed it appears to be standard practice for an insurer, where possible, to plead both defences. While this may be conceptually unsatisfactory,[146] it is well established, the rationalisation being that it is said to be part of the insured's duty of good faith to answer correctly questions on a proposal form.[147] On the other hand, there is clearly a distinction between an innocent misrepresentation, where the proposer does not know the truth, and an innocent non-disclosure, where the proposer knows the truth but does not appreciate that he should disclose the fact in question. It seems, however, that this distinction does not matter.[148]

1.38 Another reason for the relative unimportance, historically, of misrepresentation is that it applies only to those statements made before a contract is concluded which are properly mere representations and not terms of the contract. The usual, although not the only, source of such representations by the insured will be the statements he makes on the proposal form. Traditionally, by the device known as the 'basis of the contract' clause, such statements have been made terms of the contract and the law of misrepresentation is therefore irrelevant to them.[149] Nevertheless, basis clauses are less common in modern practice than they were historically and indeed are not in practice used for proposals by individual insureds,[150] at least without being qualified so that the statements thereon are representations of opinion, as discussed below, rather than statements of fact. The law on misrepresentation therefore may be more relevant now than formerly.

Most of the legal questions that arise in the context of misrepresentation, in particular the need for the misrepresented fact to be material, how materiality

---

145 See eg Treitel, *Law of Contract*, Ch 9. Until the decision of the House of Lords in *Pan Atlantic Insurance Co v Pine Top Insurance Co* [1994] 3 All ER 581, it was unclear whether or not 'inducement' was an element of misrepresentation in insurance contracts, especially because s 20 of the Marine Insurance Act 1906, codifying misrepresentation in marine insurance law and taken also to represent non-marine insurance law, does not contain it. Now it clearly is a requirement; see further below.

146 See Hasson (1975) 38 MLR 89.

147 *Everett v Desborough* (1829) 5 Bing 503.

148 *Pan Atlantic Insurance Co v Pine Top Insurance Co* [1994] 3 All ER 581, discussed further below. See Birds and Hird, (1996) 59 MLR 285. There are signs, however, that the courts will no longer allow the defence of non-disclosure to succeed when the insured has allegedly made what can only be an innocent misrepresentation. See *Economides v Commercial Union Assurance Co plc* [1999] 3 All ER 636, discussed below.

149 A modern example can be found in *DSG Retail Ltd v QBE International Insurance Ltd* [1999] Lloyd's Rep IR 483.

150 The Statement of General Insurance Practice, para 1(b), used to provide that they should not be used in consumer insurances, but this Statement was withdrawn in 2005 and there is nothing in the Insurance Conduct of Business Sourcebook that is specifically directed at basis clauses.

is judged and the possibility of excluding the remedies for a misrepresentation, are the same as apply to non-disclosure and these will be fully discussed later in this chapter. A representation of fact made before the original contract is not impliedly re-made on renewal,[151] although in *Synergy Health (UK) Ltd v CGU Insurance plc*[152] it was held that a statement made four months before renewal, that the insured would install an intruder alarm within an agreed time, which proved to be false, was impliedly misrepresented on renewal.

1.39 Section 2(2) of the Misrepresentation Act 1967 could operate as a restriction on the insurer's right to avoid for misrepresentation. That subsection gives the court discretion to award damages in lieu of rescission or avoidance. It has been held, obiter, that the discretion would never be used in respect of commercial contracts of insurance,[153] a dictum which clearly leaves open the possibility of it being available to individual insureds, and indeed the Insurance Ombudsman stated that he could use it in cases coming before him.[154] In the fairly recent case of *Economides v Commercial Union Assurance plc*,[155] which is discussed below, the insurer pleaded non-disclosure as a defence as well as misrepresentation. As we have seen such indiscriminate pleading is common practice, and if a non-disclosure defence succeeds any discussion of the Misrepresentation Act is academic, since it seems clear that the wording of section 2(2) cannot be applied to non-disclosures.[156] The defence did not succeed, however,[157] and it seems likely that it will never succeed in these circumstances. Thus the discretion to award damages may be of more importance now.

Representations of opinion

1.40 The statements made by the proposer may not be representations of fact but representations of opinion only. This is likely always to be the case as regards insurances effected by individual consumers[158] and is also quite common nowadays in commercial insurance proposal forms. A representation of opinion has been described as a statement as regards which, as it appears or should appear to the person to whom the statement is made, the

---

[151] *Limit No 2 Ltd v Axa Versicherung AG* [2008] EWCA Civ 1231, [2009] Lloyd's Rep IR 396.

[152] [2010] EWHC 2583 (Comm), [2011] Lloyd's Rep IR 500.

[153] *Highlands Insurance Co v Continental Insurance Co* [1987] 1 Lloyd's Rep 109. This view was supported by Rix LJ in *HIH Casualty & General Insurance Co Ltd v Chase Manhattan Bank* [2001] Lloyd's Rep 703 at [116].

[154] See the Annual Report for 1990, para 2.3.

[155] [1997] 3 All ER 636.

[156] See Hudson (1969) 85 LQR 524.

[157] See further below.

[158] The Statement of General Insurance Practice provided that the declaration at the foot of a proposal form should make it clear that the form was completed only to the best of the proposer's knowledge and belief, but the Statement is no longer operational.

speaker does not have sufficient information to guarantee its accuracy.[159] Even if the representor is an expert, if there could be another, reasonable interpretation, then the statement may still be of opinion. The opinion must be based upon a genuine belief, but in insurance law that belief need only be honest and the representor is not required to have reasonable grounds on which to base it.[160] The lack of a need for reasonable grounds is a fairly recent development,[161] and is out of line with the general law of contract.[162]

1.41 This was the primary holding of the Court of Appeal in *Economides v Commercial Union Assurance Co plc.*[163] In 1988, the insured effected a household contents insurance policy with the defendant insurers. He completed and signed a proposal form, which, among other things, stated the value of the contents of his flat as being £12,000 and that the total value of the valuables in the flat did not exceed one-third of this. The form stated that it was completed 'to the best of my/our knowledge and belief and concluded this proposal shall form the basis of the contract between me/us and the insurers.' There was no dispute that the statements were true at the time. In 1990, the insured's parents came to England from Cyprus, and took up residence in the flat. They brought with them some jewellery and silverware, worth, it later transpired, approximately £30,000. The insured, who at this time was 21, showed little interest in the goods, but accepted his father's advice that he ought to increase the sum insured under his policy to take account of them. His father, a retired senior policeman, suggested that an increase of approximately £3,000 should suffice. The insured asked the insurers to increase the sum insured to £16,000. The subsequent invitation to renew stated this as the sum insured.[164] The flat was then burgled and property worth £31,000 was stolen, the bulk of which was the valuables belonging to the insured's parents. He claimed under the policy, and it was only then that it became clear that the value of the parents' valuables was £30,970, much more than the sum insured, and, that their value made up considerably more than either one third of the total sum insured, or of the total value of the contents, now estimated at £40,000. The insurers denied liability, alleging both misrepresentation and non-disclosure of material facts.

The court followed earlier cases in deciding that section 20 of the Marine Insurance Act 1906 lays down the law on misrepresentation for all types of

---

159 *Hubbard v Glover* (1812) 3 Camp 313 at 314–315, per Lord Ellenborough.

160 *Economides v Commercial Union Assurance Co plc* [1997] 3 All ER 636.

161 Compare the dictum of Saville J in *Bank Leumi Le Israel BM v British National Insurance Co* [1988] 1 Lloyd's Rep 71 at 75: 'such a statement can and often does carry with it a representation that the person making the statement has an honest belief or expectation, based on reasonable grounds, that events will turn out as stated.'

162 See Bennett, 'Statements of fact and statements of opinion in insurance contract law and general contract law' (1998) 61 MLR 886.

163 Above. See also *Eagle Star Insurance Co Ltd v Games Video Co SA* [2004] EWHC 15 (Comm), [2004] Lloyd's Rep IR 867, where it was common ground that a representation as to the value of property to be insured was to be treated as a representation of opinion rather than a statement of fact.

164 It also gave a standard warning of the need to disclose material facts.

insurance.[165] Section 20(5) provides that 'a representation as to a matter of expectation or belief is true if it be made in good faith.' It was accepted that the insured had acted in good faith, but the insurers argued that the requirement of reasonable grounds was to be implied into section 20(5), relying on both general contract and insurance law cases.[166] Having distinguished most of these cases,[167] Simon Brown and Peter Gibson LJJ decided that there could not be implied into section 20(5) a requirement of reasonable grounds for belief, as this would be stretching statutory interpretation to unacceptable levels.[168] In the view of Simon Brown LJ, honesty was all that was required provided that the insured has a basis for his belief,[169] and it had been found as a matter of fact at first instance that the insured fulfilled that requirement. Any further requirement would place impossible demands on an insured. If insurers wished to place such onerous burdens on their prospective insureds, they should stipulate it expressly in the proposal form. Peter Gibson LJ considered that, even if he was wrong on the statutory interpretation point, the insured in the present case did have reasonable grounds for his belief. Sir lain Glidewell approached the issue from a slightly different standpoint, whilst arriving at the same conclusion. In his view there might be a requirement of reasonable grounds, but it was to be judged subjectively: '... could the appellant, as a reasonable man knowing the facts he knew, honestly have believed that the replacement value of the property in his flat in December 1990 was £16,000?'[170] In his judgment, the insured as a reasonable man could honestly have arrived at that conclusion, and, that being the case, was entitled to indemnification from his insurer.

1.42 While it seems clear that justice was done in *Economides* itself, with respect, the right result could have been reached without dispensing with the 'reasonable grounds' requirement. Apart from the fact that this requirement seems reasonable, it could be regarded as undesirable to have an important aspect of insurance law out of line with the general law of contract when the

---

165 See, for example, *PCW Syndicates v PCW Reinsurers* [1996] 1 All ER 774. The same view is taken as regards s 18 and the duty of disclosure.

166 *Smith v Land & House Property Corp* (1884) 28 Ch D 7 at 15 per Bowen LJ, *Brown v Raphael* [1958] 2 All ER 79 at 83 per Lord Evershed MR, *Credit Lyonnais Bank Nederland v Export Credit Guarantee Dept* [1996] 1 Lloyd's Rep 200 at 216 per Longmore J, *lonides v Pacific Fire and Marine Insurance Co* (1871) LR 6 QB 674 at 683–684 per Blackburn J, *Highlands Insurance Co v Continental Insurance Co* [1987] 1 Lloyd's Rep 109 at 112–113 per Steyn J.

167 Three of them were cases of representations of fact not opinion, and the judges considered that they were also either cases of professionals giving an unqualified opinion or individuals blindly ignoring evidence in from of them, as compared to the case of a 21 year old student taking the word of his older and wiser parent.

168 Viewing the clear dictum of Steyn J to the contrary in the *Highlands Insurance Co* case (above) as incorrect.

169 On this, compare *International Lottery Management Ltd v Dumas* [2002] Lloyd's Rep IR 237, especially at [65].

170 [1997] 3 All ER at 655.

divergence is unnecessary.[171] The law as it stands, however, is unquestionably more favourable to insureds and is clearly settled.[172]

The insurer's duty of good faith as a restriction on the right of avoidance

1.43 From the decisions examined earlier, it might be thought that there is no effective duty of utmost good faith or even just good faith on the insurer. However, recent case law has raised the issue in a different context, namely whether or not the insurer's right to avoid for non-disclosure or misrepresentation can be subject to a requirement that they exercise that right in good faith.

Although there were some indications in previous cases to this effect,[173] the issue was first clearly raised and a clear view expressed in *Strive Shipping Corp v Hellenic Mutual War Risks Association*.[174] The issue arose again in *Brotherton v Aseguradora Colseguros SA (No 2)*.[175] In both these cases the insureds had failed to disclose to their insurers that, at the time of taking out the insurance, they were under investigation for alleged fraudulent activity. Subsequently, all the allegations were proven to be false. Nevertheless, it was held that the investigations were material. The insureds argued that in exercising the remedy of avoidance in this situation the insurers were in breach of their duty of utmost good faith. In *Strive Shipping*, Colman J's view was that the right of avoidance could be refused where it would be unconscionable,[176] but the argument was rejected by the Court of Appeal in *Brotherton*. It was held that the intelligence possessed by the insured and not disclosed to the insurer was, at the time of insuring, material, thereby allowing the insurer to avoid. It was not open to the insured to try and undermine that materiality at a later date.

1.44 In contrast a differently constituted Court of Appeal took a rather different view in *Drake Insurance plc v Provident Insurance plc*.[177] The facts of the case have been given above;[178] it concerned a pre-contractual non-disclosure that actually benefited the insurer. Rix LJ, whilst accepting that there was no binding authority on the point, said that in his opinion an insurer seeking to avoid the contract could not blindly rely upon the remedy of avoidance but must show a good objective reason for doing so. He must

[171] See Bennett, (1998) 61 MLR 886 and Hird [1998] JBL 279.

[172] For a recent dictum to this effect, see Longmore LJ in *Limit No 2 Ltd v Axa Versicherung AG* [2008] EWCA Civ 1231, [2009] Lloyd's Rep IR 396 at [4].

[173] *Pan Atlantic Insurance Co v Pine Top Insurance Co* [1995] 1 AC 501 at 555, per Lord Lloyd; *Kausar v Eagle Star Insurance Co Ltd* [2000] Lloyd's Rep IR 154 at 157, per Staughton LJ.

[174] [2002] EWHC 203 (Comm), [2002] Lloyd's Rep IR 669.

[175] [2003] EWCA Civ 705, [2003] Lloyd's Rep IR 758.

[176] Above at [132].

[177] [2003] EWCA Civ 1834, [2004] Lloyd's Rep IR 277.

[178] See **1.19**.

also justify his avoidance by reference to the facts as they stood at the time of contracting. Clarke LJ agreed with this conclusion but Pill LJ dissented on this point. He said that what mattered was the actual presentation of the risk, not the reality of the position. It was accepted that it was not open to the court to overturn a valid avoidance by relying on a continuing duty of good faith – however, it was said that as a result of this duty, the insurer, must, at the time of avoidance, enquire whether there were good grounds for seeking it. Unhelpfully, there was no clear view on exactly when an insurer would be in breach by avoiding. Certainly he would be in breach if he attempted to avoid knowing that the facts relied upon did not exist, but whether he must go further than this, ie by making reasonable enquiries, is a moot point. On the facts, it was decided that the insurer was acting in bad faith by seeking to avoid. Whether or not this produces a fair result, it has to be pointed out that the reasoning is by no means clear and is in direct conflict with clear dicta of Mance LJ in *Brotherton*.[179] A right to avoid or rescind is not traditionally limited by any requirement of acting in good faith and it could be argued that this is a better view of the law as it is than that seemingly expressed in *Drake v Provident*. The argument on the other hand turns on the fact that, as we have seen, recent case-law has developed a continuing duty of good faith on both parties and there is no reason to deny the role of a doctrine of unconscionability in this situation.

The basis of the contract clause

1.45 Historically, perhaps the most common and easiest way of creating warranties in non-marine policies was the basis of the contract clause contained at the foot of the proposal form. While this device may not be so wide-ranging in its effects as it has been, because of the impact of the former Statement of General Insurance Practice, it is still of importance in commercial insurances and still appears to be used in 'consumer-type' insurances to create warranties of opinion.[180]

By making the questions and answers and declarations on a proposal form the basis of the contract, and providing that in the event of any untruth the contract could be voidable, insurers succeeded in equipping themselves with a potential defence to an action on the policy much wider than that arising

[179] See especially [2003] Lloyd's Rep IR 758 at paras 29 to 34. In *North Star Shipping Ltd v Sphere Drake Insurance plc* [2006] EWCA Civ 378, [2006] Lloyd's Rep IR 519, Waller LJ thought (at [17]) that the decision in *Drake v Provident* was likely to apply in very few cases.

[180] Even under the former Statement, it was still acceptable to use a basis clause to create promissory warranties.

by virtue of the duty of disclosure.[181] The device was first adopted in proposal forms for life insurance in the last century. In *Thomson v Weems*,[182] a question on a proposal form asked: (a) 'Are you temperate in your habits and (b) have you always been strictly so?' The proposer answered '(a) temperate; (b) yes.' The form contained a basis clause which expressly said that in the event of an untruth, the policy would be void. As the proposer was in fact a heavy drinker, the House of Lords had no difficulty in upholding the insurers' repudiation of liability. Materiality, they said, was irrelevant, even though, in fact, the matter must have been material on the facts of the case.[183]

1.46 In contrast, in *Dawsons Ltd v Bonnin*,[184] it was accepted that the incorrect answer was immaterial. A motor proposal concerning a lorry asked where it was garaged. The proposer wrongly answered that it was garaged at an address in central Glasgow, whereas, in fact, it was garaged at an address on the outskirts of the city. The proposal form merely declared that it was to constitute the basis of the contract; there was no reference to the policy being void or voidable in the event of an untrue answer, something which in the dissenting judgments was regarded as of great significance.[185] Despite this, by a bare majority, at least one of whose members[186] was not happy with the result, the House of Lords held that the insurer could repudiate all liability. 'Basis' was sufficient to render the contents of the proposal form into fundamental terms of the contract. With respect, 'basis of the contract' by itself could simply have been interpreted as the starting point on which negotiations were to be based, so that incorrect answers on the proposal form justified repudiation only if they amounted to material misstatements.[187] However, whatever criticisms may be made, the decision has long stood as authority for the simple proposition that a basis of the contract clause converts all statements on a proposal form into warranties.[188] In the Scottish case

---

[181] For a persuasive attack on the device, see Hasson, 'The basis of the contract clause in insurance law' (1971) 34 MLR 29. Hasson points out that the warranties held to be created by basis clauses in the early cases were material to the risk and these cases could therefore have been distinguished in later cases where the warranties were not material, of which *Dawsons Ltd v Bonnin*, below, is a classic example. This, however, would have been most unlikely at a time when the prevailing doctrine was freedom of contract.

[182] (1884) 9 App Cas 671. Earlier cases are *Duckett v Williams* (1834) 2 C. & M. 348 and *Anderson v Fitzgerald* (1853) 4 HLC 483.

[183] But was not the question really asking for the proposer's opinion rather than a statement of fact? See Hasson (1971) 34 MLR 29 at 34–35. It is difficult to justify the view taken in most of the cases that questions asked of the health of a proposer for life insurance can be answered factually by a non-expert: see the trenchant comment of Fletcher Moulton LJ in *Joel v Law Union and Crown Insurance Co* [1903] 2 KB 863 at 885, cited in Hasson.

[184] [1922] 2 AC 413. The other leading case is *Yorkshire Insurance Co v Campbell* [1917] AC 218.

[185] See Viscount Finlay at 430–431, and Lord Wrenbury at 436–437.

[186] Lord Dunedin at 434–435.

[187] This point is strengthened by the fact that the policy contained a condition expressly providing that material misrepresentation or non-disclosure would render it void; see Hasson (1971) 34 MLR 29 at p 36.

[188] See eg the later decision of the House of Lords in *Provincial Insurance Co v Morgan* [1933] AC 240, discussed below.

of *Unipac (Scotland) Ltd v Aegon Insurance Co (UK) Ltd*,[189] there was the following clause, 'I/We declare that to the best of my/our knowledge and belief all statements and particulars contained in the proposal are true and complete and that no material fact has been withheld or suppressed.' The insured argued that such a phrase qualified the clause, which would otherwise have been a warranty, rendering it at best a representation that the statements relating to material facts were true and complete and that no material fact had been withheld or suppressed. There was a standard basis clause on the proposal form. It was held that the effect of the basis clause was to convert the representation into a warranty once the insurance commenced. The statement regarding material facts was to be read quite distinctly.[190]

1.47 It follows that in addition to materiality being irrelevant, unless there is a term in the contract which requires this, it is also irrelevant that the proposer has answered the questions in good faith and to the best of his knowledge and belief if, in fact, answers are inaccurate. An even harsher example of this is the decision in *McKay v London General Insurance Co*.[191] The proposer for motor insurance stated on the proposal form that he had never been convicted of a motoring offence. In fact he had been fined ten shillings many months previously for driving without efficient brakes because a nut had become loose on his motorcycle. Even though this was held not to be a material fact for the purposes of the duty of disclosure, the insurers were entitled to repudiate liability for breach of warranty.[192]

Needless to say, this strict legal position has attracted considerable criticism, and it is noteworthy that judges have been as critical as other commentators.[193]

Agency

1.48 Since the 2012 Act deals with aspects of agency and many insurance contracts are concluded through agents, it is necessary to consider the position at common law regarding whose agent in law a particular intermediary is. This is not something about which it is easy to be dogmatic. As a general rule, only the agent under the direct employment or control of the insurer is the agent of the insurer, and even he may not at all times when

[189] [1999] Lloyd's Rep IR 502.
[190] See Hird [1996] JBL 404.
[191] (1935) 51 Lloyd's Rep 201.
[192] Swift J did not like the result, though; see his comments at 202.
[193] The leading criticisms are referred to by the Law Commission, Report No 104, at 7.2 and 7.3. See also the Law Commissions' Consultation Paper LCCP 182/SLCDP 134, June 2007. Even if it is the case that insurers have not generally relied on their strict legal rights, it is suggested that this fact is no answer to the necessity for reform of the law.

dealing with an insured be regarded as the insurer's agent.[194] For most purposes, all other agents are in law the agents of the insured, and this is even so in respect of Lloyd's brokers.[195] However, there have been some cases where brokers have, for particular purposes, been regarded as agents of the insurer.[196] The position of the broker[197] in these cases merits further examination.

1.49 The question is of particular importance when the broker has notice of certain matters pertaining to the insurance contract, or purports to act on behalf of the insurer. As the broker is, as we have seen, the agent of the insured, the insurer should logically not be deemed to know or be bound by his actions. It is quite clear that a Lloyd's broker is always the agent of the insured,[198] although there is clearly some judicial unease about this.[199] A broker instructed to find insurance who goes first to reinsurers is the agent of the hitherto unidentified insurers/reinsured, not the agent of the insured.[200] In two relatively modern decisions, however, it was assumed that people who appear to have been independent, non-Lloyd's brokers were agents of the insurer. In *Stockton v Mason*[201] M's father, the insured, through his wife, instructed his brokers to transfer his existing motor policy from a Ford Anglia to an MG Midget. An employee of the brokers said that this would be all right for a temporary period, which the father naturally assumed meant that the previous policy, which covered the driving of the car by any authorised driver, was thereby transferred to the new car. Subsequently, the brokers wrote saying that cover on the MG was restricted to the insured only. M was driving the MG when he negligently injured the claimant. The issue was whether, under the Road Traffic Act 1972,[202] the claimant was entitled to sue M's father's insurers[203] and thus it depended on whether the latter were bound by the oral statement of the broker's employee purporting to authorise the MG to be substituted entirely for the Anglia. The Court of Appeal, consisting of three Lords of Appeal, held that the insurers were

---

194 See the line of authority of which *Newsholme Bros v Road Transport & General Insurance Co* [1929] 2 KB 356 is the leading case, which is discussed below.

195 *Rozanes v Bowen* (1928) 32 LIL Rep 98; *Anglo-African Merchants v Bayley* [1970] 1 QB 311; *North & South Trust v Berkeley* [1971] 1 WLR 470; *McNealy v Pennine Insurance Co Ltd* [1978] 2 Lloyd's Rep 18; *Robert v Plaisted* [1989] 2 Lloyd's Rep 341.

196 *Stockton v Mason* [1978] 2 Lloyd's Rep 430; *Woolcott v Excess Insurance Co* [1978] 1 Lloyd's Rep 633 (original trial), [1979] 1 Lloyd's Rep 231 (Court of Appeal), [1979] 2 Lloyd's Rep 210 (retrial).

197 For these purposes broker includes any independent intermediary.

198 *Roberts v Plaisted* [1989] 2 Lloyd's Rep 341.

199 *Ibid* at 345, where it was commented by Purchas LJ that to the person unacquainted with the insurance industry, it may seem a remarkable state of the law that someone who describes himself as a Lloyd's broker who is remunerated by the insurance industry and who presents proposal forms and suggests policies on their behalf should not be the recipient of full disclosure. The Court of Appeal, echoing the comments of Hodgson J at first instance, thought that the matter should be referred to the Law Commission.

200 *SAIL v Farex Gie* [1995] LRLR 116; as a result knowledge obtained by the broker was not imputed to the insured.

201 [1978] 2 Lloyd's Rep 430.

202 Section 149, now replaced by the Road Traffic Act 1988.

203 The brokers were also sued in the alternative.

bound. 'A broker in non-marine insurance has implied authority to issue on behalf of the insurer, or enter into as agent for the insurer, contracts of interim insurance ... it seems to me to be quite unarguable that in saying "Yes, that will be all right. We will see to that, Mrs. Mason," the brokers were acting as agents for the insurance company and not merely acknowledging an order or request by Mrs. Mason to negotiate a contract with the insurance company on his behalf.'[204]

In *Woolcott v Excess Insurance Co Ltd*,[205] a case which involved much dispute as to the facts, being referred back by the Court of Appeal to the trial judge on this issue, it was clearly assumed beyond argument by the Court of Appeal that the knowledge of a material fact by the broker in question was imputed to the insurers, and that the latter's defence of non-disclosure of that fact failed, even if the insured did not know that the insurer had the knowledge or was deemed to know.[206]

1.50 These two decisions were clearly to be welcomed as according with the reality of the situation, particularly as that is how it is no doubt perceived by insureds. Where appropriate, the extent of the broker's authority to bind the insurer will depend upon considerations that we shall discuss further, later. It does not seem, however, that the principles of these cases are generally applicable. In both of them there was a close relationship between the brokers and the insurers, the former being actually authorised to conclude at least interim contracts of insurance. More recently, in *Winter v Irish Life Assurance plc*,[207] it was held that the knowledge of the broker, that both lives insured had cystic fibrosis, was not imputed to the insurers. As a general rule, therefore, it seems safe to say that where an insured negotiates, through a broker or other independent intermediary, with an insurer with whom the broker does not have a close relationship, unless that broker or agent has actual authority from the insurer, the insured is not entitled to rely on principles of apparent authority.[208]

Imputing the agent's knowledge

1.51 Of particular importance in the context of insurance are the rules whereby, in certain cases, the knowledge of an agent is imputed to his principal so that the latter is deemed to know what the agent knows. These will be examined here only in the context of the agent being the agent of the

204 [1978] 2 Lloyd's Rep 430 at 431–432, per Lord Diplock.
205 See **1.26**.
206 [1979] 1 Lloyd's Rep 231 at 241–242 (per Megaw LJ); see also [1979] 2 Lloyd's Rep 210 at 211 (per Cantley J).
207 [1995] 2 Lloyd's Rep 274.
208 Unless, perhaps, the insurer has previously regarded itself as bound by representations of the broker or agent. For a brief description of actual or apparent authority, see below.

insurer, that is where an insured is seeking to rely upon them, although the same principles will apply when the agent is the agent of the insured.

Most commonly, the issue will relate to material facts of which the insurer alleges non-disclosure by the insured, but which the latter claims are deemed to be known by the insurer by virtue of its agent's knowledge. *Woolcott v Excess Insurance Co*,[209] which was described earlier, is an example, and the matter was considered fully in the context of non-disclosure.[210] In general the agent's knowledge will be imputed to the insurer, because he will have been held out as having authority to receive it, but the position may well be different if an incorrect answer is given on a proposal form, even though the agent knows the truth,[211] and it is, it seems, essential that the information is received by a person who is able to appreciate its significance. In *Mahli v Abbey Life Assurance Co*,[212] the insurers had previously been told of material facts (alcoholism and malaria of the life insured) because they had declined an earlier proposal on this basis. However, the person responsible for considering the later application did not know of these facts. It was held by a majority of the Court of Appeal that the insurers had not waived their right to avoid the later policy.[213]

1.52 Another illustration would be where the agent knows of something that constitutes a breach of warranty or condition by the insured. His knowledge of the breach may be imputed to the insurer who may therefore, by subsequently accepting premiums, be deemed to have waived the breach. In *Wing v Harvey*,[214] a life policy provided that it would become void if the assured travelled beyond the limits of Europe without the insurer's consent. An assignee of the policy subsequently informed an agent of the insurer that the life assured had taken up residence in Canada. For some time after this, before the life assured died, premiums were received by the insurer. It was held that the insurer had waived the breach of warranty; they were deemed to know what their agent knew and having accepted premiums subsequently, could not rely upon the breach.

What knowledge will be imputed depends upon the status of the agent receiving it, in other words, upon his actual or apparent authority. In *Wing v Harvey*, the agent was the local representative of the insurer at a branch office. A mere canvassing or soliciting agent would probably not be regarded

[209] [1979] 1 Lloyd's Rep 231.
[210] See **1.26**.
[211] *Newsholme Bros. v Road Transport & General Insurance Co* [1929] 2 KB 356; see below.
[212] [1994] CLC 615.
[213] McCowan LJ, dissenting, thought that the situation was indistinguishable from the earlier Court of Appeal decision in *Evans v Employers Mutual Insurance Association Ltd* [1936] KB 505 on the ground that there the only requirement for imputation of knowledge was that the agent in question was authorised to receive it. With respect, this seems more persuasive. See also the earlier case of *Stone v Reliance Mutual Insurance Association* [1972] 1 Lloyd's Rep 469, which seems to support the broader ground for imputation of knowledge.
[214] (1854) 5 De GM & G 265.

as having such a wide authority, which is after all tantamount to varying the terms of the policy, but such an agent probably has authority to receive disclosures of material facts.[215] However, the knowledge of an agent is never imputed when the agent is acting in fraud of his principal.[216]

Agents and the proposal form

1.53 As we have seen,[217] a common source of insurance warranties is the proposal form that contains a basis clause. It is not uncommon, in an insurance transaction being negotiated through an agent of one sort or another, for the agent actually to fill in the proposal form. Normally this would of course be done in consultation with the proposer, but there are reported cases that show that occasionally this is not the case. If an answer is incorrect due to the fault or with the knowledge of the proposer, then obviously the insurer will be entitled to avoid liability for breach of warranty. If, however, the proposer tells the agent the truth, but the latter chooses to falsify an answer, and the proposer does not become aware of what has happened, because he does not check what the agent has done, the question arises whether the proposer is bound by what the agent has done. Certainly he is if the agent is in law his agent at all times, and it has even been held that in this case he has no right to sue the agent in damages.[218] If, however, the agent is a full-time agent of the insurer, for example, a canvassing agent or another full-time employee, it might be argued that his knowledge of the truth should be imputed to the insurer, on the basis of the authorities discussed above.

However, the common law has in general taken the opposite view.[219] This is an area that has given rise to a comparatively large number of reported cases in all common law jurisdictions. We shall here concentrate on the English decisions, but make reference to some particularly apposite Commonwealth cases.

Knowledge imputed

1.54 The first authority to be examined is perhaps the earliest in time, a Court of Appeal decision that appears at first sight to be out of line with

---

215 *Ayrey v British Legal & United Provident Assurance* [1918] 1 KB 136; *Blackley v National Mutual Life Assurance of Australasia* [1972] NZLR 1938.

216 See a series of cases arising out of various problems at Lloyd's of London where it was held that the insureds were not deemed to know of their agents' fraud, applying the general principle of *Re Hampshire Land Co* [1896] 2 Ch.743: *PCW Syndicates v PCW Reinsurers* [1996] 1 Lloyd's Rep 241, *Group Josie Re v Walbrook Insurance Co Ltd* [1996] 1 Lloyd's Rep 345, *Deutsche Ruckversicherung AG v Walbrook Insurance Co Ltd* [1996] 1 All ER 791.

217 See **1.46–1.48**.

218 *O'Connor v Kirby* [1972] 1 QB 90. Compare, however, *Dunbar v A & B Painters Ltd* [1986] 2 Lloyd's Rep 38, which is also discussed later.

219 Whether or not statute reverses this in certain cases is discussed below.

subsequent cases. *Bawden v London, Edinburgh & Glasgow Assurance Co*[220] concerned a proposal for accident insurance by a proposer who was illiterate and had only one eye. This fact was known to the agent of the insurers who completed the form for him. That form, however, warranted that the proposer had no physical deformity, which was obviously incorrect. Subsequently the insured suffered an accident in which he lost the sight of the other eye. It was held that he could recover under the policy for total loss of sight. The agent's knowledge of the truth at the time of the proposal was imputed to the insurer.

Knowledge not imputed

1.55 *Bawden* was, however, distinguished in a number of subsequent cases[221] and in particular in the leading case of *Newsholme Bros v Road Transport & General Insurance Co*[222] Here the proposal was for motor insurance and the incorrect answers, which related to previous losses, were warranted to be true. It was found as a fact that the agent who filled in the form knew of the true facts. He was an agent employed by the insurers to canvass for proposals, but he was not authorised to effect insurance whether temporary or permanent. The arbitrator held that the agent's knowledge of the truth was imputed to the insurers who could not therefore repudiate liability, but his decision was overruled by the trial judge and the Court of Appeal. Scrutton LJ, delivering the leading judgment, gave two principal reasons for the decision. First, he said,[223] if the agent filled in the form at the request of the proposer, for that purpose he must have been acting as the agent of the proposer and not of the insurers. Secondly,[224] 'I have great difficulty in understanding how a man who has signed, without reading it, a document which he knows to be a proposal for insurance, and which contains statements in fact untrue, and a promise that they are true and the basis of the contract, can escape from the consequences of his negligence by saying that the person he asked to fill it up for him is the agent of the person to whom the proposal is addressed.'

Greer LJ also relied upon the agency point,[225] but he laid greater stress upon another reason, namely, that to allow evidence of what the agent actually knew to be introduced would be a violation of the parol evidence rule whereby oral evidence is generally inadmissible to vary the terms of a written contract.[226] Here the proposal form was part of the contract because, as

---

220 [1892] 2 QB 534.
221 See eg *Biggar v Rock Life Assurance Co* [1902] 1 KB 516; *Keeling v Pearl Assurance Co* (1923) 129 L.T. 573.
222 [1929] 2 KB 356.
223 *Ibid* at 369 and 375.
224 *iIbid* at 376.
225 *iIbid* at 382.
226 *iIbid* at 379–380.

usual, it formed the basis of it and its terms were warranties. Greer LJ was thus able to distinguish the *Bawden* case on the grounds that in the latter, because of the special circumstances of the proposer's illiteracy, the court could rightly ignore the parol evidence rule or put a special meaning on the words used in the contract.[227] In contrast, Scrutton LJ came very close to saying that the *Bawden* case was wrongly decided.[228]

Authority

1.56 As to the agency point, the judges seemed particularly impressed by the fact that the agent did not have actual authority to fill in proposal forms. With respect, this should not be conclusive. The fact that agents are armed with such forms and frequently complete them, probably to the knowledge of insurers, must arguably give them apparent authority to do so unless any such authority is negatived, for example, by a notice on the proposal form[229] – yet the principles of apparent authority were ignored in the *Newsholme Bros* case. Further, even if an agent does become the agent of the proposer, or at least his amanuensis, for the purpose of filling in the form, at that stage the form is merely an offer to enter into an insurance contract and it is not easy to see why the correct knowledge of the agent should not be imputed to the insurer if the facts warrant it.[230] On this basis the strict parol evidence rule could be ignored, as the court has already admitted extrinsic evidence for the insurer that the answer on the form was incorrect.

Signing of form

1.57 However, the second reason of Scrutton LJ as described above seems valid and strictly in accordance with the law governing the signature of documents, which holds a person bound by what he has signed, except in the limited circumstances when he can plead non est factum.[231] Therefore, it is suggested that the decision in *Newsholme Bros* is correct, and cases to the contrary must either be wrong or regarded as exceptions, a point to which we shall return.

Whether the result is a fair one is an entirely separate question. The Law Reform Committee[232] certainly thought not and recommended statutory

---

227 *Ibid* at 381.

228 The *Bawden* case had previously also been subjected to considerable criticism in a number of cases in different jurisdictions. These are cited in the judgment of Scrutton LJ.

229 See *Facer v Vehicle & General Insurance Co* [1965] 1 Lloyd's Rep 113. Such a provision might not, though, survive the Unfair Terms in Consumer Contracts Regulations.

230 See Tedeschi, 'Assured's misrepresentation and the insurance agent's knowledge of the truth' (1972) 7 Israel LR 475.

231 See Treitel, *Law of Contract*, Ch 8. The *Bawden* case might thus be regarded as a case where the insured could plead non est factum because of his illiteracy and consequent inability to check the form.

232 Fifth Report, 1957 Cmnd 62.

reversal of the rule. However, their recommendation, framed in terms that the agent should be regarded as at all times the agent of the insurer may not have gone far enough. If the analysis of the true ratio for the rule given here is the correct one, the parol evidence rule and the rule relating to the signature of documents would still present problems if the contents of the proposal form are part of the written contract. The need for some reform was also pointed out in a Government White Paper in 1977,[233] and the Law Commissions have provisionally proposed reversing both limbs of the *Newsholme Bros* rule,[234] but hitherto there have been no more concrete proposals.[235]

Newsholme Bros overruled?

1.58 It was, however, decided in Canada[236] that the decision in *Newsholme Bros* has been effectively overruled by the most recent English case, namely the Court of Appeal decision in *Stone v Reliance Mutual Insurance Society*.[237] Here the claimant's fire policy with the defendants had lapsed. An inspector employed by the defendants called on the claimant's wife and persuaded her to effect a new policy. On the proposal form, the answer 'none' was put to a question asking for details of lapsed policies and previous claims. This was incorrect. The claimant had made a claim on the defendants and had previously, obviously therefore, insured with them. The inspector had filled in the proposal form as indeed he was instructed to do by the insurers. It was held that the insurers could not avoid liability for loss. Megaw and Stamp LJJ regarded the case as turning on its special facts, namely that the inspector was actually authorised to fill in proposal forms. Lord Denning's judgment could

---

233 Insurance Intermediaries, Cmnd 6715, para 16. The comment here was rather ambivalent. Having supported the Law Reform Committee's recommendation, the White Paper then said; 'But it is not the Government's intention that the proposer should be relieved of responsibility for the accuracy of statements made by him in response to questions expressly put to him in the proposal form.' The Insurance Ombudsman was prepared to depart from the rule in *Newsholme* when he thought it fair to do so.

234 See the Consultation Paper 'Insurance Contract Law: Misrepresentation, Non-Disclosure and Breach of Warranty by the Insured', LCCP 182/SLDP 134, June 2007. Although their subsequent 'Report on Consumer Insurance Law: Pre-Contract Disclosure and Misrepresentation' recommends rules to determine the status of agents, which have been enacted in the Consumer Insurance (Disclosures and Representations) Act 2012 (see Section 6.17), it does not follow up this provisional view.

235 For an interesting argument that a general regulatory provision reversed the transferred agency aspects of the *Newsholme* rule, see Adams, 'More nails for the coffin of transferred agency' [1999] JBL 215. The argument was partly based on the effect of s 39 of the Financial Services Act 1986, now replaced by s 44 of the Financial Services and Markets Act 2000. Adams' argument was largely confined to life insurance cases, which is what the 1986 Act dealt with. Given that the regime now has a wider remit because it covers the selling of general insurance, it might be arguable that this aspect of the rule is affected in all situations.

236 *Blanchette v US Ltd* (1973) 36 DLR (3d) 561. This Supreme Court case, in fact, involved the slightly different situation referred to below, namely the agent filling in a blank form after signature by the proposer.

237 [1972] 1 Lloyd's Rep 469. See also Timmins, 'Misrepresentation in insurance proposal forms completed by agents' (1974) Vict Univ of Wellington LR 217, who is also, it is suggested, over-optimistic.

be more widely interpreted, but equally it is suggested that his decision really turned on the authority of the agent, not simply as regards the imputation of knowledge of the agent, but also because he had authority to represent that the form had been correctly filled in, particularly because it was accepted that the claimant's wife with whom he dealt was a person of little education. This is sensible. If an agent is fairly senior within an insurer's hierarchy, the circumstances should be such as to allow the admittance of what he did and said and to regard him as having authority to vary the terms of a written contract.

Another reason for regarding *Stone* as merely an exception to the general rule is that the insurers themselves must have known that the answers were false and what the truth was, because they were the insurers with whom the previous lapsed policy had been held and against whom the previous claim had been made.[238] To have allowed them to repudiate liability in such circumstances would have been ridiculous. This point was not actually taken in the case itself, but it must be correct.

It is suggested therefore, that there is no mandate for regarding the decision in *Stone* as overruling that in *Newsholme Bros*. The latter remains the governing decision, but there are exceptions in the case of illiterate and possibly poorly educated proposers and, possibly, where the agent in question is more than a mere canvassing agent but can be regarded as having some authority to vary the terms of the contract.

Form signed in blank

1.59 There is some Commonwealth authority which supports a further exception, namely where the agent fills in the proposal form after it has been signed in blank by the proposer, the latter relying upon the agent's representation that he has the necessary information.[239] This is perhaps tenable, assuming that the proposer acts quite innocently and in the circumstances the agent can be regarded as having the authority to represent that the insurer would be estopped from relying upon a breach of warranty. On the other hand, it is clear that if the proposer signs the form after the agent has filled it in himself without asking any information of the proposer, the latter is bound by what he signs.[240]

Conclusion

1.60 This chapter has sought to describe the current law relating to the non-disclosure and misrepresentation of material facts. That it is clearly

---

[238] See Ritchie J, dissenting, in *Blanchette v US Ltd* (1973) 36 DLR (3d) at 572.
[239] *Blanchette v US Ltd*, above. See also *Western Australian Insurance Co v Dayton* (1924) 35 CLR 355.
[240] *Biggar v Rock Life Assurance Co* [1902] 1 KB 516.

capable of operating unfairly in the consumer context has long been apparent, as has been mentioned in a few places, and the next chapter gives detailed examination to this question and why attempts to reform the law before the Consumer Insurance (Disclosure and Representations) Act 2012 failed.

Chapter 2 Reform at Last

Peter J Tyldesley
Peter Tyldesley is a solicitor and lecturer in insurance law at the University of Manchester. Until 2007 he was a lawyer at the English Law Commission where he was responsible for the review of insurance contract law. More recently Peter has worked pro bono with consumer groups and charities presenting the case for reform. In 2002, Peter was Director of the Centre for Financial Regulation Studies when it published Insurance Contract Law Reform, *a report produced by the British Insurance Law Association. Peter has also worked in-house for several insurance companies, as a consultant to the Insurance Ombudsman and as a lecturer for the Chartered Insurance Institute, the Pensions Management Institute and Gulf Insurance Company in Kuwait.*

Introduction

2.1 Insurance contract law has long been criticised as archaic, unclear and unfair.[1] In recent years there has been particular concern regarding both the harsh impact of the law on consumers and the resulting damage to the reputation of the insurance industry.

This chapter outlines the perceived weaknesses in the law, asks why antiquated commercial law rules are applied to modern consumer insurance contracts, considers the previous official reports in this area and closes by seeking to identify why reform has now been achieved when previous initiatives failed to produce change.

Much of the current law was established in commercial cases in the 18th and 19th centuries. At that time there was no mass market for insurance. Types of cover commonly bought by consumers today, such as household and motor insurance, did not exist. Insurance was typically arranged face-to-face rather than by telephone or over the internet. Despite these clear distinctions, it is the outdated commercial law which governs present-day consumer insurance policies. It is unsurprising that this mismatch can produce unjust results.

---

1 See, for example, Peter J Tyldesley, 'Archaic, unclear and unfair – Parts 1 & 2', New Law Journal 159(2009): 961–962 and 159(2009): 1358–1360.

Change has been slow in coming. A report by the Law Reform Committee as long ago as 1957[2] identified possible reforms, and a report by the English Law Commission in 1980[3] positively recommended change and included a draft bill. Neither was implemented.

The Consumer Insurance (Disclosure and Representations) Act 2012, which will be brought into force on 6 April 2013, results from the ongoing joint review of insurance contract law commenced by the English and Scottish Law Commissions in 2006.

Criticisms of the law

2.2 What, then, are the weaknesses in the three areas of law under consideration – disclosure, representations and basis of the contract clauses?

Disclosure and representations

2.3 When consumers apply for or renew a contract of insurance the law requires them to disclose all material facts to the insurer and to refrain from misrepresenting any material facts. A material fact is one which would have an effect, not necessarily decisive, on the mind of a prudent insurer assessing the risk. Where an insurer is induced to offer cover by the non-disclosure or misrepresentation of a material fact it may, on becoming aware of the true position, avoid the contract *ab initio* – from outset – and reject any claims.

Disclosure

2.4 Seven criticisms of the law may be made:

- Consumers may be unaware of their duty of disclosure or of the consequences of breach – for most, purchasing insurance will be their only experience of contracts *uberrima fides*.
- The test of materiality requires a consumer to look into the mind of a prudent underwriter – few will have the expertise to do so.
- In law there is no obligation on the insurer to ask any questions.
- Avoidance is available to the insurer as a remedy regardless of the degree of culpability of the consumer – even innocent non-disclosure is sufficient.
- Once a policy has been avoided, any claim can be rejected, even if there is no connection between the non-disclosure and the loss.

---

2 5th Report of the Law Reform Committee: 'Conditions and exceptions in insurance policies' Cmnd 62 (1957).

3 Law Commission's Report No 104, 'Insurance Law – Non-disclosure and breach of warranty', Cmnd. 8064 (1980).

- When a policy is avoided the consumer faces a triple penalty – loss of cover, loss of any claims and a future of difficulties obtaining cover at an affordable premium.
- The law encourages poor underwriting practice. An unscrupulous insurer may limit the questions it asks when a policy is sold, but if a claim is made it can search for a non-disclosure to escape liability.

2.5 The shortcomings of the law are illustrated by the experience of Mrs Brenda Lambert. In 1974 Lambert made a claim under an all-risks policy covering her jewellery. No doubt it came as something of a shock when the claim was rejected by Mrs Lambert's insurer on the ground that she had failed to disclose that her husband had been convicted of handling stolen goods. Lambert had held the policy for over nine years and at no time had the insurer asked her any question about convictions. Although the court found in favour of the insurer, MacKenna J, as he then was, made clear his unease:

> 'The present case shows the unsatisfactory state of the law. Mrs Lambert is unlikely to have thought that it was necessary to disclose the distressing fact of her husband's recent conviction when she was renewing the policy on her little store of jewellery. She is not an underwriter and has presumably no experience in these matters. The defendant company would act decently if, having established the point of principle, they were to pay her. It might be thought a heartless thing if they did not, but that is their business, not mine.'[4]

When asked some years later whether it had subsequently paid the claim, Co-operative Insurance Society responded:

> '… the outcome of the Lambert case [is] now rather historical and we do not wish to comment'.[5]

Representations

2.6 Six criticisms of the law may be made:

- Consumers may be unaware of the consequences of misrepresentation – and, arguably, the importance of accuracy is inadequately stressed in some marketing materials.
- Questions asked by insurers are sometimes of an unclear, over-lengthy, or technical nature which may cause consumers difficulties.
- To make sales easier, some insurers have adopted application processes which may increase the risk of misrepresentations – for example, the use of pre-populated forms or 'assumptions' in place of questions.

---

4 *Lambert v Co-operative Insurance Society Ltd* [1975] 2 Lloyd's Rep 485.

5 Letter to the author dated 29 May 1997.

- Avoidance is available to the insurer as a remedy regardless of the degree of culpability of the consumer – even innocent misrepresentation is sufficient.
- Once a policy has been avoided, any claim can be rejected, even if there is no connection between the misrepresentation and the loss.
- When a policy is avoided the consumer faces a triple penalty – loss of cover, loss of any claims and a future of serious difficulties obtaining cover at an affordable premium.

2.7 The potential impact of the law is demonstrated by the experience of Mrs Michelle Barber, which was widely reported by the media in 2009.[6] Two years earlier, Barber's house had been set ablaze by her estranged husband. He was later convicted of arson and received a custodial sentence of four years. Fortunately the house was insured, and was reinstated by the insurer at a cost of £241,000. However, two weeks before Barber was due to move back into her home the insurer avoided her policy and demanded that she reimburse its outlay. It alleged that when taking out the policy she had misrepresented that she had no record of offences, when in fact she had been fined £150 in 2002 for failing to repay an overpayment of benefits. Barber argued that she was not asked a clear question about fines and that the insurer's approach was unreasonable:

> 'I wasn't arrested, the police weren't involved and I'd simply forgotten about it by the time I took out the insurance. It isn't something I would have thought would have affected the policy. Insurance companies are not making things clear enough. You could have a fine for dropping litter in the street and your home insurance becomes void. It's a nightmare.'[7]

In Barber's case the insurer claimed that it would simply not have accepted the risk had it known the truth. However the current law allows an insurer to avoid a policy even where it would have accepted the risk subject to some change in terms – perhaps an increase in premium. As the Law Commissions pointed out, in certain other jurisdictions such as France, a proportional approach may be taken in such circumstances:[8]

> 'Proportionality has long been used in French law where the insured's bad faith has not been proved. Under Article L1139 of the Code des Assurances, where a misrepresentation is discovered after a loss has occurred:

---

6 See, for example, 'Arson victim billed by insurer', BBC News, 12 October 2009, http://news.bbc.co.uk/1/hi/england/norfolk/8294336.stm (as of 21 January 2013).

7 *Daily Mail* 17 October 2009.

8 Consultation Paper 'Insurance Contract Law: Misrepresentation, Non-Disclosure and Breach of Warranty by the Insured', LCCP 182/SLDP 134, June 2007, at para 4.159.

> "the compensation shall be reduced in proportion to the rate of the premiums paid in relation to the rate of premiums that would be owed if the risks had been truthfully and exhaustively declared."

Basis of the contract clauses

2.8 Where an application form for consumer insurance contains a simple declaration that the answers given will form the basis of the contract, the effect is to turn questions and answers into warranties.[9] A warranty is a particularly onerous term of an insurance policy, with any breach discharging the insurer of all further liability immediately and automatically.[10] Consequently if an answer relating to past or present fact is incorrect the consequence is that cover simply never commences – though both consumer and insurer may be oblivious to this until a claim arises and investigations are conducted.

2.9 Four criticisms of the law may be made:

- Most consumers will be completely unaware of the impact of the words 'basis of the contract' in an application form they are completing.
- There is no requirement that there be a link between the breach and any loss that has occurred. Breach of a warranty of past or present fact will mean that cover never commenced and all claims may be rejected, and breach of a continuing warranty will mean cover ceases immediately and any subsequent claims may be rejected.
- Cover does not recommence if a breach of warranty is remedied.
- There is no requirement of materiality – breach of warranty terminates the cover even if the subject matter of the warranty is trivial or irrelevant. Indeed in one recent Scottish commercial case, the court was prepared to contemplate that even an error in a telephone number could bring cover to an end, and declined to regard this as ludicrous.[11]

2.10 In an early consumer motor insurance case, the court found that a previous conviction for a loose wheel nut on a motorcycle was not material.[12] However, on the application form – which contained a basis of the contract clause – the consumer had stated that he had no convictions. The resulting breach of warranty allowed the insurer to avoid liability, though Swift J made clear his displeasure at this result:

---

9 *Dawsons v Bonnin* [1922] 2 AC 413.

10 *Bank of Nova Scotia Appellants v Hellenic Mutual War Risks Association (Bermuda) Ltd* [1992] 1 AC 233.

11 *Unipac (Scotland) Ltd v Aegon Insurance Co (UK) Ltd* 1996 SLT 1197. See also Peter J Tyldesley. 'Pearls of wisdom' Solicitors Journal 155, No 27(2011), pp 10–11.

12 *Mackay v London General Insurance* (1935) 51 Lloyd's Law Reports 201.

> 'I am extremely sorry for the plaintiff in this case. I think he has been very badly treated – shockingly badly treated ... But I cannot help the position. Sorry as I am for him there is nothing that I can do to help him. The law is quite plain.'

Disproportionate remedies

2.11 It may be seen, therefore, that all three areas of law share a critical flaw – they provide insurers with remedies which in many circumstances will be disproportionate. Insurers have themselves recognised that this is so, and under a series of codes have agreed not to enforce their strict legal rights. Likewise regulators have issued rules and ombudsmen have issued guidance indicating that consumers should be given more favourable treatment than that for which the law provides.

The dead hand of history

Non-disclosure

2.12 Why are consumer insurance policies subject to largely the same law as business insurance contracts? Certainly if one considers the circumstances in which such rules were formed, and the apparent reasoning behind them, they seem to have little relevance to the modern consumer. Take, for example, the rules on disclosure. As set out in Chapter 1, the first clear statement of the law is found in the decision of Lord Mansfield in the 1766 case of *Carter v Boehm*:[13]

> 'Insurance is a contract upon speculation. The special facts, upon which the contingent chance is to be computed, lie most commonly in the knowledge of the insured only: the under-writer trusts to his representation, and proceeds upon the confidence that he does not keep back any circumstance in his knowledge, to mislead the under-writer into a belief that the circumstance does not exist, and to induce him to estimate the risque as if it did not exist.'

2.13 *Carter v Boehm* concerned a commercial insurance policy on trading goods belonging to Roger Carter, Governor of Fort Marlborough on the island of Sumatra. The goods were lost when the French invaded in 1760, during the Seven Years War.[14] Does it make sense for the law set down in such a case to be applied to Mrs Lambert's claim for her loss of jewellery in 1972? There are at least five factors which might lead one to conclude that the application of the same rules to the two situations is inappropriate:

---

13 (1766) 3 Burr 1905.

14 For fuller details see Peter J Tyldesley, 'Consumer insurance and the duty of disclosure' BILA Journal 123, November 2011, pp 38–49.

- **Expertise**

  In the 18th century the sharing of risk was commonplace in the City of London; a merchant might be an insurer one day and an insured the next. Consequently it was not unreasonable for prospective insureds to be expected to understand what needed to be disclosed. Contrast this with the position of a modern consumer who will typically have no knowledge of insurance law or practice. As has been seen, McKenna J specifically made this point regarding Mrs Lambert: 'She is not an underwriter and has presumably no experience in these matters'.[15]

- **Knowledge**

  Lord Mansfield suggested that 'the special facts ... lie most commonly in the knowledge of the insured only'. This carries more truth where custom policies on business risks are concerned. For standard consumer risks, insurers have access to a wide range of databases, research results and loss statistics. For example, 95% of the household insurance market is covered by the Claims and Underwriting Exchange, an industry database which records previous losses and claims and will often prove more accurate than a consumer's memory.

- **Bargaining power**

  In *Carter v Boehm*, Lord Mansfield was settling the rules to be applied to business insurances, where a prospective insured may have broadly similar bargaining power to the insurer. Nowadays, it is common for large commercial insureds to insist that the impact of non-disclosure is modified by contractual terms.[16] Indeed in June 2011 the Association of Insurance and Risk Managers in Industry and Commerce published a standard wording to be used for this purpose. A consumer simply does not have this bargaining power and will typically contract on the basis of standard policy wordings drafted by the insurer.

- **Absence of advice**

  Carter's policy was arranged by a broker. In contrast, modern consumer policies are frequently purchased over the internet or telephone without the benefit of a broker's advice.

- **Potential for misuse**

  It is often overlooked that Lord Mansfield found in favour of Carter. In doing so, he recognised that the remedy of avoidance carried risks of misuse: 'If the defendant's objections were to prevail, in the present case, the rule would be turned into an instrument of fraud'. What, one wonders, would Lord Mansfield have made of an insurer promising to

---

15 *Lambert v Co-operative Insurance Society Ltd.*

16 See, for example, the 'innocent non-disclosure' clause in *Arab Bank Plc v. Zurich Insurance Co* [1999] 1 Lloyd's Rep 262.

give 'careful and sympathetic consideration' to medical records when in reality its sole purpose was to seek any entry which might give grounds for avoiding or invalidating the policy?[17] Or the insurer who rejected a leukaemia claim under a critical illness policy for the failure to disclose mild unrelated hearing loss?[18] Most insurers act decently most of the time. Nevertheless, given the relatively weak position of consumers and the impact of avoidance, is the risk that the duty of disclosure will be misused simply too high?

2.14 As has already been noted, in 1766 mass-market consumer insurance policies did not exist. The first motor insurance policy was not issued until 1896, and certain other lines of business are much more recent – for example critical illness insurance was not available in the UK until 1984. Those personal lines products which did exist in 1766 were the preserve of the wealthy and the cover was of a rather different nature. Household policies, for instance, had been available from the 17th century but were typically limited to fire risks. Indeed with the exception of industrial branch penny policies there were no mass-market products until well into the 20th century. Modern consumer policies were simply not in Lord Mansfield's contemplation when he gave his judgment.

Current sales channels are also markedly different to those which existed in 1766. Lord Mansfield was familiar with face-to-face commercial insurance transactions in the coffee houses of Georgian London. Would he have thought that the same rules should apply to consumers buying insurance by telephone or over the internet?

Stunted law

2.15 Why then have the courts and Parliament failed to temper the law and develop separate rules for consumer insurance law cases? In part the lack of judicial intervention may result from a sparsity of opportunity. Until 1957 it was routine for consumer insurance policies to include *Scott v Avery* arbitration clauses, giving insurers the right to insist that all disputes on liability were referred to arbitration. As will be seen, in 1957 insurers entered into a voluntary agreement not to use such clauses. However, there was no monitoring of compliance and it is not known when their use finally ceased.[19]

---

17 *Cuthbertson v Friends Provident* [2006] CSOH 74.

18 Ombudsman News 27, Case 27/5.

19 From 1 July 1995 such clauses were in any event likely to be regarded as unfair and therefore not binding on the consumer by virtue of the Unfair Terms in Consumer Contract Regulations 1994. See now Schedule 2 para 1(q) of the Unfair Terms in Consumer Contract Regulations 1999 and section 91 of the Arbitration Act 1996.

After 1957 the costs for consumers to litigate no doubt provided a substantial disincentive to litigate, particularly when the law was so heavily weighted in favour of the insurer. It is not known how Mrs Lambert was funded for her trip to the Court of Appeal in 1975. However her counsel sought to argue that the court was not bound by the Marine Insurance Act 1906 or the Road Traffic Act 1934 which confirmed existing common law rules on non-disclosure. This was an all-risks insurance policy and the court had the opportunity to develop the law. Needless to say, this argument was swiftly rejected by Cairns LJ:

> 'Mr. Lewis accepted that so far as marine and motor car insurance are concerned, the rule with all its hardships applies to those branches of insurance, but he asked us to say that an exception should be made for the class of insurance with which we are dealing in this case. I can find nothing in the authorities to justify doing anything of the kind. Such injustices as there are must now be dealt with by Parliament, if they are to be got rid of at all.'[20]

In more recent years the existence of successive complaints handling schemes, culminating with the present Financial Ombudsman Service has further throttled the flow of consumer insurance cases to the courts.

2.16 There has likewise been little statutory intervention in insurance contract law – either in the three areas under discussion or more generally. The main statute is, of course, the Marine Insurance Act 1906, but this was a codifying measure. There are two main reasons for this inertia: first the lobbying power of the insurance industry and second the related failure of two formal reform initiatives.

As will be seen from the figures given by Judith Crawford in Chapter 7A, the insurance industry makes an extraordinary contribution to the financial well-being of the United Kingdom. With that contribution comes remarkable lobbying power. The industry – represented by the British Insurance Association ('BIA') until 1985, and the Association of British Insurers ('ABI') thereafter – has traditionally resisted statutory intervention. Where pressure dictates it has offered instead voluntary codes of conduct.

For example, in 1977 the Law Commission and the Scottish Law Commission published a joint report on exemption clauses. The recommendations in the report formed the basis of the Unfair Contract Terms Act 1977. It had been intended that any legislation would apply to insurance contracts. The Law Commission believed that there were good reasons for not excluding any class of contracts and the Scottish Law Commission specifically stated that the inclusion of insurance contracts was justified. Insurers, however, wanted an exemption. The BIA and Lloyd's entered into negotiations with

---

[20] *Lambert v Co-operative Insurance Society Ltd.*

the Department of Trade (DoT).[21] It was agreed that in return for an exemption, the BIA would promulgate a self-regulatory code – the Statement of General Insurance Practice ('SGIP'). Gordon Borrie, then Director-General of Fair Trading, was later to describe the exemption as 'amazing'.[22]

SGIP was followed by a similar code, the Statement for Long Term Insurance Practice. The terms of these statements were not particularly robust, compliance was not monitored and until the advent of the Insurance Ombudsman Bureau there was no route by which a consumer could enforce the rights they supposedly gave. Writing in 1977, John Birds suggested that 'it all seems a rather pointless exercise'.[23]

Insurers were, incidentally, unable to obtain a similar exemption from the Unfair Terms in Consumer Contracts Regulations, which resulted from a European directive. Nevertheless the Department of Trade and Industry ('DTI') fought successfully to limit the impact of the directive on insurance contracts. In a lecture to the British Insurance Law Association in 1994, Keith Long of the DTI explained the approach:

> 'To sum up therefore, the Department, acting as sponsors of the insurance industry, has done what it can to limit the scope of the Directive to that which is reasonable, short of complete exclusion.'[24]

In fairness, it should be noted that insurers have on occasion had good cause to resist proposed intervention, as will be seen in the consideration of the Law Commission's 1980 report below. The result of the general approach, however, is a plethora of voluntary codes and the further stunting of consumer insurance law.

Previous law reform initiatives

Introduction

2.17 Two of the previous official reports into insurance law are well-known and have previously been mentioned: the 5th Report of the Law Reform Committee: 'Conditions and exceptions in insurance policies' in 1957,[25] and the English Law Commission's Report No 104, 'Insurance Law

---

21 The Department of Prices and Consumer Protection and the Office of Fair Trading were also involved.

22 Gordon Borrie, *The development of consumer law and policy: bold spirits and timorous souls* (London: Stevens, 1984), p 110.

23 John Birds, 'The statement of insurance practice: a measure of regulation of the insurance contract', Modern Law Review, v 40, no 6 (1977), p 677–684.

24 Keith Long, 'Unfair contract terms directive', Journal (British Insurance Law Association), no 87 (1995), p 72–78.

25 5th Report of the Law Reform Committee: 'Conditions and exceptions in insurance policies' Cmnd 62 (1957).

– Non-disclosure and breach of warranty', Cmnd 8064 from 1980.[26] Often overlooked, and with good reason, is the fact that the Scottish Law Reform Committee also produced a report in 1957.[27] Each of these three reports is considered below.

The fifth report of the Law Reform Committee, 1957

Introduction

2.18 In July 1954 the Lord Chancellor asked the Law Reform Committee to consider: 'the effect on the liability of insurance companies of special conditions and exceptions in insurance policies and of non-disclosure of facts by persons effecting such policies'.

The Law Reform Committee had been established in 1952. It had a significant limitation in resources in that it did not have a full-time permanent staff other than a Secretary, D W Dobson OBE and an Assistant Secretary, K M Newman. To consider the referral, a sub-committee was formed with five part time members: Mr Justice Patrick Devlin, Lord Justice Hubert Parker, Gerald Gardiner QC, Professor Emlyn Wade and Roland Outen.[28] A second academic, Professor Dennis Browne, was co-opted as from 4 December 1954.

Writing in 1965, Chorley and Dworkin pointed out the difficulties with this type of ad hoc arrangement:

> 'The main weakness of the English Law Revision Committee system has been that, owing to the fact that the personnel has consisted of busy judges, practitioners and professors, the work has necessarily proceeded at intervals, and the results, even with three committees at work, have never been commensurate with the requirements of the situation.'[29]

It was 2½ years before the Law Reform Committee's report was ready for publication. It appears that before finalising the report the sub-committee met on seven occasions. There were also three meetings of the full Law Reform Committee to consider successive drafts. Formal written submissions were received from the BIA, Lloyd's, the Corporation of Insurance Brokers, the Law Society, the Bar Council and the Society of Labour Lawyers.

---

[26] Law Commission's Report No. 104, 'Insurance Law – Non-disclosure and breach of warranty', Cmnd 8064 (1980).

[27] The 4th report of the Law Reform Committee for Scotland: 'the effect on the liability of insurance companies of special conditions and exceptions in insurance policies and of non-disclosure of facts by persons effecting such policies', Cmnd 330, 1957.

[28] Then senior partner at Ashurst Morris Crisp.

[29] R S T Chorley and G Dworkin, The Law Commissions Act, 1965, (1965) 28 MLR 675.

Why was insurance law referred to the Committee?

2.19 The referral to the Committee arose out of a controversial consumer motor insurance case. On 24 February 1954 *The Times* reported comments made by the Divisional Court in *Coyle v Trafalgar Insurance Company Ltd.* Clause 6 of the policy under consideration appeared to deal with fraudulent claims. In fact it also required any claim to be brought within seven days of the loss occurring and barred any action on a rejected claim unless brought within three months of the rejection. The Lord Chief Justice said that this was the most extraordinary arbitration clause he had ever seen, describing it as 'a trap'. Slade J suggested most people would have assumed the court referred only to fraudulent claims. Cassels J pointed out that the policyholder had no remedy and described the situation as 'outrageous'.

Industry lobbying

2.20 Initial contact with the industry appears to have been on 7 October 1954 when Dobson and Newman were invited for lunch at the BIA. In his minute of the meeting Newman noted 'Food and drink excellent'.[30] The BIA and Lloyd's also attended the meeting of the sub-committee on 20 December 1954.

By October 1955 the BIA had established a law reform committee chaired by R A Moore, joint general manager of the Eagle Star Insurance Company. On 27 October 1955 Moore wrote to Dobson suggesting – in a manner familiar to industry observers – that, if change was contemplated, voluntary action would be preferable to legislation[31]:

> '... if the sub-committee's report is likely to call for any alterations in insurance practice, we would like the opportunity of discussing whether such alterations could best be brought about by legislation or by voluntary agreement within the industry ... we do feel very strongly that if alterations are required it would be less likely to be damaging to our business abroad and reputation in this country if they could be achieved by voluntary agreement rather than imposed by legislation'.

On 27 February 1956 Devlin met representatives of the BIA and Lloyd's in his room at the Royal Courts of Justice. A discussion took place as to whether the industry would be prepared to drop compulsory arbitration clauses from policies. The BIA and Lloyd's agreed to consider the matter further. On 1 May 1956 they wrote to the Law Reform Committee requesting another meeting with a view to agreeing that arbitration should

---

30 They were entertained for lunch at the BIA on two subsequent occasions: 13 June 1956 and 16 October 1956.

31 See, for example, the list of agreements in Appendix 8.

only be obligatory for quantum, not liability, except for reinsurance, aviation insurance and special risks.

Rather than holding a meeting Devlin submitted a proposed form of words for such an agreement. With some minor amendments this draft was accepted by the BIA and Lloyd's. In a letter dated 4 July 1956 they agreed to use their best endeavours to secure the agreement of their members and by 26 October 1956 they were able to confirm that those efforts had been successful. On 12 January 1957 *The Times* reported that the BIA and Lloyd's had agreed that 'an assured who prefers to have questions of liability, as distinct from amount determined by the Courts, to do so notwithstanding that the policy contains an arbitration clause.'

Lack of consumer input

2.21 Regrettably there was no body in existence which could put the case for reform on behalf of consumers. The group of friends which formed the basis for what is now Which? began meeting formally on 15 January 1956. However the formal launch was not until 7 October 1957[32], after the Law Reform Committee had published its report. The National Consumer Council, now part of Consumer Focus, was set up a few years later in 1963 following the recommendations of the Molony Committee.

Wade expressed his concerns on the lack of consumer input in a letter to Dobson dated 27 May 1955:

> '… the Sub-Committee is up against a real difficulty in that there is no organised source of evidence from the insured to answer the vested interests of the insurance world'.

The closest was the Society of Labour Lawyers which in its written submission to the sub-committee made the following familiar points with regard to the duty of disclosure:

> 'We have learned from clients that most laymen are wholly unaware of the doctrine of the uberrimae fidei. Very few people understand that underwriters expect any disclosures of facts as to which in their proposal forms they have made no enquiry. When the position is explained the layman puzzled since he does not know what facts would in relation to a proposal from insurance affect the mind of a prudent underwriter and it is impossible to obtain from underwriters any comprehensive statement as to what facts would affect their mind in relation to any particular risk.'

---

[32] Led by Michael Young, they initially called themselves the Association for Consumer Research. Which? today is a formidable campaigning organisation. At its outset in 1957, its remit was inevitably more limited. The focus is clear from the title of a *Guardian* article by Michael Young published the day after the launch: 'Helping the Shopper to Choose Suitable Goods, Independent Tests of Name Products'.

Split views on the sub-committee

2.22 It is clear that there was a split within the sub-committee as to the need for reform. This disagreement came to a head at the fifth meeting of the sub-committee on 6 October 1955. Amongst the documents before the meeting was a memorandum drafted by Gardiner in which he recommended six amendments to the law. Gardiner felt, for example, that the duty of disclosure should be limited to those facts which would be considered material by a reasonable insured. In this, he was supported by Brown, Outen and Wade.

However, Devlin argued that altering the law in this way raised matters of social policy falling outside the competence of the Law Reform Committee. He felt that such issues should be dealt with by Parliament and not by a committee of lawyers. With the support of Parker, he was therefore against making any such recommendations. This was the basis on which the final report was prepared though not without reservations being expressed by Gardiner in a letter to Dobson a week later:

> '... while I entirely agree that the Law Reform Committee ought not to concern itself with matters which fall under the head of "party politics" (a group of subjects which would be difficult to define but which we usually appreciate when we see them), I would not myself have thought that the law of insurance properly fell under this head'.[33]

It is this debate which led to the curiously limp wording of the Committee's final conclusions.

The Law Reform Committee's conclusions

2.23 The Law Reform Committee's brief report of just 8 pages was published on 30 January 1957. The final paragraph contained qualified conclusions rather than recommendations:

> '14 While it is not for us to determine whether legislation is desirable, we think that we can properly consider to what extent it is practicable to introduce any new provisions into existing insurance law and what form such provisions should take. We think that any or all of the following provisions could be introduced into the law and that no legal difficulties would arise in their application—
>
> (1) that for the purposes of any contract of insurance no fact should be deemed material unless it would have been considered material by a reasonable insured;

[33] Letter dated 13 October 1955.

> (2) that, notwithstanding anything contained or incorporated in a contract of insurance, no defence to a claim thereunder should be maintainable by reason of any mis-statement of fact by the insured where the insured can prove that the statement was true to the best of his knowledge and belief;
>
> (3) that any person who solicits or negotiates a contract of insurance should be deemed, for the purposes of the formation of the contract, to be the agent of the insurers. and that the knowledge of such person should be deemed to be the knowledge of the insurers.
>
> We do not propose any amendment of the law in regard to arbitration clauses in view of the new arrangements recently announced by the British Insurance Association and Lloyd's to which we have drawn attention in paragraph 13. It is true that the Association and Lloyd's cannot speak for all bodies carrying on insurance business, but we express the hope that other insurers will follow the lead which has now been given.'

Aftermath

2.24 Once the report was published, it became apparent that there had been a misunderstanding. The BIA and Lloyd's had assumed that the agreement on arbitration clauses would lead to an abandonment of any suggestion of change elsewhere. Paragraph 14 of the report, despite its timid wording, caused deep concern.

In response, the BIA and Lloyd's took three steps: first they submitted an extended memorandum to the Scottish Law Reform Committee which was still undertaking the parallel review, secondly they requested a meeting with Devlin, and thirdly they wrote to the Board of Trade expressing their concerns.

The meeting with Devlin took place on 14 May 1957. As a sign of how seriously the matter was regarded, J H Pollen, Chairman of the BIA and Sir Walter Barrie, Chairman of Lloyd's attended. Devlin pointed out that the report made no recommendations for the reform of the law, but Pollen and Barrie felt that two out of three weekly law publications had failed to appreciate this. Barrie added that the report suggested that reform was practicable, which might be taken as meaning commercially practicable. A minute of the meeting records that he went on to explain that:

> 'It was for these reasons that Lloyd's and BIA had felt it necessary to take the matter up with the Scottish Law Reform Committee for fear that the latter might make some recommendations based on the assumption that the insurance industry had not raised any objections to the proposals of the English Committee.'

The next day, 15 May 1957, the secretary to the sub-committee wrote to the Board of Trade in terms which sounded the death knell to any hopes for speedy reform:

> 'I made it clear to the British Insurance Association and Lloyd's that the Lord Chancellor has no intention of introducing legislation based on the Reports and that before any change in the existing law came to be made – which would presumably be as much a matter for the Board of Trade as for the Lord Chancellor – a further and more broadly-based enquiry would have to be made into the practice of insurance companies.'

2.25 Although the Board of Trade did attempt to suggest that the test of materiality should be amended to a reasonable insured rather than a prudent insurer basis, even this modest proposal met with objections from both the BIA and Lloyd's. On 5 June 1958 R T D Wilmot, then chairman of the BIA, wrote to the Board of Trade raising the spectre of damage to overseas business:

> 'Whilst the Association would be reluctant to express views on the legal position, it is very concerned with the practical difficulties which might arise from the changes in law outlined, and is reinforced in this view by the constant endeavour insurance companies are making to ensure that no action is taken in the United Kingdom which, through creating misunderstandings abroad, could become a threat to the maintenance of their overseas business. In view of the fact that the Law Reform Committee is clear in its intention that there is no call for legislation, it is not proposed to recite details of these difficulties, as such a statement of position could in the course of time become outdated.
>
> I am asked to request, however, that if in the future legislation on such lines should be under consideration, the Association should be given a full opportunity of explaining the nature of the problems which the insurance market and those for whom it caters would have to face in the practical application of such laws.
>
> I understand that the chairman of Lloyd's is also writing to you.'

On the same day Sir Walter Barrie, then chairman of Lloyd's, also wrote to the Board of Trade with a three-page memorandum setting out objections to the Law Reform Committee's proposals. Barrie appeared to see little wrong with requiring prospective policyholders to disclose to a standard beyond that of a reasonable insured:

> 'It is submitted that whether the belief of the insured concerned or the belief of "a reasonable insured" were adopted as the test of materiality the existing rule of "utmost good faith" would be very largely whittled away. The knowledge of insurance which might be deemed to be possessed by "a reasonable insured" might be small, but he would be

> made by law the sole judge of the facts which an insured should disclose to his Insurers (of whose business and practice he may know little and care less) because they would affect the Insurers' judgement of the risk.'

No further progress was made and reform was shelved indefinitely.

Law Reform Committee for Scotland 1957

Introduction

2.26 In January 1955 the Lord Advocate asked the Law Reform Committee for Scotland to carry out a parallel enquiry with the same terms of reference as those given to the English Law Reform Committee. The Scottish Committee set up a sub-committee[34] to deal with the matter and agreed to exchange papers with its counterpart in London.

Complacency

2.27 Extraordinarily by 25 May 1955 the Scottish sub-committee had produced a draft report. At this date the only evidence available to the sub-committee was a letter dated 9 February 1955 from Young, Dand and Reed, a firm of solicitors in Glasgow. This letter suggested that in the absence of fraud, insurers should not be allowed to repudiate liability for non-disclosure of any fact about which they had made no enquiry:

> 'Insurance is a highly skilled job, handled by experts well versed in the principles of insurance, about which most proposers for insurance know little or nothing. Most proposers for insurance also know little or nothing about materiality or non-materiality that insurers do and we think it is not unreasonable that the onus of asking for information which is material to the due assessment of any risk should be placed on the insurers.'

Nevertheless, the sub-committee concluded that reform was unnecessary as explained by the Lord Advocate in a letter which accompanied the draft report to Dobson in London:

> 'You will also see from the last paragraph of the memorandum that the sub-committee are alive to the desirability that commercial aspects of the law, such as this one is, should be as nearly as possible uniform throughout Great Britain; and that while they themselves see no reason to any alteration of the present law in this case they would, in order to preserve

---

[34] The members of the sub-committee were Hamilton Lyons B, Solicitor, Peter Maxwell BA, LLB and Thomas Young CBE, WS.

> such uniformity, consider recommending a compromise on this view if your Committee feel strongly that some change is required'.[35]

Dobson was clearly surprised to receive a copy of a draft report at such an early date. He informed the English sub-committee that the Scottish sub-committee had reached its conclusions 'without waiting for any evidence from the insurance companies or anybody else'. On seeing the draft Wade commented disapprovingly that it 'discloses complacent approval with the status quo'.

Final report

2.28 The final report was not published until December 1957. It maintained the view that no change was necessary. Indeed it went further in suggesting that the rules in the Marine Insurance Act 1906 should be applied to all types of insurance, so doing away with the advantageous status of contingency insurances under Scottish law.

It is hard to avoid the conclusion that the Committee was unduly swayed by representations made by the insurance industry. Although the Committee had sight of the representations made to the English Law Reform Committee and indeed of the resulting report, it only took direct evidence from two further witnesses – the BIA and Lloyd's. The penultimate paragraph of the Committee's report is, no doubt, what led to Wade's accusation of complacency:

> 'Irrespective of the representations made by, and the evidence given on behalf of, the British Insurance Association and Lloyd's we would have reached the conclusion that legislation on this topic was unnecessary and undesirable; but we think it right to add that we were impressed by the contention submitted by these two bodies that, having regard to the immense amount of insurance business conducted, the existing law has, over many years, worked remarkably well and with remarkably little friction. It was further submitted to us on behalf of these two bodies that there is a real danger that any legislation, which might possibly be construed as having been necessitated by a lack of integrity or fair dealing on the part of British insurers, might have a severely damaging effect on the prestige enjoyed by British insurers overseas, with a consequent falling off in the vast foreign business which they conduct. We are of course not qualified to judge whether this apprehension is well founded, but, if it is, it no doubt affords a very powerful reason for not introducing legislation on this subject.'

Small wonder, perhaps, that little reference has been made to this report in later literature.

---

[35] Letter dated 25 May 1955.

The creation of the Law Commissions

2.29 Having been a member of the Law Reform Committee when it considered insurance law, Gerald Gardiner later became disillusioned with it as an effective means for change. In 1963 he resigned and in the initial chapter of a book co-edited with Dr Andrew Martin argued that the Law Reform Committee should be replaced.[36] Elevated to the peerage he continued to champion this cause:

> 'As one who was for eleven years a member of the Law Reform Committee, I naturally do not wish to undervalue their work. We would be given a little tiny piece of law to look at, and after about two years we produced what I believe were very useful Reports, most of which at some time or other were implemented. But this work meant attending about one afternoon a quarter, after a long day's work, for about one and a half hours; and I think it was Professor Sir Arthur Goodhart who said that you simply cannot get English law into good working order in that way. One of the reasons I resigned from the Committee was because, after eleven years, I realised that this was simply scratching the surface. The truth is that, broadly speaking, nothing gets done in the field of law reform unless there is a pressure group, or the Daily Express says something about it.'[37]

Finally, as Lord Chancellor in 1965, Lord Gardiner was able to introduce the Law Commissions Bill into the House of Lords. Once enacted this abolished the English and Scottish Law Reform Committees, replacing them with the English and Scottish Law Commissions.

The English Law Commission 1980

Introduction

2.30 In 1977 the Department of Trade was considering the fifth draft of a possible European directive affecting insurance contracts.[38] The primary objective of the directive was to open up the insurance market across Europe, with obvious potential benefits for the UK. Certain articles of the directive aimed to harmonise elements of insurance contract law. Article 2 dealt with misrepresentation and non-disclosure and would, for example, have seen the introduction of the principle of proportionality.

---

36 Gerald Gardiner and Andrew Martin (eds), *Law Reform Now*, 1963.

37 Hansard, HL Deb 11 June 1964, col 1087.

38 Proposal for a Council Directive on the coordination of laws, regulations and administrative provisions relating to insurance contract, OJ 1980 C 355/30.

On 15 December 1977 R E Clarke, assistant secretary at the DoT, raised the possibility of seeking advice on these issues from the English Law Commission. At a subsequent meeting it was agreed by the Under-Secretary, M S Morris, that an approach should be made via the Lord Chancellor's Department. The minute of that meeting gives a firm picture of what the DoT had in mind:

> 'The Commissions could concentrate their studies on the present proposals in the draft insurance contract law directive, perhaps even making proposals for additional measures that might be included in this directive. … When proposing such an enquiry to the Lord Chancellor's Office it would be helpful to emphasise the value of contributing at a reasonably early stage in the debate, thereby influencing the nature of the directive.'

After a meeting with the DoT one of the commissioners, Dr Peter North, agreed that a reference could be made to the Law Commission. He indicated that the issues considered would need to be limited to non-disclosure and warranties – those matters covered by the draft directive. It was envisaged that a report would be produced by the end of 1978. A formal reference followed from the Lord Chancellor's Department on 17 May 1978.

Delay and consternation

2.31 The first sign of trouble looming was a letter dated 29 June 1978 in which Dr North informed the DoT that the Law Commission had reached the decision that the review should be handled 'in a way as little different from our normal law reform exercises as possible'. Dr North proposed to issue a working paper in November 1978, with a final report being submitted in April 1979. In the event there was further slippage. In January 1979 the DoT received an advance copy of the working paper, which was formally published in the following month.[39]

The DoT had already held discussions with the industry and had reached the view that insurers were ready to accept the terms of the draft directive, including the introduction of the proportionality principle. Consequently the contents of the working paper caused consternation. Rather than offering an analysis which could be fed into the discussion of the directive, the Law Commission argued that the directive would cause 'major difficulties' if adopted. In particular, it dismissed the principle of proportionality, suggesting that it 'would not be a desirable innovation in this country'.

---

[39] For a more detailed account of the events that followed, see Peter J Tyldesley. 'The reform of insurance contract law – why have consumers waited so long?' Insurance Research and Practice no 2(2008).

The Law Commission proposed a rather different set of reforms. These included the modification of the duty of disclosure to make it subject to a 'reasonable man' test. After reading the report, Michael Starforth, the DoT's solicitor, recorded a key concern:

> 'I have formed the view that there is not the slightest possibility of persuading our partners to abandon their own systems of law, on which the directive is founded, in order to adopt the English system. If we flatly reject the essential points of the directive, there can be no further progress on this particular bit of harmonisation.'

2.32 The DoT decided to consult with four industry bodies – the BIA, Lloyd's, the British Insurers' European Committee and the Life Offices' Association. A meeting was held at the offices of the BIA on 14 March 1979.The British Insurers' European Committee reported that the reaction of insurers had been one of bewilderment: the working paper 'seemed to ignore the fact that once the EEC Commission had initiated a draft proposal one had to consider the consequences of its possible adoption'. It felt that the industry could live with proportionality, largely on the curious basis that it could avoid applying it in practice!

The BIA representatives had little positive to say about the Law Commission's proposals. One insurer believed that what was suggested was 'hopelessly impractical' and another thought the cost would outweigh the benefits for consumers. The BIA and Lloyd's agreed that a distinction should be drawn between consumer and business policyholders – an option that had been rejected by the Law Commission.

On 4 April 1979 the DoT produced a draft response to the working paper for consideration by Clinton Davis. The covering memorandum drew attention to the difficulties over the rejection of the proportionality principle, and suggested that the Law Commission should be asked to reconsider the point. In the meantime the DoT had received a copy of the BIA's submission to the Law Commission. This extended over 15 pages and objected, sometimes in caustic terms, to almost every proposal that had been made. John Henes, assistant secretary at the DoT, accepted that some of the points made carried a lot of weight. However, the tone was such that he wrote a memorable brief note on the copy circulating within the DoT: 'To me, it seems at times to show the objective disinterestedness of a Millwall supporter.'

2.33 By April 1979 the BIA was very much on the offensive. Reports appeared in the national newspapers with headlines such as 'Insurers attack law change plan', 'An angry reaction by insurers' and 'BIA disquiet at Law Commission report'. Nor was there much support forthcoming from other interested parties. The British Insurance Brokers Association agreed that a technical case could be made out for reform but believed that the Law

Commission's proposals required complete reappraisal. The Consumers' Association said that like the industry it was disappointed with the proposals. It felt they did not go far enough.

On 3 May 1979 there was a General Election. The Conservative Party led by Margaret Thatcher ousted the incumbent Labour government of James Callaghan. As Robert Purves sets out in Chapter 3 the incoming government had very different priorities so far as financial services were concerned.

The following year, on 19 February 1980, Greville Janner MP used the 10-minute rule to introduce the Insurance Policy Holders Protection Bill into the House of Commons. This bill included two sections relating to warranties and a third which read simply: 'The duty of disclosure heretofore imposed on an insured is hereby repealed.' An order for a second reading was read on 4 July 1980, but the bill fell at the end of the parliamentary session. Janner, however, continued to press the case for fairer law over the following years.

Final report

2.34 On 20 August 1980 the chairman of the Law Commission, Mr Justice Kerr, wrote to the Lord Chancellor, Lord Hailsham, expressing concern that the recommendations in the forthcoming final report should be judged on their merits. There was particular anxiety regarding the attitude of the BIA:

> 'Whereas the BIA was openly hostile, this was by no means the position of Lloyd's. Our impression is that whereas the BIA is in effect prepared to wage something like a political campaign against any change, Lloyd's are much readier to consider our recommendations on their merits without hostility.'

Several days later, the DoT received a copy of the final report which contained a draft bill. The Law Commission had repeated its earlier view that the relevant articles of the draft directive were 'inappropriate' to English law and that the proportionality principle was 'open to serious objection' and should not be introduced. Fuller details of the recommendations are given in Chapter 3. However, they included the suggestion that a duty of disclosure should be retained, but that material facts should have to be disclosed only if a 'reasonable man in the position of the applicant' would do so.

Aftermath

2.35 A briefing note drafted by the DoT maintained support for reform but suggested it should be deferred so that the requirements of the proposed directive could be taken into account. Not all within the DoT supported this approach. Michael Wasilewski fought a rearguard action:

> 'I am not in a position to take a view on how the EEC dimension should affect the timing; but I cannot help feeling that the line proposed in … your note will be seen by many (and possibly rightly) as a polite way of throwing the report into the lumber room.'

On 29 October 1980 Lord Hailsham wrote to Henes at the DoT indicating that he felt the Law Commission's recommendations should be considered on their merits, which he regarded as 'considerable'. This received backing from Wasilewski at the DoT, who argued that it would be unfortunate if the Law Commission's proposals were 'indefinitely shelved because of the EEC angle'. He also agreed with the Law Commission's assessment that the statements of practice were not an acceptable alternative to law reform. However, a written parliamentary question was arranged so that Reginald Eyre, Parliamentary Under-Secretary of State, could put matters on hold:

> 'The Government wish to allow time for all those interested in the report to put forward views and for those views to be considered.'[40]

On 11 November 1980, the Secretary of State for Trade, John Nott, responded to Lord Hailsham stating that the DoT supported the view of the Law Commission that reform of the law of non-disclosure and breach of warranty was necessary and desirable. However, there was an understandable qualification:

> 'It would not be sensible to introduce a bill to reform a branch of the law when all concerned will know that quite different changes may have to be introduced within a few years because of a draft EC directive already put to the Council of Ministers.'

Objections, delay and vacillation

2.36 In February 1981 the National Consumer Council, the Consumers' Association and the National Federation of Consumer Groups all presented papers to the DoT giving their views on the Law Commission's final report. All three believed that the Law Commission's proposals did not go far enough. More surprisingly, all agreed that the proportionality principle should not be imported into English law. The National Consumer Council and the Consumers' Association argued that there should be a separate law of insurance for consumers.

Janner asked two further parliamentary questions regarding possible changes to the law and on 19 March 1981 received a written answer from Eyre stating that consultation was continuing.

On 31 March 1981 the BIA submitted a paper to the DoT in which it put its case against the Law Commission's proposals. The BIA pointed out that the

---

40 Hansard, HC Deb 4 November 1980, col 498W.

premium income of its members was £13,340 million in 1979, of which 35% was derived from overseas business. It argued that any changes should be limited to consumer insurances and offered to reconsider the terms of the statements of practice. Particular anxiety was expressed about the Law Commission's rejection of the draft directive:

> 'British insurers are widely represented in Europe and we are concerned with the possibility of increasing our participation in this market by way of both co insurance and freedom of services. An outright rejection by Her Majesty's Government of draft EEC legislation on insurance could only impair our prospects in this large and growing market.'

2.37 On 1 June 1981 Janner asked the Secretary of State for Trade to indicate when he expected to complete consultations. This was followed on 3 June 1981 by a debate in the House of Commons which covered both the Law Commission's proposals and the draft directive. Janner returned to the fray in May 1982 in an adjournment debate. He recognised that 'most insurers' did not take advantage of the unsatisfactory law but said he was very disturbed at a number of cases he saw and 'the often wicked way in which people are deprived of their rights'. He mentioned that his 10-minute rule bill would have a second reading in July 1982, but accepted it had no real prospect of success.

A response given by Gerard Vaughan, the minister for consumer affairs, referred to the existence of the Insurance Ombudsman Bureau as well as to European developments – though failed to mention that as at 31 March 1982 the bureau had just 38 members.[41] Janner pushed Dr Vaughan for action and received a promising reply:

> 'I am conscious of the problems and the need to take action. A good deal of uncertainty has resulted from the Law Commission's report, the consultation paper and the replies. I am aware of the damage that can be caused by drift. We shall not delay.'[42]

In January 1983, Janner asked Dr Vaughan two questions: first, whether he had any proposals to protect consumers from exclusion clauses in insurance contracts, and second, whether he would remove the exemption of insurance contracts from the Unfair Contract Terms Act 1977.[43] Dr Vaughan indicated he was considering legislation in the light of the Law Commission's report, but had no plans to amend the Unfair Contract Terms Act.

On 28 April 1983 – with an election in sight – Dr Vaughan gave a clear declaration of intent:

---

[41] IOB annual report 1982.
[42] Hansard, HC 28 May 1982, col 1199.
[43] Hansard, HC 20 Jan 1983, col 188.

'Following extensive consultations on [the 1980 report] the Government have decided to introduce a Bill, as soon as legislative time is available, broadly on the Law Commission's proposals in Cmnd 8064, but limited to private consumer insurance contracts.'[44]

2.38 Nearly a year later, on 28 March 1984, Mr Janner asked the Secretary of State for Trade and Industry[45] whether legislation reforming the duty of disclosure in insurance contracts would be introduced in that parliamentary session. John Butcher, Parliamentary Under-Secretary of State at the DTI, gave a firm commitment to the House of Commons and dismissed the possibility of the statements of practice being an acceptable alternative to legislation:

'It remains the Government's intention to introduce legislation to reform the law on non-disclosure in relation to insurance contracts affecting private consumers as soon as legislative time is available. ... We have said that we wish to introduce legislation as soon as possible. ... The Government agree with the Law Commission that voluntary undertakings by the industry are not a substitute for reforming an unfair law.'[46]

On 25 April 1984 Mr Janner asked whether the DTI had any plans to introduce legislation to subject insurance exclusion clauses to controls like the Unfair Contract Terms Act. Alexander Fletcher, Parliamentary Under-Secretary of State at the DTI, replied:

'I have no plans for legislation on insurance contract law except along the lines recommended in the Law Commission report ...'[47]

However, on 20 December 1984 Fletcher informed the House of Commons that there had been a change of heart. In answer to a written question he announced that he was embarking on discussions with the insurance industry to see whether changes could be made to the statements of practice.[48] For Dr North, who by then had left the Law Commission, this was clearly too much to stomach. He suggested that there was another question for Fletcher to answer:

'One might ask: what on earth did he think his Department had been doing for the last four years? The suspicious observer might conclude that the insurance industry lobby has been active behind closed doors and has in fact won.'[49]

---

44 Hansard, HC 28 Apr 1983, col 376.
45 The DoT and the Department of Industry had merged.
46 Hansard, HC 28 Mar 1984, cols 280–281.
47 Hansard, HC 25 Apr 1984, cols 511.
48 Hansard, HC 20 Dec 1984, cols 273–274.
49 Peter North, 'Law reform: processes and problems', Law Quarterly Review, v 101 (1985), p 338.

2.39 Over the following months, the Consumers' Association and the National Consumer Council continued discussions with the DTI. By February 1986 the Consumers' Association believed an understanding had been reached that legislation would be forthcoming after all. It was therefore a shock when on 21 February 1986 the Secretary of State for Trade and Industry, Paul Channon, announced that revisions to the statements of practice had been agreed and that there would be no reform of the law.[50] The changes in the statements of practice were limited, though notably they did include a bar on the use of 'basis of the contract' clauses.[51]

This was a missed opportunity. Insurers were clearly prepared for consumers to be treated differently to businesses, and had agreed in principle to accept the proportionality principle – though enthusiasm may have waned as it became clear that the proposed directive was not going to be pursued.[52] Even implementation of the Law Commission's proposals as they stood for consumers would have been an improvement on the existing law and entirely possible once the complicating factor of the directive had been removed.

One academic concluded that resorting to such amendments to the statements displayed a 'minimalist attitude to the problems of abusers'.[53] The Law Commission had, after all, been quite clear that it did not regard the Statements as a satisfactory substitute for reform:

> 'In our view the Statements of Insurance Practice are themselves evidence that the law is unsatisfactory and needs to be changed. As we have pointed out, the Statements lack the force of law so that an insured would have no legal remedy if an insurer fails to act in accordance with them. Indeed, the liquidator of an insurance company would be bound to disregard them. We consider that the further protection which the insured needs should be provided by legislation.'[54]

Regrettably law reform would be off the agenda for another 20 years.

---

50 Hansard, HC 21 Feb 1986, cols 356–357.

51 There was no consultation regarding these changes. The urban legend within the ABI, for which I am grateful to Martin Hoskins, was that a senior member of staff, Vic Rance, was sent home one weekend having been told to wrap a wet towel around his head and return on Monday morning having drafted suitable amendments.

52 The proposal was formally withdrawn by the European Commission on 4 August 1993. OJ 1993 C 228/4 and 14.

53 A D M Forte, 'The revised statements of insurance practice: cosmetic change or major surgery?', Modern Law Review, v 49, no 6 (1986), p 754.

54 Law Commission's Report No. 104, 'Insurance Law – Non-disclosure and breach of warranty', Cmnd 8064 (1980) at para 3.28.

Mike Harris and the GRE

Non-disclosure and basis of the contract clauses

2.40 One insurer decided not to wait for the outcome of the discussions relating to the Law Commission's report. On 3 December 1980 the Guardian Royal Exchange (GRE) circulated an internal memorandum stating that for consumer non-life insurances it would no longer rely on the duty of disclosure.[55] The move was driven by Mike Harris, Assistant General Manager, who explained his reasoning in a letter published by the Post Magazine on 14 May 1981:

> 'You cannot import into the way we handle bulk insurance products now the close contractual relationship derived from the time a ship or cargo owner dealt directly with an underwriter in a coffee house 300 years ago and bargained over a single voyage. …
>
> Defence of the traditional duty implies that although for many years we have handled hundreds of millions of transactions we still do not know all the right questions to ask. If this be so, then surely many of us should be seeking a living in some less demanding walk of life? I do not believe it is so.'[56]

The GRE reviewed this approach in 1984 and concluded it should be maintained as it had caused no difficulties in practice. With effect from 15 June 1984 the GRE also abandoned the use of basis of the contract clauses in non-life consumer insurances.

The Insurance Ombudsman Bureau

2.41 Another brainchild of Mike Harris was the Insurance Ombudsman Bureau ('IOB'), which commenced operations on 30 March 1981.[57] Harris had attended the BILA Colloquium in 1975[58], where one of the speakers was Hans Petter Lundgaard, then Head of the Norwegian Bureau for Insurance Disputes. Inspired by what he heard, Harris wrote a proposal for an ombudsman scheme.[59] However, he failed to secure support through the usual BIA channels. Eventually the GRE decided to found the IOB with two other insurers – the General Accident Fire and Life Assurance Corporation Limited and the Royal Insurance Company Limited. In an enlightened

---

55 I am indebted to Nick Feldman for a copy of this memorandum, which he drafted in his role as Accident Manager (Planning) at the GRE.

56 S M F Harris, 'Why wait for Godot?', Post Magazine, v 142, no 20 (1981).

57 Peter J Tyldesley, 'The Insurance Ombudsman Bureau – the early history', Journal of Insurance Research and Practice No 39 (2003), pp 34–43.

58 See Section 5.3.

59 Published for the first time as Appendix 1.

move the three insurers sought the views of the Consumers Association and the National Consumer Council, leading to refinements in the nature and structure of the scheme.

Membership of the IOB was voluntary, but was to grow over the following years until it included nearly all insurers offering consumer policies. One major advantage of the IOB compared with the courts was that it was empowered to look beyond the strict law in making its decisions. In particular, the Ombudsman's Terms of Reference allowed him to take into account codes of practice, good insurance practice.[60] The second ombudsman, Dr Julian Farrand indicated, for example, that he would apply a proportionate approach in cases of non-fraudulent non-disclosure[61] and in some cases award damages rather than avoidance for innocent misrepresentation.[62] Farrand also brought about an amendment to his terms of reference in 1994 allowing the ombudsman to decide cases on the basis of 'what solution would be fair and reasonable in all the circumstances'. Using this power, his successor, Laurie Slade, seemed to go further, suggesting that in the absence of clear questions at inception or renewal an insurer would be taken to have waived the requirement of disclosure.[63]

2.42 There have been suggestions that the IOB was established to deter reform. This notion appears to stem from an article written in 1988. Gradually the notion has developed, to the extent that it has even been suggested that the IOB was the result of an agreement entered into by the industry:

> 'The common law of insurance is often perceived as being weighted against the insured, a perception which has attracted the attention of the Law Commission, which in 1980 recommended reform of the most problematic part of insurance contract law, that relating to non-disclosure, misrepresentation and breach of warranty. In order to forestall this reform, the industry had to agree to the creation of the Insurance Ombudsman Bureau for the resolution of complaints involving personal lines policyholders.'[64]

This viewpoint must now be reconsidered. There was no such deal by the industry – only nine insurers were reported to have joined the IOB at outset,[65] and of those who chose not to do so, some were openly hostile.[66] Furthermore, it is quite clear that Harris had been arguing for an ombudsman since September 1975 – some two years and eight months before the Law Commission was asked to consider the subject of insurance law.

---

60 The Terms of Reference were first published in IOB Annual Report 1990, p 26.
61 IOB Annual Report 1989, pp 8–9.
62 IOB Annual Report 1990, pp 7–8.
63 IOB Annual Report 1995, p 37–38.
64 Andrew McGee, 'The Single Market in Insurance', Ashgate 1998, at p 5.
65 See, for example, 'Business Diary: Insurance's Ombudsman', *The Times*, 20 March 1981.
66 To the extent of announcing a rival arbitration scheme, PIAS, on the very day the IOB was launched.

Perhaps not surprisingly, therefore, Harris has described the suggestion that the IOB was a ploy to avoid implementation of the Law Commission's recommendations as 'complete nonsense'. Maurice Healy, who worked on the project whilst Head of Policy at the National Consumer Council, and later served on the IOB Council, supports this viewpoint: 'I agree that there was no specific intention to try to put off legislation; given the attitude of the BIA it would be hard to demonstrate that there was such an intention.'

2.43 The IOB was the first private sector ombudsman scheme, and has been the blueprint for dozens of similar arrangements for a range of professions and industries both here[67] and abroad. Few people can claim to have made a greater contribution to consumer protection worldwide than Mike Harris.

The Financial Ombudsman Service

2.44 In 2001, the IOB was one of eight complaints handling schemes replaced by the Financial Ombudsman Service.[68] Those responsible for designing the FOS were determined that it should reflect the best of the predecessor schemes.[69] Although the FOS is statutory in nature, and its remit is far broader than just insurance, it is possible to see the strong influence of the IOB in its design. Under section 228 of the Financial Services and Markets Act 2000 the ombudsman is obliged to make decisions under her compulsory jurisdiction in accordance with what she regards as fair and reasonable in all the circumstances. This has enabled the FOS to develop its own approaches to issues where the law has the potential to cause unfairness.

However, the FOS is not a complete remedy to the ills of the law. Most obviously, it cannot make binding awards in excess of £150,000.[70] It was thought that a consumer with a loss in excess of this figure would be obliged to abandon the balance of the claim.[71] A more recent case suggests it may be possible to pursue the balance through the courts – though the full harshness of the law would then apply.[72] In addition the DISP Sourcebook[73] provides

---

67 For examples, see http://www.ombudsmanassociation.org (as of 21 January 2013).

68 The eight being the Personal Investment Authority Ombudsman Bureau, the Insurance Ombudsman Bureau, the Office of the Banking Ombudsman, the Office of the Building Societies Ombudsman, the Office of the Investment Ombudsman, the Securities and Futures Authority Complaints Bureau, the Financial Services Authority Complaints Unit and the Personal Insurance Arbitration Service.

69 Clare Boyle and Nick Walker, then employed by the Securities and Investments Board, were responsible for this principled approach. Note that the PIA Ombudsman, for example, did not have a 'fair and reasonable' obligation or power: Peter J Tyldesley, 'The PIA Ombudsman – a reduction in investor protection', Solicitors Journal 138, no 23(1994), 613–614. In one area it also took a harsher view of the law than subsequently proved to be justified: Peter J Tyldesley, 'Insurers liable for mortgage advice – Martin v Britannia Life', New Law Journal 150(2000): 572–586.

70 From 1 January 2012 – previously the limit was £100,000.

71 *Andrews v SBJ Benefit Consultants* [2010] EWHC 2875.

72 *Clark v In Focus Asset Management & Tax Solutions Ltd* [2012] EWHC 3669 (QB).

73 Part of the FSA Handbook.

a range of grounds on which cases may be dismissed without consideration of the merits. One practical consequence of the FOS being unable to take evidence under oath is that they may decline to deal with a case where there is a significant dispute on the facts.[74]

Furthermore, the overall impact of the conflicting layers of law, self-regulation, statutory regulation and ombudsman guidance is the risk of some confusion.

The Law Commissions' current review of insurance law

Introduction

2.45 The English Law Commission announced the current review of insurance contract law in its Ninth Programme published in March 2005:

> 'PROJECT 7: INSURANCE CONTRACT LAW
>
> The current law is incoherent and arguably unfair to the insured. It is made tolerable only by codes of practice that in effect disapply parts of the law. The result is not comprehensible to the consumer, while businesses are not covered by the codes of practice. The law also contains uncertainties that encourage unnecessary litigation. It has been suggested that these defects are adversely affecting confidence in the UK market. This review will ensure the law reflects the need of modern insurance practice and allows both insured and insurer to know their rights and obligations'.

A Scoping Paper was issued on 18 January 2006. This confirmed that it would be a joint review with the Scottish Law Commission. Some Law Commission projects result from referrals from Government departments. However the Law Commissions also have the power to initiate their own reviews, as they did in this case. The Scoping Paper gave one of the main reasons for doing so:

> 'A major factor in our decision to return to this area was the publication of a report by the British Insurance Law Association ("BILA") in 2002. This report was prepared by a sub-committee with an impressive breadth of membership – academics, brokers, insurers, lawyers, loss adjusters, a self-regulatory body and trade associations. It included the text of lectures given by two senior members of the

---

[74] Consultation Paper 'Insurance Contract Law: Misrepresentation, Non-Disclosure, and Breach of Warranty by the Insured', LCCP 182/SLDP 134, — June 2007 at para 3.5.9

judiciary, and a foreword contributed by a third. BILA declared itself "satisfied that there is a need for reform" and put forward detailed proposals for change.'[75]

There was at this time also considerable disquiet about critical illness insurance – with reported cases starkly highlighting the impact of bad law.

Critical illness insurance

2.46 One notorious case was reported by the FOS as early as 2003. Mr and Mrs C held a joint critical illness policy. When Mrs C was diagnosed with leukaemia, the resulting claim was rejected on the basis that she had misrepresented her health on the original application form by failing to disclose mild hearing loss. Had the insurer been aware of the true position it would simply have imposed an exclusion relating to her hearing. The FOS concluded the misrepresentation was inadvertent and required the insurer to meet the claim in full.

Some insurers were alert to the damage that such cases were causing to the reputation of the insurance industry generally. Writing in Money Marketing in November 2005 Nick Kirwan – then Protection Market Director at Scottish Widows – stated that the announcement that the Law Commissions were to review insurance law was 'long overdue' and set out why he felt reform should be 'another step on the long road towards winning back the trust of consumers'.[76] In the following month the *Daily Mail* began its ongoing campaign on the issue with a steady stream of case studies where consumers, already facing life changing illnesses, appeared to have been dealt with harshly by insurers. Both the *Daily Mail* and LifeSearch, an insurance intermediary, also obtained and published data for individual insurers showing the percentage of critical illness claims rejected for non-disclosure and overall. On 22 March 2006 BBC South East Today highlighted the case of multiple sclerosis sufferer Jasmine Tucker and interviewed both Peter Hinchliffe from the FOS and Hugh Beale, then Law Commissioner.

The ABI initially responded to concerns with the issue of Application Form Design in 2006.[77] In 2007, Nick Kirwan joined the ABI and, as described by Melissa Collet in Chapter 4,[78] worked with the ABI to produce further guidance. Non-Disclosure and Treating Customers Fairly was issued in 2008 and upgraded in 2009.[79]

---

75 'Insurance Contract Law, A Joint Scoping Paper', The Law Commission and the Scottish Law Commission, 2006, para 1.6.
76 Nick Kirwan, 'Application of the law', Money Marketing, 17 November 2005.
77 See Appendix 6.
78 See Section 4.10.
79 See Appendix 7.

Consultation and research

Scoping Paper

2.47 The Law Commissions received 118 responses to their Scoping Paper. In August 2006 they published their analysis of these responses and their decisions on scope. By this time the Law Commissions had already given 6 lectures and attended 35 meetings to discuss aspects of the project. It was decided that the first issue to be looked at would be the pre-contractual provision of information by the consumer – that is disclosure, representations and basis of the contract clauses. A three-stage approach was to be taken, in the knowledge that it would be familiar to insurers from the similar structure of some Financial Services Authority consultations:

- Issues Paper[80]
- Consultation Paper
- Final Report.

Where appropriate the Law Commissions took account of the Code of Practice on Consultation – so, for example, allowing a minimum time for responses of 12 weeks.

Issues Paper

2.48 The Issues Paper on disclosure, representations and basis of the contract clauses was issued in September 2006 and covered both business and consumer insurances. The purpose of the Issues Paper was stated to be to 'promote discussion of some of the main matters within the review, and give a focus for debate at seminars that we are holding'. It would 'list our tentative conclusions and proposals' but these would be 'reviewed in the light of submissions we receive and discussions at the planned seminars'.

Once the Issues Paper had been published, the Law Commissions undertook a further round of lectures, seminars and meetings. The English Law Commission also conducted a survey of relevant cases at the Financial Ombudsman Service.

Financial Ombudsman Service

2.49 As noted above the ombudsman is obliged to make decisions under her compulsory jurisdiction in accordance with what she regards as fair and reasonable in all the circumstances. This has led to the FOS developing the

[80] In the FSA nomenclature this would be a Discussion Paper, but the term was already in use by the Scottish Law Commission for what the Law Commission calls a Consultation Paper.

approaches to non-disclosure, misrepresentation and basis of the contract clauses in consumer cases that are set out in Chapter 4.

The FOS gave the Law Commissions access – subject to a confidentiality agreement – to a sample of decisions in non-disclosure cases. This enabled the Law Commissions to carry out the sort of work envisaged by Lord Justice Longmore in the Pat Saxton Memorial Lecture he gave on 5 March 2001:

> 'The first [way] is to do some empirical research in order to discover whether insureds have suffered injustice in the areas I have been considering. In this respect the records of the Ombudsman Bureau will be an early port of call.'

Consultation Paper

2.50 The Consultation Paper on disclosure, representations and basis of the contract clauses was issued in July 2007 and again covered both business and consumer insurances. It included a report on the research conducted at the FOS which explained its purpose:

> 'Our aim was to understand the issues involved in these disputes. We therefore set out to read around 200 final ombudsman decisions dealing with non-disclosure and misrepresentation. The FOS located around 300 decisions for us, and we read 197 cases about this area of law. The great majority of these cases were brought by private consumers: only 7 of the 197 cases (4%) were brought by small businesses.'

It was clear that the Law Commissions were impressed with the approaches developed by the FOS:

> 'For consumers we propose a mandatory regime which is based largely on existing FOS practice.'

Consumer Action Group

2.51 In 2009 it became known that a Final Report containing a draft Bill would be published towards the end of the year. The anticipated proposals, based on the FOS approaches, seemed adequately to address the worst faults in the law. A number of consumer groups and charities were potentially interested in the Law Commissions' work and so in July 2009 the author suggested a meeting to discuss how best to press the case for change.

The Institute of Advanced Legal Studies has taken an interest in this area of law reform[81] and very kindly agreed to provide a room for an initial meeting.[82] A second meeting was hosted by Which? on 23 October 2009 and a strategy was agreed for the campaign. In all, there were to be nine members of this informal action group: Age UK, British Heart Foundation, Consumer Focus, Macmillan Cancer Support, the Multiple Sclerosis Society, the Trading Standards Institute, the author, UNLOCK and Which?.[83] Mike Hobday and Ron Gainsford describe some of the actions taken in Chapter 7B and 7F respectively.

Final report

2.52 On 15 December 2009 the Law Commissions' Final Report was published. Unlike the Issues Paper and the Consultation Paper it dealt only with consumer insurance. This was a canny move. Business risks are considerably more varied and complex than standard consumer risks, and typically have far greater values at risk. There is nervousness amongst insurers and no doubt at HM Treasury at any move which might put the industry at a disadvantage or threaten the substantial flow of overseas earnings. There is a certain affection for the devil that is known – the Marine Insurance Act 1906 – though oddly that legislation itself met with strong opposition when first mooted.

The recommendations within the report were as expected and immediately gained widespread support. Under a subsequently agreed protocol, the Government was obliged to respond within one year:

> 'The Minister will provide a full response to the Commission as soon as possible after delivery of the interim response and in any event within one year of publication of the report unless otherwise agreed with the Commission. The response will set out which recommendations the

---

81 Julian Harris, Editor of Amicus Curiae and Assistant Research Fellow at the Institute of Advanced Legal Studies, has been particularly supportive of the campaign for change. See lectures by Professor John Birds on 10 December 2003: 'Good Faith in the Reform of Insurance Law' and by Peter Tyldesley on 27 March 2006: 'Archaic, unclear, inaccessible and unfair – Should insurance contract law be reformed?'. See also Peter J Tyldesley, 'Insurance law – unfair, unclear, archaic and inaccessible', Amicus Curiae no 64 (2006) p 1; Peter J Tyldesley, 'Consumer insurance law – reform at last?' Amicus Curiae no 81 (2010) pp 1–3; Peter J Tyldesley, 'Utmost Good Faith – Unintended Injustice?' Amicus Curiae no 86 (2011) pp 1–2.

82 Thanks are due to Belinda Crowther for this facility.

83 Age UK: Jane Vass and Lucy Malenczuk; British Heart Foundation: Mubeen Bhutta, Katie Chruszcz, Maura Gillespie, Beatrice Brooke and Amy Smullen; Consumer Focus: Jill Johnstone, Lola Bello and John Cottrill; Macmillan Cancer Support: Mike Hobday and Leonora Miles; the Multiple Sclerosis Society: Isabel Arthur, Laura Weir and Dan Berry; Trading Standards Institute: Jessica Tangye, David Sanders, Suzanne Kuyser, Irja Howie and Lizzi Piggins; UNLOCK: Christopher Stacey, Julie Harmsworth and Chris Bath; Which?: Lucy Widenka, Phil Jones, Vera Cottrell, Alice Lythgoe-Goldstein and Teresa Fritz.

> Minister accepts, rejects or intends to implement in modified form. If applicable, the Minister will also provide the timescale for implementation.'[84]

There were however two doubts – would the recommendations be supported by insurers, represented by the ABI, and what would happen if there was, as expected, a change of administration at the forthcoming election.

Implementation

Industry support

2.53 As Judith Crawford sets out clearly in Chapter 7A, the ABI had taken a cautious approach to the possibility of law reform. In 2010 it appeared that a position of neutrality had been adopted, though some of the ABI's formal statements left it less than certain which way it would jump:

> 'We share the Law Commissions' desire that customers should be treated fairly. The insurance industry is committed to ensuring that customers understand their rights and obligations, and have their genuine claims paid quickly. We are pleased that the Law Commissions recognise that best practice throughout the industry, supplemented by FSA regulation and the approach of the Financial Ombudsman Service, already protects the consumer. The Commissions' proposals give legal status to existing best practices, and brings them together in one place in a clear format.'[85]

This was worrying because the best chance of gaining Parliamentary time for the reforms to be enacted would be to use a new Special Procedure for Law Commission Bills. However, as will be seen, this requires Bills to be uncontroversial. An objection from the ABI would certainly have rendered the Bill controversial and unsuitable for the procedure.

2.54 The breakthrough came at a meeting of the All-Party Parliamentary Group on Insurance and Financial Services on 1 December 2010. Weather conditions were treacherous and consequently the meeting, chaired by Jonathan Evans MP, was poorly attended. However, Kate Carr (Assistant Director, Markets & Regulation, General Insurance) was present for the ABI. In response to direct questioning from Evans, Carr confirmed that the ABI supported the Bill and that she was happy to put this in writing to him. Formal minutes of the meeting do not exist but Evans later confirmed the exchange on the floor of the House of Commons during the Third Reading:

---

84 Protocol between the Lord Chancellor (On behalf of the Government) and the Law Commission, 29 March 2010, HC499.

85 Erfan Hussain, ABI spokesperson, 16 March 2010.

'I wish to detain the House briefly in order to place on record the contribution to this Bill of the all-party group on insurance and financial services, which I chair. The group met on 1 December 2010 at the request of the consumer bodies to which my hon. Friend the Minister referred. I am glad the shadow Minister referred to multiple sclerosis, because the Multiple Sclerosis Society was one of the groups that asked us to examine this area of the law.

We were told that this area of the law has, in fact, been under review since 1980. In the 1980s and 1990s the shortcomings of the operation of consumer law were apparent. A scoping paper was produced in 2006. The Law Commission then produced its proposed legislation, but it was not enacted, despite the fact that in 2009 a request to do so was made to the last Labour Government. The reason for that was—[Interruption.] No, this is not a party political point. The reason was that the Association of British Insurers had responded in a letter, expressing its broad support for the recommendations but adding that there were still issues that needed to be addressed

> "before we could support the Bill entering the process for uncontroversial Bills."

That sets the context for the all-party group's contribution. We had our meeting on 1 December, and we heard from Mr David Hertzell, the law commissioner who is the author of this legislation. He also attended the special Public Bill Committee that was set up as part of this process. We also heard from Mr Peter Tyldesley, a senior lecturer in insurance law at Bedfordshire university, a consultant to the Financial Ombudsman Service and a lawyer at the Law Commission. Both of them told us it was necessary to have the buy-in of the ABI before we would be able to make use of the uncontroversial Bills process.

This is the first Bill that has gone through that new process. As a result, there was no Second Reading on the Floor of the House and there was a mere 29-minute Committee sitting, and in the Lords there was a special Public Bill Committee. That was possible because the legislation is uncontroversial.

Following our meeting with David Hertzell and Mr Tyldesley, we contacted the ABI and it came back within three days clarifying that its letter had been misinterpreted, and that as far as it was concerned the Bill could proceed on the current basis. Within a few weeks, that happened.

As there is a review taking place of all-party groups, I wish to stress the constructive contribution that this all-party group made in this instance. I pay tribute to my colleagues on that group for their contribution to this excellent measure.'

Political will

2.55 Once the ABI's support was confirmed, only one question remained – would the Government implement the Bill? The coalition Government took office on 6 May 2010. It would perhaps not have been surprising if the Law Commissions' proposals, published on 15 December 2009 under the previous administration, had been shelved. Attention was understandably on the need to deal with the financial crisis.

Instead on 16 May 2011, little more than a year later, the reform Bill was receiving its first reading in the House of Lords under the Special Procedure. Much of the credit for this speed and for the successful enactment of the measure must go to Mark Hoban MP – then Financial Secretary to the Treasury – and his team.

Special Procedure

2.56 As has been noted, the Bill was introduced into Parliament under a new Special Procedure which is of some general interest. The procedure resulted from long-standing concerns regarding the implementation rate for Law Commission reports.[86] An earlier step, the Jellicoe Procedure, had achieved little.[87] In 1997, the English Law Commission therefore set out what it saw as the argument for a new approach:

> 'The Law Commission's recommendations are the subject of extensive consultation before they are included in a final report. The Law Commission starts a law reform project by investigating the law and the deficiencies in it. This involves informal pre-consultation with Government departments and users of the law in question. Then the Commission issues a consultation paper summarising the present law, its defects, the relevant law of other jurisdictions, some options for reform and the Commission's own provisional recommendations. The paper is published by The Stationery Office and copies are sent to representatives of users and other persons thought likely to be interested to respond (including the judiciary, practising lawyers, academics, Government bodies and professional organisations). The responses to the consultation are analysed and a final report published, accompanied by a draft bill prepared by Parliamentary Counsel attached to the Commission. The Law Commission does not undertake formal consultation on its final report, but its final recommendations are based on the options put forward in the consultation document. From start to finish the entire process may take three or more years.

---

86 See *Law reform in England and Wales: a shattered dream or triumph of political vision?*, The Hon Mr Justice Etherton, Amicus Curiae Issue 73 Spring 2008

87 In the Quinquennial Review of the English Law Commission in 2003, John Halliday noted that the Jellicoe Procedure had not been used since the previous review.

> Since the recommendations for reform will have been the subject of extensive scrutiny before legislative proposals are introduced into Parliament, bills based on Law Commission recommendations are in general, in the Law Commission's submission, appropriate for some streamlined Parliamentary procedure.'[88]

In 2008 the House of Lords Procedure Committee reported that:

> 'Since 1991 some 54 Law Commission reports with bills have been published. Most have been implemented, normally by incorporating them into relevant Government bills, as and when opportunities arise within the Government's legislative programme. However, such opportunities are limited, and as a result the rate of implementation has not kept pace with the production of reports. Eight reports, which have been accepted by Government, are still awaiting implementation; Government responses to another 12 reports are pending.'

2.57 The Procedure Committee recommended that a new procedure proposed by the then Leader of the House of Lords, Baroness Ashton, should be adopted, initially for a trial involving two Bills. This recommendation was approved by the House of Lords on 3 April 2008. The two Bills selected for the trial were:

- The Perpetuities and Accumulations Bill. This Bill was based on recommendations set out in the Law Commission's 1998 report *The Rules Against Perpetuities and Excessive Accumulations*[89]. The Bill was introduced under the procedure on 1 April 2009 and received the Royal Assent on 12 November 2009.[90]
- The Third Parties (Rights against Insurers) Bill. This Bill was based on the recommendations set out in joint report of the English and Scottish Law Commissions: *Third Parties – Rights against Insurers*.[91] The Bill was introduced under the procedure on 23 November 2009 and received the Royal Assent on 25 March 2010.[92]

Following the success of the trial the House of Lords Constitution Committee and the Chief Executive of the English Law Commission recommended that the new procedure – modified to extend to Scottish Law Commission bills – should be made a permanent fixture. This proposal received the agreement of the House of Lords on 7 October 2010.

---

88 Modernisation of the House of Commons – First Report, 23 July 1997, Appendix 3, Memorandum submitted by the Law Commission.

89 (Law Com 251) HC 579.

90 Brought into force on 6 April 2010 by The Perpetuities and Accumulations Act 2009 (Commencement) Order 2010.

91 (Law Com No 272; Scot Law Com No 184).

92 To be amended and unlikely to commence until 2014 – see 'Report on the implementation of Law Commission proposals', Ministry of Justice, January 2013.

The procedure does not 'fast-track' Law Commission bills through Parliament. It does, however, make the introduction of such measures – and thus ultimately implementation – more likely. The differences between the procedure and the normal process for a Law Commission bill are underlined in the table below. It will be seen that the only differences occur in the House of Lords. In particular, the second reading debate and committee stages take place in committee rather than requiring time to be found on the floor of the House:

New procedure for uncontroversial Law Commission Bills	**Normal procedure for a Law Commission Bill**
HOUSE OF LORDS	
Introduction and First Reading in House of Lords	Introduction and First Reading in House of Lords
Second Reading debate in Committee, followed by formal motion for Second Reading on floor of the House	Second Reading debate on the floor of the House, followed by formal motion for Second Reading
Special Public Bill Committee	Grand Committee or Committee of the Whole House
Report	Report
Third Reading	Third Reading
HOUSE OF COMMONS	
(Introduction on same day as Third Reading in House of Lords)	(Introduction on same day as Third Reading in House of Lords)
Second Reading debate in Committee, followed by formal motion for Second Reading on floor of the House (HoC Standing Order 59)	Second Reading debate in Committee, followed by formal motion for Second Reading on floor of the House (HoC Standing Order 59)
Committee	Committee
Report and Third Reading	Report and Third Reading

2.58 There are three important aspects of the procedure:

- It may only be used for Bills which are 'uncontroversial'. In 2008 the House of Lords Procedure Committee gave the following pledge:

> 'Before introduction of any bill, there will be full consultation within the usual channels to determine whether or not it is suitable for these procedures. If in the course of proceedings on the bill it becomes clear, for example during debate on second reading, that it does after all contain controversial provisions, the new procedures will be halted and it will then be for the Government business managers to decide whether or not to proceed with the bill under the normal procedures applying to any other public bill.'

- It may only be used to consider one Bill at a time.
- It may be used to consider Bills produced by either the English Law Commission or the Scottish Law Commission – or those which have been jointly produced.

Enactment

2.59 Having received its First Reading in the House of Lords on 16 May 2011,[93] the Bill passed successfully through the Special Procedure and received the Royal Assent on 8 March 2012. It will be brought into force on 6 April 2013.[94]

The Consumer Insurance (Disclosure and Representations) Act 2012

Main provisions

2.60 How will the Act address the perceived flaws in the law? Chapter 6 and Appendix 14 provide the details, but the approach may be briefly summarised. The duty of disclosure is abolished and basis of the contract clauses are rendered ineffective. For misrepresentation the requirement that a fact be material in objective terms is abandoned and a proportionate approach to remedies is adopted:

- For deliberate or reckless misrepresentation the insurer may avoid the policy ab initio as at present and reject any claims.
- For careless misrepresentation the remedy will depend on what the insurer would have done had it known the true facts. So, for example, if it would have included an exclusion clause, that clause will be added to the policy with retrospective effect and any claim will be assessed accordingly. If the insurer would have declined to offer cover, the policy can be avoided and any claims may then be rejected.
- For innocent misrepresentation, the insurer has no remedy. The policy will remain in force and any claims must be paid.

These changes represent a major step forward in consumer rights. An unrealistic requirement that a consumer disclose information is replaced with a reasonable and easily understood obligation on the consumer to take reasonable care to answer questions accurately. Section 2(2) of the Act is at the centre of this approach:

---

93 Peter J Tyldesley, 'Reform at Last?', New Law Journal 161(2011) pp: 843–844.

94 'Report on the implementation of Law Commission proposals', Ministry of Justice, January 2013.

> 'It is the duty of the consumer to take reasonable care not to make a misrepresentation to the insurer.'

Despite these reforms, there remains the possibility of hard cases. For example, a consumer may carelessly give incorrect information on a point which is crucial to the insurer involved, but not to the insurance market as a whole. The consequence may be that the insurer is entitled to avoid the policy and reject a claim – even though there is no connection between the information and the loss that has occurred, and despite the fact that the consumer would readily have been able to obtain cover with other insurers.

Marketing

2.61 Attention is therefore likely to focus on whether questions are clear and whether the importance of giving accurate answers has been made plain. Existing difficulties with consumer insurance law are exacerbated by the conflict between marketing imperatives and sound underwriting practices. There are two aspects to this issue – advertising and the application process.

Advertising

Consumer insurance advertising does not stress the need for painstaking care when completing insurance applications. Indeed some advertising downplays the process. At the time the Law Commissions began their review one insurer was running television advertisements in which it apparently delivered a bliss-inducing motor insurance quotation to a consumer who telephoned and simply stated 'It's a hatchback, and I want you to quote me happy'. During the passage of the Consumer Insurance (Disclosure and Representations) Bill through the House of Lords, a billboard campaign from another insurer proclaiming 'Car Insurance Quotes in 60 seconds – More Time to Ride' was drawn to the attention of the Special Public Bill Committee. Does this type of advertising go too far in stressing ease of application over the serious nature of the underwriting process?

Application form design

The design of application forms is of more direct impact. Criticism in recent years has drawn attention to a range of potential problems:

- Questions which are unclear, over-lengthy or use technical terms which may be inaccessible to consumers.
- Online applications which in place of questions give a set of assumptions which can be confirmed or rejected with a single click.
- Online application forms which are partly pre-populated with answers.

- Application forms which include cross-selling marketing question amongst underwriting questions, potentially leaving the consumer as to which questions are material to the insurer's decision.

The Association of British Insurers has made valuable progress in this area with its publication in 2006 of guidance Application Form Design.[95] However this only applies to life and health protection insurances.

Section 3

Under section 3 of the Act some of these marketing issues may become relevant when considering whether a consumer has met the requirement to take reasonable care not to make misrepresentions:

'3

(1) Whether or not a consumer has taken reasonable care not to make a misrepresentation is to be determined in the light of all the relevant circumstances.

(2) The following are examples of things which may need to be taken into account in making a determination under subsection (1)—

(a) the type of consumer insurance contract in question, and its target market,

(b) any relevant explanatory material or publicity produced or authorised by the insurer,

(c) how clear, and how specific, the insurer's questions were,

(d) in the case of a failure to respond to the insurer's questions in connection with the renewal or variation of a consumer insurance contract, how clearly the insurer communicated the importance of answering those questions (or the possible consequences of failing to do so),

e) whether or not an agent was acting for the consumer.

(3) The standard of care required is that of a reasonable consumer: but this is subject to subsections (4) and (5).

(4) If the insurer was, or ought to have been, aware of any particular characteristics or circumstances of the actual consumer, those are to be taken into account.

(5) A misrepresentation made dishonestly is always to be taken as showing lack of reasonable care.

---

95 See Appendix 6.

Reform at last

2.62 Why has the Law Commissions' current review of insurance law succeeded in producing reform where earlier initiatives failed? Eight interrelated factors seem to be in play:

- **Financial Ombudsman Service**

  For the present review, the Law Commissions have been able to draw on the experiences of the Financial Ombudsman Service. Past decisions provided hard evidence of the issues under consideration and the Law Commissions were able to use the FOS approaches as the bases for their recommendations. As a consequence the reformed law is based on tried and tested solutions to which insurers are accustomed – it is not a leap in the dark.

  In contrast, at the time of the 1957 and 1980 reports, there was no ombudsman dealing with insurance complaints.[96] As noted above, it was not until 30 March 1981 that the Insurance Ombudsman Bureau opened its doors.[97]

- **The critical illness insurance scandal**

  The critical illness cases that were reported brought home the real cost of bad law in a way that was readily accessible without the need for technical knowledge. Concerns about such cases also led influential medical charities to become involved in the campaign for change – the British Heart Foundation, Macmillan Cancer Support and the Multiple Sclerosis Society.

  The backdrops to the 1957 and 1980 reports were distinctly dryer and less newsworthy – concern regarding the use of arbitration clauses and the impact of an anticipated European directive on motor insurance respectively.

- **Sound consultation**

  The Law Commissions conducted prolonged consultations on their proposals, with dozens of lectures, seminars and meetings. An Issues Paper and a Consultation Paper were published, with the latter attracting 107 formal responses. Respondents could see that their comments were taken into account and in some cases led to fine-tuning of the proposals.[98]

---

96 There was an Industrial Assurance Commissioner with limited remit and powers.

97 Peter J Tyldesley, 'The Insurance Ombudsman Bureau – the early history' Journal of Insurance Research and Practice No 39 (2003), pp 34–43.

98 See, for example, the abandonment of non-contestability periods as an option, following representations from insurers: 'Consumer Insurance Laws Pre-Contract Disclosure and Misrepresentation', Cm 7758, paras 10.20–10.28.

In 1957 and 1980 just 11 and 39 submissions were received respectively and there appears to have been very little in the way of external activities.

- **Strong recommendations**

  The Law Commissions' recommendations were strong, clear and based on well-established approaches applied by the FOS. Dealing with consumers separately side-stepped the concerns of industry and HM Treasury regarding business insurances and overseas earnings.

  In 1957 and 1980 the conclusions and recommendations were relatively weak – there was no attempt to abolish the duty of disclosure or introduce the concept of proportionality. Consumers were not separated from businesses in 1957, and only limited differences in their treatment were suggested in 1980.

- **Industry support**

  Partly, no doubt, as a result of some of the above factors, the Law Commissions have been successful in gaining the support of the insurance industry.

  In 1957 and 1980 the proposals were implacably opposed by insurers. As related above, one Whitehall mandarin declared the BIA in 1979 to be demonstrating 'the objective disinterestedness of a Millwall supporter'.

- **Consumer support**

  From 2009 onwards a range of consumer organisations and charities have worked effectively together to bring about consumer insurance law reform: Age Concern, British Heart Foundation, Consumer Focus, Macmillan Cancer Support, the Multiple Sclerosis Society, the Trading Standards Institute, the author, UNLOCK and Which?.

  In 1957 there was no consumer involvement at all, and in 1980 it was simply the three consumer organisations which took an interest: the National Consumer Council, the Consumers' Association and the National Federation of Consumer Groups.

- **Political will**

  On 6 May 2010 the current Government took office. By 16 May 2011 the Bill was receiving its first reading in the House of Lords. It passed through both Houses and on 8 March 2012 received the Royal Assent. On 6 April 2013, less than three years after the Government came to power, the Act will be in force. This feat was accomplished at a time when the Government was contending with the financial crisis and with the need to restructure the financial regulatory system. As has been noted above, much of the credit for this impressive achievement lies with Mark Hoban MP – then Financial Secretary to the Treasury – and his team.

In contrast, the absence of effective Government action following the 1957 and 1980 reports condemned consumers to face the harshest aspects of insurance law for more than 55 years.

The 1957 report was simply shelved and the 1980 report led to the Government dithering for more than five years before finally settling for mere changes to the voluntary statements of practice. It is, of course, true that the reform proposals in these reports were strongly opposed by the industry and were weaker than those put forward in 2009. Additionally, the 1980 report was undermined by a lack of pragmatism with regard to the anticipated European Directive. Nevertheless the lack of mettle displayed by the Government was disappointing.

- **Special Procedure**

  The final hurdle for the Bill to overcome was the need to obtain Parliamentary time. Here the timing was serendipitous, since the new Special Procedure for 'uncontroversial' Law Commission Bills had recently been agreed.

  In 1957 and 1980 there was no special treatment available for Law Reform Committee or Law Commission Bills.

Conclusions

2.63 The Consumer Insurance (Disclosure and Representations) Act 2012 is a major step forward in consumer protection and should enhance the reputation of the insurance industry. Nevertheless much still remains in consumer insurance law that is archaic and has the potential to cause injustice.

The Law Commissions' review is expected to conclude at the end of this year with a Final Report and draft Bill covering all the remaining issues which are to be considered – for both business and consumer insurances. Will further reform for consumers be held back by the need for the Government to consider proposals for businesses at the same time? And in those areas, such as insurable interest, where the FOS has little experience to share, will it be more difficult to convince industry and Government that any reform proposals are sound and workable?

In the long term the aim should surely be to create a complete consumer insurance law code, a single source of the basic law which clarifies the position for consumers and insurers alike, and places the UK in a strong position to argue its corner as the slow move towards European harmonisation of insurance law continues.[99] Given that some issues remain entirely outside the current review, that objective may have to wait until the Law Commissions next return to this area of law.

[99] See, in particular, the Principles of European Insurance Contract Law and the Commission Decision of 17 January 2013 on setting up the Commission Export Group on a European Insurance Contract Law (2013/C 16/03).

Chapter 3 The Impact of FSA Regulation

Robert Purves

Dr Robert Purves is a barrister at 3 Verulam Buildings, Gray's Inn, with strong specialism in financial services law and regulation. Robert practised as an Attorney in South Africa and Solicitor in England, before transferring to the Bar. From 1999 to 2003 Robert was a legal adviser to the Financial Services Authority. From 2003 to 2007, Robert was Chief Counsel, Insurance and Prudential Policy at the Financial Services Authority.

Introduction

3.1 The United Kingdom has a long history of statutory intervention in the content and operation of contracts of insurance. Two examples from 1774, which remain in force to the present day, set the scene. By the Life Assurance Act 1774, s 1,

> 'no insurance shall be made ... on the life or lives of any person or persons, or on any other event or events whatsoever, wherein the person ... for whose ... benefit ... such policy ... shall be made, shall have no [insurable] interest, or by way of gaming or wagering'.

The Fires Prevention (Metropolis) Act 1774, s 83 provides that 'in order to deter and hinder ill-minded persons from wilfully setting their house or houses or other buildings on fire with a view of gaining to themselves the insurance money', the governors or directors of any insurance company by which any house or building is insured against fire are required, in case of loss or damage by fire and under specified conditions, to apply the insurance proceeds to reinstate the property.

There is a correspondingly long history of later intervention to ameliorate the effect of earlier intervening statutes, as new social conditions and concerns emerge and the nature of insurance business changes. For example, the Life Assurance Act 1774, s 2 provides that 'it shall not be lawful to make any policy ... on the life ... of any person ... or other event ... without inserting in such policy ... the ... persons [sic] name ... interested therein, or for whose use, benefit, or on whose account such policy is so made or underwrote'. But the Insurance Companies (Amendment) Act 1973, s 50 modifies the effect of that provision to accommodate group life insurance business:

> 'a policy for the benefit of unnamed persons ... [is not invalid] if the class or description [of policyholder] is stated in the policy with sufficient particularity to make it possible to establish the identity of all persons who at any given time are entitled to benefit under the policy.'

3.2 The Consumer Insurance (Disclosure and Representations) Act 2012 ('the 2012 Act') is a part of that long practice of intervention and counter-intervention: amongst other things, the 2012 Act mitigates (for consumer-insureds at least) the harsh consequences of an innocent or negligent pre-contractual misrepresentation or non-disclosure, as codified in the Marine Insurance Act 1906.

But the 2012 Act also has its own context. An important part of that context is the United Kingdom's increasing reliance on regulation as a means of achieving the outcomes that the UK as a society requires from its financial services industry. In particular, the 2012 Act partly supersedes and partly operates alongside the system of insurance regulation operated by the Financial Services Authority ('the FSA'), under the Financial Services and Markets Act 2000 ('FSMA 2000'). Much of the detail of that system of insurance regulation takes the form of subordinate legislation, made by the FSA and published in the form of the FSA's Handbook of Rules and Guidance.

This Chapter explores how the FSA became involved in the issues that are the subject matter of the 2012 Act, and how the 2012 Act can be expected to impact on the future regulation of insurance business, whether by the FSA or by its successors (the Prudential Regulation Authority and the Financial Conduct Authority), once the Financial Services and Markets Act 2012,[1] which received the Royal Assent on 19 December 2012, comes fully into effect.

The involvement of the FSA in the regulation of the terms of consumer insurance contracts has a complex history. The intertwined strands of that history are first, the regulation of insurance companies ('insurance firms' in FSA jargon); second, the regulation of insurance brokers ('insurance intermediaries' in EU, and hence FSA, jargon); and third, the direct regulation of contract terms.

1 On which, see HM Treasury, 'A new approach to financial regulation: the blueprint for reform', Cm 8083, June 2011.

The regulation of insurance companies before 1984[2]

3.3 Although an Office of Assurances was established in the 1500s, during the reign of Queen Elizabeth I, the regulation of insurance business in the UK really only began in earnest in 1870. Until that point the UK Government played virtually no role in the day-to-day activities of insurers or their agents.[3] The Life Assurance Companies Acts 1870 to 1872, were, put broadly, a response to the failure of a number of life insurance companies. They did not apply to general insurance, but did apply to the many composite insurance companies writing both life insurance and general insurance business.

The Life Assurance Companies Acts 1870 to 1872 introduced four main requirements. First, they required the separation of the assets supporting an insurer's life and annuity business into a long-term fund, separate from the insurer's other assets including its shareholder funds. Second, they required actuarial scrutiny of the adequacy of the assets in the long-term fund, by way of an actuarial report, once every five years. Third, they introduced Court-supervised systems of life insurance business transfers and the winding up of insurance companies. Finally, they required the annual revenue accounts and the balance sheet of insurance companies, in a prescribed form and with the abstract of any actuarial report on the valuation of the life business, to be deposited with the Board of Trade and made available to policyholders and shareholders on request. Novel as these requirements were, they did not intrude far into the contractual relationship between an insurance company and its policyholders. As Ford[4] notes:

> 'Although prior approval of insurance products and premiums was required in certain US states such as Massachusetts and New York, and supported in Germany and later in Japan and a number of other countries, neither the 1870 Act nor any later legislation required prior approval of premiums or products. … The UK Government had been persuaded that companies should be left relatively free to act as they saw fit, with very limited governmental supervision, as long as they made available sufficient information about their financial position to enable the public to make informed choices about their insurers. This "freedom with publicity" policy remained central to the regulation of insurance in the UK until responsibility for the regulation of insurance passed to the Financial Services Authority in 1999.'

General insurance companies were brought within the framework of the 1870 to 1872 Acts by the Assurance Companies Act 1909, which replaced

---

2 See generally Ford, R, 'History: a history of insurance regulation in the UK' in Burling, J and Lazarus, K (eds), *Research Handbook on International Insurance Law and Regulation* (Edward Elgar, 2011), p 251, from which this historical outline is, in part, extracted.

3 Ibid, p 252.

4 Ibid, p 254.

the 1870 Act and subsequent legislation. After World War II, the Assurance Companies Act 1946 extended the 1909 Act to marine, aviation and transport insurance. It divided the eight existing classes of insurance into two divisions: long-term business (life and bond investment) and general business (all other classes, including motor vehicle, employers' liability, marine, aviation and transport, fire and accident). In 1958, the year in which the European Union was established, the existing requirements under the Acts passed between 1909 and 1946 were consolidated (with some changes) into the Insurance Companies Act 1958, but the regulatory reach of the 1958 Act remained limited:

> 'at a time when most of the world's sophisticated insurance jurisdictions boasted comprehensive regimes governing the licensing and supervision of insurance companies, the Insurance Companies Act 1958 still required merely the maintenance of a derisory minimum capital, the separation of funds, and the deposit of annual accounts with the Board of Trade.'[5]

3.4 By 1973, the year in which the UK acceded to the treaties establishing the European Union, the system of insurance regulation had undergone refinement and was now set out in the Insurance Companies Act 1973, later consolidated into the Insurance Companies Act 1974. But the fundamental philosophy underlying that regulation (at least as expressed by the Government of the day in 1980) had not changed very much since the 1870s:

> 'The Insurance Companies Act 1974 was a consolidation measure covering the Acts dealing with insurance companies. It has provided the framework for the Secretary of State to authorise and supervise undertakings carrying on insurance business, and if necessary to intervene in their affairs …
>
> A phrase often used to describe the United Kingdom approach to regulation by the Government of its insurance industry is "freedom with publicity". The phrase serves to bring out some clear and continuing features of that regulation over the last century. In general, there has been no Government control of premiums or other conditions of contract between insurers and policyholders; there has not been Government direction of the investment of insurance companies; there has been a wish to see the insurance industry expand the range and volume of its business in the United Kingdom and in other countries; but there have been requirements for insurance companies to make substantial returns to the Department of Trade and its predecessors, for those returns to give details of companies business in a form allowing

---

5 Young, J (ed), *A Practitioner's Guide to the FSA Regulation of Insurance* (3rd ed, City and Financial Publishing, 2008), preface.

position and performance to be assessed, and for those returns to be available to policyholders and to the public at large.'[6]

Moreover, as pointed out in the same Commons debate[7], there was at that time little if any statutory regulation of the conduct of insurance business, an issue to which we will return below. In summary, therefore, the statutory system of insurance regulation in place at the end of the 1970s did not address directly the formation or content of the contractual relationship between an insurer and its policyholder, except to the extent that the resulting contract of insurance gave rise to liabilities that had to be taken into account in assessing the adequacy of the company's assets to meet its liabilities. Control of the exercise by an insurance company of its contractual rights and obligations remained, therefore, largely a matter for the common law, which, as regards contracts of insurance had been codified in the form of the Marine Insurance Act 1906.

3.5 The UK's accession to the EU[8] in 1973 did not immediately change the, largely prudential, focus of UK insurance regulation. This was for three main reasons.

First, as a matter of technicality, the earliest EU insurance legislation[9], enacted between 1964 and 1979, took the form of directives. In the legal framework established under the treaties giving effect to the EU, legislation in the form of a directive is binding, as to the result to be achieved, upon each Member State to which it is addressed, but leaves the national authorities 'the choice of form and methods'[10] by which that outcome is to be achieved.

Second, as a matter of policy and priority, EU insurance legislation was initially focussed on the establishment of an EU single market[11] in insurance. The earliest insurance directives (enacted between 1964 and 1979[12]) were concerned primarily with establishing uniform descriptions, or 'classes' of

---

6 Hansard, HC Deb 2 February 1981, vol 998 cc 103–20, The Under-Secretary of State for Trade (Mr Reginald Eyre), on the Second Reading of the Insurance Companies Bill 1980.

7 *Ibid*, Mr Clinton-Davis, at col. 111: 'I turn to another matter – the conduct on insurance business – which is extremely important. I am disappointed – again, I express no great surprise about it – that the Bill has nothing to say about this topic, in particular about the selling of insurance by non-broker intermediaries.'

8 In 1973, the formal title of the EU was of course the European Economic Community ('the EEC'). For convenience I have chosen, in this Chapter, to use the current terminology and to cite the relevant articles of the current EU Treaties and founding documents.

9 And also the majority of subsequent EU legislation relevant to insurance.

10 The Treaty on the Functioning of the European Union ('the TFEU'), Art 288.

11 The Treaty of the European Union ('the TEU'), Art 3(3) commits the EU to establishing an internal market: 'an area without internal frontiers in which the free movement of goods, persons, services and capital is ensured in accordance with the provisions of the Treaties'. Under TFEU, Art 57, a 'service' includes an activity of a commercial character that is normally provided for remuneration. Insurance business is a service in this sense and is treated as such in EU legislation.

12 The First Reinsurance Directive (64/225/EEC), the First Non-Life Insurance Directive (73/239/EEC) and the First Life Assurance Directive (79/267/EEC).

insurance business that would be recognised in in each Member State of the EU, and with setting out the conditions under which insurance companies (in EU jargon, 'insurance undertakings') that were nationals of one Member State (meaning that an undertaking had its establishment or head office in that 'home' state), could pursue their business in other Member States, by becoming authorised in those 'host' states.[13]

Third, as will be seen below, the European Commission, which is usually[14] the only body in the EU legal system with the right of legislative initiative, had elected to pursue policyholder protection by a range of other means, including the harmonisation of insurance contract law across EU Member States.

The regulation of insurance intermediaries from 1977

3.6 The EU did not legislate for conduct of business requirements in respect of insurance brokers (as above, 'insurance intermediaries' in EU jargon) until 2002.[15] That left the UK with a considerable degree of legislative freedom in this field, untrammelled by EU requirements. In the UK, before 1977, 'anyone could lawfully describe himself as an insurance broker. No professional body existed to secure the maintenance of professional standards on the part of those who so described themselves.'[16]

The Insurance Brokers (Registration) Act 1977, which came into force in stages between 1 December 1977 and 1 December 1981, established the Insurance Brokers Registration Council. The Council was charged with the registration of 'insurance brokers' (and associated 'enrolled bodies corporate') and with the regulation of their professional standards. The 1977 Act was general in its scope as regards different classes of insurance business: as defined in section 29 of the 1977 Act, the term 'insurance broker' is to be construed by reference to a definition of 'insurance business' of any class relevant for the purpose of Part I of the Insurance Companies Act 1974, other than industrial insurance business. The classes of insurance business set out in section 1 of the 1974 Act included both 'ordinary long-term insurance business' and a wide variety of general insurance business.

The Council was empowered[17] to draw up and maintain 'a statement of the acts and omissions which, if done or made by registered insurance brokers … constitute in the opinion of the Council unprofessional conduct'. Once this

---

13 See generally, Purves, R, 'Europe: the architecture and content of EU insurance regulation', in Burling, J and Lazarus, K (eds), *Research Handbook on International Insurance Law and Regulation* (Edward Elgar, 2011), p 634.

14 TEU, Art 17(2).

15 The Insurance Mediation Directive (2002/92/EC).

16 *Pickles v Insurance Brokers Registration Council* [1984] 1 All ER 1073, *per* McCullough J, giving the judgment of the Court, at p 1073j.

17 Insurance Brokers (Registration) Act 1977, s 10(1).

code of conduct (or any amendment to it) had been approved by order of the Secretary of State[18] it applied to registered insurance brokers. In addition, the 1977 Act provided for the Council to make rules relevant to the carrying on of business by insurance brokers. These included, for example, rules as to the maintenance of the register and discipline, rules as to adequate capital and rules as to professional indemnity insurance.[19] In particular, section 11(1)(c) required the Council to make rules to ensure 'that the number of insurance companies with which … [practising insurance brokers] place insurance business, and the amount of insurance business which they place with each insurance company, is such as to prevent their business from becoming unduly dependent on any particular insurance company'.

3.7 The 1977 Act gave the Council disciplinary powers in relation to registered insurance brokers, by reference to the code of conduct and the rules, but the scope of its regime was markedly limited. Although the 1977 Act made the use of any style, title or description consisting of or including the expression 'insurance broker' an offence unless the person using it was registered under the Act,[20] it did not reach persons who carried on the activity of insurance broking under a different title. The 1977 Act therefore created a binary regime, in which those who used or wish to use the title 'insurance broker' were subject to a statutory code of conduct, while those who chose, for whatever reason, to trade under another title were not subject to the code.

The first statement of the code of conduct to be approved under the 1977 Act came into force in 1978.[21] Section 10(2) of the 1977 Act made a breach of the code of conduct set out in that statement indicative only: 'the statement shall serve as a guide to registered insurance brokers … but the mention or lack of mention in it of a particular act or omission shall not be taken as conclusive of any question of professional conduct'. The statement[22] set out seven 'fundamental principles governing the professional conduct of insurance brokers … [breach of which might] in the opinion of the Council constitute unprofessional conduct'. The principles were as follows:

'(A) Insurance brokers shall at all times conduct business with utmost good faith and integrity.

(B) Insurance brokers shall do everything possible to satisfy the requirements of clients and shall, subject to Principle C, place the

18 *Ibid*, s 27.

19 See, for example, the Insurance Brokers Registration Council (Accounts and Business Requirements) Rules Approval Order (SI 1979/489).

20 Insurance Brokers (Registration) Act 1977, s 22, which came into force on 1 December 1981.

21 The Insurance Brokers Registration Council (Code of Conduct) Approval Order 1978 (SI 1978/1394).

22 *Ibid*, Schedule.

interests of clients before all other considerations. Subject to these requirements and interests, insurance brokers shall have proper regard for others.

(C) Insurance brokers shall not directly or indirectly do anything in the course of practising as insurance brokers which compromises or impairs, or is likely to compromise or impair, the good repute of insurance brokers or the insurance broking profession.

(D) Statements made by or on behalf of insurance brokers when advertising shall not be misleading or extravagant.

(E) Insurance brokers shall conduct their relationship with the Council, their professional body, with propriety.

(F) Insurance brokers shall organise and control the internal affairs of their insurance broking business in a responsible manner, and where staff are employed ensure that they are competent, suitable, and under adequate day-to-day supervision by a registered insurance broker.

(G) Insurance brokers should be familiar with, and in carrying on business should be mindful of guidance as to proper professional conduct contained in any Practice Notes issued or endorsed by the Council.'

The principles were supported by examples:

> 'The following are some specific examples of the application of these principles:
>
> …
>
> (20) In the completion of the proposal form, claim form, or any other material document, insurance brokers shall make it clear that all answers or statements are the client's own responsibility. The client should always be asked to check the details and told that the inclusion of incorrect information may result, inter alia, in a claim being repudiated. On request, a client shall be supplied with a copy of the proposal form or other relevant document at the time of completion.'

As example (20) demonstrates, the basic premise underlying the application of the code of conduct was that the customer should take responsibility for his actions, in the expectation that the full rigour of English insurance contract law would or might apply to any misrepresentation or non-disclosure. The IBRC code of conduct was, however, an interesting early application of regulation by reference to principles, breach of which might be a basis for regulatory action, but which did not give rise to a right of action by the person who claimed to have been affected by the breach.

The regulation of insurance contract terms in the late 1970s: EU proposals, domestic legislation and self-regulation

3.8 In August 1975 the Law Commission and the Scottish Law Commission put forward proposals[23] for the control by statute of 'exemption clauses' – contractual provisions that could be invoked by a person who had, in the course of business,[24] entered into a contract with a consumer or a standard form contract.[25] 'Exemption clauses' were broadly defined to include two types of provisions. First, provisions which excluded or restricted the exercise of a right or remedy or any liability arising out of the breach of any obligation in a contract. Second, and more important for present purposes, clauses that had the effect of 'preventing the obligations to which they relate from arising or … providing that such obligations are to arise only in a restricted or qualified form.' The Commissions indicated that the mischief of such clauses was that:

> 'they deprive the persons against whom they are invoked of contractual rights which those persons legitimately expected to enjoy. They can be so expressed that the promisee may think that the promisor is undertaking an obligation which more valuable to the promisee than in fact it is.'

The problem, put succinctly, was 'the likelihood (in light of the surrounding circumstances including the way in which the contract is expressed) that the promisee might reasonably have misunderstood the extent of the promisor's obligation.'[26] The recommended form of control for such clauses was a 'reasonableness test'.[27] Birds noted at the time that 'although insurance itself was hardly mentioned by the Law Commissions in the Report and the preceding Working Paper, it was clearly intended to be covered by their general recommendations.'[28]

The Commissions' analysis was plainly relevant and applicable in principle to the problems created by the insurer's ability to avoid liability under (very often standard form) contracts of insurance, in response to a pre-contractual misrepresentation or non-disclosure, or in response to a consumer-insured's

---

23 The Law Commission and the Scottish Law Commission, 'Exemption Clauses Second Report', Law Com No 69, HMSO, 5 August 1975.

24 *Ibid*, Part IV, para 137.

25 *Ibid*, para 147.

26 *Ibid*, para 143.

27 *Ibid*, para 158.

28 Birds, J, 'Codes of Practice – the Statement of Insurance Practice – a Measure of Regulation of the Insurance Contract', (1977) 40 Modern Law Review 677, at p 677, n 4. See also The Law Commission '(Law Com No 104) Insurance Law: Non-disclosure and Breach of Warranty', October 1980, at p 4, footnote 11: 'In the Second Report of the Law Commission and the Scottish Law Commission on Exemption Clauses … the Law Commission had recommended that the proposals in the report, on which the 1977 [Unfair Contract Terms] Act was based, should be applied to contracts of all types: see paras 240–247.'

breach of warranty. Birds commented with some justification, therefore, that 'potentially the most far-reaching recommendation [for control over the terms and conditions of insurance policies or for reform of insurance law] … was that in the Law Commissions' Second Report … that the terms and conditions of insurance policies be subject to the fair and reasonable test in the … draft Bill'.[29]

3.9 The potential impact of the Law Commissions' recommendations (in the form of the Unfair Contract Terms Bill) was not lost on Parliament. On 4 May 1977, the Secretary of State for Trade was asked, having regard to that Bill and to the possibility that contracts of insurance might be excluded from its scope, to make a statement 'concerning the protection afforded to insurance policy holders from unfair treatment as a result of the terms of insurance contracts'. In response, the Under-Secretary of State for Trade said the following:

> 'In general I consider that the insurance industry has a good record in treating policy holders fairly.[30] But, in view of the proposed new legislation on contract terms in other fields, I asked the British Insurance Association[31] and Lloyd's to consider drawing up a statement of practice in the field of personal non-life insurance to cover certain matters. I welcome the fact that the BIA and Lloyd's have now drawn up the following statement of insurance practice which they are recommending to their members. … The Chairman of the Life Offices' Association has also written to me, on behalf of the three Life Associations[32] involved, to express their willingness to consider drawing up within the next few weeks a parallel statement of practice relating to life assurance.'

The Statement of General Insurance Practice ('the SGIP'), presented to Parliament on 4 May 1977, and the Statement of Life Insurance Practice ('the SLIP') which followed it and was presented to Parliament on 28 July 1977[33] went some way to addressing the types of concerns that had been raised by the Law Commissions in relation to exemption clauses in consumer and standard form contracts, set out above. At their broadest, both the SGIP and the SLIP set out a framework to enable effective compliance by a consumer with his pre-contractual duty of disclosure about the risk, and restricting the ability of an insurer unreasonably to repudiate its liability under a contract of insurance with a consumer.[34] For present purposes, the operative text of the SGIP was as follows:

---

29 *Ibid*, p 677.
30 'Treating policyholders fairly' is of course, a phrase that is now a cornerstone of FSA insurance conduct of business regulation.
31 Now the Association of British Insurers ('the ABI').
32 Now part of the ABI.
33 Hansard, HC Deb, 28 July 1977, vol 936, cc 641–4W.
34 The Law Commission and the Scottish Law Commission, 'Insurance Contract Law Issues Paper 1: Misrepresentation and Non-Disclosure', September 2006, paras 3.8–3.12.

'1. Proposal Forms

(a) The declaration at the foot of the proposal form should be restricted to completion according to the proposer's knowledge and belief.

(b) If not included in the declaration, prominently displayed on the proposal form should be a Statement:

  (i) drawing the attention of the proposer to the consequences of the failure to disclose all material facts, explained as those facts an insurer would regard as likely to influence the acceptance and assessment of the proposal;

  (ii) warning that if the proposer is in any doubt about facts considered material, he should disclose them.

(c) Those matters which insurers have found generally to be material will be the subject of clear questions in proposal forms.

(d) So far as is practicable, insurers will avoid asking questions which would require expert knowledge beyond that which the proposer could reasonably be expected to possess or obtain or which would require a value judgment on the part of the proposer.

...

2. Claims

...

(b) Except where fraud, deception or negligence is involved, an insurer will not unreasonably repudiate liability to indemnify a policyholder:

  (i) on the grounds of non-disclosure or misrepresentation of a material fact where knowledge of the fact would not materially have influenced the insurer's judgment in the acceptance or assessment of the insurance;

  (ii) on the grounds of a breach of warranty or condition where the circumstances of the loss are unconnected with the breach.

The previous paragraph does not apply to Marine and Aviation policies.'

As regards proposal forms, the SLIP was in broadly similar terms. The material in the SLIP about claims was more succinct, but to broadly similar effect:

'1. Claims

(a) An insurer will not unreasonably reject a claim. (However, fraud

> or deception will, and negligence or non-disclosure or misrepresentation of a material fact may, result in adjustment or constitute grounds for rejection). In particular, an insurer will not reject a claim on grounds of non-disclosure or misrepresentation of a matter that was outside the knowledge of the proposer.'

3.10 If the purpose of the SGIP and the SLIP was that contracts of insurance would be excluded from the scope of legislation limiting the efficacy of exclusion clauses in consumer contracts, then they were a success. The Unfair Contract Terms Act 1977, s 3[35] embodied the Law Commissions' 1975 proposal in relation to exclusion clauses in consumer and standard form contracts, but by s 1(2) and Schedule 1, paragraph 1(a), section 3 (amongst others) did not extend to 'any contract of insurance (including a contract to pay an annuity on human life).'

The Law Commissions have suggested that the SGIP and the SLIP were a response primarily to the advent of the 1977 Act:

> 'It appears that these Statements were introduced as part of an agreement with the Government, under which insurance contracts were exempted from key provisions of the Unfair Contract Terms Act 1977. We are told that the title "Statement" was chosen in preference to "Code" to make it clear that in the industry's view the provisions merely confirmed current practice.'[36]

This is a view supported by Birds:

> 'It does seem, though, that the threat of inclusion [in the 1977 Act] was sufficient to persuade the insurance industry (as represented by the British Insurance Association and Lloyd's) to agree upon a code of conduct (officially called a Statement of Insurance Practice) with respect to their dealings with private non-–life insureds.'[37]

3.11 There was, however, at least one other important factor in play when the SGIP and the SLIP were first produced. That factor was Europe. By the mid-1970s the EU member states and the European Commission were discussing draft proposals on the co-ordination of insurance law in the EU. The production of a mutually agreeable directive was not easy. As Ellis noted, towards the end of the decade, 'so far, five drafts have been produced

---

35 '(1) … as between contracting parties where one of them deals as consumer or on the other's written standard terms of business. (2) As against that party, the other cannot by reference to any contract term … (b) claim to be entitled (i) to render a contractual performance substantially different from that which was reasonably expected of him, or (ii) in respect of the whole or any part of his contractual obligation, to render no performance at all, except in so far as … the contract term satisfies the requirement of reasonableness.'

36 The Law Commission and the Scottish Law Commission, 'Insurance Contract Law Issues Paper 1: Misrepresentation and Non-Disclosure', September 2006, para 3.6

37 Birds, J, 'Codes of Practice – the Statement of Insurance Practice – a Measure of Regulation of the Insurance Contract', (1977) 40 Modern Law Review 677, at p 678.

of the harmonisation directive and as none has found favour in its entirety, a sixth is being produced.'[38] However, the various drafts were themselves influential. In the UK, on 17 May 1978, the Lord Chancellor asked the Law Commission to consider the effect 'on the liability of an insurer, and on the rights of an insured' of (amongst other issues) non-disclosure, misrepresentation or breach of warranty by the insured.

The Lord Chancellor requested that the Law Commission consider those issues particularly in the light of the EU proposals.[39] It must have been evident at the time that any harmonisation of insurance contract law at EU level would inevitably deal with the impact of pre-contractual disclosure about the risk on the performance of the contract and might well adopt an approach very different to that of the common law. Given that background, together with the insurance industry's statements of practice, it is perhaps not surprising that Parliament accepted that the Unfair Contract Terms Act 1977 should not extend to contracts of insurance.

When finally published in July 1979 the draft harmonisation directive[40] made clear that the European Commission saw the harmonisation of the insurance contract law of the Member States (at least insofar as applicable to consumer insurance contracts)[41] as an important means of balancing the freedoms inherent in the creation of the single market with consumer protection:

> 'such coordination, by establishing a balance between the interests of the insurer on the one hand and the protection of the policyholder and the insured person on the other, is likely to enable freedom of choice to be extended and thus to facilitate the exercise of the freedom to provide services.'[42]

The draft directive identified that 'among the fundamental problems posed by legislation on insurance contracts are the consequences resulting firstly from the conduct of the policyholder at the time of the conclusion ... of the contract ... concerning the declaration of the risk.'[43] Article 3 of the draft directive, which is the most relevant for present purposes, set out four proposals relevant to pre-contractual disclosure of the risk: (a) a duty on the insured to disclose to the insurer all material circumstances known to the insured (that is, any circumstance that would influence the judgment of the actual insurer in assessing the risk); (b) an entitlement for the insurer to

38 Ellis, T, *European Integration and Insurance (Creating a Common Insurance Market)* (Witherby, 1980), p 146.
39 The Law Commission '(Law Com No 104) Insurance Law: Non-disclosure and Breach of Warranty', October 1980, at p 1.
40 Commission of the European Communities, 'Proposal for a Council Directive on the coordination of laws, regulations and administrative provisions relating to insurance contracts', COM(79) 335 final, 6 July 1979.
41 Marine, aviation and transport insurance were excluded from the scope of the draft directive.
42 COM(79) 335 final, above, preamble.
43 *Idem*.

propose a higher premium or different terms of cover if material circumstances which should have been disclosed subsequently come to light; (c) an entitlement for the insurer to repudiate all liability under the policy if the insured acted fraudulently in breaching his duty of disclosure; and (d) an entitlement for the insured to make a partial recovery of his claim if he breached his duty of disclosure and in doing so 'may be considered to have acted improperly'.

3.12 When the Law Commission reported, in 1980, it concluded[44] that on a purely local level, leaving aside any question of harmonisation at EC level, legislative reform of the English law of insurance was long overdue and required to address four main issues. First, to cut back the insured's stringent duty of pre-contractual disclosure,[45] recognising that an honest and reasonable insured might be quite unaware of the existence and extent of that duty and even if he was aware of it, might have great difficulty in forming any view as to what facts a prudent insurer would consider to be material. Second, to address the 'trap' created by the insured's residual duty to disclose further or additional material facts (a) going beyond matters covered by the specific questions in the proposal form; and (b) in any event, on renewal. Third, to control the insurer's ability to repudiate the policy for breach of warranty, whether or not the warranty in question was material to the risk, and whether or not any breach of warranty had any causal connection with the claim. Fourth, to control the use of 'basis of the contract clauses' and similar contractual devices, by which all statements, and all answers given by the insured to questions in proposal forms, are converted into warranties, thereby enabling subsequent avoidance of the contract.

The Commission was trenchant in its conclusion that the draft directive was an 'unsatisfactory instrument for the reform of the law of insurance'[46] and no substitute for local legislative reform. The Commission set out eight reasons[47] for this conclusion, of which three are most relevant for present purposes. First, the draft directive dealt with a relatively narrow area of insurance law. Although it touched on issues of pre-contractual disclosure, the Commission felt that the draft did not address that issue sufficiently or adequately. It was 'generally too favourable to the insurer and in some respects still harsher on the insured than our present law'. It imposed no requirement to alert the insured about the duty of disclosure, for example by including relevant warnings in proposal forms. The draft directive drew 'unsatisfactory distinctions between breaches of the insured's duty of disclosure when these have

---

44 The Law Commission '(Law Com No 104) Insurance Law: Non-disclosure and Breach of Warranty', October 1980, at p 101, para 9.3.

45 Which required every insured to disclose any fact which a prudent insurer would consider to be material, and entitled the insurer to repudiate the policy and to reject any claim in the event of any breach of this duty.

46 The Law Commission '(Law Com No 104) Insurance Law: Non-disclosure and Breach of Warranty', October 1980, at p 10, para 1.21.

47 *Ibid*, at pp 103–104, para 9.5.

occurred innocently, or when the insured "may be considered to have acted improperly".' Second, the draft directive did not address the local problems created by basis of the contract clauses and the strict legal consequences of a breach of warranty.

Third, a central feature of the draft directive was the 'proportionality' principle. The Commission accepted that this addressed the insurer's ability to repudiate the policy and to reject any claim in the event of a non-disclosure, by providing instead that the insurer would be liable to pay such proportion of any claim as equalled the proportion which the actual premium paid bore to a notional premium which would have been charged by the insurer if the non-disclosure had not occurred. But, in contrast to the approach eventually adopted in the 2012 Act, the Commission concluded that:

> 'In our view the ascertainment of the sum payable on this basis presents great practical difficulties and would be likely to lead to much litigation, particularly in this country where premium tariffs are virtually unknown and there is no administrative control over the content of insurance policies.'

3.13 More generally, the Commission noted that the provisions of the draft directive were sufficiently prescriptive in their drafting as to be 'maximum harmonising', with the result that the implementation of the draft directive:

> 'would preclude Parliament from enacting any further legislation within the domain of the Directive, in particular any legislation for the protection of the consumer insured. The enactment of the Directive would therefore freeze our law indefinitely in an unsatisfactory state.'

The Commission was equally trenchant that the SGIP and the SLIP were insufficient substitutes for legislative reform of insurance law. As to non-disclosure[48], the Commission concluded that 'the mischiefs which we have noted in the law relating to the duty of disclosure imposed upon applicants for insurance are not cured by the Statements of Insurance Practice'. Indeed, in the Commission's view 'the Statements of Insurance Practice are themselves evidence that the law is unsatisfactory and needs to be changed'. The Commission observed that the most important provision of both Statements was to the effect that insurers will not 'unreasonably' repudiate liability or reject a claim for non-disclosure or misrepresentation. But, this left 'insurers as the sole judges of whether repudiation or rejection is unreasonable in any given situation', and in the Commission's view, this was unsatisfactory.

The SGIP and the SLIP did not themselves change the law, but were intended merely to set out existing insurance practice. This had the result

48 *Ibid*, at pp 27–29, paras 3.23–3.30.

that insurers were 'always entitled to invoke their strict legal rights to repudiate policies and reject claims for non-disclosure'. However, since the Commission's primary conclusions included that the existing English law of non-disclosure was unfair, it seemed to the Commission 'unacceptable that insurers should have what is in effect a discretion to repudiate policies and reject claims on grounds which are in themselves unsatisfactory.'

3.14 As to breach of warranty[49], the Commission noted that the only provision in the SGIP and the SLIP which was relevant exclusively to the law of warranties was to be found in paragraph 2(b) of the SGIP, which indicated that except where fraud, deception or negligence was involved an insurer would not unreasonably repudiate liability to indemnify a policy-holder where there has been a breach of warranty or condition but the circumstances of the loss are unconnected with the breach. As in relation to non-disclosure, the Commission concluded that:

> 'this provision in effect confers a discretion on insurers to repudiate a policy on technical grounds if they suspect fraud but are unable to prove it. For the same reasons as those stated … [in relation to non-disclosure] we have concluded that the protection of the insured requires more than measures of self-regulation by the insurance industry and that reform of the law of warranties is necessary.'

Although the Commission plainly concluded that self-regulation (through the SGIP and SLIP) was an insufficient substitute for legislative reform, the Commission unearthed no substantial evidence to suggest that the insurance industry routinely abused its strict legal rights. Such evidence as there was suggested, therefore, that the SGIP and the SLIP did in fact reflect the insurance industry's actual practice in relation to consumer policyholders. Moreover, many of the Commission's ultimate legislative recommendations 'follow lines broadly similar to the provisions of the Statements of Practice, in particular with regard to proposal forms'.[50]

The Commission's recommendation in relation to proposal forms (which duly reflected paragraph 1(b) of the SGIP) included[51] that an insurance proposal form should contain clear and explicit warnings to the insured, presented in an explicit manner, about (a) the standard of answer required of him; (b) the existence and extent of his duty to volunteer information apart from answering the questions in the form; and (c) the consequences of a failure to fulfil either of these obligations. The Commission added a further recommendation: that the Secretary of State should be provided with a residual statutory power to prescribe by Order the specific form and content of warnings to be included by an insurer in a proposal form or renewal

---

49 *Ibid*, at pp 82–83, para 6.10.
50 *Ibid*, at p 29, para 3.30.
51 *Ibid*, at p 108, para 10.14.

notice 'as well as warnings concerning any further aspects of the insured's duty of disclosure as appear to ... [the Secretary of State] to be appropriate.'[52]

3.15 Given the UK legislature's historical caution about statutory intervention in the conduct of insurance business, or in the terms of individual contracts of insurance, encapsulated in the policy of 'freedom with publicity', the Commission's proposal that reform of the law should be backed up by powers of regulatory intervention as to the content of the warnings to be given to policyholders was novel. Perhaps more novel, and more important for the longer term, was the Commission's more general position that statutory regulation of insurance business might be a viable alternative to the statutory reform of insurance law:

> 'The present law as to non-disclosure is defective. The mischief in the present law cannot be cured by measures of self-regulation by the insurance industry such as Statements of Insurance Practice. In the absence of effective administrative control of underwriting, reform of the law is therefore required.'[53]

Conduct of business regulation and principles-based regulation up to 1998

3.16 As it happened, events intervened to ensure that neither option was immediately pursued. In 1979, a new Conservative government, under Margaret Thatcher, initiated an era of privatisation, reform of the public sector and reform of the regulation of financial services. In 1981 the Secretary of State for Trade was able to inform Parliament[54] that the ABI (building on the apparent success of the SGIP and the SLIP) had published self-regulatory codes of practice[55] for the selling of insurance by 'non-broker intermediaries' – those intermediaries who could not (or chose not to) operate under the title 'insurance broker' and were therefore ineligible for registration under the Insurance Brokers (Registration) Act 1977.

The codes, which members of the ABI undertook to enforce as a condition of membership, purported to provide a framework of general principles within which intermediaries and ABI members would sell insurance, including provisions as to the handling of complaints. The general insurance code of conduct required, for example that in obtaining the completion of a proposal form or any other material, an intermediary would (a) avoid influencing the prospective policyholder and make it clear that all answers

52 *Ibid*, at p 110, para 10.27.
53 *Ibid*, p 107, para 10.5.
54 Hansard, HC Deb 19 January 1981, vol 997 c 75W, The Under-Secretary of State for Trade (Mr Reginald Eyre), on Insurance Intermediaries (Codes of Practice).
55 The General Insurance Business – Code of Practice for all Intermediaries (Including Employees of Insurance Companies) other than Registered Insurance Brokers and the Life Assurance Selling – Code of Practice.

and statements were the policyholder's own responsibility; and (b) ensure that the consequences of non-disclosure and inaccuracies were pointed out to the policyholder by drawing his attention to the relevant statement in the proposal form.

The general insurance code of practice for non-broker intermediaries therefore emphasised the policyholder's individual responsibility in the same way as the Insurance Brokers Registration Council Code of Conduct that applied to registered intermediaries, and sought to maximise the utility of the warning statements in the proposal form, required under the SGIP.

3.17 In parallel the Government embarked on two important legislative initiatives relevant to the regulation of insurance business.

First, a programme to implement the EC insurance legislation in force at the UK's accession to the Community in 1973 – at first by regulations under the European Communities Act 1972 and then by the Insurance Companies Act 1981 and regulations under that Act. Parliamentary time was then taken up with a new consolidating Insurance Companies Bill, which became the Insurance Companies Act 1982. Some disquiet was expressed by opposition Members of Parliament that the new legislation had 'nothing to say' about the conduct of insurance business, particularly by non-broker intermediaries,[56] but that was perhaps unsurprising given the largely prudential focus of the relevant directives and the (no doubt carefully timed) introduction of the codes of practice.

Second, in July 1981, the Secretary of State for Trade commissioned Professor L C B Gower, a research adviser on company law to the Department of Trade and Industry, to undertake a review of investor protection in the United Kingdom. Public participation in newly privatised entities, including by way of the ownership of shares was an important part of the economic strategy of the new Conservative government. An appropriate degree of investor protection was therefore an important part of the legislative agenda. The purposes of the Gower review were threefold[57]: to examine the existing statutory protection required by private and business investors in securities and other properties such as unit trusts and open-ended investment companies; to consider the need for statutory control of dealers in securities, investment consultants and investment managers; and finally, to advise on the need for new legislation.

---

[56] Hansard, HC Deb 2 February 1981, vol 998 cc 103–120, Mr Clinton Davis (Insurance Companies Bill).

[57] See generally, Pimlott, G 'The reform of investor protection in the UK: an examination of the proposals of the Gower Report and the UK Government's White Paper of January, 1985', Journal of Comparative Business and Capital Market Law 7 (1985), p 141.

3.18 Professor Gower published a Discussion Document[58] in January 1982 and a Report[59] in January, 1984. The report raised a number of concerns about the marketing of certain long-term insurance products that had a significant investment element. The Report advocated a regulatory system based on Self-Regulatory Agencies ('the SRAs'), each responsible for supervising a particular area of activity, but with statutory backing, in the form of an Investor Protection Act ('the IPA'). Under the IPA, a governmental agency would be responsible for overall surveillance and residual regulation of investment business. Day-to-day regulation would be the province of the SRAs or the governmental agency, for those investment businesses that needed to be, or wished to be, regulated directly by the governmental agency. The Report recommended that 'investments' and 'investment business' should be defined widely and should include long-term insurance products with an investment component. It would be a criminal offence to carry on an unregistered investment business. In relation to insurance selling, the Report recommended that a Code of Conduct should be established to impose 'cooling off' periods, to regulate cold-calling, and to ban unsuitable salespersons. The Report further recommended that independent intermediaries should be registered and that insurance companies should be held responsible for the intermediaries that they employed.

3.19 Given these developments, it is perhaps not surprising that the legislative reform of insurance law took a back seat in the meantime. On 20 December 1984, the Secretary of State announced[60], in response to Parliamentary questions about the Government's intentions as to the draft legislation accompanying the Law Commission's 1980 report, that he was 'embarking on discussions with the insurance industry to see whether changes to their statements of insurance practice can be made to deal with the problems in those areas.' He indicated that he would 'review whether legislation is appropriate and feasible in the light of whatever changes may be agreed.'

In January 1985, the UK Government published a White Paper on the reform of the regulation of investment business, which formed the basis for subsequent legislation in the form of the Financial Services Act 1986, which came into force that year. In line with the recommendations in the Gower Report, the powers of the Secretary of State under that Act were delegated to the Securities and Investments Board ('the SIB'), as the designated government agency for the supervision of investment business in the UK. The SIB then recognised five (later reduced to three) self-regulatory organisations ('the SROs'): the Personal Investment Authority ('the PIA'), the Investment Management Regulatory Authority ('IMRO') and the Securities and Futures Authority ('the SFA').

---

58 Gower, L C B, 'Review of Investor Protection: A Discussion Document' (London, HMSO, 1982).

59 Gower, L C B, 'Review of Investor Protection', Cmnd 9125, 1984.

60 Hansard, HC Deb 20 December 1984 vol 70 cc 273–4W, Mr Fletcher (Insurance Contracts).

3.20 The implementation of FSA 1986 therefore completed an inelegant patchwork of regulatory and self-regulatory arrangements applicable to insurance business. The prudential regulation of both long-term and general insurance business remained the responsibility of the Department of Trade and Industry (later HM Treasury), under the Insurance Companies Act 1982.

Insurance intermediaries who traded under the title 'insurance broker' and who sold either contracts of general insurance, or contracts of long-term insurance without an investment element (usually called 'pure protection contracts') were regulated by the Insurance Brokers Registration Council and subject to the Code of Conduct made under the Insurance Brokers (Registration) Act 1977.

Intermediaries selling contracts of general insurance and non-investment contracts of long-term insurance who traded under other titles (for example, 'insurance consultant') were not subject to statutory regulation: the Government was instead content 'to look to insurance companies to enforce – and where appropriate improve upon – the standards set out in the industry's self-regulatory code of practice for the selling of insurance by non-broker intermediaries.'[61] This code was later supplemented by other codes, including the ABI life insurance (non-investment business) selling code of practice.

Companies and intermediaries advising on or arranging deals in long-term insurance products within the scope of FSA 1986 (ie products with an investment element) were compelled to bring themselves within the framework set out in that Act. A product provider could achieve that result by obtaining membership of an SRO, or direct authorisation by the SIB. Membership of an SRO entailed submission by statute to the rules of the SIB and contractual submission to the rules of that SRO, as approved by the SIB. Distributors of long-term insurance products within the scope of FSA 1986 were required to choose between 'tied agent' or 'independent adviser' status.

A tied agent was either a company representative employed by the provider, or an independent firm for whom the provider had accepted responsibility as an 'appointed representative' under FSA 1986. A tied agent could only distribute the products of the life company to which it was tied, but in return did not require separate authorisation under FSA 1986.

Those intermediaries that wished to distribute long-term insurance products within the scope of FSA 1986 but also to remain independent had either to seek membership of an SRO in their own right, or to obtain registration under the Insurance Brokers (Registration) Act 1977. The latter option was

---

[61] Hansard, HC Deb 22 October 1984 vol 65 cc 445–6W, Mr Alex Fletcher.

available once the Insurance Brokers Registration Council had been designated as a Recognised Professional Body under FSA 1986[62] and could therefore authorise appropriately qualified insurance brokers to carry on investment business within the scope of FSA 1986.

3.21 Parliament turned again to the conduct of insurance business (and the possible legislative reform of insurance law) on 21 February 1986, shortly after the publication of a revised SGIP and SLIP. The Secretary of State informed Parliament[63] that:

> 'the insurers have informed me that they are willing to strengthen the non-life and long-term statements of insurance practice on certain aspects proposed by the Department [of Trade and Industry]. These concern the limitation of the duty of disclosure, warranties, disputes procedures and, in the case of the long-term statements the payment of interest on life insurance claims. The statements apply to insurances taken out by private consumers. ...
>
> These changes are in the right direction. I am well aware of the arguments, advanced amongst others by the representatives of consumers, in favour of legislation on non-disclosure and breach of warranty. But I consider that on balance the case for legislation is out-weighed by the advantages of self-regulation so long as this is effective. I look to all insurers, whether or not they belong to the Association of British Insurers which has promulgated the statements, to observe both their spirit and their letter.
>
> In the light of the insurers' undertakings I do no consider there is any need for the moment to proceed with earlier proposals for a change in the law. My Department will however keep the situation under review in order to ensure that self-regulation is working adequately and will reconsider the question of legislation if problems continue to arise.'

Three principal changes were made to the revised SGIP. First, the addition of a prohibition on 'basis of the contract clauses' and similar devices:

> 'Neither the proposal form nor the policy shall contain any provision converting the statements as to past or present fact in the proposal form into warranties. But insurers may require specific warranties about matters which are material to the risk'.

Second a re-working of the material in relation to claims-handling to so that an insurer no longer retained the discretion to repudiate liability when, in the insurer's discretion, it was 'not unreasonable' to do so, even if the

---

62 Designation as an RPB was facilitated by decisions such as that in *Pickles v IBRC* [1984] 1 All ER 1073, in which McCullough J observed (at 1074j) that the aim of the IBRC 'clearly, is that in time registered insurance brokers will enjoy the reputation and standing of people who conduct their calling by professional standards'.

63 Hansard, HC Deb 21 February 1986 vol 92 cc 356–7W, Mr Channon (Insurance Contracts).

insured's purported non-disclosure, misrepresentation or breach of warranty was otherwise unobjectionable, or unconnected with the loss in question. Third, by the addition of a requirement that the provisions of the SGIP should be taken into account in any disputes between a policyholder and an insurer relating to matters dealt with in the SGIP.

The SLIP was significantly expanded, bringing its content into line with that of the SGIP. For present purposes, perhaps the most significant expansion was in the material about claims handling:

> '3. CLAIMS
>
> (a) An insurer will not unreasonably reject a claim. In particular, an insurer will not reject a claim or invalidate a policy on grounds of nondisclosure or misrepresentation of a fact unless:
>
> (i) it is a material fact; and
>
> (ii) it is a fact within the knowledge of the proposer; and
>
> (iii) it is a fact which the proposer could reasonably be expected to disclose.
>
> (It should be noted that fraud or deception will, and reckless or negligent non-disclosure or misrepresentation of a material fact may, constitute grounds for rejection of a claim.)
>
> (b) Except where fraud is involved, an insurer will not reject a claim or invalidate a policy on grounds of a breach of warranty unless the circumstances of the claim are connected with the breach and unless:
>
> (i) the warranty relates to a statement of fact concerning the life to be assured under a life of another policy and that statement would have constituted grounds for rejection of a claim by the insurer under 3(a)above if it had been made by the life to be assured under an own life policy or;
>
> (ii) the warranty was created in relation to specific matters material to the risk and it was drawn to the proposer's attention at or before the making of the contract.
>
> ...'

To take (at least partial) account of the new regime under FSA 1986, the revised SLIP included a caption to the effect that 'Nothing in this statement should be interpreted as conflicting with or overriding the rules of LAUTRO [an SRO, later subsumed into the PIA] in respect of long-term insurance policies which are treated as investments for the purposes of the Financial Services Act 1986'.

3.22 Once the system of regulation under FSA 1986 began operating, the SIB rulebook grew rapidly in its complexity and density. As a reaction to this complexity, the then chairman of the SIB, Sir David Walker, secured the passage of a series of amendments to FSA 1986, by way of the Companies Act 1989. In particular, the 1989 Act inserted FSA 1986, s 47A, which gave the Secretary of State the power to:

> 'issue statements of principle with respect to the conduct and financial standing expected of persons authorised to carry on investment business'.

FSA 1986, s 47A(2) provided that failure to comply with a statement of principle was a ground for taking disciplinary action or exercising powers of intervention, but did not of itself give rise to any right of action by investors, or affect the validity of any transaction.

The SIB then promulgated ten principles for business and forty 'designated rules', which were directly applicable to members of the SROs and formed the backbone of SIB's regulatory rulebook.[64] As noted above in relation to the Code of Conduct issued by the Insurance Brokers Registration Council, the notion of regulation by reference to general principles, breach of which might be a basis for regulatory action but which did not give rise to a right of action by the person who claimed to have been affected by the breach, was not new. The principles set out in the IBRC Code of Conduct continued to apply alongside the principles enacted by the SIB. Reflecting the patchwork nature of the regulatory regime, the last version of the IBRC Code of Conduct to be approved (in 1994[65]) included an additional principle (H) in the following terms:

> 'Insurance brokers who are authorised by the Council to conduct relevant investment business shall comply with any statements of principle issued under section 47A of the Financial Services Act 1986.'

The establishment of the FSA and the regulatory regime under FSMA 2000: 1990 to the present day

3.23 Prompted by a series of failures of financial services firms, the Labour government that came into power in May 1997 announced that it would establish a single financial regulator as the successor to the SIB, operating under new legislation to replace FSA 1986.

The Financial Services Authority, in corporate terms the re-named SIB, was formally launched on 27 October 1997. Over the following months the

---

[64] See generally Blair, M, et al, *Financial Services Law* (2nd ed, Oxford, 2009), Ch 5, from which this material is taken.

[65] The Insurance Brokers Registration Council (Code of Conduct) Approval Order 1994 (SI 1994/2569).

Government confirmed that the FSA would become responsible not only for the regulation of investment business, but also for the regulation of other financial services sectors and institutions, including banking, insurance building societies, friendly societies and Lloyd's of London.

By July 1998, HM Treasury had produced a series of Consultation Papers, including an outline Financial Services and Markets Bill. As the new legislation progressed through Parliament, the SROs established under FSA 1986 continued to report to the FSA (in its guise as the former SIB). Under the Bank of England Act 1998, the FSA assumed formal responsibility for the supervision of banks, listed money market institutions and related clearing houses from 1 June 1998 (a date christened 'N1'). The functions of the DTI and HM Treasury as prudential insurance regulator were sub-contracted to the FSA in 1999.

The Financial Services and Markets Act 2000 ('FSMA 2000') received Royal assent on 14 June 2000 and the FSA assumed formal responsibility for the supervision of all financial services business within the purview of FSMA 2000 from 1 December 2001 (a date christened 'N2').

3.24 In the midst of all this regulatory change, the broking of general insurance and non-investment long-term insurance occupied an odd, isolated backwater. Following consultation in 1998 on the need for statutory regulation of insurance brokers and other general insurance intermediaries the Government announced on 27 July 1998 that it would repeal the Insurance Brokers (Registration) Act 1977 in FSMA 2000 and so end the statutory status of the IBRC and the artificial distinction between 'brokers' and other intermediaries. This was followed, on 13 April 1999, by Government evidence to the Joint Committee on Financial Services and Markets,[66] to the effect that proposed regulation of general insurance was to be limited to the authorisation and prudential oversight of insurance companies and Lloyd's. The Government was, therefore, looking to the insurance industry to develop effective voluntary standards of professional practice for general insurance business.

By 1 July 1999 an HM Treasury news release[67] recorded that:

> 'a broad-based range of support has developed for the General Insurance Standards Council … a new voluntary body to promote high standards of professional conduct among general insurance intermediaries … It plans to complement the statutory responsibilities of the Financial Services Authority … while stripping away unnecessary regulatory requirements on general insurance intermediaries.'

[66] Reports of the Joint Committee on Financial Services and Markets in Session 1998–99 HC 328 – Draft Financial Services and Markets Bill (Report), 29 April 1999, paragraph 88.

[67] HM Treasury News Release 109/99, 1 July 1999.

3.25 The GISC was formally launched on 3 July 2000. Its rules included a 'Private Customer Code', which was intended to ensure that general insurance customers were treated fairly and reasonably. The requirements of the Code extended to matters such as explaining the service offered, matching the customer's requirements to the products and services offered, giving appropriate information, confirming the cover, observing service standards (for example as to the handling of claims), issuing documentation, observing confidentiality and handling complaints.

More controversially, and in an attempt to ensure that the GISC would in practice have the authority of the general insurance broking community behind it, GISC membership rules provided that where an intermediary was not a member of the GISC, an insurer member could deal with that intermediary only if the intermediary became an agent or sub-agent of the insurer. This rule quickly attracted legal challenge on the grounds that it was anti-competitive.[68] Perhaps paradoxically, although the rule survived the challenge, the GISC itself (and more particularly the strategy of self-regulation that underpinned it[69]) was overtaken by external events.

3.26 First, on 22 October 2001, HM Treasury announced its intention to bring long-term care insurance products within the scope of FSA regulation, following the recommendation of a Royal Commission on long-term care for the elderly.[70]

The basic purpose of long-term care ('LTC') products is to help consumers provide for all or part of the cost of long-term care if they need to move into a residential home or need nursing care in their own home. Some LTC products took the form of investments or packaged products (for example impaired life annuities or investment bonds linked to an insurance contract). The sale and marketing of LTC products of this type (ie products with an investment element) fell within the existing conduct of business regime for investment business.

However, other LTC products took the form of 'pure protection contracts': insurance-only products with no investment element. In principle, such insurance products could be written either as contracts of long-term insurance or contracts of general insurance, but were generally written as long-term insurance Class IV (Permanent Health Insurance). Such long-term contracts fell outside both the existing investment business regime and the proposed GISC regime, which was limited to contracts of general insurance. HM Treasury's preferred option, that the regulation of such contracts should

---

68 See *Institute of Independent Insurance Brokers v Director General of Fair Trading*, Competition Commission Appeal Tribunal, Transcript, 17 September 2001.

69 Since 'self-regulation' would be unlikely to meet the EU requirement that insurance mediation should be subject to authorisation – ie conducted within a legislative framework imposed and enforced by the home-state.

70 See Financial Services Authority, 'Consultation Paper'.

be brought within the remit of the FSA, highlighted that the selling of non-investment long-term insurance business (which included a substantial body of health insurance business[71]) fell uncomfortably between the investment business regime under FSMA 2000 and the GISC regime and remained subject only to industry (ie ABI) codes of practice.

3.27 Second, on 26 November 2011 the EC Council of Ministers agreed the text of a directive that would, once agreed by the EU Parliament and formally adopted, require Member States to introduce regulation of persons conducting insurance and reinsurance mediation (ie broking) business.

With the new directive in mind, on 12 Dec 2001 the Government announced that the scope of FSMA 2000 would be extended[72] to make the FSA responsible for the regulation of 'general insurance broking'. In practice, of course, since the directive would require the regulation of the mediation of both general and long-term insurance and reinsurance contracts, the FSA would also acquire responsibility for the regulation of the selling of non-investment long-term insurance contracts.

In response to the announcement, Howard Davies, the then chairman of the FSA, said[73]:

> 'We recognise the merits of bringing … general insurance brokers within the FSA's scope, providing a single regulator for such firms and greater protection for consumers. Smaller firms, in particular, have told us that the current mix of statutory and non-statutory regulation imposes extra costs and burdens on them. The requirements of the new regimes must be proportionate to the risks faced by consumers and ensure that the benefits of competition and innovation are retained. The Government have said that they will consult on the timetable for implementation of the new regimes and expects that they will come into force simultaneously. We hope that voluntary industry arrangements will be retained in the meantime to provide protection to consumers, and we will work, in full consultation with all concerned, towards a smooth transition to the new regimes.'

Regulation under FSMA 2000

The FSA's functions and statutory objectives

3.28 FSMA 2000, ss 2(1) and (4) give the FSA a number of 'general functions'. For present purposes, these include (a) its function of making

71 For example, permanent health insurance (or income protection), critical-illness insurance and private medical insurance.

72 By designating new 'regulated activities' as necessary.

73 Financial Services Authority, Press Release FSA/PN/168/2001, 12 December 2001.

rules; (b) its functions in relation to the giving of general guidance; and (c) its function of determining the general policy and principles by reference to which it performs particular functions. To this end, FSMA 2000 gives the FSA the power to make rules (technically, subordinate legislation in the form of instruments made by the FSA Board) and express general guidance, which is generally but not exclusively collated and set out in the FSA's Handbook of Rules and Guidance ('the Handbook'). The FSA's rules are generally, but not exclusively, binding on persons carrying on the wide range of 'regulated activities' defined by or under FSMA 2000. [74]

The FSA's particular functions are all those specific tasks that fall within its remit, for example in our case, the prudential regulation of insurance firms and the regulation of the conduct of general and long-term insurance business. FSMA 2000, s 2(1) requires that in discharging its general functions the FSA must so far as is reasonably possible, act in a way (a) which is compatible with the FSA's regulatory objectives; and (b) which the FSA considers most appropriate for the purpose of meeting those objectives.

The FSA's regulatory objectives are set out in FSMA 2000, s 2(2). They are market confidence; financial stability; the protection of consumers; and the reduction of financial crime. For present purposes the two most relevant objectives are market confidence and the protection of consumers. The market confidence objective means, under FSMA 2000, s 3(1), maintaining confidence in the UK financial system, including financial markets. The consumer protection objective means, under FSMA 2000, s 5(1), securing the appropriate degree of protection for consumers. FSMA 2000, s 5(2) provides that:

> 'In considering what degree of protection may be appropriate, the Authority must have regard to—
>
> (a) the differing degrees of risk involved in different kinds of investment or other transaction;
>
> (b) the differing degrees of experience and expertise that different consumers may have in relation to different kinds of regulated activity;
>
> (ba) any information which the consumer financial education body has provided to the Authority in the exercise of the consumer financial education function;]
>
> (c) the needs that consumers may have for advice and accurate information; and

[74] See in particular the Financial Services and Markets Act 2000 (Regulated Activities) Order 2001 (SI 2001/544).

(d) the general principle that consumers should take responsibility for their decisions.'

Under FSMA 2000, s 425A and 425B, a 'consumer' is widely defined. At its most basic the definition includes 'persons who use, have used or may use any services provided by authorised persons in carrying on regulated activities under FSMA 2000.'

3.29 It follows that an important difference between the FSA regime and earlier regimes applicable to the conduct of insurance business is that the FSA's fundamental regulatory objectives extend to the protection the all users of financial services, whether, those users act in their private capacity, or in a commercial capacity.

That point must be tempered, however, by the following observations. First, the FSA's objective is to deliver an appropriate degree of protection, so that it is open to the FSA to provide different degrees of protection to different classes of users of financial services. Second (and confusingly), the term 'consumer' has as narrower meaning in the FSA Handbook than the wide definition in FSMA 2000. The Glossary to the Handbook defines as consumer as 'any natural person acting for purposes outside his trade, business or profession.' Some parts of the Handbook, including the Insurance Conduct of Business Sourcebook, discussed below, provide greater protection for consumers than for other commercial users of financial services. Third, FSA rules draw an important distinction between 'clients' and 'customers'[75] of financial services firms. The degree of protection afforded to clients who are customers is generally higher than that afforded to clients who are not customers. Fourth, it is fundamental to the FSA regime that consumers should take responsibility for their own decisions. As a minimum, this imposes some responsibility on a consumer to engage actively with an authorised firm and to seek to understand the advice and information being given.[76]

3.30 Under FSMA 2000, s 2(3), in discharging its general functions the FSA must have regard to a range of factors, including the following:

'(a) the need to use its resources in the most efficient and economic way;

---

75 The Glossary to the FSA Handbook defines a 'customer' differently in different contexts. In relation to the conduct of investment business (which includes some types of long-term insurance business), an authorised firm must classify each user of its services as (a) a retail client; (b) a professional client; or (c) an eligible counterparty. In general, only retail clients and professional clients are 'customers'. The position is somewhat different in relation to the conduct of insurance business that is not investment business (so including all general insurance business and non-investment long-term insurance business): in relation to that business, all policyholders and potential policyholders are 'customers'.

76 See Financial Services Authority, 'Discussion Paper DP08/5: Consumer responsibility', January 2008, and Financial Services Authority, 'Feedback statement FS 09/2: Consumer responsibility: Feedback on DP08/5', September 2009.

(b) the responsibilities of those who manage the affairs of authorised persons;

(c) the principle that a burden or restriction which is imposed on a person, or on the carrying on of an activity, should be proportionate to the benefits, considered in general terms, which are expected to result from the imposition of that burden or restriction;

(d) the desirability of facilitating innovation in connection with regulated activities;

(e) the international character of financial services and markets and the desirability of maintaining the competitive position of the United Kingdom;

(f) the need to minimise the adverse effects on competition that may arise from anything done in the discharge of those functions; [and]

(g) the desirability of facilitating competition between those who are subject to any form of regulation by the Authority.'

One important consequence of these 'have regard' factors (taken together with the scope of the consumer protection objective and the practical reality that the FSA has a wide range of functions but limited resources) is that the FSA generally conducts itself as a risk-based regulator. At bottom, this means that the FSA will direct its resources to those firms, sectors or issues which prospectively or actually pose an identifiable risk to the attainment of the FSA's regulatory objectives.

3.31 Although the FSA is required to balance the achievement of its consumer protection objective against its other objectives, including that of protecting the UK financial system, the achievement of the consumer protection objective has been a very significant driver of FSA policy and rule-making in relation to the conduct of regulated business.

The conduct issues that gain the most FSA attention are, therefore, those that are evaluated to have resulted in significant consumer detriment, or to pose the greatest risk of detriment to consumers generally. The corollary to this risk-based approach is that, beyond making rules and exercising supervisory powers to address potential areas of consumer detriment, the FSA is very unlikely to intervene in, or to respond to the failure of, an individual transaction between a consumer and a firm, unless that transaction or its failure are indicative of an issue of regulatory significance.

Such an issue might include, for example, a series of related failures indicating a systematic failure of compliance by a regulated firm, or evidence of detriment to a number of the firm's consumers. To this end, the FSA has formal arrangements in place between it, the Financial Ombudsman Service ('the FOS') and the Office of Fair Trading ('the OFT'), intended to assist the

FSA to identify and respond effectively to issues of regulatory relevance that may be referred to or identified by the OFT, or which may emerge from the consumer complaints and applications for redress that are dealt with by the FOS.[77]

Similar considerations dictate that the FSA does not routinely scrutinise the terms on which firms contract with their customers. Allied to this, in the insurance field, the insurance directives actively prohibit member states from requiring the systematic approval or prior notification of policy conditions. For example the Solvency II Directive[78] (replicating the equivalent provisions in its predecessor directives) provides as follows in Article 21:

> 'Member States shall not [subject to limited exceptions] require the prior approval or systematic notification of general and special policy conditions, of scales of premiums, of the technical bases, used in particular for calculating scales of premiums and technical provisions, or of forms and other printed documents which an undertaking intends to use in its dealings with policy holders or ceding or retroceding undertakings.'

FSA Principles for Business

3.32 Reflecting the FSA's SIB heritage, the FSA Handbook is replete with 'principles', most notably the FSA Principles for Business, set out in the PRIN module of the Handbook:

> '1. Integrity: A firm must conduct its business with integrity.
>
> 2. Skill, care and diligence: A firm must conduct its business with due skill, care and diligence.
>
> 3. Management and control: A firm must take reasonable care to organise and control its affairs responsibly and effectively, with adequate risk management systems.
>
> 4. Financial prudence: A firm must maintain adequate financial resources.
>
> 5. Market conduct: A firm must observe proper standards of market conduct.
>
> 6. Customers' interests: A firm must pay due regard to the interests of its customers and treat them fairly.
>
> 7. Communications with clients: A firm must pay due regard to the

---

77 See Financial Services Authority, 'Discussion Paper DP10/01: Consumer complaints (emerging risks and mass claims)', March 2010, and Financial Services Authority, 'Feedback Statement FS 11/2: Consumer complaints (emerging risks and mass claims): Feedback on DP10/01', March 2011.

78 Directive 2009/138/EC of 25 November 2009 on the taking-up and pursuit of the business of Insurance and Reinsurance (Solvency II) (recast).

information needs of its clients, and communicate information to them in a way which is clear, fair and not misleading.

8. Conflicts of interest: A firm must manage conflicts of interest fairly, both between itself and its customers and between a customer and another client.
9. Customers: relationships of trust: A firm must take reasonable care to ensure the suitability of its advice and discretionary decisions for any customer who is entitled to rely upon its judgment.
10. Clients' assets: A firm must arrange adequate protection for clients' assets when it is responsible for them.
11. Relations with regulators: A firm must deal with its regulators in an open and cooperative way, and must disclose to the FSA appropriately anything relating to the firm of which the FSA would reasonably expect notice.'

In analytical terms, the Principles for Business are simply high-level FSA rules that are the product of the ordinary legislative processes under FSMA 2000. The relevance of the Principles for Business to the FSA and its successor regulators is discussed further below.

COBS and ICOBS

3.33 The FSA's rules for the conduct of insurance business fall into two parts: first, the Conduct of Business Sourcebook ('COBS'), and second, the Insurance Conduct of Business Sourcebook ('ICOBS'). COBS applies to a regulated firm with respect to 'designated investment business' and 'long-term insurance business in relation to life policies', carried on from an establishment maintained by it, or its appointed representative, in the United Kingdom. The overall effect is (subject to one exception) to include within the scope of the conduct of business regime for investment business (a) any contract of direct long-term insurance that is not a pure protection contract; and (b) any pension policy[79]. The exclusion of 'pure protection contracts'[80] is intended to remove from the scope of investment conduct of business regulation those contracts of long-term insurance that have no investment element.

---

79 Defined in the Glossary to the Handbook as 'a contract under which a right to benefits results from contributions made to an occupational pension scheme or to a personal pension scheme, where the contributions are paid to a long-term insurer.'

80 Defined in the Glossary to the Handbook as 'a long-term insurance contract in respect of which the following conditions are met: (a) the benefits under the contract are payable only on death or in respect of incapacity due to injury, sickness or infirmity; (b) the contract has no surrender value, or the consideration consists of a single premium and the surrender value does not exceed that premium; and (c) the contract makes no provision for its conversion or extension in a manner which would result in it ceasing to comply with (a) or (b).'

The exception implements the policy preference, set out in October 2001 and prefaced above, that in view of the risk of consumer detriment arising from long-term care insurance contracts, the sale of such products should be brought within the scope of the conduct of business regime for investment business, whether or not such contracts of insurance have any investment element. Accordingly, if a pure protection contract is also a 'long-term care insurance contract'[81] it falls within the definition of a 'life policy' and within the investment business regime applicable to packaged products.[82]

3.34 ICOBS applies to a regulated firm with respect to insurance mediation (and other) activities when carried on in relation to a 'non-investment insurance contract', that is 'a contract of insurance which is a general insurance contract or a pure protection contract but which is not a long-term care insurance contract.' ICOBS imposes the obligations required to implement the Insurance Mediation Directive[83] ('the IMD'), but also goes beyond the requirements of the IMD, in particular because it carries forward and imposes on insurers some of the obligations previously set out in the SGIP.

In 2002, the FSA noted[84] that its discussions with the FOS had revealed that private customers had a number of concerns about claims handling. The concerns included: customers having to request a claim form a number of times before eventually receiving one; apparently unnecessary delays in the claims handling process; customers not understanding why they were being offered an amount that was less than the amount initially claimed; and claims not being handled fairly.

The FSA made a number of proposals as to how it might address these issues. In relation to the fair handling of claims, the FSA observed[85] that 'the ABI's Statement of General Insurance Practice affects the way in which insurance companies treat claims by removing the harsh consequences of strict interpretation of contract law [in relation to non-disclosure, misrepresentation and breach of warranty] when applied to insurance claims.' The FSA indicated that was 'minded to include these provisions in … [FSA] rules as they are important provisions in ensuring that customers' claims are treated fairly.'

---

81 Defined in the Glossary to the Handbook as 'a long-term insurance contract: (a) which provides, would provide at the policyholder's option, or is sold or held out as providing, benefits that are payable or provided if the policyholder's health deteriorates to the extent that he cannot live independently without assistance and that is not expected to change; and (b) under which the benefits are capable of being paid for periodically for all or part of the period that the policyholder cannot live without assistance; where [in each case] "benefits" are services, accommodation or goods necessary or desirable for the continuing care of the policyholder because he cannot live independently without assistance.'

82 See generally Financial Services Authority, 'Consultation Paper 200: Regulation of long-term care insurance', September 2003.

83 Directive of 9 December 2002 on insurance mediation (2002/92/EC).

84 Financial Services Authority, 'Consultation Paper 160: Insurance Selling and Administration: the FSA's high-level approach to regulation', December 2002, p 81.

85 *Ibid*, p 83.

The resulting rules are now set out in ICOBS 8.1, as follows:

> 'ICOBS 8.1.1R: An insurer must:
>
> (1) handle claims promptly and fairly;
>
> (2) provide reasonable guidance to help a policyholder make a claim and appropriate information on its progress;
>
> (3) not unreasonably reject a claim (including by terminating or avoiding a policy); and
>
> (4) settle claims promptly once settlement terms are agreed.
>
> ICOBS 8.1.2R: A rejection of a consumer policyholder's claim is unreasonable, except where there is evidence of fraud, if it is for:
>
> (1) non-disclosure of a fact material to the risk which the policyholder could not reasonably be expected to have disclosed; or
>
> (2) non-negligent misrepresentation of a fact material to the risk; or
>
> (3) breach of warranty or condition unless the circumstances of the claim are connected to the breach and unless (for a pure protection contract):
>
> > (a) under a "life of another" contract, the warranty relates to a statement of fact concerning the life to be assured and, if the statement had been made by the life to be assured under an "own life" contract, the insurer could have rejected the claim under this rule; or
> >
> > (b) the warranty is material to the risk and was drawn to the customer's attention before the conclusion of the contract.'

3.35 With two exceptions, the investment conduct of business requirements applicable to long-term contracts of insurance and long-term care insurance contracts does not mirror the insurance conduct of business requirements in ICOBS. The first exception is that in order to implement the IMD, COBS 7.1 (Insurance mediation) imposes on an intermediary selling a life policy (so including a long-term care insurance contract) the minimum information disclosure and other obligations required under the IMD. Second, in relation to the sale of a long-term care insurance contract, COBS 17 imposes claims handling requirements, including the following at COBS 17.1.3R, which follows the text of the ABI SLIP:

> 'An insurer and a managing agent [in respect of insurance business written at Lloyd's] must not:
>
> (1) unreasonably reject a claim; or
>
> (2) except where there is evidence of fraud, reject a claim for:

(a) non-disclosure of a fact material to the risk which the policyholder could not reasonably have been expected to disclose; or

(b) misrepresentation of a fact material to the risk, unless the misrepresentation is negligent; or

(c) breach of warranty, unless the circumstances of the claim are connected to the breach, the warranty is material to the risk and was drawn to the policyholder's attention before the conclusion of the contract.'

Remedies for a consumer-insured

3.36 Both the FSA's Principles for Business (which, as above, are high-level rules) and the specific conduct of business rules in ICOBS and COBS are binding on insurers and intermediaries, as are a range of other FSA rules that may be relevant to insurance business and insurance broking. It does not follow, however, that a breach of an FSA rule is necessarily actionable by anyone other than the FSA. FSMA 2000, s 150(1) provides that a contravention by an authorised person (for example an FSA-authorised insurer or insurance intermediary) of certain types of FSA rule is actionable 'at the suit of a private person who suffers loss as a result of the contravention, subject to the defences and other incidents applying to actions for breach of statutory duty'. The scope of that right of action is extended in limited cases to non-private persons,[86] but FSMA 2000, s 150(2) also gives the FSA the power to disapply a private right of action. The FSA has exercised that power so that, for example, breach of the FSA's Principles for Business and breach of the FSA's high-level systems and controls rules are not actionable by a private person. The net result, however is that in relation to some FSA rules (in particular most rules in COBS and ICOBS) breach by an insurer or insurance intermediary in principle gives a consumer-insured (and sometimes a commercial insured) a right of action in tort, for breach of statutory duty.

In practice, however, that private right of action has been little used. The Law Commissions concluded that private action for breach of regulatory rules:

> '… would be a difficult, unusual and expensive course of action. There have been very few reported cases where [s 150] has been applied, and we are not aware of any concerning ICOBS 8.1.2.'

One reason for the limited take-up of the private right of action under FSMA 2000, s 150 is that a consumer-insured is perhaps more likely to proceed by lodging a complaint with the FOS. Typically, the FOS will not

---

[86] See in particular the Financial Services and Markets Act 2000 (Rights of Action Regulations) 2001 (SI 2256/2001), and *Titan Steel Wheels Ltd v Royal Bank of Scotland plc* [2010] EWHC 211 (Comm).

rely on the breach in determining such a complaint. Under FSMA 2000, s 228 the FOS is obliged to determine cases within its compulsory jurisdiction, not by the application of the law, but on the basis of what the Ombudsman regards as 'fair and reasonable in all the circumstances of the case'. As can be seen in Chapter 4, this has led the FOS to develop its own distinctive approach to non-disclosure, misrepresentation and basis of the contract clauses, independent of the FSA's rules and indeed independent of the law more generally.

The FSA's approach to the SGIP and the SLIP

3.37 The available FSA policy materials do not indicate whether the FSA considered adopting other parts of the SGIP and the SLIP, along with the material now reflected in ICOBS 8.1 and COBS 17. Obvious candidates would have included other parts of the SGIP and the SLIP, including perhaps the prohibition on basis of the contract clauses. Perhaps, very simply, the FSA simply selected only the material directly relevant to the issue of consumer claims handling, with which it was most concerned when ICOBS 8.1 was adopted. One might also speculate, however, that the remaining material in the SGIP and the SLIP (both of which were discontinued in January 2005 when the regime in ICOB came into force) was not considered essential in the context of other pressures bearing on the FSA at the time ICOBS was implemented.

In a speech to the FSA in June 2005, Sir David Arculus (then head of the Better Regulation Task Force) captured the mood of the time in this way:

> 'it's much too easy for … regulators to react to events … by producing yet another equivalent of the dangerous dogs act. Most times there is already a law in place which is perfectly adequate but which is not being followed properly. Sometimes of course there does need to be a change in the law, and when that is the case, [the BRTF proposes] … that a compensatory simplification measure be brought in.
>
> Simplification might mean deregulation or it might mean consolidation of an existing regulation or it might mean rationalization – using horizontal regulation (such as a general duty not to trade unfairly) to replace a variety of sector specific regulations. Alternatively, it might mean a targeted sectoral guide'.[87]

There was, therefore, a growing pressure on the FSA to rationalise its rulebook and make the most of existing general duties, as a deliberate substitute for making additional specific rules, driven by the political, commercial and common-sense desire for better regulation. That pressure

[87] The speech can be found at http://www.fsa.gov.uk/Pages/Library/Communication/Speeches/2005/0705_sda.shtml.

led the FSA to re-visit and re-invigorate a policy of 'principle-based regulation', an idea whose time had come before, most notably under the auspices of the SIB, under the Chairmanship of Sir David Walker.

In March 2005, the FSA (in partnership with the Financial Services Practitioner Panel) launched a study of the costs of FSA regulation, in parallel with a Government review of the costs of regulation generally. The results of the FSA study[88] were published in 2006. In July 2005, the FSA outlined[89] its strategy for reviewing its Handbook. The FSA commented that a key reason for undertaking a review of the Handbook was that it wanted the Handbook to reflect its vision and values, which include:

> 'an approach to rule-making based as far as possible on principles rather than prescription; a focus on senior management responsibility; and acting in a proportionate and risk-based way.'

The future

3.38 As noted above, the FSA Handbook is replete with Principles. The power of the FSA Principles for Business[90] does not lie in their legal nature as such. They are, after all, merely high-level rules that are the product of the legislative processes under FSMA 2000. From a regulatory point of view, the power of principles lies in their generality. First, principles are aimed at outcomes or behaviours that are required from a number of (or indeed, all) regulated firms, no matter how diverse their business, structure or governance. For example, under PRIN firms must 'act with integrity', 'treat their customers fairly', 'maintain adequate financial resources'. Second, principles are specific as to outcome, but not as to the method by which each firm is to achieve that outcome. Third, deciding whether (or not) a firm has achieved the outcome required by a principle almost always requires judgment by the regulator. The central role of that judgment is reflected in the language in which principles (including those in PRIN) are drafted: for example, capital must be adequate, behaviour must be reasonable or fair. Fourth, because principles are rules, they are capable of being breached. Breach can be the basis for the exercise of supervisory or enforcement powers by the FSA. Indeed, since the middle of the last decade, FSA supervisory and enforcement actions have increasingly been framed in terms of breach of the Principles for Business and less reliant on breaches of specific underlying rules.

The price for this regulatory power is, of course, paid by firms in the increased cost of compliance. The more principle-based regulation is, the

---

88 Deloitte, 'The Cost of Regulation Study', June 2006.
89 Financial Services Authority, 'Consultation Paper 05/10: Reviewing the FSA Handbook', July 2005.
90 On which see Blair, M, et al, *Financial Services Law* (2nd ed, Oxford, 2009), Ch 5.

more difficult it becomes to draw bright rule-based lines between compliance and non-compliance and the more compliance becomes the outcome of culture rather than form filling. In the present climate, however, it is very likely that the cost of tougher, more nuanced, value-driven compliance will be seen as a cost worth imposing on the financial services industry.

Now that the Financial Services and Markets Act 2012 has become law, the functions of the FSA will be divided between the Bank of England, a new Prudential Regulatory Authority ('the PRA') (which will be a subsidiary of the Bank) and a new Financial Conduct Authority ('the FCA'), which will be the corporate successor to the FSA. The prudential regulation of insurance firms will be the responsibility of the PRA, but the FCA will be responsible for the regulation of all aspects of the conduct of business. It is too soon to tell whether the FCA rules will be materially different from those of the FSA. Early indications are, however, that the FCA intends to be more activist, interventionist and intrusive as a regulator. It seems, therefore, that principle-based regulation will be here to stay.

Chapter 4 The Financial Ombudsman Service: the History and Development of its Approach to Non-Disclosure[1]

Melissa Collett, Ombudsman[2]

Melissa Collett is an ombudsman at the Financial Ombudsman Service, leading the medical, travel and specialist insurance teams. She is a frequent presenter at insurance conferences and events, authored articles on insurance practice, and has been involved in the development of industry-wide guidance. She has worked closely with the English Law Commission on the reform of the law on non-disclosure. Prior to joining the Financial Ombudsman Service, she was a solicitor at Hogan Lovells specialising in insurance litigation and regulation.

The growth of consumer insurance and the formation of the Financial Ombudsman Service[3]

4.1 The Consumer Insurance (Disclosure and Representations) Act 2012 ('the 2012 Act') marks the culmination in the reform of the law of non-disclosure that has taken decades to achieve. Other contributors to this book have explained the history of the Act and the factors that led to the change of the law pertaining to consumers. The purpose of the first part of this chapter is to explain the important role of the Financial Ombudsman Service[4] in the reform of the law. The second part of this chapter will explain the ombudsman's current approach to non-disclosure.

---

1 For simplicity, references to 'non-disclosure' throughout this chapter refer to misrepresentation as well as non-disclosure. This also reflects how the ombudsman service tends to refer to both.

2 While this chapter discusses the ombudsman service's approach, it was written in my own personal capacity, and any views expressed are my own.

3 I am indebted to the editor, Peter Tyldesley, for his research into the history of the Financial Ombudsman Service.

4 Throughout this chapter the word 'ombudsman' refers to the ombudsmen of the Financial Ombudsman Service or the Insurance Ombudsman Bureau, as relevant.

4.1 *Consumer Insurance Law*

Insurance law evolved over the centuries in large part to respond to the needs of the marine insurance industry and the commercial environment in which it operated. Although insurance for individuals existed for hundreds of years, more and more insurance products began to be designed for and sold to consumers in the latter part of the 20th century.[5]

It is against this background of growth in consumer insurance that the concept of an insurance ombudsman came into being. The rigours of insurance law (as set out in earlier chapters), especially the duty of utmost good faith and the remedy of avoidance[6] for breach of this duty, did not sit well with consumer insurance contracts. Ordinary people were not aware what facts were material to a prudent insurer and needed to be disclosed. Insurers could invoke the draconian remedy of avoidance of the contract from the start even if the non-disclosure was innocently made. Consumers, unlike businesses, were not often professionally advised by brokers. They had no bargaining power with insurers, and were forced to accept the insurer's standard terms. If their claim was declined, they had little recourse except to the courts, which was expensive and impractical unless large sums were at stake.

4.2 The Law Reform Committee recognised these problems and identified in its report of 1957 reforms of insurance law that it felt could usefully be undertaken.[7] Its suggestions, however, were not taken up. In 1975 the English and Scottish Law Commissions recommended legislation against unfair contract terms,[8] but the British Insurance Association (BIA) (now the Association of British Insurers) opposed the application of the proposals to insurance contracts. Instead, the BIA agreed to self-regulate in return for insurance being exempt from what became the Unfair Contract Terms Act 1977. The BIA subsequently produced two codes of practice: the Statement of General Insurance Practice (SGIP) and the Statement of Long-term Insurance Practice (SLIP). The purpose of both was to ameliorate the harshness of the law towards consumers. Both codes effectively abolished the general duty of disclosure in favour of insurers asking clear questions about matters they considered to be material. The codes also prohibited the avoidance of a contract for non-negligent non-disclosure. Insurers were required to provide warnings on application forms about the duty of disclosure and the consequences of breach.

These codes represented a significant step towards reform, but as industry codes they were unenforceable. This was recognised by a few insurers who agreed to form an independent Insurance Ombudsman Bureau (IOB) in

---

5 Malcolm Clarke, *Policies and Perceptions of Insurance Law in the Twenty-first Century* (2005).

6 This means cancelling the policy from the start and treating it as though it never existed. This usually means returning any premiums paid.

7 Fifth Report of the Law Reform Committee (1957) Cmnd 62.

8 English and Scottish Law Commissions, 'Exemption Clauses: Second Report' (1975) Law Com No 69.

1981 to handle disputes with consumers.[9] Although voluntary, within a short time, most personal lines insurers signed up. A significant advantage of the ombudsman scheme over the courts was that the ombudsman was empowered to look beyond the strict law. The ombudsman was also able to take account of the industry codes, effectively making them binding on insurers. Subsequently, the ombudsman's Terms of Reference were amended to allow it to take account of what was 'fair and reasonable in all the circumstances'. Early ombudsmen set out their approach to non-disclosure in the IOB's Annual Report. The second ombudsman, Dr Julian Farrand, indicated he would apply a proportionate[10] approach to all unintentional[11] non-disclosure. His successor, Laurie Slade, suggested that in the absence of clear questions, the insurer would be treated to have waived the requirement of disclosure.[12]

4.3 The Financial Services and Markets Act 2000 ('FSMA 2000') replaced the IOB with the Financial Ombudsman Service, amalgamating it with a number of other ombudsman schemes covering other financial services. Unlike the IOB, the Financial Ombudsman Service was not a voluntary scheme and it had statutory powers. Under s 228 of FSMA 2000, the ombudsman is required to make decisions by reference to what is, in the opinion of the ombudsman, fair and reasonable in all the circumstances of the case. In deciding what is fair and reasonable in all the circumstances, the ombudsman will take into account relevant law and regulations; regulators' rules, guidance and standards; codes of practice; and (where appropriate) what he considers to have been good industry practice at the relevant time.[13]

Development of the Financial Ombudsman Service's approach to non-disclosure

4.4 The Financial Ombudsman Service's approach to non-disclosure is based on the approach formulated by the early ombudsmen. It requires insurers to ask clear questions at the point of application and applies a proportionate approach to negligent non-disclosure. Over the years, it has sought to categorise types of non-disclosure in order to decide which remedy is appropriate. The evolution of the categorisation is the subject of discussion below.

---

[9] Peter J Tyldesley, 'The Insurance Ombudsman Bureau – the early history', Journal of Insurance Research and Practice No 39 (2003), pp 34–43.

[10] For an explanation of the proportionate approach see Section 4.39 below.

[11] Annual Report 1989, para 2.17. Unintentional non-disclosure is now referred to as negligent non-disclosure.

[12] Annual Report 1995, p 37.

[13] The Financial Services Authority's Dispute Resolution Sourcebook (DISP) Rule 3.6.4.

Categories of non-disclosure

4.5 Like the IOB's Annual Report, the ombudsman's approach towards different types of cases is set out in its publication, Ombudsman News. In the April 2003 issue of Ombudsman News[14] an article was published setting out four categories of non-disclosure: (1) innocent, (2) inadvertent,[15] (3) clearly reckless and (4) fraudulent or deliberate. The innocent category applied if the questions were not clear and/or it was reasonable for the consumer to have overlooked the fact(s) non-disclosed. Fraudulent and deliberate non-disclosure entitled the insurer to keep the premiums and seek to recover any money paid in relation to previous claims. The two categories of inadvertent and clearly reckless non-disclosure were to distinguish between minor carelessness on one hand, and having no regard for accuracy on the other. A proportionate remedy only applied to the former, whereas the latter was considered akin to deliberate non-disclosure and entitled the insurer to avoid the policy from the start and treat it as though it never existed. However, it was felt to fall short of fraud so insurers were required to return the premiums.

Problems in practice

4.6 This approach was over-enthusiastically adopted by many insurers, who were quick to label any mistake as 'clearly reckless', entitling them to avoid the policy. Often insurers did not even bother to enquire why the consumer had made an error – or if indeed it was the consumer's, rather than their own agent's fault. Poor questions, the use of tick-boxes, hasty online application processes, and lack of prominent warnings led to a steady flow of complaints about non-disclosure. It was common practice, for instance, for some insurers to trawl through a consumer's medical records at the point of claim, looking for anything, however minor, that could be used to avoid the policy. Non-disclosure of unrelated, minor matters was being used to defeat valid claims for serious illnesses and death, with often devastating results. Articles often appeared in the media about such injustices.[16]

Although the ombudsman continued to overturn a sizeable number of insurers' decisions, these complaints gave no sign of abating. There were many instances of poor practices and there seemed no impetus for insurers to improve the application and claims process to make things fairer for consumers.

4.7 In light of this, it became clear that the ombudsman's approach needed to be clarified externally by publishing a further article in Ombudsman

---

14 Issue 27.

15 Now referred to as 'negligent' following the introduction of the ABI Code.

16 See for example 'The sickness at the heart of insurance' by Richard Dyson, *Daily Mail*, 2 October 2006.

News. Although articles about non-disclosure had been published in Ombudsman News after 2003, it was obvious that insurers were still misunderstanding the categories. In particular, the 'reckless' category was being overused and wrongly applied. In the May/April 2007 issue of Ombudsman News[17] an article was published referring to how the law defines recklessness as a state of not caring whether a disclosure is true or false. This was contrasted with the situation where a lack of sufficient care and attention resulted in an incorrect answer being given, regardless of how incorrect the answer may be. It went on to state:

> 'For us to conclude that a consumer's non-disclosure or misrepresentation when applying for a policy was reckless rather than inadvertent, we must be satisfied from all the evidence (including that relating to any conversation, marketing documentation, other advice or paperwork available at the time to the consumer), that in answer to a clear question the consumer:
>
> - did not care whether their answer was true or false and
> - understood, if only in a limited way, that an answer was required, that it was important to the insurer and that there was a consequence to it.'

Insurers had the burden of proving recklessness and the threshold was high. In essence, recklessness was akin to fraudulent or deliberate non-disclosure. This clarification of the ombudsman's approach confirmed that insurers had no remedy for innocent non-disclosure, proportionate remedies applied to inadvertent non-disclosure, and the remedy of avoidance applied to reckless and deliberate non-disclosure – effectively, three categories instead of four. In spite of this, there continued to be large numbers of complaints where insurers were not taking the ombudsman's approach on board.

Law Commission survey of Ombudsman decisions

4.8 Around this time, the English Law Commission was finalising a survey of the ombudsman's decisions that had been conducted the year before. They read over a hundred ombudsman decisions about non-disclosure and drew heavily on these in its 2007 consultation paper, 'Misrepresentation, Non-Disclosure and Breach of Warranty by the Insured'[18]. Many ombudsman decisions featured as case studies in the paper and were used in support of its recommendations for reform. The Law Commission largely endorsed the ombudsman's existing approach, concluding that the proportionate approach that the ombudsman had devised was workable and just.

---

17 Issue 61.

18 The Law Commission Consultation Paper No 182 and The Scottish Law Commission Discussion Paper No 134, July 2007.

Non-disclosure in the media

4.9 Despite the number of insurers' decisions the ombudsman was overturning, insurers were continuing to avoid policies unfairly, citing non-disclosure. As well as referring their disputes to the ombudsman service, a steady stream of consumers complained to the media about how they were being treated by their insurers. A number of highly critical articles appeared in the national press[19], especially about declined critical illness and death claims. Stories about cancer victims whose insurance claims were being denied because of alleged non-disclosure of trivial health matters such as back pain did not endear insurers to the public. The reputation of the industry suffered a severe blow, and critical illness insurance sales went down as a result[20]. Certain independent intermediaries started calling for claims statistics to be published and, after much resistance, the industry released claims data showing that between 10 and 20% of critical illness claims were being declined due to non-disclosure.

Things came to a head in August 2007 when an ombudsman's decision hit the headlines. Scottish Widows had declined a widow's claim for death benefit after her husband died of leukaemia on the grounds of non-disclosure. Although she stormed Scottish Widows' Annual General Meeting dressed as *the* Scottish Widow, the insurance company refused to relent. She subsequently brought a complaint to the ombudsman service. The ombudsman found that during the online application, the sales adviser (acting as the insurer's agent) had incorrectly input the start date of her husband's symptoms. Due to this mistake, he was erroneously accepted for cover. The ombudsman concluded that the non-disclosure was innocent, as it was due to the fault of the agent, and that Scottish Widows should pay the claim in full. The decision was widely reported in the media, notably featuring in several articles in the *Mail on Sunday*[21], and the widow's story subsequently featured on the 'Tonight' programme on ITV. This led some commentators to call for a re-thinking of the industry's approach.

ABI Guidance on Non-Disclosure and Treating Customers Fairly[22]

4.10 It was against this background of intense media criticism of the industry's stance on non-disclosure and the Law Commissions' endorsement

---

19 See for example 'Widow cast into the cold' by Jeff Prestridge, *Mail on Sunday*, 29 May 2005.

20 See for example 'Critical cover crisis?' by Barbara Cockburn, Cover Magazine, 1 September 2006, 'A new dawn', Cover Magazine, 1 September 2007, and Swiss Re's Term and Health Watch Report 2006.

21 Written by Jeff Prestridge, who had campaigned for a number of years on behalf of consumers who felt they had been treated unjustly by their insurer.

22 Full title: 'ABI Guidance on Non-Disclosure and Treating Customer Fairly – Claims for Long-Term Protection Insurance Products'.

of the ombudsman's approach in their 2007 consultation paper that the ombudsman[23] decided to approach the ABI with its concerns. The ombudsman put it to them that the number of complaints concerning non-disclosure was unacceptably high and insurers were not taking the ombudsman's approach into account when assessing claims. A meeting was arranged with Nick Kirwan, Assistant Director of Health and Protection Insurance at the ABI. Kirwan had a long career in the insurance industry, notably at Scottish Widows. He had been on a number of ABI committees before assuming this post, and was involved in drafting the ABI Code of Practice on Genetic Testing.

Kirwan was receptive to the ombudsman's suggestions, and a joint working party was set up to draft guidance on non-disclosure for insurers. The aim of the guidance was to ensure consumers were treated fairly at the point of claim and to align the industry's and the ombudsman's approach more closely. The working party adopted the ombudsman's requirement that insurers ask clear questions about facts they regarded as material. It also embraced the ombudsman idea of proportionate remedies for negligent non-disclosure. Its three-part classification system for non-disclosure owed much to current ombudsman thinking, effectively endorsing the refinement of the categories referred to in the section above, with a slight change in terminology. 'Inadvertent' was now referred to as 'negligent', and 'reckless' was now referred to as 'without any care'. The over-enthusiastic use of the term 'reckless' in the past, and its pejorative connotations, were behind this change.

Other notable aspects of the guidance included the requirement that insurers seek explanations from consumers to understand why the non-disclosure occurred before making any decision about the claim. It also suggested that trivial non-disclosures[24] should automatically be dealt with proportionately and that the Total Permanent Disability (TPD) element of critical illness cover and waiver of premium should be treated as severable from other benefits. So if the non-disclosure affected the TPD cover only, the rest of the cover should be left intact. This was an important protection so that, for example, non-disclosure of back pain did not invalidate a cancer claim. Furthermore, it recognised that insurers are responsible for intermediaries acting on their behalf. This was an important point that previously insurers frequently overlooked. Insurers often relied on the fact that an intermediary was separately regulated to disclaim responsibility for it, without acknowledging that such an intermediary could nevertheless act as their agent.

---

23 Represented by the then lead ombudsman for insurance, Peter Hinchliffe, and the author of this chapter.

24 Attracting a rating of no more than +50% (or £1 per mille) for the applicable life assured (per mille = per £1,000 of cover).

Arguably, where the guidance was most radical was on information-gathering at the point of claim. The ombudsman had been critical of insurers trawling through medical records at the point of claim, rather than at application stage when they could have checked to see whether consumers had fully disclosed. This was referred to, in a pejorative sense, as 'fishing'. The guidance explicitly frowned on this practice of underwriting at the claims stage. It stated that insurers needed a legitimate reason to look back at a consumer's medical records at the point of claim[25] and it provided examples of what was acceptable practice. It referred to the joint British Medical Association (BMA)/ABI guidance, 'Medical Information and Insurance'[26], which addressed this subject in further detail.

ABI Code on Non-Disclosure and Treating Customers Fairly[27]

4.11 The Guidance was published and took effect on 1 January 2008[28], which represented a remarkably fast turnaround for the development, drafting and, ultimately, agreement of guidance by the ABI Board. This reflected the importance the ABI and the industry as a whole attached to this issue, which was continuing to provoke negative press and was the subject of frequent ombudsman criticism both at industry conferences and in decisions. The publication of the ABI Guidance attracted a great deal of positive comment within the industry and the media alike. Within a year, it led to a near halving of the number of non-disclosure complaints about critical illness insurance referred to the ombudsman.[29] It also made it much easier to assess the complaints still being received, as the ombudsman could make reference to the categories and remedies set out therein.

In recognition of the Guidance's widely acknowledged success, the ABI decided to upgrade the ABI Guidance to the status of a Code, to take effect on 1 January 2009. This made it binding, rather than just good practice, on all ABI members. It also was extended to cover group[30] insurance. Otherwise, its provisions were left unchanged, and as at the date of publication of this book, it still represents the prevailing approach to non-disclosure as applied by protection[31] insurers and ombudsmen alike. It represents a significant achievement in terms of the benefits it has brought to consumers

25 Paragraphs 3.6 and 3.7 of the guidance.
26 Last updated 1 March 2010 (also commonly referred to as 'The Blue Book').
27 Full title: 'ABI Code of Practice – Managing Claims For Individual and Group Life, Critical Illness and Income Protection Insurance Products'.
28 Applies to all claims made after this date.
29 'ABI and FOS tackle non-disclosure', Money Marketing, 15 January 2009.
30 This refers to insurance taken out by a company on behalf of its employees.
31 This is an umbrella term referring to life, critical illness, and income protection insurance.

by aligning the industry's and ombudsman's approach. It also shows what can be achieved when the industry is willing to enter into dialogue with the ombudsman.

Effect on law reform

4.12 Whilst the impact of the ABI Code on law reform has been discussed in detail by other contributors, it is worth noting again that the ABI's adoption of the ombudsman's approach gave significant support to the Law Commissions' proposals that the law do a similar thing. Indeed, by issuing the Code, it made it very difficult for the ABI to maintain its original stance against law reform.[32] The ABI subsequently reversed its original stance and publicly endorsed the recommendations for reform. The lack of any real opposition to law reform made it possible for the Treasury to fast-track the Bill, and for it to be adopted without any substantive amendment.

Effect on general insurance[33]

4.13 Whilst complaints about non-disclosure in protection insurance never returned to the previous high levels experienced in the years 2005–2007, complaints about non-disclosure in general insurance, especially motor and household, continue apace[34]. This largely reflects the fact that there is no guidance or code covering non-disclosure in general insurance. The ombudsman's approach to non-disclosure complaints in general insurance is the same as that applied to protection/long-term insurance. This is set out in detail in the next part of this chapter.

Current approach[35]

Introduction

4.14 The ombudsman service sees a significant number of complaints about non-disclosure each year[36]. Such complaints arise across the spectrum of insurance products, including both long-term and general. Typically, non-disclosure arises in life and critical illness insurance as well as motor and

---

32 'Summary of responses on consumer insurance contract law', April 2008, p 9.

33 Refers to short-term insurance contracts (monthly or annual), as opposed to long-term insurance contracts as defined by the FSA Handbook.

34 There were around 1,000 complaints in the year ending March 2011 about non-disclosure in general insurance (not including long-term protection insurance).

35 I am grateful to my colleague Robert Short, ombudsman, for sharing his insights about the ombudsman's approach to general insurance.

36 It is difficult to give precise figures because complaints are recorded by product and complaint issue but 'non-disclosure' is not generally listed as a sub-category. As a rough estimate, between 10 and 30% of insurance complaints relate to non-disclosure.

household, but also arises in travel, private medical and even pet insurance[37]. Commercial insurance products also give rise to complaints about non-disclosure. If there is any disclosure element on the application form or in the application process, then this can give rise to allegations by the insurer of non-disclosure, usually at the claims stage. If the insurer denies coverage and the consumer (or small business)[38] believes this is unfair, this can ultimately result in a complaint being referred to the ombudsman service, if the parties cannot resolve their disagreement themselves.

'Fair and reasonable'

4.15 The ombudsman determines complaints by reference to what is fair and reasonable in all the circumstances, having regard to all the matters set out in Section 4.3 above. Ultimately, it is this fair and reasonable jurisdiction which allows the ombudsman to develop approaches which result in fair outcomes in individual complaints even where these depart from the strict legal position.

Three-stage approach

4.16 The ombudsman's long-standing approach to complaints about non-disclosure is a three-stage one:

- Was there a clear question, and was it answered incorrectly?
- Was the insurer induced?
- What kind of non-disclosure was it?

The rest of this chapter discusses in detail each aspect of these stages.

Clear questions and information-gathering

4.17 Examining whether a clear question has been asked is all about whether the insurer's information-gathering process is fair. For reasons already explained, the ombudsman does not consider it reasonable to expect consumers to volunteer information, rather it is up to the insurer to ask.

It is recognised that insurers are entitled to seek such information from applicants in order to assess the individual risk they are underwriting.

---

[37] Although many of these insurances use exclusions for pre-existing conditions instead of underwriting based on information disclosed on a proposal form.

[38] In the rest of this chapter, the word 'consumer' also includes 'small business'. In general, the small businesses that come within the ombudsman's remit are essentially treated no differently than consumers by the ombudsman service if they are small enough and are without the benefit of professional advice.

Traditionally insurers use paper application forms to obtain the information they need. The paper application may be filled in by the consumer themselves, or by an intermediary, often during a face to face meeting with the consumer.

Increasingly, however, insurers are using online information-gathering where a consumer is asked a series of questions over the internet and answers are selected via a drop-down list. Often there is little if any space for free text entries. Such applications can be completed directly by a consumer, or by an intermediary using a computer during a face to face meeting.

There are pitfalls and advantages in each of these methods of information-gathering. It is common (and understandable) that insurers often choose the least expensive and fastest method of information gathering. The speed at which a policy can be underwritten and put into force is a major factor in process design. Systems which allow the policy to be underwritten instantly, depending on the information given, are often preferred.

The method of gathering information can be important to the outcome of the complaint. Often the complaint will turn on whether the process was straightforward and clear, or if it was confusing for consumers.

Clear questions (and wrong answers)

4.18 As explained in the first part of this chapter, the starting point for reviewing a complaint about non-disclosure is whether clear questions were asked. If an insurer wishes to rely on non-disclosure as a valid defence to a claim, it must first demonstrate that it asked the consumer at least one clear question to which a wrong answer was given.

Burden of proof

4.19 It is up to the insurer to prove on balance that a clear question was asked, and answered wrongly. This reflects the fact that an insurer is relying on non-disclosure as a defence to an otherwise valid claim. The requirement to establish that a clear question was asked is discussed at length below. Equally, the insurer is required to show that the answer was, in fact, wrong, incomplete, or only partially true. Without evidence to show that the answer was inaccurate, misleading or otherwise inadequate, the defence will not succeed.

Warnings about the consequences of non-disclosure

4.20 Concurrently with the duty of asking clear questions, insurers must also carefully explain the importance of disclosing material facts and the serious consequences of not doing so: the policy may be avoided and the claim refused. This reflects long-established good industry practice[39] as well as current regulatory rules.[40] However, many application forms that the ombudsman sees do not make this warning prominent enough, and it is just one more sentence in almost an entire page of sentences in 8 point font on the declaration and signature page. Commonly, at least half of the small print on the declaration page concerns data protection, rather than the potentially dire consequences of non-disclosure. The declaration page usually also doubles as a direct debit mandate form, which again can distract from and dilute the importance of the declaration that the consumer must sign which states: that to the best of the applicant's knowledge and belief, the information included in the proposal is true and correct.

Basis of the contract clauses

4.21 In the past, insurers often turned the above declaration into a warranty of the contract. This is known as a 'basis of the contract' clause. The intended effect of this was to enable the insurer to regard any non-disclosure as a breach of warranty, as well as a breach of the duty of utmost good faith. The remedy for a breach of warranty was to discharge the insurer from liability under the contract from the date of the breach, which in this case, pre-dates the contract. This effectively gives insurers a double remedy in the event of non-disclosure and is unnecessarily harsh on consumers. To their credit, consumer insurers have largely recognised this, and generally have not sought to rely on basis of the contract clauses. An ombudsman would not regard an insurer's reliance on such a clause as fair. As explained in earlier chapters, the Bill now abolishes such clauses in consumer insurance.

Problems with questions

4.22 Over the years, the ombudsman has seen many examples of poor questions, or poor application form design, which has led to information needed by insurers not being captured. The ABI has recognised this problem and has issued guidance on application form design[41], which goes some way towards rectifying the problem, as least in protection insurance. Common flaws include 'memory test questions': 'Have you ever suffered from …' which asks consumers to recall episodes of ill health potentially dating back to birth. Other 'laundry list' or 'catch-all' type questions contain a series of unrelated conditions together: 'Do you have any problems with your heart, lung, liver, spleen, digestive system, urinary tract, eyes, ears or nose, or

---

39 As set out in SLIP and SGIP. Although these are no longer published on the ABI website, the ombudsman still regards them as good industry practice.

40 ICOBS Rule 5.1.4.

41 Application Form Design for Life and Health Protection Insurance – Guidance, February 2006. See Appendix 6.

throat, allergies, back pain or spinal trouble?' Other questions use ambiguous phrases such as 'Have you ever had a back, spine or joint disorder'? The use of the word 'disorder' in this context connotes something serious and lasting whereas insurers may be simply trying to capture an episode of lower back pain. Other examples from general insurance are questions that ask the applicant whether they had any claims in the past year, but do not mention losses that did not give rise to claims even though the insurer expects the applicant to disclose this information. Likewise a common question on motor insurance applications, 'Do you have any motoring convictions?', may not mention fixed-penalty offences, even though the insurer expects disclosure of this information.

Problems with layout

4.23 Other problems with applications arise from the layout. Boxes that are too small to capture the extent of information an insurer is seeking are a typical problem. This often leads to under-disclosure of information. For instance, the question 'Have you seen your doctor in the past three years?' often has space the size of a matchbox for the applicant who ticks the "yes" box to list all appointments in the past three years (if the question was taken literally). Clearly, the small size of the box is inviting the applicant to edit their response to include only important or material visits. Just what is important or material to the applicant is, however, very subjective. What seemed a minor symptom or episode at the time can often turn out later, with hindsight, to be the start of a serious illness. In the circumstances, it is arguably unrealistic to expect a layperson to know what doctor's appointments are significant to an underwriter and what are not.

Also, some application forms refer the applicant to a blank page at the end of the form where they can provide additional information. Again, this may be unsatisfactory, not only because the instructions are usually in small print and therefore not always noticeable, but also from the point of the view that the information that is provided is very much left up to the applicant's judgment, which does not always match up with what an underwriter is interested in knowing.

Problems with face to face interviews

4.24 The ombudsman has seen many complaints over the years arising from applications made via face to face meetings with sales advisers. Often set up to arrange a mortgage or a re-mortgage, these meetings can also result in the sale of life and critical illness insurance to cover the mortgage loan in the event that a mortgage applicant dies or falls ill and cannot afford the monthly repayments. These meetings often take place in banks with mortgage advisers who use a particular insurer's (or reinsurer's) own underwriting system (such as Swiss Re's 'Magnum'), which automatically sets up the life and critical illness (or mortgage payment protection) policies. Such meetings can also take place at the office of an independent financial adviser (IFA), or even an applicant's home, as many IFAs conduct home visits.

4.25 If the insurance is being sold alongside a mortgage, the insurance is often secondary to the main purpose of the meeting, which is in most cases to obtain a mortgage to finance a house move. The insurance is usually 'sold' to the consumer – in other words, the consumer does not ask for the insurance, it is offered to them by the adviser. The consumer (or consumers, as it is often purchased jointly) is encouraged to take out the same level of cover, for the same number of years, as their mortgage loan, often on a decreasing basis, as this is less expensive than level (ie fixed) term cover. The application process tends to consist of the adviser asking questions from a computer screen, and the oral answers from the applicant are input back into the computer. Tick boxes and drop down lists are widely used to speed up the process and make it more uniform. There is very little scope for free text entries, and often the applicant does not see the questions on screen or written down at all throughout the process.

Depending on the answers given, additional questions may be generated. Equally, if the answers are negative, the additional questions are not posed. This makes the initial questions very important – effectively acting as a 'gatekeeper' question for the more detailed questions within the system. However, the 'gatekeeper' questions often have the same problems as identified above, ie they can be ambiguous or be 'memory test' type questions. Or there may be too many conditions listed in one question for an applicant to take in when it is being read aloud. Remembering the time pressure both the applicant and the adviser are often under to get the mortgage loan documentation completed within the course of the meeting, one can imagine how the intricacies and nuances of the insurance questions can be sometimes be overlooked, with catastrophic results: if something is missed during the application process and then someone dies, the insurance might not pay out as a result.

After the question and answer session, the consumer is usually asked to sign a declaration page. The rest of the application may or may not be printed out for the consumer to check; the process varies from insurer to insurer. The declaration page usually requires the applicant to give the insurer the right to obtain a medical report from their doctor, and they can tick a box as to whether they wish to see the report before it is sent to the insurer. The ombudsman says it is good practice for an insurer to inform the applicant that a medical report might not be obtained, but insurers often do not make this clear. Many consumers believe that an insurer will obtain a report from their doctor as a matter of course, and are surprised when this is not the case.

The declaration itself usually states that all information in the form is given 'to the best of my knowledge and belief', which has important ramifications, to be discussed in the 'innocent' non-disclosure section below.

4.26 Face to face meetings as described above are rarely recorded and can often lead to disputes about what was said during the meeting. A common complaint is that a consumer told the adviser about a doctor's visit or a symptom, but the adviser said it was not necessary to disclose, and therefore it was not included or input into the computer system. Alternatively, the consumer says that the adviser asked the question differently than posed on the application system, such as 'Do you smoke?' rather than 'Have you smoked in the last 12 months?' Either way, it is very difficult to prove exactly what happened during a meeting, which may have occurred many years previously, in the absence of a recording. Very rarely, the ombudsman may convene an informal hearing where the both the consumer and adviser attend to give oral evidence about exactly what happened during the meeting. But in the vast majority of cases, the ombudsman tries to work out what happened based on the documentation and the written testimony of both parties.

Tele-underwriting in protection insurance

4.27 Given the multifarious disputes that can arise as a result of face to face meetings as described above, for the past several years protection insurers have increasingly used tele-underwriting. This is effectively a telephone-based application process. There are numerous advantages of completing the application (or at least the medical part) over the phone: primarily that the exact questions asked and answers given are recorded, leaving no room for doubt about what was said. It also gives greater flexibility for capturing additional information disclosed during the conversation, since the whole conversation is recorded and not just the specific answers to questions. It also removes the embarrassment factor that is present in face to face meetings, making it is easier to discuss and disclose sensitive and personal medical details. The telephone call is individual to each applicant, so again, a husband need not disclose embarrassing or private medical matters in front of his wife and vice versa. A number of tele-underwriters are trained nurses, so know what is medically significant and what is not. The emphasis in tele-underwriting is on probing the applicant to obtain sufficient information, rather than rapid-fire questions and answers in order to get a sale completed. Removing the medical questions and answers from the sale also has the advantage of freeing up the adviser to concentrate on the financial aspects of the sale, which is more within their field of expertise than medical underwriting.

Problems with price comparison websites

4.28 A common issue with complaints about non-disclosure in general insurance involves the growing use of price comparison websites (also called aggregators) to purchase common types of insurance, especially motor and household. These websites appear to provide a quick and easy way of finding the best quote. But there are pitfalls. From a non-disclosure point of view, the most concerning aspect of these websites is the way they capture information to generate a quote. Often, there is a list of assumptions – which sometimes can be long – which the consumer may have to confirm are correct. Unless the consumer actively changes the drop down boxes or ticks that are set by default, the information fed into the quote system may not be accurate for their particular circumstances.[42]

Furthermore, the consumer does not see the interface between the comparison site and the insurer. Therefore, the consumer does not know what questions the insurer is asking – these may be different from the ones posed by the comparison site, which by definition is gathering information on a 'one size fits all' basis. The ombudsman has seen cases where the question asked by the comparison website was different from the one posed by the insurer, and therefore whilst the answer the consumer gave to the former may have been true, it was not an accurate answer for the purposes of the insurer, such as 'Are you the owner of the car?' which gets recorded by the insurer as 'I am the owner/registered keeper' which may not necessarily be true. As the comparison website effectively drops out of the equation when the insurance is set up, the consumer is left to fend for themselves when it comes to insurers alleging non-disclosure. The consumer will find it difficult to prove that they responded accurately to the question as the comparison website is constantly changing and it is difficult for it to recreate the exact interface that was online when the sale took place.

4.29 The ombudsman would expect insurers in such circumstances to prove that the information provided by the consumer at the point of sale was inaccurate, and the ombudsman will request details of the precise questions answered by the consumer via the comparison website. Otherwise, the ombudsman expects the insurer to show that a copy of the questions and answers in written form was sent to the consumer to check. If the insurer is unable to supply either of these, the ombudsman is unlikely to accept that a non-disclosure occurred.

Often an insurer will send an applicant a list of statements (often called a 'confirmation schedule'), rather than questions and answers, that supposedly reflect what the consumer disclosed at the point of sale. The ombudsman will ask for proof that the statements are a true reflection of the questions and answers at the point of sale. Consumers do not expect to have to go through

---

[42] This is also a common problem with insurers' and intermediaries' websites generally.

a disclosure exercise twice, and in most cases it would be reasonable for a consumer to assume that the statements reflect the information they provided at the outset. The ombudsman would therefore not expect consumers to have to meticulously check through these statements for accuracy, especially given the plethora of documentation that is usually sent out with them. Consumers should be entitled to expect that the information was recorded accurately the first time. If the statements are inaccurate due to the insurer slightly rephrasing the questions and answers originally posed, the ombudsman is unlikely to hold the consumer responsible for this inaccuracy.

The Financial Services Authority also recognises the problems with disclosure associated with price comparison websites[43] and agrees that too much onus is put on the consumer to check that the disclosure information is correct. It highlights the fact that many of these websites are acting in breach of ICOB 5.1.4 in not ensuring a consumer knows or is informed what must be disclosed. They state:

> 'We are concerned consumers may find they are not covered by the policy purchased because a standardised or short set of questions used on the firm's website may not be sufficient to accurately capture all relevant eligibility or risk information for that individual. We are also concerned that in many cases questions are pre-populated with default answers eg a presumption of an absence of relevant convictions as a material risk, or a presumption that a certain age group indicates particular employment or education status.'

The FSA also regards it as unfair under the Unfair Terms in Consumer Contracts Regulations 1999 for websites to exclude or limit their liability for the insurance not paying out if the consumer misunderstands their disclosure obligations. For all these reasons, consumers may also have grounds to bring a formal complaint against a price comparison website if it has caused them to suffer loss, provided the website is regulated by the FSA and comes within the ombudsman's jurisdiction.

Information gathered from third parties

Information in medical records

4.30 In applications for certain types of insurance, insurance companies often seek information from other parties as well as from the consumers themselves. In particular, life and health insurers regularly seek information from a consumer's doctor at the underwriting stage, or require the consumer

---

[43] 'Proposed Guidance on the Selling of General Insurance Policies Through Price Comparison Websites', June 2011, p 10.

to undergo a medical examination by a healthcare professional. This can give rise to disputes where the information obtained from the third party turns out to be inaccurate.

A typical example the ombudsman sees is where the insurer has obtained a medical report from an applicant's General Practitioner (GP), perhaps prompted by something the consumer has disclosed in the application form. If the GP omits to mention, say, a recent medical investigation, an insurer might later attempt to avoid the contract if it finds out about the investigation from reviewing the consumer's medical records, if this would have led it to postpone or decline offering terms. In this scenario, the consumer has also omitted to disclose the information on the application form.

In such a situation, the ombudsman might conclude that the GP, in reviewing the consumer's medical records and completing the medical report for the insurer in return for a fee, is acting as an 'agent to know' on behalf of the insurer. In other words, the insurer cannot say that it did not know about the investigation noted in the medical records because its agent, the GP, had knowledge of it but decided it was immaterial to include in the medical report. Another way of looking at it would be to conclude that the consumer's non-disclosure was innocent because if the GP did not consider it significant enough to mention, then the consumer had reasonable grounds for reaching the same conclusion. The GP's omission also lends credence to the consumer's argument that the GP attached little significance to and/or reassured the consumer about it.

Depending on the circumstances, the ombudsman might regard the GP's omission as unreasonable or negligent, but consider that this negligence should not prejudice the consumer as an innocent party. In such cases, the ombudsman would consider the insurer's remedy lies not against the consumer but against the GP (or their professional indemnity insurers). The ombudsman's understanding from a discussion with the British Medical Association (BMA)[44] is that they too would regard this as a matter between the GP and the insurer, and the consumer's rights under the contract should not be affected.

Information held in databases

4.31 A significant amount of information held by insurers is shared across the industry, especially pertaining to claims. Most general insurers subscribe to the Claims and Underwriting Exchange ('CUE') which operates as a central database for industry-wide claims information. The database can be accessed by individual insurers to check a consumer's previous insurance claims history.

44 Joint ABI/BMA/FOS meeting, 26 August 2009.

Over the years the ombudsman has seen a number of complaints arising from insurers checking CUE at the claims stage, discovering undisclosed past claims, and subsequently avoiding policies for non-disclosure. Given that this past claims history is accessible to insurers at all times, the ombudsman has often questioned why this information is not routinely checked at underwriting stage, rather than relying on the consumer to precisely recollect and disclose these details on the application form. It seems that if the information is readily obtainable by the insurer then arguably the insurer can be treated as knowing this information. It also seems contrary to the principle of treating customers fairly, as well as the bilateral duty of utmost good faith, to only look at the database in order to invalidate an otherwise valid claim. (See also the discussion in Sections 4.56–4.58 below.)

Information held by the insurer

4.32 The ombudsman sometimes sees cases where the consumer has made a previous application to the insurer for cover, or may already hold cover with the insurer to which they are applying. If the information allegedly non-disclosed on the latest application form is information that the insurer already holds, then the ombudsman is unlikely to find that any non-disclosure has in fact occurred.

Whether it is reasonable to expect the insurer to access this information when considering a new application very much depends on the circumstances in each particular case. For instance, where a consumer has made reference to a previous policy, often in response to a direct question on the new application form, then the ombudsman is likely to regard the information held in relation to that previous policy to be within the insurer's knowledge.

When a consumer applies for a top-up policy, to increase the level of cover already held, it is commonly assumed by the consumer that the insurer already knows the information disclosed on the previous application form, and that it is only necessary to disclose 'new' information relating to the period after the previous policy started. Insurers need to make it clear if they are expecting consumers to disclose everything afresh.

Also, if it is apparent from a subsequent application form that information may have been omitted or mis-stated on a previous application form, then the ombudsman would expect an insurer to request clarification from the consumer. If an insurer is put on notice of a potential non-disclosure but does not make such enquiries, and continues to treat the original policy as valid, the ombudsman may conclude that the insurer has effectively affirmed the contract and waived its right to avoid it later for non-disclosure.

Inducement

4.33 Fundamental to non-disclosure is the concept of inducement. If the insurer cannot demonstrate that it was induced to offer terms it would not have offered had the information been disclosed, then it cannot rely on the non-disclosure to avoid the contract and defeat a claim. 'Inducement' is an insurance term which means the insurer's underwriting decision was affected or influenced by the non-disclosed information.

Proof of inducement

4.34 The insurer has the burden of proving inducement – this is no different to the position at law. The insurer must show, by reference to its contemporaneous underwriting guidelines, that its decision was affected by the non-disclosed information. Commonly insurers do this by providing a copy of its 'underwriting retro sheet', an internal document setting out what its retrospective underwriting decision would have been had it known the non-disclosed information. This is normally prepared by a senior underwriter, and is supported by a copy of an extract from the relevant page(s) in the contemporaneous underwriting guidelines.

Where such guidelines are unavailable, an underwriter will normally provide a statement of what the decision would have been, according to the 'underwriting philosophy' at the time. Ideally, the underwriter giving the statement will have personal knowledge of the philosophy previously applying because they were the relevant underwriter at that time.

In most cases, providing the evidence described above does not present any difficulties for insurers, and cases do not often turn on the issue of inducement. However, where the retrospective underwriting decision seems overly harsh or out of line with other similar cases, the ombudsman will not necessarily take the underwriter's statement at face value, and may ask questions or request further evidence to support such an underwriting stance. It should be borne in mind that in insurance litigation, cases often turn on the issue of inducement.

In court, the actual underwriter of the risk may be called to give evidence and will be subjected to searching cross-examination questions. Although the ombudsman service decides cases on paper without a hearing, its inquisitorial remit means that it will evaluate the evidence with the same scepticism as the courts. Insurers therefore should be chary of providing unsupported, self-serving evidence that would not convince a judge.

Deferred underwriting decisions

4.35 The ombudsman occasionally comes across cases where the insurer says it would have deferred its underwriting decision had it known the non-disclosed information, eg a referral for a medical test. Problems can arise if the consumer never actually took the test. Had it been disclosed, the insurer would in all likelihood have made the test a precondition for insurance. In such circumstances, and in line with the ABI Code, the ombudsman would consider whether the likely outcome of the test could be determined by the surrounding circumstances. So if someone was recorded as habitually consuming excess alcohol at the time they were referred for a liver function test, the ombudsman might conclude that the test, had it been taken, is likely to have been abnormal. Whereas, if someone was recorded as being in reasonably good health and drinking modestly or not at all, then the ombudsman might conclude that the liver function test is likely to have been normal.

Like other complaints, the ombudsman decides these on the balance of probabilities. Sometimes it might be necessary to seek more evidence from the consumer's doctor about the likely outcome of any test. If it is not possible from all the surrounding evidence, including the doctor's expert opinion, to determine what the likely outcome would have been, then the ombudsman might conclude it was reasonable to assume that no cover would have been in place while the test was outstanding.

Types of non-disclosure

4.36 Once it has been determined that there was non-disclosure, ie the consumer was asked a clear question that was answered incorrectly, and that the insurer was induced by this, then the next question is, what type of non-disclosure was it? The insurer's remedy, if any, will depend on the categorisation of the non-disclosure. The ombudsman service categorises non-disclosure as innocent, negligent, or deliberate.

No non-disclosure

4.37 It is worth reiterating that the categorisation only occurs where, in simplest terms, there has been a clear question answered wrongly. Essentially, if there is no relevant question that would have captured the information, the insurer has not passed the first hurdle in establishing non-disclosure has occurred. This is equally the case if the allegedly non-disclosed information is already known to the insurer. In both cases, there can be no non-disclosure and the ombudsman's consideration of the complaint is likely to stop there. The ombudsman does not need to go on and consider inducement, although if clearly there has been no inducement then this provides an additional reason to uphold the complaint.

Innocent non-disclosure

4.38 The ombudsman has long held that consumers are only expected to disclose 'to the best of their knowledge and belief'. Indeed, this is usually how the declaration on the proposal form is phrased, above where the consumer signs. It would not be fair to penalise a consumer if they genuinely (but erroneously) believed their disclosure was correct. Where non-disclosure is treated as innocent, the insurer has no remedy, and should pay any valid claims in full based on the original terms.

Another way of looking at innocent non-disclosure is the concept of reasonableness. Was it reasonable for the consumer to have non-disclosed the information? As explained above, if the consumer had good reasons for believing the information was correct, then the consumer's answer to the question is likely to be regarded as reasonable, even if strictly speaking incorrect. 'Reasonable' in this context is synonymous with 'innocent'.

The Law Commissions list a number of factors to be taken into account when determining whether a non-disclosure is reasonable or not. These include the type of insurance and its target market; the insurer's explanatory material and publicity; how clear, and how specific, the insurer's questions were; and whether the consumer was using an agent. These are factors that the ombudsman also takes into account.

The Law Commissions describe any reasonable non-disclosure as a 'non-qualifying misrepresentation'. There is no category of innocent non-disclosure. This reflects the ombudsman's position that there is no difference in remedy between an innocent non-disclosure and no non-disclosure. Although the innocent category is retained to cover instances where the disclosure is technically incorrect but this is not the consumer's fault, there is in practice little difference in substance between innocent non-disclosure on the one hand, and no non-disclosure on the other. In both cases the consumer acted reasonably.

The ombudsman's determination of what is 'reasonable' is very much based on what is reasonable in the circumstances the consumer finds themselves in. That is not to say that the ombudsman takes into account the consumer's own particular characteristics and abilities where these are unknown to the insurer. Like the Law Commissions, the ombudsman does not consider the consumer's lack of fluency in English or learning disabilities should be taken into account, if the insurer is not aware of this. However, the ombudsman does consider how a reasonable person, standing in the shoes of the consumer, would have answered the question, taking into account the surrounding circumstances. So it is an objective test, but one in which the ombudsman has regard to the consumer's testimony and their explanation for what led them to non-disclose. A genuine belief that their disclosure was correct may be sufficient, but in order to accept the belief is genuine it is likely to be underpinned by good reasons for holding such a belief.

Negligent non-disclosure and proportionate remedies

4.39 If the ombudsman concludes that the non-disclosure was not innocent but negligent – ie owing to an unreasonable error or mistake on the consumer's part – then the ombudsman regards the appropriate remedy to be a proportionate one. That means the parties should be put into the position as though the non-disclosed information had been disclosed at the outset.

If the non-disclosed information would have resulted in the insurer adding an exclusion to the policy, then the exclusion is added. The effect of adding an exclusion depends on the circumstances, and whether a claim has been notified. If the claim is unaffected by the exclusion, then the claim would be payable in full. Alternatively, if the claim fell within the scope of the exclusion, it would be reasonable for the insurer to decline it. Or the insurer may not have offered any cover at all. In such cases, the insurer should return all premiums paid with interest. Obviously, no claim would be payable if the contract would never have come into being.

Alternatively, the non-disclosure might have led to the policy being rated: in other words, a higher premium being imposed. In such cases the ombudsman would require the insurer to pay the claim proportionately: that is, to pay the claim in proportion to the premium that was paid. If the premium actually paid was half of what the correct premium should have been, then half the sum assured is payable.

Or the non-disclosed information may have led the consumer to be rated higher on a mortality chart. In which case, the ombudsman asks the insurer to calculate how much cover would have been offered for the premium actually paid.

As explained above, sometimes the non-disclosed information would have resulted in the offer of terms being postponed or deferred, pending the outcome of a medical or other test. In such cases, the ombudsman tries to determine what the outcome of the test would have been based on the available medical evidence, and then determines what cover would then have been offered. If the cover would have been heavily rated (ie a significantly higher premium imposed) then the ombudsman tries to determine whether the consumer would have indeed still purchased the cover from the insurer, or whether it would have been unaffordable. If the latter, then the ombudsman might agree with the insurer that the consumer would never have purchased the cover had they known the true price, therefore it is fair to treat the policy as void.

Deliberate non-disclosure

4.40 Where the consumer deliberately misrepresented or withheld information from the insurer, knowing that information to be wrong and relevant to the insurer, then the appropriate remedy is for the contract to be avoided from the outset and the premiums returned. The insurer is entitled to decline any claims arising under the contract.

Another way of looking at deliberate non-disclosure is that it is fraud, in that the consumer knows the non-disclosed information is likely to make a difference to the premium or whether cover is offered at all, and intentionally withholds it in order to gain what they are not entitled to. This is why it is reasonable for the harsh remedy of avoidance to apply to such cases. The insurer would not have entered into the contract had it known the consumer's intention to mislead it, even if the non-disclosed information would have only made a modest difference to the premium. Like the ombudsman, the Law Commissions believe it is appropriate for fraudulent behaviour to be sanctioned in this way by avoidance of the contract and the declinature of the claim.

Retention of the premium?

4.41 The Law Commissions also consider that, in general, the insurer should be entitled to retain the premium when avoiding the contract for deliberate non-disclosure.[45] This penalty reflects the opprobrium attached to the consumer's behaviour. Whilst this may be justifiable in the abstract, it may not be appropriate on a practical level. Often in cases that come before the ombudsman, the insurer has already avoided the contract and returned the premiums in full. It may or may not be alleging deliberate non-disclosure. Some insurers avoid policies whenever *any* non-disclosure has occurred. Others take the view they are entitled to avoid the policy even where the non-disclosure is merely negligent. Given that it is relatively rare for the ombudsman to make a finding of deliberate non-disclosure (for reasons to be explained below), returning the premiums when avoiding makes sense if it is likely a finding of negligent non-disclosure is going to be made.

If insurers followed the Law Commissions' approach and kept the premiums prior to an independent decision being made by an ombudsman or a court, then this would undoubtedly lead to injustices. Given that insurers often do not get the decision on avoidance right, wrongfully keeping the premiums

[45] For more detailed discussion of the Law Commission's rationale behind this approach, see sections 6.40–6.53 of 'Consumer Insurance Law: Pre-contract Disclosure and Misrepresentation', 2009.

could compound the injury. This is why it continues to be fair and reasonable in practice for premiums to be returned (with interest) if a contract is avoided.

Burden of proof

4.42 The insurer has the burden of proving a non-disclosure is deliberate. Given that deliberate non-disclosure is fraud, this can be a difficult burden to discharge. Although the ombudsman decides cases based on the civil standard of proof – the balance of probabilities – the inherent unlikelihood that a mistake on an application form was due to fraud means that the evidence required to prove this must be particularly strong. Moreover, because the penalty is so severe if such a finding is made, it is not a conclusion that is reached lightly.

Effectively, an insurer must demonstrate that the consumer knew the information was wrong, and knew it was relevant to the insurer (in that it would affect the price/terms of the insurance), and yet went ahead and failed to disclose anyway. In practice, this kind of behaviour arises very infrequently. There are several reasons for this.

First, most consumers do not really know what is relevant to the price of insurance. Although insurers say that by asking a specific question on the application form this indicates the information is relevant, consumers do not necessarily appreciate that. They may have little idea why the questions are being asked and what the significance of them is. They may misinterpret the questions, believing insurers are seeking disclosure of significant or serious matters only. Unless a reasonable person standing in the consumer's shoes would know to disclose the information, then the ombudsman is unlikely to conclude the consumer knew it was relevant.

Second, consumers often have to sign a declaration that gives insurers the right to seek more information from third parties or databases about them. Therefore, by simply applying for the insurance, the consumer knows the insurer can access their records, eg their medical records or claims history. In such circumstances, it is going to be very difficult to say that the consumer deliberately concealed from the insurer anything held in these records. Often the consumer will be unaware whether the insurer has accessed these records or not. Many consumers assume that the insurer will access this information at the point of application before offering terms. In reality, insurers seem to rarely access information held by third parties except at the claims stage. This often comes as a huge surprise to consumers who believed the insurers had obtained the information they needed at the outset, before offering cover. Insurers sometimes include warnings on the application that they will not invariably access this information, but these are rarely prominent enough. And by making consumers give their consent to access this information, and setting out at length what information could potentially be obtained, the insurer actually gives the consumer the positive impression that the information *will* be accessed, when in truth this is rarely the case.

Third, even if consumers knew that the insurer would *not* seek a report from their doctor or look at their previous claims history, they would understand that the insurer could in any event check this information at claims stage. Therefore, what would be the point of taking out insurance more cheaply if it is going to be invalidated when they come to make a claim? Most consumers would recognise this as nonsensical.

Of course, where the information is only known to the consumer and is difficult for the insurer to check, or the consumer is unaware of data being held centrally, a dishonest consumer might attempt to deliberately conceal it. This is more likely where the insurance is compulsory and the consumer has no intention of claiming. However, it is doubtful whether in the former case such deliberate non-disclosure would ever come to light, bearing in mind the difficulty of detection.

4.43 For all these reasons, the likelihood that a consumer's non-disclosure is deliberate is to be regarded as a remote one. More often than not, when consumers non-disclose it is because they did not realise the information was wrong or did not realise it was relevant, rather than from a conscious decision not to disclose for personal gain. As discussed above, application forms and processes can cause confusion for many consumers and this, in the ombudsman's experience, is at the heart of most cases of non-disclosure.

The myth of widespread consumer fraud at proposal stage

4.44 Nevertheless, the notion that there is widespread fraudulent non-disclosure continues to inform the insurance industry's approach to consumers and their claims. The fight against fraud is a constant refrain in many insurance conference speeches and publications. Obviously, this also refers to fraud at the claims stage, the existence of which is supported by countless studies and statistical data. But it also encompasses fraud at the application stage which, for reasons explained above, is not as clear cut as it may seem.

In practical terms, the myth of widespread fraud leads many insurers to take the 'avoid first, ask questions later' approach to claims handling, which can lead to injustice towards consumers. The ombudsman has often found there to be an innocent reason for the non-disclosure, but the consumer was never asked for an explanation until the complaint was investigated by the ombudsman. Because the ombudsman overturns such a large number of these complaints, especially in general insurance,[46] many consumers have to wait months or years before receiving what is rightfully theirs under the

[46] Nearly 50% of complaints about non-disclosure in motor and household insurance were upheld in the six months ending March 2011.

policy. The ombudsman knows that, for a number of reasons, many consumers are reluctant to make a formal complaint,[47] therefore there are likely to be many more unfair insurer decisions for each one the ombudsman overturns.

The failure of insurers to properly investigate alleged non-disclosure was recognised by the ABI Code which made it mandatory to seek an explanation from the consumer for any non-disclosure. Following the introduction of this Code, many insurers started making telephone contact with the claimant as part of their process. This led to fewer claims being declined for non-disclosure. Insurers, particularly protection insurers, also seemed to have stopped the insensitive practice of writing curt one-line letters to consumers stating their contract was avoided for non-disclosure at the first indication that any non-disclosure may have occurred.

Reckless/without any care non-disclosure

4.45 In the Law Commissions' recommendations, deliberate non-disclosure is grouped together with reckless non-disclosure. The phrase 'without any care' is used in the ABI Code, but for all intents and purposes, 'reckless' and 'without any care' are synonymous. If the consumer was reckless as to whether the information was wrong and relevant, then the insurer has the same remedy as that for deliberate non-disclosure. Likewise, if the consumer does not care whether the information is wrong/relevant the same remedy applies.

Although the ombudsman used to use 'reckless' as a category of non-disclosure, the ombudsman's thinking has evolved and there now seems little justification for it. There is no difference in remedy whether the non-disclosure is reckless or deliberate, so there seems to be little point in trying to differentiate between the two categories. Ultimately, whilst hypothetically it can be imagined that some consumers might try to conceal information for personal gain, it seems highly artificial to conceive of a consumer 'not caring' whether the information disclosed is wrong and/or relevant. If they didn't care, then why would they bother taking out the insurance? After all, for most consumers, taking out insurance represents a prudent step, a decision to protect their finances against unforeseen losses. It seems evident that the vast majority of consumers would approach the application for such insurance with a degree of care commensurate with the decision to take out insurance in the first place.

The adoption of the category of 'reckless' by the Law Commissions therefore seems on reflection a retrograde step, especially since the ABI Code has

---

47 Financial Ombudsman Service – Annual Review 2010/11, p 20.

already distanced itself from it. 'Reckless' connotes criminality[48], and is not a word that fits readily into a consumer protection legislative environment.

Special concessions for protection insurance

4.46 The ABI Code has introduced special concessions that apply to protection insurance covered by the Code. These concessions require insurers to apply additional leniency into how they consider certain claims involving non-disclosure. The ombudsman agrees with these concessions as being part of a fair and reasonable overall approach to claims handling. It should be noted, however, that these concessions have not been incorporated into the new Act.

Low materiality

4.47 Where the non-disclosed information would have made only a very modest/trivial difference to the premium charged, equating to not more than a +50% rating[49], then the insurer should treat the non-disclosure as negligent (unless of course it is innocent!). All this means is that the insurer will not, under any circumstances, seek to avoid a policy for a trivial non-disclosure. This is certainly a welcome innovation, since regrettably the ombudsman has come across cases in the past when insurers did just that, which was invariably wrongful and unfair.

Multi-benefit policies and severable benefits

4.48 Where the non-disclosed information would have only affected one part of the cover, for example the Total Permanent Disability (TPD) benefit under the critical illness section, then the insurer should treat the non-disclosure as negligent (if it is not innocent) and the benefit as severable.[50] Thus, an insurer should not avoid a multi-benefit policy (such as a life and critical illness cover) on the basis of a non-disclosure of something (eg back pain) that would only lead to the exclusion of one benefit (eg TPD). This reflects the idea that relatively minor non-disclosure should not invalidate the entire insurance. Moreover, consumers should not be prejudiced by taking out multiple benefits under the umbrella of one policy.

Other relevant issues

4.49 There are a number of other issues that arise when dealing with complaints about non-disclosure.

---

48 Although 'recklessness' in a criminal context does not have the same meaning.
49 Paragraph 8.3.2 of the ABI Code.
50 Paragraphs 6.1–6.2 of the ABI Code.

Continuing duty of disclosure

4.50 The continuing duty of disclosure arises where there is a delay between the completion of the application form and the start date of the insurance. This delay can be anywhere from a few days to several months, depending on the type of insurance. The delay can arise due to the time it takes for insurers to complete the underwriting process or because the commencement of the insurance is timed to coincide with something else, eg the completion of a house purchase. Sometimes the process is also delayed while insurers seek medical reports from the consumer's doctor, or require them to have specific medical tests or a medical examination.

However understandable this gap might be, it nevertheless can give rise to problems. This is because the insurer, usually unrealistically, expects the consumer to continue disclosing material facts right up until the start date of the cover. The consumer, on the other hand, normally feels that once they have completed the application form, they have done what is necessary to enable the insurer to process the application and start the cover. Consumers are not aware of the different stages of the application process, and the subtle distinction between acceptance and commencement of the risk. And many consumers are not even aware of when their policy starts, as this date is often determined by their financial adviser, and not them.

4.51 This divergence of views and misunderstanding leads to a significant number of complaints. The ombudsman's long-standing approach is that the continuing duty of disclosure is both significant and onerous. It therefore must be clearly brought to the consumer's attention throughout the application process in order for the insurer to be able to rely on it. Regrettably, despite reiterating this point over a number of years, the ombudsman still sees many examples of insurers inadequately highlighting this duty to consumers.

In such cases, much depends on the wording of the application documentation and subsequent correspondence. Protection insurers often request consumers to disclose 'any change in health' without further explanation. In the ombudsman's experience, this phrase is ambiguous and subjective, and is widely misunderstood by consumers. As a result, the ombudsman expects insurers to be much more specific about the disclosure they expect. They also need to highlight this duty to the consumer and not just the consumer's financial adviser, who is not best placed to know whether the consumer has visited their doctor, let alone suffered a 'change in health'. The insurer must also make it straightforward for consumers to notify it of any changes to the application form answers by actually enclosing a copy of the completed application form that they are asking consumers to check. It should also provide a telephone number and/or email address on which it can be easily contacted. These steps may seem obvious, but it is astonishing how many insurers still do not observe these simple steps to obtain the further disclosure they say they require.

Some insurers have dispensed with the continuing duty of disclosure altogether and underwrite the policy based on the disclosures in the application form (and any subsequent medical report) only. This seems an eminently practical step, given the problems highlighted above. Also any underwriting process that allows for immediate acceptance has the obvious advantage of eliminating the need for a further disclosure period.

Role of intermediaries

4.52 Insurance has traditionally been an area in which intermediaries have played an active part. Most of this chapter has been concerned with insurers, but often insurance is purchased via an intermediary rather than directly from an insurer. In resolving a complaint about non-disclosure that involves an intermediary, the first question to ask is, for whom is the intermediary acting: the insurer or the consumer? If the intermediary acts for the insurer, then the complaint is set up against that insurer. If the intermediary acts for the consumer, then the complaint is set up against the intermediary.

The question of whom the intermediary is acting for is one that has been explored extensively by the Law Commissions. Ultimately, their recommendations reflect the ombudsman's existing approach. The ombudsman tends to regard the intermediary who sells the products of one or a small number of insurers to be acting on behalf of the insurer when arranging the policy. Conversely, the ombudsman tends to regard the intermediary who sells the products of a range of insurers across the market to be acting on behalf of the consumer.

4.53 For instance, the ombudsman generally considers independent financial advisers (IFAs), who advise on products across the market and are not tied to any insurer, to be acting on behalf of the consumer. Thus, if the consumer alleges that the IFA completed the application form incorrectly, leading to the insurer avoiding the policy for non-disclosure, then the ombudsman would set up the complaint against the IFA. If the ombudsman agreed that the IFA was at fault, then the ombudsman would expect the IFA to compensate the consumer accordingly. This might mean the IFA paying an amount equivalent to the claim that was declined because of the IFA's error, or an amount equivalent to the sum assured the consumer could have obtained elsewhere. Equally, there might be no financial loss if the consumer was uninsurable. However, the ombudsman might make an award for distress and inconvenience to reflect the upset and hassle suffered by the consumer as a result of the IFA's mistake.

On the other hand, the ombudsman tends to regard banks and building societies which are tied to a particular insurer or panel of insurers as acting on behalf of the insurer in arranging the cover (even if they are separately regulated by the FSA). By 'tied', the ombudsman means effectively acting as the insurer's agent. The bank and/or building society is not giving the consumer a choice of products from different providers, or doing a 'fair analysis of the market' (using the phraseology of the EU Insurance Mediation Directive). The insurer and the bank will have entered into an agreement whereby the bank agrees to sell the insurer's products to its customer base. For all these reasons, the ombudsman does not regard the bank as acting on behalf of the consumer in this transaction. The ombudsman would also treat intermediaries who 'white-label'[51] products in a similar way (eg high street retailers, as well as those with delegated underwriting authority (such as car insurance services)) as acting for the insurer.

This approach avoids the inconsistencies and ambiguities, identified by the Law Commissions in their report[52], in trying to discern and follow the current law of agency as pertaining to insurance. In any event, the ombudsman considers it reasonable to treat consumers differently from commercial entities, whose professional, arms-length dealings with brokers comprise most of the case law on this subject.

4.54 A further issue arises with the ABI Code. In general, if the intermediary is truly independent, then mistakes in collecting and passing information to the insurer by the intermediary are the responsibility of the intermediary. However, for the purposes of the ABI Code, the ombudsman considers that whether the consumer or the intermediary acting for the consumer is negligent, then the insurer should still assess the claim proportionately. This is because the ombudsman views the consumer and their agent as one entity vis-à-vis the insurer. However, the consumer would need to pursue the intermediary if there was any shortfall in the claim payment arising as a result of the intermediary's negligence. The ombudsman regards this approach as reflecting the principles of the law of agency, and the ABI agrees. [53]

Severability of cover in joint policies

4.55 Often consumers take out life insurance jointly with another party (usually a partner or a spouse). Where the ombudsman concludes that a consumer's non-disclosure is negligent, and if the remedy in that case is avoidance, the ombudsman considers it would be unfair if the cover for the other party, who is not at fault, is also avoided. In such cases, the

---

[51] This means to brand the insurance with the (usually) more recognisable name of the intermediary.
[52] See footnote 18 above.
[53] Discussions with Nick Kirwan, then Assistant Director of Health and Protection, ABI, in 2009.

ombudsman would ask the insurer to sever the joint policy, avoid the cover for the party that non-disclosed, but keep the cover for the other party intact. Obviously the premium for the other party will need to be revised to take into account that the policy now only covers one life.

Most insurers accept this approach and will offer to continue the other policyholder's cover on revised terms. There may be instances where it can be established that the joint policyholder can be held equally responsible for the other's non-disclosure and therefore it is fair to avoid the policy as a whole, but these cases are rare. It would not be fair to assume that a joint policyholder knows in sufficient detail the medical or claims history of their partner or spouse.

Collection of evidence at the claims stage

4.56 An insurer is entitled to ask for and obtain information in order to properly assess a claim, and this right is often expressly included as a term in the policy. This is also sometimes referred to as a claims cooperation clause. However, indiscriminate trawling through a consumer's medical or other records to underwrite at claims stage or to find reasons to reject a claim is clearly unacceptable. This kind of behaviour runs counter to the insurer's duty of good faith to the insured: it is often forgotten that the duty of good faith is a bilateral one.

Given that applicants for protection insurance must sign a declaration giving the insurer the right to obtain their medical information via their doctor (usually without them even having sight of such a report), it is also arguable that if insurers do not obtain such a medical report, they may possibly be waiving their rights to seek this information at the claims stage in any event.

The ABI has recently recognised the legal and reputational problem of underwriting at the claims stage and its inconsistency with fairness. This is reflected in its Code. The ABI Code sets clear parameters for insurers who must be able to justify their requests for information at the point of claim, and evidence this via an audit trail.

The ABI Code recognises and gives effect to the principles agreed between it and the British Medical Association on obtaining medical information for insurance purposes, which can be found in the joint guidance entitled 'Medical Information and Insurance'[54]. In any event it is questionable whether seeking information beyond that necessary to assess the validity of a claim is consistent with the consent given by consumers when they apply for a policy and complete a claim form under contemporary data protection principles.

---

54 See footnote 26 above.

4.57 For all these reasons, the ombudsman agrees with the ABI Code that insurers should not be requesting information which extends beyond the time period applicable to the insured event and its assessment of the claim. Logically, insurers' questions should be confined to the information necessary to establish a valid claim. This would in essence simply comprise the information that would be needed to obtain summary judgment in court had the insurer refused to pay the claim.

According to the ABI Code, gathering information beyond that necessary to validate a claim would only be justified if the insurer had reason to suspect non-disclosure may have occurred. Notification of an early claim is not a sufficient reason in itself for such a suspicion, a position the ABI Code itself endorses. Clearly, an early claim involving a chronic or end stage medical condition such as ischaemic heart disease or alcoholic liver disease could prompt a legitimate request for further information about the history of the condition if neither the condition nor the symptoms were disclosed on the application form. Likewise, new medical information included on the claim form might also legitimately prompt enquiry into why the information was not disclosed at the application stage. Normally, however, the ombudsman would expect an insurer to restrict its request for information to that particular medical condition claimed for rather than simply obtain a copy of the full medical records or a wide-ranging medical report.

4.58 The ombudsman would also look askance at claim forms which ask questions which go beyond the scope of legitimate enquiry. An example of this is where the claim form asks so-called 'lifestyle' questions about smoking and alcohol consumption, height and weight, which on the face of it have nothing to do with establishing whether a claim for a particular critical illness, eg heart attack or stroke, has occurred. The ombudsman would not normally permit an insurer to rely on such information (or rely on further enquiries prompted by the information), whether asked in the claim form filled in by the consumer, or in the claim form sent to the consumer's doctor.

Similarly, in general insurance, the ombudsman would look critically at an insurer checking a central claims database at the claims stage purely to seek information with which to avoid a claim. If an insurer can easily check the claims database at the application stage but chooses not to, then it will be up to the insurer to demonstrate why it was reasonable for it only to check it at claims stage and why this did not amount to bad faith. Unless the insurer had a reasonable suspicion that information had been withheld at the outset, it is difficult to see how checking previous claims on the claims database is relevant to the assessment of the validity of a current claim. The ombudsman is aware of at least one insurer that, as matter of good practice, routinely checks the central claims database at the application stage, thus preventing disputes arising at the claims stage about non-disclosure of past claims.

Distress and inconvenience awards

4.59 When the ombudsman finds a consumer's claim has been wrongly declined and their policy avoided on the grounds of alleged non-disclosure, the ombudsman will consider whether an additional award for distress and inconvenience is warranted. Such awards are generally made by the ombudsman in recognition of distress and inconvenience caused to the consumer by the mishandling of the claim. The distress can be extreme where a policy bought for peace of mind and financial protection has been dishonoured, and the consumer's (or their late spouse's or parent's) honesty has been called into question. Wrongful declinatures can have catastrophic financial consequences, especially where the sum assured was intended to cover the mortgage in the event of death of the family breadwinner. Even where the circumstances are not so severe, the delay in receiving payment can make the whole experience a very worrying time for the consumer.

For this reason, distress and inconvenience awards are common where non-disclosure complaints are upheld. This is in addition to any award of interest on the sum assured. Distress and inconvenience awards in this area range from the modest (£150) to the exceptional (£1,000), depending on the circumstances of each case. Often the award is merely a token sum, in comparison with the sum assured that is awarded, which can be up to £100,000 (or £150,000 for complaints received from 1 January 2012), with a recommendation for payment of sums assured in excess of this. Nevertheless, the ombudsman considers it important to recognise and compensate consumers for the hassle, grief and suffering caused by the unreasonable handling of a claim.

Conclusions

4.60 Ombudsmen have used their discretion over the past thirty years to ensure, as far as possible, that disputes between consumers and insurers are resolved fairly and reasonably. In the area of non-disclosure, this has meant departing from the law where necessary to produce a just result. After all this time, it seems the law has finally caught up with the ombudsman. The ombudsman service welcomes the reform of the law of non-disclosure, which by and large reflects its existing approach.

The ombudsman is pleased that the proposals for reform have been largely unopposed by the insurance industry and enjoy widespread support amongst lawyers, academics, consumers, public bodies and other stakeholders. Although a few expressed concerns that the ombudsman would use law reform as a stepping stone to make further changes, there is little need for the ombudsman to change its approach now that the law has recognised it as the fair one. It is expected that the ombudsman service will continue to resolve the bulk of consumer disputes about non-disclosure, rather than the courts.

However, consumers whose claims are in excess of the ombudsman's £150,000 limit will now not risk losing out if they go to the courts. The subtle nuances of difference that might remain are largely academic ones and unlikely to arise very much in practice, if at all. The ombudsman does not foresee that the new law will make an increase in complaints likely; in fact, it expects the opposite: namely, that it should lead to a fall in the number of complaints about non-disclosure now that the industry can be left in no doubt about how these claims should be handled.

Chapter 5 The British Insurance Law Association

Alison Green
Alison Green is a barrister specialising in Insurance Law at 2 Temple Gardens, The Temple, London and is a Vice President of BILA and Chairman of the BILA Charitable Trust. She acts as an arbitrator and mediator in insurance disputes.

BILA's role in reforming consumer insurance law

5.1 BILA's impetus for promoting reform of insurance law came in the 1990s and led to the publication in September 2002 of what has been referred to as its landmark report entitled 'Insurance Contract Law Reform – Recommendations to the Law Commissions.' This report was presented to the Law Commissions with a view to urging them to consider proposals for reform in this area of the law. The Law Commissions acknowledged in their Report on Consumer Insurance Law in 2009 that:

> '... a major factor in our decision to return to this area was a report by the British Insurance Law Association (BILA) in 2002. The report was prepared by a sub-committee with an impressive breadth of membership – academics, brokers, insurers, lawyers, loss adjusters and trade associations. BILA declared itself "satisfied that there is a need for reform." '[1]

Before looking at BILA's approach to the Law Commissions, it is worth recording BILA's early interest and influence in relation to insurance law reform.

BILA's early interest in law reform: the 1960s

5.2 From its formation back in February 1964 BILA was interested in the reform of certain aspects of insurance law. BILA's two founders, Professor Hugh Cockerell OBE and Gordon Shaw, were keen that the UK should continue to be one of the foremost centres for insurance and reinsurance. They both believed that law was destined to assume ever greater importance

[1] 'Consumer Insurance Law: Pre-Contract Disclosure and Misrepresentation 2009', CM 7758, page 2.

in the transaction of insurance and appreciated the qualities of English law and lawyers.[2] They recognised, however, that there were certain deficiencies in English insurance law and practice. Their appreciation of the need for discussion about these defects, the desirability of looking at how other countries dealt with such matters and the need for some reform came from their depth of knowledge of insurance law. Gordon Shaw, though practising as an insurance broker, had qualified as a barrister. Hugh Cockerell was a professor of law and for many years Secretary (now called Director General) of the Chartered Insurance Institute (CII). They gathered an initial membership of BILA made up of insurance practitioners, academics, barristers and solicitors interested in insurance law. Professor Cockerell wrote various papers regarding the harshness of English law on disclosure, particularly so far as consumers were concerned. One paper entitled 'Erosions of the duty of disclosure' was very influential[3]. He pointed out the pitfalls for consumers when seeking to give disclosure to insurers and how this had been somewhat mitigated and might be reformed.

From its early days BILA had close contacts with the Law Commission of England and Wales. One of the first presentations to BILA came from Professor L C B Gower, then a newly appointed Law Commissioner, who explained the role of the recently established Commission and the implications of its work for those concerned with insurance law.[4] BILA's early bulletins and journals contain numerous references to discussions, lectures and papers regarding possible reforms of the law. Working parties presented reports to the Law Commissions on a variety of topics.[5] Hugh Cockerell was heavily involved in preparing BILA working party reports long after he retired from academic life and from the Directorship of the Chartered Insurance Institute.

The 1970s

5.3 In the 1970s reform of consumer insurance law was championed by Professor Aubrey Diamond who was appointed a Law Commissioner in 1971 and later became President of BILA. Professor Diamond addressed the BILA AGM in September 1970 on the subject of 'Law and the Insurance Consumer'. He dwelt on the heavy burden of disclosure borne by an ordinary consumer, the unfairness of basis of contract clauses and was critical

---

2 See Hugh Cockerell's article, 'The Future of BILA', in BILA Journal No 76.

3 It was published in BILA Journal No 44, 1979, and in the Post Magazine and Insurance Monitor.

4 Address in 1966 reported in BILA Bulletin No 6.

5 Examples of reports from working parties include a Memorandum presented to the Law Commissions on exclusion of liability for negligence and exemption clauses, see BILA Journal No 28, another on interest, see BILA Journal No 39, one on the OFT's General Duty to Trade Fairly, see BILA Journal No 64, and others on Conditional Fees, Third Parties (Rights against Insurers) Act 1930, and the Life Assurance Act 1774.

of the doctrine of insurable interest.[6] Professor Diamond was an eminent authority on consumer law and wrote one of the most readable law books entitled *The Consumer, Society and the Law* back in 1963. He served as a member of the Consumer Council for many years and was President of the National Federation of Consumer Groups. He was a modest self-effacing man but his voice was very influential in this area.

In July 1975 the topicality of consumerism as a subject for high-level discussion was demonstrated by BILA's Colloquium in London, which took place over several days and included delegates from 22 different countries. Speakers representing seven countries delivered papers on three aspects of the subject, namely:

1. What the consumer expects from insurance
2. What the consumer gets from insurance
3. Where do we go from here?

Mr John Methven, the then Director General of the UK Office of Fair Trading spoke at the Colloquium and was critical of certain ways that insurers dealt with consumers.[7] This Colloquium proved to be influential in the setting up of the Insurance Ombudsman Bureau as different foreign speakers spoke of the success of independent complaints systems in their countries, such as the ombudsman system in Norway. This inspired Mike Harris of GRE and others to promote the concept of an Ombudsman Bureau for handling insurance complaints in England and Wales.[8]

As recorded elsewhere in this book, in May 1978 the Lord Chancellor requested the Law Commissions to consider various aspects of insurance contract law, including misrepresentation and non-disclosure. This request was prompted by the EEC producing a draft Directive on insurance contract law, which dealt, inter alia, with the effects of non-disclosure, misrepresentation and breach of warranty.

By January 1979 the Law Commissions had produced a Working Paper specifically directed to non-disclosure, misrepresentation and breach of warranty. The Chairman of the Law Commission of England and Wales was the redoubtable Mr Justice Kerr, as he then was. He gave a lunchtime address to BILA entitled 'Insurance law – non-disclosure and breach of warranty'. He reported to BILA[9] that the Commission was currently in the process of drafting its report, which would shortly be submitted to the Lord Chancellor, who would proceed with preparation of an appropriate Bill. He observed that Insurance had been exempted from the Unfair Contract Terms

6 BILA Journal No 24, October 1970.

7 See P V Saxton's report of the Colloquium in BILA Journal No 36.

8 Peter J Tyldesley, 'The Insurance Ombudsman Bureau – the early history' Journal of Insurance Research and Practice No 39 (2003), pp 34–43.

9 BILA Journal No 46.

Act 1977 in exchange for the code of conduct addressed by the market but that this was unsatisfactory.[10] He considered that the answer was to legislate so that no one abused their rights in respect of non-disclosure or warranties.[11]

BILA submitted a response to the Law Commissions on their report.[12] Unfortunately a draft Bill was never presented to Parliament. Lord Justice Longmore in the Pat Saxton Memorial Lecture explained the unfortunate demise of the Law Commissions' proposals.[13]

The 1980s

5.4 After the failure of the reform proposed by the Law Commissions, BILA recognised that impetus for reform in this area might come from Europe, particularly as the European Commission and European Parliament were concerned about consumer rights in the fields of sales and services. In the 1980s, as in the present decade, there was some appreciation or apprehension that if the UK did not reform certain aspects of insurance contract law the European Commission might forge ahead with contract law reform, including that of insurance law. Back in the 1980s some members of BILA expressed concern about reform being instigated from Europe. There was a lively discussion following a BILA lunchtime meeting where the BILA Committee had given the speaker the title of the talk, namely 'The EEC – what has it done for us so far'. Mr W E Pool, Head of the Insurance Division of Taxation of the European Commission, gave the main speech in which he addressed various European Directives, which had an impact on insurance law.

During the 1980s BILA was involved in presenting papers and speeches on the then-proposed draft Insurance Contract Law Directive. Gordon Cornish, who became Chairman of BILA, spoke on this draft Directive at many venues.[14]

Towards the end of the 1980s interest in the duty of disclosure in English law became more of a subject of discussion in the wake of the decision in *CTI v Oceanus* [1984] 1 Lloyd's Rep 476. That decision in the Court of Appeal did not follow the decision of Mr Justice Kerr (as he then was) in *Berger v Pollock* where he considered the materiality test laid down in s 18(2)

---

10 This is a reference to the ABI statements of insurance practice which were to be applied by members of the ABI but which were not legally binding. These have since been replaced by provisions in the Insurance Conduct of Business Rules.

11 BILA Journal No 46.

12 See BILA's Honorary Secretary's Report 1980/81.

13 See 'An Insurance Contracts Act for a new century?' by Lord Justice Longmore in BILA Journal No 106.

14 Eg at a joint meeting of BILA's Scottish Branch and the Scottish Law Societies European Group in Edinburgh in 1982, see BILA's Honorary Secretary's Report 1981/82.

of the Marine Insurance Act and stated this required a Court to consider the impact that the undisclosed facts would have had on the mind of the *particular* underwriter had the facts been disclosed to him at the time of placing the risk. He held that it was insufficient to call an independent expert underwriter to give his opinion on the materiality of any particular undisclosed fact. The Court of Appeal in *CTI v Oceanus* held that an insurer was entitled to avoid an insurance contract if there was a failure to disclose any circumstance which a prudent underwriter would take into account in reaching his decision whether or not to accept that risk or what premium to charge. The emphasis was firmly placed on the prudent underwriter's opinion rather than the actual underwriter's.

During the 1980s there was disquiet in some quarters regarding the outcome of some large cases, particularly ones going to arbitration in the 1980s where some brokers may not have been too scrupulous about disclosing matters and certain underwriters did not spend much time considering and enquiring into risks that they were writing, as their attention was more concerned in securing business and large premiums. When some of this business produced disastrous claims, certain insurers sought to avoid such insurance and relied on evidence from a 'prudent underwriter' to say that he would not have written the insurance or certainly would not have written it on those terms. I recall being involved in litigation of this kind where it was apparent that the actual underwriter would have written the business if he had known about matters which were not disclosed and/or were misrepresented. Nevertheless insurers were found to be entitled to avoid the insurance on the basis of evidence from an expert witness, usually an active or recently retired underwriter, who would say that such matters would have affected his decision to write the business or to do so on those terms

5.5 At the end of the 1980s BILA held a very successful Colloquium at University College London over 3 days in July 1989 which had as its subject 'The Making and Breaking of Insurance Contracts', which reviewed English law on non-disclosure and misrepresentation and compared it with the law of other jurisdictions. Speakers came from Australia, the USA and Europe. Michael Gill from Australia was the first to speak. He explained the Australian Insurance Contracts Act of 1984, which had replaced common law (largely based on English law principles) by introducing a statutory code on non-disclosure and misrepresentation. This Act set a new test of materiality more favourable to insureds. Ray Hodgin of Birmingham University followed with a talk on the state of English law on non-disclosure and misrepresentation. He considered that the present rules of disclosure weighed heavily against the insured. He felt that with the Law Reform Committee Report of 1957 and The Law Commission Report of 1980, both of which were gathering dust on the shelves, it was perhaps time to address the problem in a comprehensive way as had been achieved in Australia. Papers were given on the issue of disclosure by speakers from the

USA, Hungary, France, Denmark and Germany. Preference for the remedy of avoidance or for a principle of proportionality was debated at some length. On the final day there was an interesting moot conducted by Counsel, dealing with a factual situation involving non-disclosure by the insured. Judgment was given according to how it would be dealt with in different jurisdictions, with the Insurance Ombudsman and a professor from Germany adopting a proportionality approach and one British judge finding for the insured and another for the insurer.

The early 1990s

5.6 In May 1991 BILA and the CII held a joint conference on Utmost Good Faith with papers presented by various participants, including Ray Hodgin, Peter Madge and John Butler. The latter examined the judgment in the preceding year of Mr Justice Waller (as he then was) in *Pan Atlantic v Pine Top*, which was destined to become the leading case on non-disclosure and misrepresentation.

At BILA's Annual Conference on 17 September 1991 there was a lively debate. The motion proposed by Professor John Birds of Sheffield University, seconded by Derrick Cole, was that:

> 'The House considers current insurance contract law in the UK to be weighted in favour of insurers and to be in urgent need of reform.'

Opposing the motion were Duncan McMillan, Claims Director of a Lloyd's syndicate, seconded by Tony Tudor of the CII. Adrian Hamilton QC chaired that debate. There were many comments from the rest of 'the House'. Ultimately the proposition was put to the vote, but notwithstanding the powerful arguments put by Professor Birds and Derrick Cole, the motion achieved only one third of the votes and failed.

Spurred on by these discussions and the debate, certain members of BILA were keen for BILA to take a more active role in considering the current state of insurance contract law.

BILA's First Report on insurance contract law in 1993

5.7 Both Pat Saxton, a former BILA Chairman and Director General of the CII, and Derrick Cole, a retired insurance broker and expert witness, were concerned about the state of insurance law as it affected consumers and small businesses. A year after becoming Editor of the BILA Journal Derrick Cole wrote an article for the Journal about duty of care and disclosure under household policies.[15]

---

15 BILA Journal No 65.

In 1992 Derrick Cole, then Chairman of BILA, proposed to the BILA Committee that there should be a working party or subcommittee looking into some current problems in UK insurance contract law. Pat Saxton and Derrick Cole wished to have a lawyer on the working party and asked me to join them in this task. The full Committee agreed to the formation of this working party, with its terms of reference being to examine current insurance contract law in the UK. The objective of this task was to expose the problems and point to possible solutions. The three of us had regular meetings during 1992 and 1993 in which we discussed particular aspects of insurance law and practice and produced short papers. In between these meetings we did research on various topics and on how certain other leading European countries, as well as the US and Australia, had been dealing with similar problems.

Our working party was conscious that certain members of the BILA Committee were diffident about BILA resurrecting the issue of law reform in this area, so it was decided to produce a report to the Committee dealing with those aspects considered to be most in need of reform with a view to getting the Committee to agree to a more formal report to the Law Commissions and other bodies that might be interested in reform.

In 1993 our working party finalised our report and presented it to the BILA Committee that year. The report was published in the BILA Journal of May 1994.[16] It examined various topics, but concentrated much of its attention on insurers' entitlement to avoid an insurance contract for material non-disclosure and misrepresentation. The report favoured changing the test for materiality to the approach that the insured should disclose every matter that a reasonable person should be expected to know in his particular circumstances. It was critical of the 'all or nothing' approach of avoidance, as lacking flexibility and recommended that this should be changed. Although the report considered that insurers should be entitled to avoid in the case of fraud, it proposed that innocent negligent or reckless misrepresentation or non-disclosure should be dealt with by a form of judicial discretion based on proportionality.

In its conclusions the report voiced concern that:

> '… notwithstanding the Law Commission Report of October 1980, and their recommendations, no attempt has been made to rationalise insurance contract law which has resulted in the UK falling behind developments taking place in other parts of the world. This could have a serious knock-on effect by discouraging foreign industrialists placing business in the London Market subject to UK law'.

The report ended:

---

[16] BILA Journal No 85.

'If we wish to avoid this type of situation and other problems detrimental to the market, reform is necessary and urgent.'

5.8 The BILA Committee considered this report and, despite a few voices being reluctant for BILA to be seen to be actively initiating and promoting law reform, it was agreed that a further subcommittee could be formed with a view to exploring the matter further and producing a final report which could be submitted to the Law Commissions and/or other interested bodies.

The landmark decision of the House of Lords in *Pan Atlantic Insurance Co Ltd v Pine Top Insurance Co Ltd* [1995] 1 AC 501 was delivered after that BILA report. As has been written elsewhere, this decision ameliorated the test for materiality in that insurers could not avoid insurance based purely on the viewpoint of a prudent insurer, but also had to show that the actual underwriter was induced by the misrepresentation or non-disclosure involved. That judgment produced more discussion about this area of the law.

In the mid-1990s BILA became in closer contact once more with the Law Commissions. When I became BILA Chairman in 1994 I asked Peter Goldsmith QC (as he then was) to speak on problems with the Third Parties (Rights against Insurers) Act 1930.[17] He had asked the Law Reform Committee of the Bar Council, of which I was a member, to recommend to the Law Commissions that there should be reform, which the Bar Council duly did. BILA joined forces in supporting that reform and was involved in a Conference on this topic at St John's College, Cambridge. As part of this review, I was approached by the Law Commissions to comment on drafts for possible reform of this Act before such drafts were made public. This led to closer collaboration between BILA and the Law Commissions, particularly with Professor Hugh Beale when he was appointed a Law Commissioner in 2000.

BILA's report to the Law Commissions

5.9 Following on from the BILA working party's report, a further BILA subcommittee was formed to consider reform of insurance contract law. It was agreed that BILA members should look into different aspects of insurance law that might require reform. Derrick Cole became the Secretary of this subcommittee which would have distinct subgroups of BILA members under different Chairmen, who would each prepare a report on their respective area. I was Chairman of the group that considered utmost good faith and material non-disclosure, and misrepresentation. Our group also looked at problems concerning warranties in insurance contracts.

[17] His talk to BILA is published in BILA Journal No 88.

Derrick Cole headed the group looking at problems concerning intermediaries, particularly brokers. Tim Hardy was Chairman of the group that considered matters from a reinsurance angle. Richard Hanson-Jones headed the sub-group looking at claims and David Taylor headed a group considering marine insurance. A notice went out to BILA members as to whether they wished to become members of these groups and various members volunteered.

The Chairmen held meetings with their members who investigated their designated area and produced individual reports. Some groups met more often than others. Our sub-group met about every six weeks. All sub-groups eventually produced reports on their research and deliberations. Early on Derrick Cole and I considered that it was important to have someone eminent in insurance law circles to assist in presenting the final report, as that would give additional weight to the final submissions. We thought it might be awkward for a serving judge to be asked to do so, although there was support from some quarters of the judiciary for reform, notably from Sir Andrew Longmore and Sir Jonathan Mance (as he then was). I suggested that we ask Adrian Hamilton QC if he would be prepared to assist as he had been leading Counsel in the *Pan Atlantic* case and had a wealth of experience in this area of the law. He had led me as a silk in various insurance and reinsurance law cases and I knew he was interested in insurance law reform. Incidentally he had been Pupil Master to Lord Justices Longmore and Mance and was very highly regarded. Adrian Hamilton QC agreed to become Chairman of the subcommittee and considered all the reports from the different working groups and was instrumental in putting together the final report for presentation to the Law Commissions.

In July 1999 Pat Saxton died. He had been one of the most active members in BILA for many years. He had been Chairman of BILA, then a Vice President and finally Chairman of the BILA Charitable Trust. It was decided by the remaining charitable trustees, namely Derrick Cole, Ken Davidson and myself, that it would be appropriate to have a reception which would include a memorial lecture in his memory and that this should address insurance law reform.

Thus it was that the BILA Charitable Trust arranged for Lord Justice Longmore to give a lecture on 5 March 2001 at the CII which made a compelling case for it being time to reform the Marine Insurance Act 1906. His speech was entitled 'An Insurance Contracts Act for a new century?'[18] He stated that the case for reform in the areas he had discussed, which included non-disclosure and misrepresentation, was 'extremely strong'. Apart from BILA members, there were a number of influential attendees including other members of the judiciary, members of the Law Commission and the Insurance Ombudsman.

---

[18] This lecture appears in BILA Journal No 106.

Following this lecture it was more generally accepted within BILA that there was a need for reform and for BILA to promote this. The doubters on the BILA Committee, who had not been inclined to progress a report from BILA, accepted that BILA should move forward with presenting a report to the Law Commissions.

5.10 The BILA Committee decided that the September 2001 Annual Conference would be largely devoted to the topic of 'Reform of Insurance Contract Law'. The chairman of each sub-group gave the provisional findings of their particular group to the Conference. Summaries of these provisional findings were published in the BILA Journal.[19] Derrick Cole and I devised a Questionnaire for delegates to this Conference, which asked their views concerning possible reforms of insurance law, so we could get some measure of the level of support for reform within the membership. The completed questionnaires showed a fairly high level of support.

On 19 December 2001 Lord Justice Rix gave a lecture to BILA entitled 'Good faith: To be or not to be?' in which he raised the question whether the UK should look again at the problems of how the principles of good faith operate in the insurance context, particularly after the insurance contract has incepted.

From the time of the formation of the BILA subcommittee and the subgroups Derrick Cole had been very active in persuading the working groups to make progress and deliver their reports. To a large degree it was thanks to his energy and enthusiasm that this project finally came to fruition. He acted as coordinator and made sure that all the material was properly presented to Adrian Hamilton QC.

5.11 In September 2002 (nearly 10 years after the first BILA report on insurance law reform) the final BILA Report was published. It was decided that it should not be too lengthy or make detailed recommendations regarding many areas, as that might make it less 'punchy' and less digestible when it came to persuading others to read about law reform. Apart from a summary of BILA's recommendations for reform, the Report contained a foreword from Lord Justice Mance, as he then was, and appended to the Report were the lectures given to BILA from Lord Justice Longmore and Lord Justice Rix, to which I have referred.

Rather than reciting details of the sub-groups' deliberations, it was decided that the best course was largely to support the Law Commission's draft Bill from 1980 with some suggested alterations. It was considered that it was more likely to get legislative reform on this basis rather than by suggesting an extensive overhaul of the Marine Insurance Act 1906. The Report stated that:

---

19 Bila Journal No 107.

> 'We do not believe that it would be helpful to attempt to codify fully the law of insurance at the first stage. This would appear to be a recipe for delay.'

The following were the main recommendations of the BILA 2002 Report so far as non-disclosure and misrepresentation was concerned:

(1) A new test for materiality, namely whether a reasonable insured would have considered the undisclosed matter (or misrepresentation) to be material to a prudent underwriter;

(2) To allow insurers to avoid where there has been fraudulent or reckless misrepresentation/non-disclosure; reckless in the sense of blind eye recklessness not caring whether a representation was true or false;

(3) To introduce proportionality as a remedy for other types of misrepresentation and non-disclosure;

(4) Abolition of basis of contract clauses.

BILA's proposals for reform were directed at all types of insurance save for marine, aviation and transport risks, as in the 1980 draft Bill. The types of insurance excluded were essentially those where the insured would be insuring in a market where he would be professionally represented by a broker.

Hugh Beale, still serving as a Law Commissioner, expressed his clear interest in the BILA Report. The Law Commissions asked, as they did annually, for topics to be proposed for law reform. The topic of Insurance Contract Law reform was put on the proposed list. As Vice Chairman of the Law Reform Committee of the Bar Council I suggested that that Committee lend its support to this topic being reviewed by the Law Commissions, which it did. On 17 May 2004 I spoke in favour of reform of insurance contract law in the consumer context at a conference entitled 'Protecting the consumer – is there a need for insurance law reform?'[20] I set out and explained the proposals that BILA had put forward for reform. The consensus of those at that conference was that reform of insurance law was required. In 2004 the Law Commissions were prepared to undertake a scoping study into insurance contract law reform and got the go ahead from the Treasury to review this area of law.

BILA's support of Law Commissions' reform of insurance contract law

5.12 BILA has supported the Law Commissions in its review of insurance contract law in various ways. Firstly, BILA's Law Review subcommittee has

[20] Conference organised by the London Metropolitan University.

submitted written responses to issues papers and reports produced by the Law Commissions on insurance contract law reform. Some BILA members have been invited to take part in discussions with the Law Commissions on issues papers prior to such papers being released. Secondly, BILA has been involved in staging lectures and conferences on the topics being addressed by the Law Commissions, usually in collaboration with the Law Commission. The most recent BILA Conference took place on 26 June 2012 as a joint conference with the Law Commissions and University of Southampton in the Willis Building. The full day conference examined issues that had been raised by recent Law Commission papers with different panels of commentators for each issue. Lord Justice Rix, and Lord Justice Aiken chaired two of the sessions and gave the audience the benefit of their views on certain legal points. David Hertzell, the Law Commissioner currently heading the Insurance Contract Law project, addressed the Conference on the Commissions' most recent proposals. There were lively discussions both within the panels and from the floor.

Thirdly, BILA has organised mock trials which have illustrated problems with the present law. I acted as a barrister in one such mock trial in 2005, which revolved around the Court of Appeal's judgment in *Sprung v Royal Insurance (UK) Ltd*[21] *('Sprung')*. That case confirmed that an insured could not recover damages in respect of losses he had suffered as a result of insurers unreasonably delaying payment of a valid claim. In my practice at the Bar I had had to explain to mystified clients why such damages were not recoverable. I suggested to Bob Moxon Browne QC that the problem behind this case should be brought to wider attention and we should devise a scenario for the mock trial based on *Sprung,* which we did. In order not to appear partisan, we appeared for the insurers and Michael Crane QC and Sioban Healy appeared for the insured. Adrian Hamilton QC presided over proceedings in the Lord Chief Justice's Court after court hours. Bob and I were not dismayed that the majority found in favour of the insured and 'overruled' *Sprung*. The airing of arguments for and against *Sprung* seemed to generate much greater interest in this point. Certainly the Law Commissions recognised the need for reform on this issue in their Consultation Paper on Post Contract Duties.[22]

Finally, BILA members have made their individual views known to the Law Commissions, notably Derrick Cole and Geoffrey Lloyd, who as former insurance practitioners have sought to persuade the Law Commissions of the need for reform so far as consumers and small businesses are concerned, as well as reform regarding insurance intermediaries.

---

21 [1999] 1 Lloyd's Rep 111.

22 Insurance Contract Law: Post Contract Duties and Other Issues, December 2011.

BILA's support of the Consumer Insurance (Disclosure and Representations) Act

5.13 BILA was consulted by the Law Commissions on the draft Consumer Insurance (Disclosure and Representations) Bill. I and a few other BILA members appreciated having the opportunity to comment on early drafts of the Bill. BILA has welcomed the speedy way in which the Bill passed through Parliament under the procedure for uncontroversial Bills. It is quite some achievement to see this Bill receive the Royal Assent by March 2012. Although some of us in BILA may have wished the reforms to cover small businesses or at least micro businesses, consumers will not have to face the prospect of their insurance contracts being avoided for non-disclosure or misrepresentation unless there has been a deliberate or reckless misrepresentation. BILA is pleased that the more flexible proportionality approach has been introduced in the case of careless misrepresentations. The outlawing of basis of contract clauses in consumer contracts was well over due. It is desirable that the law as applied in the courts is perceived as fair and reflective of good practice.

5.14 BILA regards the Consumer Insurance (Disclosure and Representations) Act 2012 as a worthy step on the road to reform of some perceived deficiencies in UK insurance law. It hopes that some of the other deficiencies of our insurance law will also be remedied by future legislation so that those making insurance contracts continue to favour choosing our law and our courts.

Chapter 6 The Consumer Insurance (Disclosure and Representations) Act 2012

David Hertzell
David Hertzell was Managing Partner of city law firm DAC until 2006. He was appointed a Law Commissioner in 2007. He previously chaired the AIRMIC (the UK risk managers association) Captive Insurance Focus Group and was a member of the BSI drafting committee on risk management. He is a pension fund trustee and sits as the independent member on the audit and risk committee of the Judicial Appointments Committee. As Law Commissioner David is responsible for commercial and common law projects, including those to reform the law of insurance and sale of goods.

Background

6.1 It has taken many years to reform the law on what a consumer must tell an insurer before taking out insurance. There have been many calls for reform: by the Law Reform Committee in 1957; the English Law Commission in 1980; and the National Consumer Council in 1997. In 2002, the British Insurance Law Association (BILA) put forward strong arguments for change, and encouraged the Law Commissions to look at the area again.[1]

In 2006, following the BILA report, the Law Commission and Scottish Law Commission set up a joint review of insurance law. In 2007, the two Commissions carried out a wide consultation on potential reform, which identified the law on consumers' duties of disclosure as the most serious problem to be addressed. Therefore, in 2009, the Commissions published a report and draft Bill targeted at this particular issue, entitled 'Consumer Insurance Law: Pre-Contract Disclosure and Misrepresentation'. The Bill was introduced into the House of Lords in May 2011, using the Law Commission procedure for uncontroversial bills, was passed with minor

---

1 For references to these reports, see Joint Report, paras 1.5 to 1.7.

amendment and received the Royal Assent on 8 March 2012. A commencement order is anticipated in March 2013. The text of the Act is very similar to the draft in the report.

Much of the pressure for change came from consumers, particularly those who had been refused claims under critical illness policies because the insurer argued that they had not revealed some apparently minor aspect of their medical history. However concern was by no means limited to consumer groups and consumer champions. The industry too believed that the law was inappropriate. What then is the problem and why has the law failed to adapt?

The strict law

6.2 The existing law, as set out in the Marine Insurance Act 1906,[2] requires a consumer to volunteer information to insurers. The consumer is obliged to tell the insurer about anything which would 'influence the judgment of a prudent insurer' in fixing the premium or deciding whether to take the risk.[3] The insurer does not need to ask questions – it is up to the policyholder to work out what the insurer would want to know.

It is clearly important that insurers receive the information they need to assess risks. Information from policyholders is often the basis of underwriting decisions on whether to accept risks at all, and if so, at what price and on what terms. But the obligation to volunteer information does not correspond to the realities of a modern consumer insurance market. Most consumers are unaware that the law imposes such a duty. Even if they are aware of it, they usually have little idea of what an insurer might think relevant. And consumers suspect that, even if they were to telephone the call centre to mention something, the staff would be ill-equipped to process the information.

If a consumer fails to disclose something which the prudent underwriter would consider relevant then the 1906 Act is quite clear. The insurer is entitled to 'avoid the contract': they may treat the contract as if it never existed and to refuse to pay all claims. It is irrelevant that the consumer's mistake was honest and reasonable.

As its name suggest, much of the 1906 Act is concerned with marine matters. The legislation codified the rules developed over the eighteenth and nineteenth centuries, between sophisticated insurers and brokers, largely meeting face to face in London. It did not anticipate a mass consumer

---

2 Although this Act appears to apply only to marine insurance, the courts have held that it codifies the common law, and therefore embodies the principles which apply to all insurance.

3 Section 18(2).

insurance market, developing during the era of post war affluence. Nevertheless the courts have held that the 1906 Act has general application, including to consumers.[4]

Overlapping attempts to mitigate the strict law

6.3 The insurance industry has long recognised that the Act is not appropriate for consumer insurance. Unfortunately attempts to redress the situation have led to overlapping and inconsistent industry statements, regulatory rules, ombudsman discretion and codes of practice:

- *Statements of Practice* were issued in 1977 and strengthened in 1986. Insurers agreed not to rely on their strict legal rights in some circumstances.

- The *Financial Services Authority* (FSA) has incorporated some principles in the Statements of Practice into its rules. For example, the rules state that except where there is evidence of fraud, an insurer must not refuse to meet a claim for a non-negligent misrepresentation.[5] The FSA rules do not amend the law. Instead, courts are required to apply the 1906 Act. In theory, an insurer could rely on its legal rights, win its case before a court, and then face the threat of an FSA fine, though this has never happened.

- The *Financial Ombudsman Service* (FOS) has a statutory power to determine complaints according to what is 'fair and reasonable in all the circumstances'.[6] The FOS is not bound to decide cases according to the strict law. Instead it has developed its own approach, which goes further than the FSA rules. Where the insurer has failed to ask about an issue, the FOS does not require consumers to volunteer information. Furthermore, where a consumer has answered a question carelessly, the FOS does not allow the insurer to avoid the policy. Instead, the FOS applies a compensatory remedy, based on what the insurer would have done had it known the truth.

- In January 2008, the ABI issued formal Guidance on non-disclosure in long-term protection insurance.[7] This responded to public disquiet about refusal rates in critical illness insurance. The industry recognised that insurers should not necessarily refuse claims for careless errors.

---

4 See, for example, *Lambert v Co-operative Insurance Society Ltd* [1975] 2 Lloyd's Rep 485.
5 Insurance Conduct of Business Sourcebook, Rule 8.1.2(2).
6 Financial Services and Markets Act 2000, s 228(2).
7 ABI Guidance, 'Non-Disclosure and Treating Customers Fairly in Claims for Long-Term Protection Insurance Products', January 2008. See Appendix 7.

Instead, insurers should consider what they would have done had they known the full facts. The Guidance was upgraded to the status of a Code in January 2009.[8]

Most consumer insurance disputes are now resolved by the FOS, applying its own rules. In effect we now have two separate insurance schemes in the UK, one applied by the FOS to consumers and one applied by the courts to businesses. Use of the FOS has steered cases away from the courts. This has prevented the courts from developing the law as it applies to consumers, even if they had the flexibility to do so within the constraints of the 1906 Act.

Separate rules for consumers

6.4 The Commissions have decided to adopt the concept of two sets of rules. The 2012 Act covers only consumers: businesses will be subject to a different legal regime. This is a significant change from the previous 'one size fits all' approach.

This division between consumer insurance and business insurance does not appear to cause any difficulty in practice. In response to the Law Commissions' 2007 consultation, most respondents supported the division. Many justified the distinction on the basis that businesses are in general more sophisticated purchasers of insurance than consumers and are more often advised by informed brokers. That may well be correct. However there are other fundamental differences.

Consumer insurance is more often affected by social policy. Certain types such as motor are compulsory. It may be in the future that insurance will be expected to take on more of the financial burden around the provision of social services such as long term care for the elderly. Social policy exists with business insurance too. Employers' liability insurance is an obvious example. However business insurance covers a vast range of activities where social policy plays little part.

Consumer insurance caters for the mass market, where the risk pools are large and the likely losses are relatively stable and predictable. Consumer insurance is sometimes referred to as 'portfolio insurance' for this reason. Insurers tend to have reliable information about consumer risks. For example, over 90% of the household insurance market is covered by the Comprehensive Underwriting Exchange, a system which records previous losses and claims and which is often more accurate than the consumer's memory.

---

8 See ABI Code of Practice, 'Managing Claims for Individual and Group Life, Critical Illness and Income Protection Insurance Products', January 2009.

By contrast, businesses vary greatly both in size and in terms of the risks they represent, leading to a wide variety of potential exposures. Business losses can be much larger and therefore the insurer's experience is more volatile. Insurers cannot be expected to know the risks of every business process, and the specific knowledge of the insured is more important.

It is therefore appropriate to impose less onerous disclosure rules on consumers than on businesses.

The problems the 2012 Act addresses

6.5 The 2012 Act is designed to solve four problems with the 1906 Act:

- *The duty to disclose may operate as a trap for consumers.* Consumers are usually unaware that this duty exists or, even if they know that they should disclose facts, they may have no idea what is relevant to the insurer.
- *Policyholders may be denied claims when they have acted honestly and reasonably.* If the untrue statement is deemed to be one of fact rather than belief, it does not matter that the consumer tried their best to get it right.
- *The remedy for misrepresentation and non-disclosure may be overly harsh.* The law entitles the insurer to 'avoid' the policy. This means that the insurer may refuse all claims, even claims which the insurer would have paid had it been given full information. This is appropriate where consumers are deliberate or reckless, but not appropriate where they act reasonably or are merely careless.
- *A statement on a proposal form can be converted into a warranty using obscure words that most policyholders do not understand.* If a prospective policy-holder signs a statement on the proposal form stating that the answers form 'the basis of the contract', this converts all the answers into warranties. If any statement is incorrect, the insurer may refuse all claims, even if the mistake is of no importance to it.

The 2012 Act

6.6 The 2012 Act is short and targeted. It applies only to consumer insurance contracts: that is, to insurance bought by individuals for purposes wholly or mainly unrelated to their trade, business or profession. Furthermore, it only deals with the issue of what a consumer must tell an insurer before entering into or varying an insurance contract.

The Act follows FOS practice in abolishing the consumer's duty to volunteer information. Instead, the insurer must ask appropriate questions, and the consumer must take care to answer them honestly and carefully. If the consumer does say something which is not true, the Act distinguishes between three types of misrepresentation: those which are 'reasonable', 'careless' or 'deliberate or reckless'.

- Where a misrepresentation is *reasonable*, the insurer must pay the claim.
- Where a misrepresentation is *careless*, the insurer has a compensatory remedy, based on what the insurer would have done had the question been answered fully.
- Where a misrepresentation is *deliberate or reckless*, the insurer may treat the policy as if it did not exist and decline all claims. The insurer would also be entitled to retain the premium, unless there was a good reason why the premium should be returned.

The Act also gives guidance about when an intermediary acts for an insurer rather than a consumer. It abolishes 'basis of the contract clauses' and includes special rules for group insurance. The Act also provides that the rules are mandatory: insurers may not use contract terms to put consumers in a worse position.

The Law Commissions' 2009 Report discusses the policy behind the recommendations in detail. This paper gives a quick summary of each provision. The Act is best thought of as a series of hurdles which an insurer needs to jump in order to obtain a remedy, as illustrated in the flow diagram opposite.

When does the 2012 act apply?

6.7 Section 1 defines 'consumer insurance contract', 'consumer' and 'insurer'. The definitions in the 2012 Act are not exactly the same as those in the draft bill attached to the 2009 Report. Consultees were concerned that the definitions should mirror those used by the FSA: they feared that differences would lead to unnecessary confusion and additional costs. The Law Commissions therefore liaised closely with the FSA to find acceptable wording.

The definition of a consumer follows the general approach of European law, as imported into UK consumer legislation by EU directives. A consumer must be an 'individual'; that is, a natural rather than legal person. Unlike other consumer definitions, the definition in the 2012 Act expressly provides for 'mixed use contracts', where the insurance is mainly for personal use, but also includes some element of business use. For example, personal car insurance may include an extension for some business use; or home contents insurance may include some business equipment. The definition states that the consumer must purchase the insurance for 'purposes wholly or mainly unrelated to the individual's trade, business or profession'. That will generally

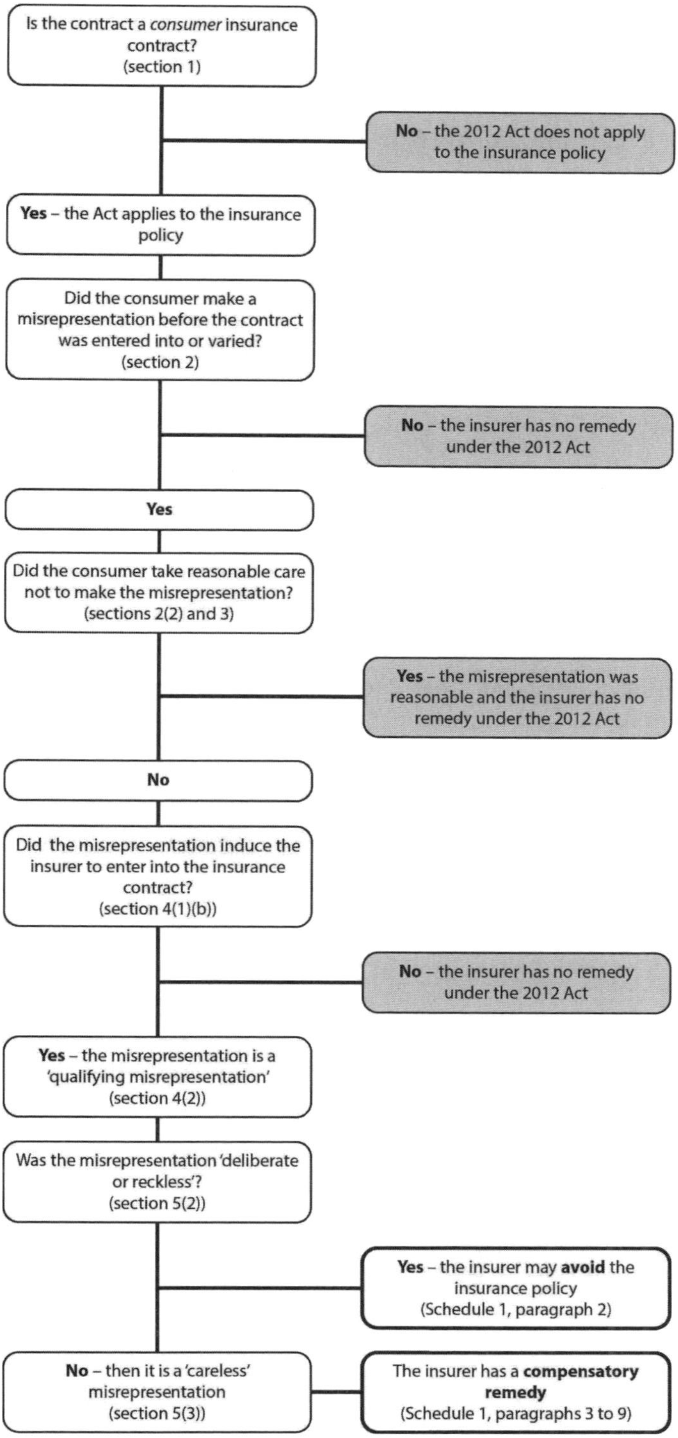
Is the contract a *consumer* insurance contract? (section 1)
No – the 2012 Act does not apply to the insurance policy
Yes – the Act applies to the insurance policy
Did the consumer make a misrepresentation before the contract was entered into or varied? (section 2)
No – the insurer has no remedy under the 2012 Act
Yes
Did the consumer take reasonable care not to make the misrepresentation? (sections 2(2) and 3)
Yes – the misrepresentation was reasonable and the insurer has no remedy under the 2012 Act
No
Did the misrepresentation induce the insurer to enter into the insurance contract? (section 4(1)(b))
No – the insurer has no remedy under the 2012 Act
Yes – the misrepresentation is a 'qualifying misrepresentation' (section 4(2))
Was the misrepresentation 'deliberate or reckless'? (section 5(2))
Yes – the insurer may **avoid** the insurance policy (Schedule 1, paragraph 2)
No – then it is a 'careless' misrepresentation (section 5(3))
The insurer has a **compensatory remedy** (Schedule 1, paragraphs 3 to 9)

be obvious but ultimately is a question of fact to be decided by the court or ombudsman after considering the main purpose of the insurance policy.

The 2012 Act refers to the 'business of insurance', but does not define insurance. The definition is left to the common law. Most companies who carry out insurance business must be authorised by the FSA under the Financial Services and Markets Act 2000, but this is not decisive. The Act expressly states that the insurer may or may not be authorised by the FSA.[9] Authorisation includes some activities (such as pension fund management) which are not necessarily insurance. And a small group of contracts (such as funeral plans) do not require FSA authorisation, even if they are traditionally regarded as insurance and would be covered by the principles behind the 1906 Act. By relying on the common law definition of insurance, they are included within the Act.

The Act is also clear that the party contracting with the consumer must be acting in the course of business. The Act does not apply to private arrangements between individuals.

Abolishing the duty of disclosure

6.8 Section 2 abolishes the duty currently imposed on consumers to volunteer material facts. Instead, consumers are required to take reasonable care not to make a misrepresentation. This new duty is central to the 2012 Act. It means that consumers must take reasonable care to answer insurers' questions fully and accurately. If consumers do volunteer information, they must take reasonable care to ensure that the information is not misleading.

The Act confirms that the duty also applies when an existing contract is varied. No explicit mention is made of renewals. As renewals are treated by the law as new contracts, the duty will apply.

A particular concern arises where a consumer is asked to confirm or amend information that has been supplied previously. This is most likely to arise when a policy is renewed although it could arise in other circumstances too. Depending upon the facts, the Act confirms that the consumer's failure to answer the insurer's questions in such a situation could amount to a misrepresentation.

What is reasonable care?

6.9 The question will then be: did the consumer take reasonable care?

---

9 The authorisation requirements are set out in the Financial Services and Markets Act (Regulated Activities) Order 2001 (SI 2001/544).

Section 3 states that the standard applied to decide whether the consumer has taken reasonable care is an objective one: it is that of the reasonable consumer. In other words, the standard of care is that which could be expected from an average consumer with no special skills or knowledge. The particular characteristics of the actual consumer are not relevant, unless the insurer knew or ought to have known about those characteristics. For example, a consumer who does not speak English is judged by the standards of the average consumer (who does speak English), unless the insurer knew or ought to have known that this particular consumer was struggling to understand the question. If so, the court must ask, what would a reasonable consumer who does not speak English have done in the circumstances?

In deciding whether a consumer has acted reasonably the Act requires all relevant circumstances to be taken into account. It provides an indicative non-exhaustive list of the kind of matters that should be considered. These include the type of insurance contract, the sales material provided by the insurer, how clear the insurer's questions were and whether or not an agent was acting for the consumer.

Section 3(2)(d) was added by the House of Lords at Report Stage. Peers were concerned that consumers may not realise that, as a renewal constitutes a new contract, they must take the same care on renewal as when they first take out insurance.[10] It is now common for insurers to send out renewal notices which ask the consumer to notify them if any of the facts they gave previously have changed. If the consumer fails to respond, the insurance is renewed automatically. Automatic renewal is convenient (especially in car insurance where the consumer who allows insurance to lapse commits a criminal offence[11]). But it does make it easier for a consumer to make a misrepresentation inadvertently, by failing to read or respond to a letter. Following the amendment, the Act includes a new factor for the court to consider in these circumstances: how clearly the insurer communicated the importance of responding, or the consequences of failing to do so.

Section 3(5) confirms that if a consumer acted dishonestly, that will always show a lack or reasonable care. It covers the situation where a well-informed consumer acted dishonestly while an average consumer might have made a reasonable mistake about the same issues.

'Qualifying misrepresentations'

6.10 If there has been a misrepresentation, section 4 describes the circumstances in which an insurer is entitled to a remedy. First the consumer must be in breach of the duty in section 2. The consumer must have failed to take

---

[10] Hansard (HL), 20 December 2011, vol 733, col 1746.

[11] See section 22 of the Road Safety Act 2006, which amends the Road Traffic Act 1988.

reasonable care not to make a misrepresentation. Second the insurer must show that it was induced to enter the contract by the misrepresentation.

The 2012 Act codifies the current law on inducement as developed following *Pan Atlantic Insurance Co Ltd v Pine Top Insurance Co Ltd.*[12] The insurer must establish that had it known the true facts it would have done something different, either by not entering into the contract (or agreeing to the variation) at all, or by requiring different terms or a higher premium. The Act does not preserve the current law set out in section 20 of the 1906 Act that a misrepresentation must also have influenced the judgment of a hypothetical 'prudent insurer'. It is the effect on the particular insurer which matters.

The 2012 Act uses the phrase 'qualifying misrepresentations' to describe misrepresentations where the consumer has not acted reasonably which also induced the insurer to enter the contract on the agreed terms.

The Insurer's remedies

6.11 Where an insurer has been induced by a 'qualifying misrepresentation' to enter into an insurance contract, the insurer's remedy will depend on the consumer's state of mind.

Under section 5, there are two types of qualifying misrepresentation: those which are (i) 'deliberate or reckless' or (ii) 'careless'. 'Deliberate or reckless' is defined under the Act, while 'careless' is the residual category. A misrepresentation is careless if the consumer did not act reasonably (and made a 'qualifying misrepresentation'), but was not deliberate or reckless.

Deliberate or reckless: the contract may be avoided

6.12 The Commissions consulted widely on possible definitions of 'deliberate or reckless'. The ABI Code largely adopted the definition proposed in the consultation paper, which is now in the 2012 Act.

For a misrepresentation to be considered 'deliberate or reckless' the insurer must show on the balance of probabilities that the consumer:

- knew that the statement was untrue or misleading, or did not care whether it was or not; and
- knew that the matter was relevant to the insurer, or did not care whether it was or not.

---

[12] [1995] 1 AC 501.

This definition follows the law as established in *Derry v Peek,*[13] where Lord Bramwell put the definition of fraud in the following terms:

> 'A man who makes a statement without care and regard for its truth or falsity commits a fraud. He is a rogue.'[14]

The court distinguished this from making a statement which one genuinely thinks to be true without taking sufficient care to check the facts. That is careless rather than reckless.

Normally, the onus of proving that a misrepresentation was 'deliberate or reckless' is on the insurer. However, the insurer is helped by the two presumptions in section 5(5). It is presumed that:

- The consumer had the knowledge of a reasonable consumer, and
- The consumer knew that a matter about which the insurer asked a clear and specific question was relevant to the insurer.

Where the presumptions apply, the burden of proof is reversed.

The effect of the presumptions may be illustrated by an example. Take the case where a consumer fails to mention a heart attack in response to a clear and specific question. As most reasonable people would know that they had suffered a heart attack, the insurer does not need to prove that the consumer acted deliberately or recklessly. Instead, it is up to the consumer to show that he or she did not know about the heart attack, or did not understand the question. Thus the consumer might explain that the doctor failed to mention a minor heart attack, or might provide other evidence of lack of understanding.

Under Schedule 1, paragraph 2, where the misrepresentation is deliberate or reckless, the insurer may 'avoid the contract and refuse all claims'. The insurer would also be entitled to retain the premium, unless there was a good reason why the premium should be returned. The Law Commissions comment that there may be a good reason to return the investment element in life insurance, where the misrepresentation is not relevant to the investment.

Careless misrepresentations: a compensatory remedy

6.13 Under the 1906 Act, the remedy for misrepresentation is avoidance. This can be harsh. If a consumer taking out critical illness insurance acts carelessly in failing to mention hearing loss and later develops breast cancer, the insurer can refuse the cancer claim. This is so even if, had the insurer been aware of the hearing loss, it would merely have excluded hearing

13 (1889) LR 14 App Cas 337.

14 *Ibid*, at p 350.

problems from the policy and would have paid the cancer claim. This represents a glaring injustice under the current law.

For many years, the FOS has been prepared to grant proportionate remedies, based on what the insurer would have done had the consumer taken care to answer the question. But these remedies had no basis in law. Until recently, the FOS has applied them cautiously. In the Law Commissions' 2006 survey of ombudsman decisions on non-disclosure and misrepresentation, the consumer received a proportion of the claim in only 8 out of 190 cases (4%). In a further five cases, an exclusion was applied which did not affect the claim.[15] It appears that insurers are now accepting proportionate remedies, and are much more prepared to offer them. The Act provides a statutory basis for this approach.

The details of how compensatory remedies work are set out in Schedule 1:

- Where an insurer would have declined the risk altogether, the policy may be avoided, the claim refused and the premiums returned (paragraph 5).
- Where the insurer would have applied an exclusion, the insurer is not obliged to pay claims that would fall within the exclusion. For example, if a consumer carelessly failed to reveal hearing loss, and the insurer would have excluded hearing loss from the policy, the insurer is not be obliged to pay claims related to the loss of hearing. But the insurer must pay other claims. Similarly, if an insurer would have imposed a warranty or excess, the claim should be treated as if the policy included that warranty or excess (paragraph 6).
- Where an insurer would have increased the premium, the claim should be reduced proportionately. For example, if an insurer only charged £1,000 but should have charged £1,500, the consumer would receive two thirds of the claim. This is often referred to as a 'proportionate' settlement (paragraphs 7 and 8).

Most disputes about misrepresentation concern whether a claim should be paid. But under paragraph 9, the insurer may also terminate the contract for the future. Where an insurer discovers a careless misrepresentation, it has a choice. It may notify the consumer that it intends to treat the contract as subsisting on different terms. Alternatively, it may terminate the contract by giving reasonable notice and refunding any premium that relates to the rest of the contract term.

There is an exception for life insurance: if an insurer discovers a careless misrepresentation before the consumer dies, the insurer must continue the policy and meet a proportion of the claim. Life policies often include accelerated critical illness cover, for example, to allow consumers to claim

15 CP, Appendix C, paras 79 to 87.

when diagnosed with cancer. If an insurer who discovers a careless misrepresentation in the course of such a claim could cancel the life cover, the consumer would not be able to obtain other insurance and would lose a valuable benefit.

Basis of the contract clauses

6.14 Section 6 abolishes 'basis of the contract' clauses.

Under the current law, as strictly applied, insurers may include a declaration in the proposal form or policy that the consumer 'warrants' the accuracy of the information supplied, or that the information forms 'the basis of the contract'. Such clauses turn the consumer's representations into warranties. Under the 1906 Act, a breach of warranty automatically discharges the insurer from any further liability, even if it is not material or has been remedied. The effect is to allow an insurer to refuse all claims because of a minor mistake on the form, however innocent, and however irrelevant to the insurer's decision to write the policy.

Basis of the contract clauses therefore have the potential to undermine the whole policy of the 2012 Act. Consultees told us that insurers did not rely on their strict rights in these circumstances and that the FOS would not permit them to do so. The Act therefore brings the law into line with best practice.

Section 6 prevents insurers from relying on contract wording to convert representations into contract terms. It does not prevent specific warranties being used in insurance contracts. The problems caused by specific warranties will be considered again in a third consultation paper to be published by the Law Commissions this summer.

Group insurance

6.15 Section 7 makes special provisions for group schemes, where one party (typically an employer) arranges insurance to benefit members of the group (typically employees). This is an underdeveloped area of law. The Act brings the law into line with good practice by providing that where a group member makes a misrepresentation, the misrepresentation has consequences only for that individual, not for others within the group.

Insurance on the life of another

6.16 Section 8 deals with situations where one consumer takes out insurance on the life of another. A husband and wife would be a typical example.

In these circumstances it is common for the person whose life is being insured ('L') to be asked questions about their age and state of health. The insurer may rely on this information. However, as L is not a party to the contract, L would not normally owe a duty to take reasonable care to give correct information. Section 8 imposes the same duties on L as section 2 imposes on the policyholder. Where L provided the information, the issue is whether L (rather than the policyholder) was reasonable, careless, or deliberate or reckless.

The result is that where a consumer takes out insurance on the life of another, both the consumer and the life insured are under a duty to take reasonable care not to make a misrepresentation. If either (or both) fails in this duty, the insurer has a remedy.

Intermediaries

6.17 Insurance is often bought through intermediaries, who may use a variety of titles (such as 'broker', 'agent' or 'consultant'). It is not unusual for consumers to blame the intermediary for giving inaccurate or misleading information to insurers. An intermediary might, for example, give poor advice about what to include on a proposal form, or write down the consumer's answers incorrectly.

In law, if an agent acts for the consumer, the consumer is held responsible for the agent's actions. This means that if the consumer's agent acted deliberately or recklessly then, under the Act, the insurer could avoid the claim. If the agent acted carelessly, a compensatory remedy would be applied. The consumer would then need to bring an action against the intermediary, either through FOS or through the courts, showing that the intermediary was at fault. On the other hand, if the intermediary acted as an agent for the insurer, the insurer would be required to pay the claim. It could then pursue its own remedy against the intermediary.

It is therefore important to know for whom an intermediary acts when helping a consumer complete an insurance application. Unfortunately, the law in this area is uncertain, as the courts and the FOS have struggled to apply early twentieth century cases to a rapidly changing market place.

This is a difficult issue, and the Law Commissions have amended their policy since publication of the consultation paper. It has not proved possible to produce a bright line to distinguish whether an intermediary acts for the consumer or for the insurer. Instead the decision depends on a range of factors, and will change as the market develops new ways of providing advice.

Section 9 introduces a statutory code, based largely on the existing law, as supplemented by FOS practice and industry understanding. The aim is to give greater guidance, while retaining flexibility for the FOS and the courts to adapt to new arrangements.

Under Schedule 2, an intermediary is considered to act for the insurer if:

- the intermediary is the appointed representative of the insurer;
- the insurer has given the intermediary express authority to collect the information as its agent; or
- the insurer has given the intermediary express authority to enter into the contract on the insurer's behalf.

In other cases, the intermediary is presumed to act for the consumer unless it appears that it acts for the insurer. The issue would need to be determined by looking at all the circumstances. Schedule 2 lists factors which may be relevant, but the courts and the FOS would be able to consider new factors as the market changes.

The Act suggests that factors which might indicate that an agent is acting for the consumer include an undertaking to provide impartial advice, undertaking a fair analysis of the market and being paid a fee by the consumer. Conversely factors which indicate that the agent is acing for the insurer include the agent placing insurance with only one of the available market, being under a contractual agreement which restricts the available market, where the agent uses the insurer's name or 'white-labelling' where the insurance is marketed in the name of the agent.

In order to ensure that the Act does not become out of date given changes in how insurance is intermediated, HM Treasury is provided with a power to amend the list of factors by statutory instrument.

And finally...

6.18 Insurers may not contract out of this scheme. Section 10 provides that terms are of no effect if they would put the consumer in a worse position than the 2012 Act.

Section 11 amends the 1906 Act to ensure that consumer marine insurance (such as insurance on private yachts) is in line with the new consumer regime. It also makes changes to section 152 of the Road Traffic Act 1988. Section 152 is a complex rarely used provision, described in detail in the Report.[16] The amendment clarifies that insurers may not avoid a consumer motor insurance policy under the 1988 Act unless they have a right to avoid under the 2012 Act.

---

16 Report, para 9.21 to 9.35.

Under section 12, the 2012 Act applies throughout the UK – to England and Wales, to Scotland and to Northern Ireland. The Act will commence at a time decided by HM Treasury. However there will be at least a year between Royal Assent and commencement.

Conclusion

6.19 The 2012 Act was passed 106 years after the 1906 Act became law. The insurance market today is very different from that which existed in 1906, and it needs different laws. For many years, problems in the law have been patched up by codes, regulation and voluntary agreements, but these are confusing. They also fail to protect those who are unable to use the FOS, such as those with claims above the FOS limits.[17] They have not proved a complete answer to obsolete legislation.

Over the last few years, insurance law has been reformed across the globe, from Chile to China. In the EU there are moves to provide an optional code based on civil law principles. The UK's patchwork of inconsistent rules has begun to look vulnerable. New legislation should enable the UK once again to become the benchmark of best practice. This, we hope, will strengthen the international negotiating position of the UK government and the UK insurance industry.

17 The FOS monetary limit is currently £150,000: FSA Handbook, DISP 3.7.4.

Chapter 7A A View from the Association of British Insurers (ABI)

Judith Crawford
Judith Crawford is Policy Adviser for Regulation and Distribution in the Financial Conduct Regulation Directorate at the ABI. The ABI is the voice of insurance, representing the general insurance, protection, investment and long-term savings industry. It was formed in 1985 to represent the whole of the industry and today has over 300 members, accounting for some 90% of premiums in the UK.
Judith studied International Relations at St Andrews, before moving to Brussels to work as a Parliamentary Assistant to John Purvis MEP. She spent six years there, focusing on financial services legislation, before taking a year out in the US and India. She then relocated to London and began her role at the ABI in early 2011. As part of the ABI's newly formed Conduct Regulation team, she covers regulatory developments affecting general insurance, and has been leading the ABI's work on the Consumer Insurance Act.

Introduction

7A.1 The ABI has always recognised the need for a higher level of protection for retail consumers than for commercial customers. It is obvious that the insurance market and consumer expectations have changed materially since 1906. Customer service standards and regulatory requirements now go well beyond what the law actually requires. Insurers rarely, if ever, bring the strict legal position into play for consumer claims. The balance of knowledge between insurer and consumer has also changed: due to technological advances, insurers have access to a great deal more information about their potential and actual customers than 100 years ago.

Right from the start, the ABI has taken an active and close interest in the Law Commissions' review of insurance contract law, carefully considering and commenting at every step of the process. Beginning with their initial exploration of the potential for productive reform, all the way through to debating a new Bill in Parliament, and now finally to ensuring the smooth and successful implementation of a new Act of law, the ABI has been fully engaged in this historic process.

The UK insurance industry and the ABI

7A.2 Before providing an overview of the ABI's commitment to the Consumer Insurance (Disclosure and Representations) Act 2012 it is worth first giving a flavour of the wider context within which it has an impact. The UK insurance industry is the third largest in the world and the largest in Europe. It is a vital part of the UK economy, managing investments amounting to 26% of the UK's total net worth and contributing £10.4 billion in taxes to the Government. Employing over 290,000 people in the UK alone, the insurance industry is also one of this country's major exporters, with 28% of its net premium income coming from overseas business. Every day, ABI members pay out £147 million in benefits to pensioners and long-term savers as well as £60 million in general insurance claims.

The ABI and reform of the Marine Insurance Act (MIA) 1906

7A.3 The UK insurance industry has grown and changed over the course of the 20th Century. As more and more insurance products were developed and designed for personal risks, insurers gradually moved away from a strict application of the duty of disclosure towards taking on risks on the basis of answers to pre-defined questions. The ABI's Statement of General Insurance Practice (SGIP), which was first published in 1977 and revised in 1986, laid the foundation for a number of important departures from the MIA in the retail context and set down insurer obligations that strengthen consumer protection. Examples include the ban on 'basis of the contract' clauses, recognition of the limitations of what a 'reasonable' consumer would be likely to know, and the suggestion that facts considered material to the insurer should be actively requested from the consumer at policy inception.[1] Later, the creation of the Insurance Ombudsman Bureau (IOB) in 1981, the Financial Ombudsman Service (FOS) in 2001, and the introduction of FSA Insurance Conduct of Business Sourcebook (ICOBS) in 2005 added yet more layers of protection for consumers.

Despite this, or perhaps because of this, the ABI's initial response to the Law Commissions' review was cautious. We agreed that the strict legal position no longer represented market practice, that retail customers *should* have a higher degree of regulatory protection and that consumer standards already went well beyond the law. However, we highlighted the need to be clear on the rationale for new legislation.

---

1 See Appendix 2.

Better regulation

7A.4 Firstly, we weren't convinced it was necessary to introduce an alteration to the law that would involve disruption to the industry, but without any corresponding benefit to consumers over and above that already provided by regulation. We argued that the regulatory environment created by ICOBS and the FOS as well as industry good practice standards already provided sufficient protection for consumers.

We were also concerned about the cost of change. It is the role of the insurance industry to try to ensure a fair balance amongst the interests of the insured population as a whole. Any rebalance of the relationship between insurer and insured will inevitably have consequences on the cost and number of claims paid, and a corresponding impact on premium prices. Whilst this is not necessarily a bad thing, such consequences should therefore be measured. The establishment of a new regulatory regime under the Financial Services Authority in 2005 had taught firms an essential lesson about the importance of not underestimating the cost of change. It was forcefully argued that any proposals for legal reform should therefore be subject to a robust cost-benefit analysis to ensure the impact of any change would be properly understood.

The ABI had itself commissioned research to look at the costs and benefits of reforming insurance contract law. This was conducted by Pricewaterhouse-Coopers (PwC), and concluded that whilst the overall impact of the proposals was expected to be limited, there could be significant ongoing costs for the life/protection industry and for commercial general insurance product lines.[2]

Flexibility

7A.5 We were also concerned that bringing such changes into primary legislation would remove the flexibility that the industry and their customers had so far enjoyed. The dispute resolution powers of the FOS, coupled with FSA rules and industry guidance, allow market-based solutions with a greater degree of flexibility than codified reform in that they allow the insurance market to react and adapt to changed circumstances. Those actually working in the market on a daily basis are able to participate in identifying and addressing perceived problems.

---

2 ABI Research Paper 5, 'The Financial Impact of the Law Commission's Review of Insurance Contract Law', Report by PricewaterhouseCoopers LLP, November 2007, ISBN 1-903193-34-6.

Fraud

7A.6 Insurance fraud was (and is) a growing problem for insurers and consumers. It currently costs insurers over £2 billion a year, adding on average £50 to every household's annual insurance bill. It is also extremely difficult to prove. Added to this is the growing trend for consumers to compare and purchase insurance online. Behavioural attitudes towards fraud are complex, and it is understood to be easier to make a misrepresentation to a computer than to a person; evidence suggests that consumers are more willing to adjust their answers to online proposal forms in order to get a cheaper insurance quote. Any dilution of standards could therefore lead to a higher incidence of insurance fraud, so it was felt important that the right to avoid policies be protected. If the proposals were to make it easier for an insured to make fraudulent claims by putting an insurer in the position where it is too difficult or not economically viable to take on fraudsters, the inevitable result will be a higher incidence of fraud, increased insurer costs, and higher premiums for the insured population as a whole.

There was also growing unease around apparent (and unrealistic) expectations surrounding the development of technology and databases. The ABI's early input to the Law Commission expressed concern that too much emphasis was placed on the use of anti-fraud and other databases. Information obtained from enquiries of a database is not a panacea in itself. It should merely put the insurer on notice that further enquiries of an applicant should be made. Some databases are limited in the number of classes of insurance that are collected and shared. They are also not currently subscribed to by all of the personal lines market. Despite ongoing improvements in technology and data-sharing, the insured still generally has more information about their own personal circumstances than their insurer.

Making reform work

7A.7 As the Law Commissions' work progressed and their proposals were adapted and refined in response to feedback from the industry and other consultees, the ABI's position in turn evolved. In 2008, working closely with the FOS, the ABI published their Good Practice Guide on non-disclosure for long-term protection products.[3] This was developed in response to public concern, and was driven in large part by the industry. The following year, this became an ABI Code of Conduct, and a condition of membership of the ABI. This was a significant development, and received praise from the Law Commissions.

By the time they published their Final Report and draft Bill in 2009, the industry's advance adoption of their model for law reform had in effect

[3] See Appendix 7.

allowed the Law Commissions to firm up their preliminary proposals. The ABI was ready to give its support to the report, in the belief that bringing the law into line with existing practice would plug gaps not yet covered by FSA rules. ABI concern did remain over the potential rigidity of a new law, as well as any impact on the incidence of fraud. Additional concerns also surfaced around the fact that this was not the only regulatory change being undergone by the insurance industry, with the impact of the Retail Distribution Review, the *Test Achats* judgment, and the EU Solvency II Directive being some examples of increasingly tangible changes on the horizon. However, the ABI concluded that the reputation of the industry would be strengthened overall if the law of consumer insurance were to be reformed and contained in a single accessible code that met consumers' expectations. If both sides were to know their rights and obligations, this could only improve contract certainty.

7A.8 From a practical point of view, consumers in the UK today have become more and more accustomed to using comparison websites and blogs to compare insurance products and firms, and then to conduct the actual purchase online. Today's consumer does not want to spend time filling out forms, and this is a key consideration for anyone who wishes to compete in this market. A commercial balance is always being sought between the amount of information needed in order to assess a risk, with the time spent collecting this information, and the risk that the consumer may feel frustrated and walk away from the sale. Comparison websites analyse 'drop-off' rates – the points in the sales process where consumers are more likely to quit. It was important that the proposals allow for such developments.

We suggested the new law should simplify matters, reducing complexity and bureaucracy for consumer and insurer alike. It should take the form of high level principles as opposed to prescriptive rules which, it was hoped, would leave some market flexibility. It should take account of existing regulatory requirements, such as the FSA's Treating Customers Fairly (TCF) initiative, Unfair Terms in Consumer Contracts Regulation (UTCCR) 1999, and FOS' approach to non-disclosure. We also asked the Law Commission to take account of developments at EU level in the area of contract law, and to be wary of rushing on ahead with reform that might shortly be superseded by EU legislation. We were concerned about putting UK firms at a competitive disadvantage compared to their continental counterparts. Although plans to address contract law remain on the EU agenda today, they have not as yet materialised, and we do not expect any movement on this front in the near future.

7A.9 We actively supported the Bill as it travelled through Parliament, providing briefings for parliamentarians and the government about why the proposed Act should be passed. We explained the benefit of the changes to MPs, and were able to respond to specific individual enquiries from different members of both Houses. We were pleased to be able to support it when it finally received Royal Assent on 8 March 2012.

Insurers across the UK have been reviewing the questions they ask at policy inception (whether on paper, online, or by phone) and their claims handling processes in preparation for the Act becoming law on 6 April 2013. The ABI has been working with our members and the FOS on improving question sets and customer-facing wording. In December 2012 we published a number of recommendations for sales practices – telephone, online and face to face – to bring them into line with the Act. This included recommendations covering common practices around the use of, for example, assumptions, default answers, helptext or warnings. It also included recommendations for clearer wording on certain questions that the FOS have found are often misunderstood by customers, and thus more likely to lead to misrepresentations. This has been distributed to the wider insurance market, and has received a high level of industry support.

ABI's position on specific issues

7A.10 Having given a brief overview of the narrative behind the ABI's commitment to the Consumer Insurance Act, it may be useful to offer some more detailed comments regarding particular aspects of the Act itself.

Definition of consumer

7A.11 Much debate surrounded the definition of consumer as proposed by the Law Commissions. The ABI saw no reason to depart from the FSA definition of a retail customer, namely;

> 'an individual acting for purposes which are outside his trade, business or profession.'

We felt that the Law Commissions' proposed definition would create uncertainty through its reference to the idea of insurance purchased '*mainly* for purposes unrelated to his business'. In addition, having different definitions of 'consumer' creates a number of unnecessary complexities and costs for firms aiming to comply with regulations and laws. However, on balance, we were able to accept the Law Commissions' reasons for taking forward the definition that has now been incorporated in the Act.

Reasonable insured and materiality

7A.12 The SGIP had already moved away from requiring consumers to know what is in the mind of a prudent underwriter by looking instead at what a consumer could reasonably be expected to know. When the SGIP was incorporated into the FSA's general insurance rules handbook (ICOBS 7.3.6), the rules stated that the insurer:

> '... must not unreasonably reject a claim made by a customer for a disclosure of a material fact that they could not reasonably be expected to disclose, or for misrepresentation (unless negligent).'

ICOBS 4.3.2 on the other hand, and indeed insurance advising and selling standards in general, require intermediaries, when assessing the demands and needs of a customer, to explain to the customer his duty to disclose all the circumstances material to the insurance, and the consequences of failing to do so. They must also explain that the duty of disclosure runs throughout the contract, and make it clear what customers are expected to disclose.

Despite this, the 'duty of disclosure' has in reality been transformed to a requirement to answer any questions honestly. Thus the ABI was able to support the Law Commissions' proposal that the only duty on a consumer should be that of taking 'reasonable care' not to make a misrepresentation.

Proportionate remedy

7A.13 The ABI has long recognised that the remedy of avoidance for a breach of the duty of disclosure can be overly severe, especially where there is no causal link with the loss being claimed for. Whilst we believed that a combination of the SGIP, FOS and ICOBS had been able to temper the potential harshness of this remedy for many years, the ABI was supportive of the proportionate remedy as proposed by the Law Commissions.

We continue to favour avoidance as a back-stop for fraudulent misrepresentation, as set out in the Act. We welcome the fact that the bar has been set at 'deliberate or reckless' misrepresentation, as fraud is very difficult to prove. However, we do foresee difficulties in ever proving that the insured 'knew or realised that the risk was material and did not care whether it was or not'. As with the initial concerns over the potential dilution of standards, we do not want to send a message to the insured that they will get a partial claim payment even if they deliberately misrepresent, for example, their smoking habits. This would only add to the cost of premiums for the majority of honest policyholders.

We are currently considering how proportionate remedies as set out under the Act might apply to different common claims scenarios for general insurance products such as motor, property and travel. This process has uncovered a number of unexpected complexities, which expose the fact that in practical terms, the proportionate remedy may not be the best solution for all insurance product lines. In general, however, we welcome the fact that it is much fairer than pure avoidance.

Basis of the contract clause

7A.14 Under the MIA an insurer could include a declaration in the proposal form that would convert all the answers to questions into a warranty, thus allowing the insurer to avoid the whole policy on the basis of a misrepresentation, even if not material to the risk and with no connection to the loss occurring. This does not accord with consumers' reasonable expectations. As mentioned earlier, the SGIP disallowed the use of basis of the contract clauses. They may also be unfair under the UTCCR, contrary to TCF and are disallowed by the FOS. There can be no justification for the use of these in consumer insurance, and the ABI fully supports the Law Commissions' proposals to remove these for consumer insurance.

Agency

7A.15 In 2006, the ABI felt the issue over agency and distributor responsibilities was best dealt with by regulation rather than primary legislation. This was not because the ABI denied any problems in this area. On the contrary, the ABI fully accepted that there were issues that needed resolving. However, agency relationships in the general insurance market can be complex, as regulatory responsibility between intermediary and provider is not always clearly delineated or understood, either by market players, or by regulators themselves. The FSA has attempted to address such issues as and when they arise, whether through conflict of interest rules, redress requirements or disclosure rules. Given the evolutionary and complex nature of intermediary relationships, we felt it would be difficult to define these in a meaningful way within primary legislation.

Schedule II of the Act therefore, which attempts to address this topic, proved to be one of the more challenging aspects of the legislation for the ABI to grapple with. A certain level of ambiguity remains around how it fits with FSA rules. In practice, it still seems uncertain when insurers will bear the responsibility for misrepresentations caused by intermediaries.

Conclusion and future

7A.16 The ABI has played an active role in the development and formation of the Consumer Insurance Act. It is a result of a combination of external changes in the regulatory dimension, greater willingness on the part of insurers to improve their services to customers, and the collaborative and tireless efforts of the Law Commissions that has brought us to this historic point in time. Now, as insurance law is amended to reflect good practice, we hope and expect the FOS to accordingly finally be able to apply the letter of the law to their cases.

Chapter 7B Macmillan Cancer Support

Mike Hobday
Mike is Macmillan's first Director of Policy & Research, appointed to lead the charity's work in influencing Government and the NHS. Previously, he was Macmillan's Head of Campaigns, Policy & Public Affairs, where he led a multi-award winning team which had successfully pushed for free prescriptions for cancer patients, for the new cancer drugs fund and to save cancer networks from the threat of abolition. Mike's background includes over 20 years of professional public affairs work, and he joined Macmillan from the League Against Cruel Sports where he led the campaign against fox hunting. Mike has an MA from the University of Cambridge and an MBA at the University of Hertfordshire. Mike tweets for Macmillan at http://twitter.com/MikeHobday.

Introduction

7B.1 Macmillan Cancer Support is delighted to have been involved in the successful campaign to bring about essential reforms to consumer insurance contract law.

One in three of us will be diagnosed with cancer at some point in our lives and Macmillan exists to push for better cancer care and to provide practical, medical and financial support. Insurance can play a vital role in relieving cancer patients and their dependents of financial concerns. Unfortunately the law currently applicable to consumer insurance contracts is archaic and unfair. Most insurers act ethically and do not rely on their strict legal rights. However in recent years Macmillan has been concerned by the difficulties encountered by some cancer patients when making insurance claims relating to their condition – most commonly under critical illness insurance policies. These difficulties are well illustrated by the experiences of Jane Smith.[1]

1 Names changed.

Jane Smith

7B.2 Jane Smith was diagnosed with ovarian cancer in 2007. Self-employed, and with a mortgage to pay, Jane was forced to stop work whilst she was treated. Fortunately she had taken out critical illness insurance against just such an eventuality. However, her claim was rejected for alleged non-disclosure. Jane complained to the Financial Ombudsman Service ('FOS') which held that any non-disclosure was careless and ordered that the insurer should pay Jane over £40,000, the greater part of her claim.

Payment was received by Jane some thirteen months after making the claim. Deprived in the meantime of the funds, Jane was obliged to go back to work earlier than recommended by her doctor – and also had to borrow money. Writing in 2009, Jane described the strain these events caused:

> 'What shocked me was the horrific way my insurance company dealt with me over it. They branded me a liar, failed to return my calls and, to add insult to injury, in a letter to me referred to my diagnosis as breast cancer not ovarian cancer.
>
> To add to this, the anomaly in my policy the insurer was referring to didn't remotely relate to my diagnosis and it turns out even if I had answered that one question correctly I would have been covered, albeit with increased premiums.
>
> As well as the whole process being extremely stressful, I also (to be frank) didn't know whether I would be alive to be able to see it through. I had always felt extremely safe in the knowledge that, if the worst happened, I would be able to be financially secure, and that the last worry on my, or my partner's mind, would be money. That I was not able to concentrate on my health, and give myself the space to deal with my diagnosis, is something I still feel a sense of loss about.'

Macmillan was pleased to offer support and a grant to Jane. However, the latter was only necessary as a result of the rejection of her insurance claim in its entirety. Although this was permitted under the present flawed law, it breached guidance from both the FOS and the Association of British Insurers ('ABI'). Jane had prudently made provision against ill-health by purchasing critical illness cover, and it is regrettable that she did not promptly receive the benefit to which she was entitled and for which she had paid.

Sustained criticism

7B.3 Although insurers typically act decently, Jane Smith's experience is far from unique. Shortly before the Law Commissions commenced their current review of this area of law, the *Daily Mail* published statistics relating to six insurers. In 2005 these insurers rejected in total around 10% of all critical illness claims for non-disclosure, and another 10% on other grounds.[2] A sustained campaign continues to be run by the *Daily Mail* which has reported a variety of individual cases, many involving cancer patients. Much of the concern results from the perception that insurers have a perverse incentive to pore over medical records once a claim is received – since discovery of a non-disclosure or misrepresentation entitles them in law to avoid liability, even where the consumer has acted reasonably and honestly.

In 2006, a Scottish case involving a multiple sclerosis patient added weight to these concerns when it emerged that the insurer had promised to give 'careful and sympathetic consideration' to the patient's medical records when as the judge noted:

> '… the only purpose of recovering the GP records was to see whether within those notes there was any entry which might give [the insurer] grounds for avoiding or invalidating the policy under which the claim was being made.'[3]

Jeff Prestridge, *Financial Mail* personal finance editor, highlighted the damage caused to the reputation of the industry when enquiries were deferred until a claim was made:

> 'The right of insurers to "trawl" back through a claimant's medical records in this way is the unacceptable side of the insurance industry. Indeed, I think it is wholly counter-productive because by turning down valid claims, the insurance industry merely gives protection insurance a bad name. It puts most people off buying it.'[4]

In an interview with the BBC Watchdog programme on 11 April 2007, Walter Merricks, then Chief Ombudsman at the FOS, gave some idea of the potential scale of the issue when he suggested that one in five of those holding critical illness cover had policies which could in law be set aside for non-disclosure.

Perhaps in response to the growing criticism, the ABI issued two sets of guidance – 'Application Form Design' in 2006,[5] and 'Non-Disclosure and Treating Customers Fairly' in 2008.[6] The latter was upgraded to a code in January 2009, meaning that compliance became compulsory for ABI members.

---

2 Richard Dyson, 'All I could do was sob', *Daily Mail*, 7 December 2005.

3 *Valerie Cuthbertson v Friends' Provident Life Office* [2006] CSOH 74. See also Peter J Tyldesley, 'The reform of insurance contract law – why have consumers waited so long?', Journal of Insurance Research and Practice, January 2008.

4 Jeff Prestridge, 'A reputation that needs protection', *Financial Adviser*, 24 Sept 2007.

5 Appendix 6.

6 Appendix 7.

Self-regulation, regulation and ombudsman guidance

7B.4 Macmillan believes the insurance industry is to be commended for these voluntary steps, but questions whether they were ever a satisfactory alternative to law reform. There have, of course, been previous attempts to ameliorate the harshness of the law. In 1977 the insurance industry issued statements of practice, which were updated in 1986.[7] Provisions in these statements relating to non-disclosure and misrepresentation for general and pure protection insurance were later incorporated into the ICOBS section of the Handbook issued by the Financial Services Authority ('FSA').[8] However the impact was limited. The rules are relatively weak. For example, they modify rather than abolishing the duty of disclosure. And if a consumer pursues a breach of rules through the courts – whether through choice or because the matter is outside the jurisdiction of the FOS – a remedy is only available via a relatively complex action for breach of statutory duty.[9]

Since 2001 consumers have been best protected by the availability of the FOS for the resolution of disputes. Under s 228 of the Financial Services and Markets Act 2000 the FOS is obliged to make decisions under its compulsory jurisdiction 'by reference to what is, in the opinion of the ombudsman, fair and reasonable in all the circumstances of the case'. In 2005 the FOS issued guidance indicating that it would be departing from the law to apply a fairer approach to non-disclosure and misrepresentation cases.[10] It is this approach, described in detail in Chapter 4, which strongly influenced both the ABI's code 'Non-Disclosure and Treating Customers Fairly' and the Law Commissions' proposals for the reform of the law.

At the time that 'Non-Disclosure and Treating Customers Fairly' was upgraded to a code the ABI stressed that it had already led to a significant fall in the number of non-disclosure disputes referred to the FOS. It stated that in the four quarters of 2008 such referrals fell from 85, to 78, to 48 and finally to an anticipated 32. ABI spokesperson Kelly Ostler-Coyle said the upgrade was to let people know 'once and for all that this isn't optional, it is a code, it's mandatory'. She added: 'One year on, and the referral figures to the FOS have dramatically dropped since the guidance has been in place. Before it was seen as optional, which it isn't, it never has been and all our members are using what is now the code.'[11] Certainly the steps taken by the industry do appear to have led to improvement. In 2013 under the headline 'We won a better deal for customers over claims' the *Mail on Sunday* reported that 92% of critical illness claims were being met compared with 80% when it started its campaign seven years earlier.[12]

---

[7] Appendices 2 and 3.
[8] Appendix 4. See also Chapter 3.
[9] Financial Services and Markets Act 2000, s 150.
[10] Ombudsman News 46. See also Chapter 4.
[11] 'ABI and FOS tackle non-disclosure', Money Marketing, 15 January 2009
[12] Jeff Prestridge, 'I never thought my claim would be challenged', *Mail on Sunday*, 12 January 2013.

Although compliance with 'Non-Disclosure and Treating Customers Fairly' is mandatory as a condition of membership of the ABI, such membership is not itself compulsory. Since the high profile resignation of Skandia in 2008, the ABI states that its membership accounts for around 90% of premiums in the UK domestic market. In any event, whether an insurer is an ABI member or not, enforcement in individual cases will ultimately be a matter for the FOS since the code explicitly states that it 'does not purport in any way to replace the Law'.[13]

Problems therefore remain where cases simply fall outside the jurisdiction of the FOS or where the limits on awards – originally £100,000, but increased to £150,000 on 1 January 2012[14] – may be exceeded. In 2005, the *Daily Mail* covered the case of Kevin Mullane,[15] a skin cancer patient whose critical illness claim for £180,000 was rejected for alleged non-disclosure. And in 2013, it reported the experiences of Mark Cannon, whose claim for £280,000 was rejected.[16] Whatever the rights or wrongs of these cases, it is clear from them that the FOS does not offer a full solution. And, given that many critical illness insurance disputes arise when the consumer has been diagnosed with a serious medical condition, there is a further problem. An investigation by the FOS takes time. So as Jane Smith experienced, even where the FOS is able to consider a complaint and finds in favour of a cancer patient, a heavy price will be paid in the stress and financial losses caused by the inevitable delays. And as the Law Commissions have recognised, there is also a danger that this layering of bad law, FSA rules, industry codes and FOS guidance may lead to confusion – for consumers and insurers alike.

Macmillan therefore fully supported the superseding of this patchwork of measures by the Consumer Insurance (Disclosure and Representations) Act 2012. The Act will still leave a role for rules, codes and the FOS, but will establish a baseline of fair and clear law.

Action group

7B.5 Macmillan was pleased to work with a range of organisations to bring about these reforms. The informal action group included representatives of Age Concern, the British Heart Foundation, Consumer Focus, the Multiple Sclerosis Society, the Trading Standards Institute, UNLOCK and Which? as well as Peter Tyldesley (first at the University of Bedfordshire and then at the University of Manchester).

---

13 Appendix 7, paragraph 1.5.

14 FSA Handbook, DISP 3.7.4.

15 Richard Dyson, 'All I could do was sob', *Daily Mail*, 7 December 2005.

16 See footnote 12.

Group and individual campaign letters were sent to the press[17] and Macmillan also produced real case studies which could be used by journalists to demonstrate the harm being caused in practice by bad law. When the All-Party Parliamentary Group on Insurance and Financial Services indicated it would be discussing the Law Commissions' work at a meeting on 1 December 2010, we prepared a joint submission. As Jonathan Evans MP later recorded, it was at this meeting that it became clear that the ABI would support the reforms.[18]

The Consumer Insurance (Disclosure and Representations) Bill was introduced into the House of Lords under a special procedure,[19] and received its first reading on 16 May 2011. Our support for change was mentioned by Lord Sassoon on 13 June 2011 when it was moved that the Bill be considered by the Special Public Bill Committee:

> 'We believe that the Bill will shift the balance of the law in favour of the consumer. The Marine Insurance Act is, in some parts, heavily biased in favour of insurers. This Bill attempts to rectify that bias. It removes a sometimes unreasonable level of duty on the consumer so that responsibility for accurate disclosure lies somewhere between consumer and insurer. Our replacement has received support from a range of consumer groups, including Which?, the British Heart Foundation, Consumer Focus, Macmillan and Age UK.'[20]

On 10 October 2011 we submitted joint evidence to the Special Public Bill Committee.[21] And when the Bill passed to the House of Commons we submitted a joint position statement to the Public Bill Committee. Our views were mentioned by Mark Hoban MP – then Financial Secretary to the Treasury – when the Committee sat on 22 February 2012:

> 'I do not think there is very much to add to what the hon. Gentleman has said, save that the Bill is supported by Age UK, the British Heart Foundation, Consumer Focus, Macmillan Cancer Support, the Multiple Sclerosis Society, the Trading Standards Institute, the university of Manchester, Which? and UNLOCK, which demonstrates the wide support commanded by the Bill.'

Finally, on 6 March 2012, during the Third Reading debate in the House of Commons, Chloe Smith MP – then Economic Secretary to the Treasury – referred to one of our campaign letters and our position statement when urging support for the measure:

---

17 See Appendix 7.
18 Hansard, 6 March 2012, Columns 789–790.
19 See Section 2.56 for details.
20 Hansard, 13 June 2011, Column GC90.
21 HL Paper 219, Consumer Insurance (Disclosure and Representations) Bill [HL], 10 November 2011, pages 25–30.

'In October 2010, a letter with a range of signatures was sent to The Times in support of the Bill. It described the current law as designed to

> "govern face-to-face commercial insurance deals in the coffee houses of Georgian London."

... I hope that Members will accept the advice of consumer representatives who wrote to the Committee – including Age UK, the British Heart Foundation, Consumer Focus, Macmillan Cancer Support, the Trading Standards Institute, Which? and UNLOCK – and will give the Bill its Third Reading.'[22]

Looking forward

7B.6 Macmillan will maintain a keen interest in insurance as a product which can provide valuable benefits to those diagnosed with cancer. The Law Commissions' review continues, and some of the questions they have raised, such as whether damages should be awarded for losses caused by the late payment of claims, are potentially of particular significance. Problems remain. Uncertainty exists as to how insurers will deal with claims under policies which were taken out under the current law – since technically these contracts will remain subject to the existing rules on non-disclosure and misrepresentation unless and until renewed. And there is still much of consumer insurance law that is archaic, unclear and unfair.

Additionally, Macmillan is working with a number of major insurers and banks, seeking to encourage them to change their policies and procedures to more closely reflect the needs of people affected by cancer. A key objective for 2013 is for firms to start to redesign their application forms to reduce non disclosure cases by making them easier to understand and only asking for information that the purchaser is likely to have.

The Consumer Insurance (Disclosure and Representations) Act 2012 is nevertheless an excellent start to the necessary reforms. Macmillan looks forward to it being brought into force.

---

[22] Hansard, 6 March 2012, Columns 786–787.

Chapter 7C Which?

Lucy Widenka
Lucy Widenka is Financial Services Senior Advocate at Which?. She has worked on a number of campaigns to help secure a better deal for consumers, including insurance law reform, PPI and bank reform.

Introduction

7C.1 I work in the personal finance campaigns team at Which? Personal finance has been a priority for some years now for us, where we have focused on issues ranging through mis-sold endowment mortgages, payment protection insurance, pension reform and financial regulation. Many of the issues we campaign on have the potential to cause – and often have caused – massive consumer detriment. Whether it be a relatively small number of people affected in a big way (endowment mortgage mis-selling, which saw redress payouts of over £2.4bn) or millions of consumers with smaller individual claims (payment protection insurance mis-selling), when problems arise in financial services the detriment to consumers can be enormous and have long-term consequences. The unfair law currently applicable to consumer insurance is no different.

Why is reform important?

7C.2 Which? has recognised for a number of years that legal rules which were never intended for use in insurance transactions with consumers needed urgent reform. The current law is based on legislation drawn up more than 100 years ago[1] to facilitate negotiations between experts, not consumers and experts. It is difficult for consumers, who know little of insurance law, to recognise that they are under a duty to volunteer information, let alone understand what information needs to be disclosed. By 2009 consumer organisations, some insurance industry bodies and the English and Scottish Law Commissions agreed that the law needed to be updated to ensure that consumers know their rights and can be confident in the insurance product they are buying – and so that both consumers and insurers enjoy the benefits of fair law.

---

1 Marine Insurance Act 1906.

Through our discussions with other organisations, such as Macmillan Cancer Support and Age UK, we heard evidence of critical illness insurance claims being turned down because the policyholder failed to disclose a medical condition that they honestly did not consider relevant. The case of one lady, who was denied a critical illness payout for leukaemia because she had not declared a prior ear infection, illustrates the unfairness of the law as it stands and displayed to us how important it was to get the law changed. It is not adequate to rely on best practice codes established by the industry. Nor is it enough to say that the vast majority of insurance providers follow the codes, when there is potential for such huge consumer detriment such as that experienced by the lady with leukaemia. The current law risks undermining the purpose of insurance and damages confidence in the insurance industry's willingness to deliver a fair and trustworthy service.

How was Which? involved?

7C.3 Reform of the law had been discussed by Which? over a number of years and we spoke in favour of change at a conference entitled 'Protecting the consumer – is there a need for insurance law reform?' organised by Peter Tyldesley in 2004[2]. Some seventeen months later the Law Commissions started their joint review of this area of the law, a lengthy process with Issues Papers leading to Consultation Papers leading to Final Reports.

Things stepped up a pace when on 28 July 2009 Which? wrote to the shadow leaders of the House of Commons to highlight the anticipated publication in December 2009 of the Final Report of the Law Commissions on disclosure, representations and basis of the contract clauses in consumer insurance.[3] We urged them to press the Government to include this important reform in its legislative plans. The Law Commissions had been working towards their proposals for three years and had consulted widely. And a short draft Bill was to be included in their final report. So we believed that implementing the legislation should be straightforward. It was nevertheless important to try and get cross-party support for reform to ensure as smooth a process as possible for the Bill.

Which? attended a meeting of consumer groups and charities hosted by Peter Tyldesley at the Institute of Advanced Legal Studies on 27 August 2009. The meeting discussed ways in which the anticipated recommendations for consumer insurance law reform could be supported. On 23 October 2009 Which? hosted a further roundtable event with consumer representatives to set out a plan to press for urgent change to the law and gather intelligence about consumers who had been turned down for insurance payouts as a result of the loopholes in the law.

---

2 17 May 2004.

3 'Consumer Insurance Law: Pre-Contract Disclosure and Misrepresentation', Cm 7758.

A letter from HM Treasury dated 29 July 2010 seeking the views of interested parties on the Bill gave us the impetus to step up our campaign. With the support of consumer groups from a broad range of backgrounds, including MoneySavingExpert.com, we set about raising the issue within Parliament, and also in the media. A few journalists have shown a marked and very welcome interest in an issue which is often difficult to explain simply, and this helped to keep the issue in the news. A joint letter published in the *Financial Times* on 2 October 2010 and one published from Peter Vicary-Smith, Chief Executive of Which?, in the *Times* on 7 October 2010 no doubt helped to ensure that this somewhat 'techie' insurance issue was shown to be important and worth keeping on the parliamentary reform agenda. The strength in our argument was to use real-life stories of people who had been refused payouts – such as the lady with leukaemia and the unrelated ear infection, or the heart attack victim who made a claim under his critical illness policy which was rejected due to undisclosed and unconnected problems with his back and neck.

All Party Parliamentary Group

7C.4 As momentum was once again building up around reform, the All Party Parliamentary Group for Insurance and Financial Services ('APPGIFS'), decided to hold a short inquiry into the issue. David Hertzell from the English Law Commission and Peter Tyldesley were invited to give evidence to the Group on 1 December 2010. Peter was keen to involve a consumer body at the evidence session, and so I attended the panel too. In advance of the session, we thought it worthwhile to put together a joint written briefing for members of APPGIFS from the broad range of consumer bodies who were calling for reform[4]. The briefing reflected our key messages around the adverse impact that lack of reform was having on individual consumers, and the need to reform the law as a matter of priority. It pulled together some case studies the various organisations had gathered (including those referenced above).

We re-iterated the case we put together in our written evidence at the oral evidence session, and were delighted that the Association of British Insurers, who had up until then abstained from publically supporting or disagreeing with the proposed Bill, announced that they would be supportive of the proposals. This was a major step towards reform, as to pass the Bill via special procedures[5] set out for 'non-controversial' bills there would need to be sufficient and strong evidence that the Bill would pass without objection.

---

4 Age UK, British Heart Foundation, Consumer Focus, Macmillan Cancer Support, MS Society, Trading Standards Institute, Peter Tyldesley (then at the University of Bedfordshire), UNLOCK and Which?.

5 See Section 2.56.

Following the inquiry, APPGIFS published its report, supporting the Law Commissions' Bill and so helping to pave the way for its introduction to parliament.

Next steps

7C.5 As a campaigner in financial services, I have found consumer insurance law reform to be an eyeopening and yet ultimately rewarding experience – being able to see a clear and worthwhile goal in an often complex and frustrating area of campaigning. Looking back through various files at Which? relating to insurance law reform, I uncovered a letter from 22 years ago from the then head of our in-house legal team to an MP who had successfully secured a place in a Private Members' Bill Ballot. The letter urges the MP to consider taking up the cause for a Bill based on the English Law Commission's draft proposals from 1980. It states:

> 'How can the consumer possibly know what might affect the judgement of a prudent insurer? He or she has no expert knowledge. And surely the consumer is entitled to conclude that what the insurers haven't asked for in their proposal form matters they don't need to know.'

Well, quite. And how telling that all these years later, the same arguments for reform were still being borne out. One doesn't like to think about how many consumers since 1980 have fallen foul of the loophole, and how their lives may have been profoundly affected on an individual level as a result of it – but thankfully, with reform at last on its way, consumers can feel safe in the knowledge that they will not fall foul of an archaic and out-of-date law any more.

Chapter 7D The Consumer Insurance (Disclosure and Representations) Act: Some (Lateral) Thoughts of a Claims Lawyer

Richard Buttle

After 27 years in private practice, for most of that time as Insurance Litigation Partner in a City of London law firm, Richard Buttle joined Swiss Re in 1998, initially as Legal Services Manager, and more recently focusing exclusively on claims as Claims Counsel. In that role he has worked closely with the English Law Commission in relation to these reforms.

A brief overview

7D.1 It is perhaps a fitting tribute to its work that the Consumer Insurance (Disclosure and Representations) Act 2012 largely (although by no means entirely) codifies what has been the FOS's approach to life in this context over recent years. Faced with old law that was almost universally perceived as outdated, capable of being harshly applied towards consumers, and in short, generally not fit for purpose, the FOS over time developed its own body of 'jurisprudence' to address and at the same time mitigate the inadequacy and potential harshness of the old law: much of which 'jurisprudence' has now been enshrined in the Act.

More recently, the Life and Health Protection industry, working closely with the FOS, embraced in advance (and in certain material respects went beyond) the Law Commissions' model for law reform, in the ABI 'Code of Practice on Non-Disclosure and Treating Customers Fairly' of January 2009.

All that said, it is instructive to look beyond the text of the Act to the Law Commissions' preparatory and consultative works that preceded it: specifically, at the outset of their deliberations, their Joint Consultation Paper of June 2007 ('the JCP 2007'), and their Joint Report of December 2009 ('the

JR 2009'): not least because these serve to highlight certain as yet unresolved issues as to how the FOS will choose to conduct itself in response to the new legal landscape going forward.

The FOS approach going forward

7D.2 Possibly first and foremost amongst these issues is the extent to which the FOS will henceforth consider itself as constrained to follow that new legal landscape: on the basis that there is an inherent difficulty in suggesting that such law is either unfair or unreasonable.

For the purposes of their determination of complaints the primary consideration will of course remain what the FOS considers 'fair and reasonable in all of the circumstances of the case'. The FSA Handbook (at DISP 3.6.4) goes on to state, however, that for those purposes the FOS '… will take into account … relevant law … codes of practice …' and the like. If the decision of the FOS in any way misinterprets the law, and/or a relevant code of practice, and/or other material consideration, it will have arguably failed to take it into account, and will to that extent be susceptible to proceedings for judicial review. But otherwise the FOS enjoys relative complete freedom of movement in its decision making.

However, the Law Commissions' dialogue with the FOS, specifically as evidenced by the JCP 2007 and JR 2009, provides some grounds for cautious optimism in this regard.

In the JCP 2007 (at 3.71) the Law Commissions stated as follows:

> 'We believe that it is undesirable that the FOS is routinely obliged to replace the most fundamental principles of insurance contract law with its own approach. Discretion is a valuable supplement to legal rules, but it is a poor substitute for them, for two reasons.
>
> (1) The FOS may develop its approach without public debate or wide consultation.
>
> (2) As the FOS is able to change its approach at will, there is a continuing degree of uncertainty.'

These sentiments were echoed by the FOS itself when writing to the Law Commissions for the purposes of the JR 2009 as follows (as quoted at 3.42):

> 'Our preference is for our decisions to be based on law and for our decisions on what is "fair and reasonable" to coincide with the law. It is much easier to defend and justify our decisions when they are consistent with the legal position and it is advantageous to all our potential users if our decisions can be predicted …'

Finally, when responding to ABI concerns in this regard in July 2009, the Law Commissions stated that:

> '... the FOS has assured us that it will start on the basis that the recent will of Parliament, as enshrined in the Act, would form the basis of what is considered fair and reasonable.'

The relevance of all of this is arguably not confined to the strict content of the Act alone; not least because the Law Commissions conducted an exhaustive review of the directly relevant wider legal landscape in which all of this sits, only effectively to reaffirm the continued validity of that wider law as it stands.

FOS declining to entertain complaints in favour of the courts

7D.3 The FSA Handbook (at DISP 3.3.4 (10)) states that 'The Ombudsman may dismiss a complaint without considering its merits if he considers that ... it would be more suitable ... to be dealt with by a court, arbitration or another complaints scheme.'

Typical circumstances in which that discretionary entitlement has arisen for consideration historically have included cases turning on disputed evidence from a third party (eg a broker, former salesperson, or other representative of a firm/insurer) who needs to be cross-examined. In submissions to the Law Commissions for the purposes of the JCP 2007 (as quoted at 3.59), the FOS stated that it has in the past been reluctant to exercise this power, as to do so would force complainants back into the courts, and result in their case there being decided 'upon an entirely different basis ... that we do not regard as fair or reasonable or as representing good practice in the sector': ie within the terms of the old law, which was then (but no longer is) significantly different from the FOS's approach to complaints.

With the advent of the new law it remains to be seen whether the FOS going forward may be more disposed to consider exercising that power than they have perhaps been historically.

The conduct categories – dishonesty and the onus of proof

7D.4 For the purposes of the JCP 2007 the Law Commissions conducted a detailed review of around 200 ombudsman final decisions involving allegations of misrepresentation or non-disclosure, and (at 3.41) observed that 'It was clear from our survey that ombudsmen are reluctant to accuse consumers of dishonesty.' Those findings accord with the industry's experience historically.

Again (at 4.56) of the JCP 2007 the Law Commissions stated that:

> 'We think that it is right to describe a person who has deliberately or recklessly given incorrect information to another, knowing or not caring that the other may act on it, as not acting "honestly", but we do not want to import criminal definitions or standards of proof.'

The Law Commissions' concerns in this regard may in part have been driven by the fact that some confusion had arisen in the past out of certain judicial dicta suggesting that the standard of proof for the purposes of civil proceedings may vary with the gravity of the misconduct alleged, or even the seriousness of the consequences for the person concerned: ie that a higher standard of proof was required for the purposes of dishonest than negligent non-disclosure.

That confusion has since largely been resolved in The House of Lords' (as it then was) decision of *In Re B (Children)* ([2008] UKHL 35) in which Lord Hoffmann made it quite clear that 'there is only one (binary) rule of law, namely that the occurrence of the fact in issue must be proved to have been more probable than not (and that) ... Common sense, not law, requires that in deciding this question regard should be had, to whatever extent appropriate, to inherent probabilities.' – ie that the standard of proof on the balance of probabilities is not in fact a potentially movable feast (as was previously thought to be the case) according to the gravity of the misconduct alleged, but a constant.

Leaving aside regard for personal and social sensitivities, the FOS's reluctance historically to find dishonesty present may in part have stemmed from the above confusion as to the standard of proof at law, and in part may have been driven by a perhaps understandable reluctance stemming from the fact that in all but a very few cases complaints are considered on the basis of written submissions alone. Whatever may have been the situation in the past, however, with the advent of the new law, it is perhaps not unreasonable to hope that in appropriate cases where an insurer alleges dishonesty, the FOS might be more disposed than historically to consider exercising its entitlement to dismiss a complaint as more suitable to be dealt with by a court of law.

Certain other 'legacy' industry/FOS issues hopefully now resolved

7D.5 There have also been certain areas in which the FOS's approach to life historically markedly differed from the Law Commissions' model for law reform, as now enshrined in the Act, although the FOS have recently unequivocally confirmed that these no longer apply. They include the following:

- The test for materiality. Under the old law, misrepresentation/non-disclosure was of course only actionable if it was material, in that it would have influenced the judgment of a hypothetical prudent underwriter. That concept has not been preserved: and it is now enough for the insurer to be able to show that it was induced by the misrepresentation, and that a reasonable consumer would not have made it. The insurer does not have to show that the misrepresentation/non-disclosure would also have influenced other underwriters in the market.

- With the abandonment of the hypothetical prudent underwriter test it is understood that the FOS have also now abandoned their historical practice of on occasion seeking the hypothetical views of other insurers.
- The Act makes it quite clear that the standard of care is generally the objective one of the reasonable consumer, and that that test does not take into account the particular characteristics or circumstances of the consumer except to the extent that the insurer was or ought to have been aware of them.
- Schedule 2 of the Act helpfully provides a non-exhaustive list of factors that may tend to show whether an agent is acting for the consumer or the insurer. Furthermore, subject to the matters addressed at Schedule 2 clause 2, a general presumption is applied to the effect that the agent is acting as the consumer's agent.

The way forward

7D.6 The Act is the product of what has perhaps unusually been almost universal consensus as to the need for law reform, and as such has been eagerly awaited by all stakeholders. In overhauling and updating the law it has gone a long way in significantly simplifying and at the same time harmonising the labyrinthine patchwork of statute and case law and regulatory/FOS/industry guidance, codes and practice that have applied in this context. In so doing it will hopefully provide a firm foundation for more fairness in terms of consumer outcomes before the courts, and greater certainty and predictability for the consumer and industry alike before the FOS.

Chapter 7E Forming the Law on Consumer Insurance: Creating a Strong Foundation for Professionalism

Laurence Baxter
Laurence Baxter is Head of Policy and Research at the Chartered Insurance Institute (CII). He has extensive experience of leading research and policy projects on issues relevant to Government and the financial services sector; and successfully established a dedicated policy influence and thought leadership programme for the CII where he leads on several projects including responding to the insurance contract law reforms. Prior to joining the CII, Laurence was Senior Policy Advisor for the Council of Mortgage Lenders, and before this was the financial services campaigns policy adviser for the consumer group Which?. Previous roles include being a policy adviser to the Canadian government and later to HM Treasury.

Support for the Law Commissions' work

7E.1 The CII welcomed and supported the Law Commissions' review of the law covering misrepresentation, non-disclosure and breach of warranty in consumer insurance contracts. We believe that the law governing insurance contracts in this area needed reform and modernisation in line with current best practice and to reflect the regulatory landscape.

The Marine Insurance Act 1906 may have been a worthy craft for its time but it was clearly in need of a refit. The reforms will bring greater clarity around claims-handling and improve public trust and confidence in the general insurance sector.

Failure in the legal clarity of service to consumers has had a direct impact on the industry's reputation. The Consumer Insurance (Disclosure and Representations) Act 2012 will contribute to improved peace of mind that a claim will be paid even if a consumer makes an innocent mistake. Greater clarity over the handling of claims by insurers will result in improved consumer confidence in the insurance industry, a more proportionate response to negligent misrepresentation and a targeted approach to cases of deliberate insurance fraud. It will also offer a continuing encouragement to improve clarity and questions in the underwriting process.

By distinguishing deliberate misrepresentations from honest mistakes made by customers, the changes strike a sensible balance between protecting consumers with limited financial capability and protecting insurers from proportionate financial loss due to carelessness or even fraud.

Most importantly, as a result of these changes, the underlying contract law will provide a modern and stable foundation on which higher standards of practitioner professional knowledge and ethical conduct can be built in line with the public interest.

7E.2 The process to bring about these reforms was lengthy as it was iterative, with much discussion from various quarters of the market. The central issue discussed concerned developing a range of remedies proportionate to the nature of the non-disclosure or misrepresentation. A second issue emerged on proposed reforms to the law of agency relationship in relation to intermediaries with respect to customers or providers on disclosing information. We will look at each in turn.

Proportionate remedies

7E.3 Under the 1906 Act, insurance contracts were made under the principle of utmost good faith. This means that the insurer relied on the integrity of information provided by the policyholder to assess risks, and if any information emerged at any time that this was not robust, then the insurer could void the entire insurance contract, reject any claims and decline to do business with that customer again.

The result was a propensity for some insurers to wait for the claim stage before any underwriting is undertaken. The law provided an incentive for insurers to go back and look for any evidence of non-disclosure or misrepresentation on the part of the policyholder. If any evidence of either emerged, then the insurer could decide not to honour the claim, leaving customers without a payout. In the words of Jeff Prestridge, Personal Finance Editor in the *Financial Mail on Sunday*:

> 'The right of insurers to "trawl" back through a claimant's medical records in this way is the unacceptable side of the insurance industry. Indeed, I think it is wholly counter-productive because by turning down valid claims, the insurance industry merely gives protection insurance a bad name. It puts most people off buying it.'[1]

---

1 'A Reputation that needs protection' *Financial Adviser*, 24 Sep 2007.

The biggest problem was that there was a significant lack of clarity in the consumer's mind about what constitutes material information to be disclosed, so the likelihood of such avoidance could be very high. Some material information might be quite obvious – the serviceability of a burglar alarm in a home and contents policy for example. However, other facts are less evidently material. Moreover, the insurer not asking for disclosure was no defence against non-disclosure. So the onus lay squarely on the customer to know what needed to be disclosed, not on the insurer to ask appropriate questions.

Revising this law was therefore essential to improving consumer trust and confidence. The 2012 Act sets out 'a duty of the consumer to take reasonable care not to make a misrepresentation to the insurer' and establishes a set of proportionate remedies insurers are able to use:

- **Deliberately or recklessly misleading:** insurers remain entitled to avoid a policy and reject a claim if they can prove the policyholder provided information knowing it was untrue or misleading – or not caring whether or not it was so.
- **Honest and reasonable:** if a misrepresentation is deemed a reasonable mistake based on the type of insurance contract and the clarity of the insurer's questions, then an otherwise valid claim must be paid.
- **Careless misrepresentation:** if the consumer fails to take sufficient care to understand what the insurer wanted to know or to check the facts, then the insurer is able to apply a 'compensatory remedy'. This is based on what the insurer would have done had it known the correct information, such as applying relevant exclusions, or a proportionate claims settlement based on the increased premium that would have been charged.

This approach is exactly what we called for. For misrepresentation or non-disclosure, the 2012 Act introduces a range of remedies that are proportionate to the nature of the offence. To void the contract, the insurer would have to prove that the misrepresentation was deliberate or reckless. On the other hand, customers who are careless warrant proportionate action and those who make innocent mistakes should face no penalty.

Law of agency relationship

7E.4 The second element of reform concerned the law of agency relationship when an intermediary is involved in the consumer insurance transaction. Clearly this is much more complex because technically an intermediary may have greater knowledge of the insurance risks involved and can help the customer disclose the correct information.

However existing law under the old Marine Insurance Act 1906 was clearly not designed for mass market consumer contracts. The onus was on the consumer to ensure the insurer received full and correct information. This arrangement may be appropriate where the intermediary is acting on behalf of the customer, but even then there are no safeguards reflecting the consumer's more limited knowledge. It is definitely not appropriate if the intermediary is receiving a commission from the insurer.

During the 2007 consultation, the Law Commission proposed changing the law of agency relationship so that for the purposes of gathering information, the intermediary acted as agent of the insurer. A starting point in the argument for doing this was the view that whilst consumers are clear with single-tied and fully independent intermediaries, there exists significant uncertainty around parts of the market where the party for whom the intermediary is acting is unclear. This is correct, but changing the law of agency relationship would add more complexity to this issue, not less.

Any law reform in this area must instead focus on clarifying the distinction between independent and restricted advice, in line with current regulatory initiatives such as the Financial Services Authority's reform of the retail investment advice sector, and the move towards enhanced professionalism amongst financial advisers.

Consumers do need to be better informed about their legal rights. This can be addressed through the following measures:

- Clarification statements that summarise the law of agency relationship and remind consumers that their signature indicates their approval of the information in the statement. We believe these would be in line with the industry best practice, such as the Association of British Insurer's application form design for life and health protection insurance.
- Ensuring that the sales process on insurance includes reference to reminding customers of the implications of the law of agency. This would involve applying the principles of business including treating customers fairly and suitability into the insurance conduct of business review that is currently under way.
- Significant further work is necessary to clarify the intermediary/agency relationship, especially the complexities around confidentiality and changes in broker appointments identified in the British Insurance Brokers' Association consultation response.

The 2012 Act amends the law of agency relationship between insurance intermediaries, insurers and policyholders (for the purposes of gathering information, not other aspects of the law of agency relationship). The intermediary is presumed to be an agent of the insurer where it is acting in its capacity as an appointed representative or has express authority to collect information or enter into the contract on behalf of the insurer. While this is still not ideal, because customers will face the difficulty of bringing a claim against an independent intermediary that acts deliberately or recklessly, this is a clearer relationship that is consistent with other regulatory practices as we had called for in the consultation.

Raised standards of intermediary professionalism

7E.5 Many of the issues raised in this aspect of the Law Commissions' work could be addressed in part through greater professionalism amongst the intermediaries themselves. The Law Commissions did note a need for improved market discipline, and we believe the best way to bring this about is by raising the bar in the sector so that all advisers selling insurance policies must adhere to the appropriate standards of professionalism and conduct.

Our view stems from a desire to improve customers' access to good quality advice which would increase public trust and confidence in the industry. We believe this outlook is largely shared by a sizeable representation of industry practitioners and observers. The current level of professional standards within the financial advice sector is not on par with other professions such as accountancy and the law, and is therefore not sufficient to deal with some of the issues raised by the Law Commissions in their consultation exercise.

The CII has been striving to raise professional standards. This might be through regulatory developments, such as for retail investment advisers in the case of the Retail Distribution Review which came into force on 1 January 2013; but more importantly through voluntary initiatives in the general insurance profession. Our approach throughout the process has been to help to build consensus within the industry around positions that will increase professionalism, build a more confident and trusted market as viewed by the public, and ultimately ensure there is an expanding market and increasing numbers of consumers with access to quality advice. That is the prize for both general insurance and retail investments.

Chapter 7F Trading Standards Institute

Ron Gainsford OBE

Ron joined the Trading Standards Institute as its Chief Executive in February 2002. He welcomed and has enjoyed the opportunity to help lead the trading standards profession, the Institute and its not-for-profit companies after spending a decade at the heart of local government's national and international coordinating machinery. His professional background is in trading standards and local government with broad experience in working in a variety of local authorities and in UK, EU and international regulation of trading standards and associated consumer protection issues. He is well versed in European and international collaboration and has represented UK interests on several European enforcement and influencing groups involving consumer protection counterparts and other professionals from member states, EU institutions and other overseas agencies. He has been an adviser to a number of overseas governments on public protection and market surveillance issues. Ron was made a Fellow of the Institute in 1999 for his services to trading standards and awarded the OBE in 2010 for services to consumers and to business. He was given freedom of the City of London in 2008 and is a member of the World Traders livery company.

Introduction

7F.1 The Trading Standards Institute ('TSI') welcomes the fairer rights for consumers that will be introduced by the Consumer Insurance (Disclosure and Representations) Act 2012 and is pleased to have been part of the campaign to bring about these changes.

TSI is a training and membership organisation that has represented the interests of the Trading Standards profession since 1881, both nationally and internationally. We aim to raise the profile of the profession while working towards fairer, better informed and safer consumer and business communities.

Insurance law has long been regarded as unduly weighted in favour of insurers and so capable of causing injustice, particularly where consumers are involved. In 1997 a report on consumer insurance law from the National

Consumer Council recommended a range of reforms.[1] Regrettably it met with the same fate as the reports of the Law Reform Committee in 1957[2] and the English Law Commission in 1980[3] – it was simply never implemented.

TSI was encouraged when the English and Scottish Law Commissions took the decision in 2005 to undertake a new review of this problematic area. By 2009 it was clear that the Law Commissions had developed sound proposals for the reform of the law relating to disclosure, representations and basis of the contract clauses in consumer insurance contracts. A report and draft Bill was awaited. TSI concluded that enactment of such a measure would be advantageous for consumers and insurers alike. Consumers would gain clearer and fairer rights, and insurers would benefit through an increase in confidence in the insurance industry. We therefore organised a meeting of the All Party Parliamentary Group for Consumer Affairs and Trading Standards ('APPG-CATS') at the House of Commons on 29 May 2009 to discuss the need for change.[4]

APPG

7F.2 APPG-CATS has six main aims:

- To increase the awareness and raise the level of debate in both Houses of Parliament and Government on issues concerning consumer affairs and the trading standards profession.
- To encourage members of the APPG-CATS to become advocates on issues that affect consumers and the trading standards profession.
- To inform MPs and Peers of the key issues affecting consumers and the trading standards profession and encourage them to raise issues during relevant parliamentary sessions.
- To foster dialogue between the Group and key stakeholders in the fields of consumer affairs and trading standards.
- To encourage stakeholders (both individuals and organisations) to support and attend relevant APPG-CATS meetings.
- To endeavour to collaborate with other All-Party Parliamentary Groups on issues of mutual interest.

---

1 'Insurance Law Reform – The consumer case for a review of insurance law', National Consumer Council, May 1997.

2 5th Report of the Law Reform Committee, 'Conditions and exceptions in insurance policies', Cmnd 62 (1957).

3 Law Commission's Report No 104, 'Insurance Law – Non-disclosure and breach of warranty', Cmnd 8064 (1980).

4 TSI provides the Secretariat for APPG-CATS.

The meeting on 29 May 2009 was attended by a number of MPs and Peers – including APPG-CATS chairman, Austin Mitchell MP, and incoming TSI President, Baroness Crawley. Also present was Lord Borrie, who was later to make an invaluable contribution as a member of the Special Public Bill Committee which considered the Consumer Insurance (Disclosure and Representations) Bill. Attendance would perhaps have been higher but for the febrile atmosphere in the House of Commons – this was, memorably, the day on which Michael Martin MP resigned as Speaker.

TSI was represented at the meeting by a small team headed by our deputy chief executive, Paul Ramsden. A briefing note prepared on behalf of TSI by Peter Tyldesley of the University of Manchester had been circulated in advance.[5] Representatives from the Association of British Insurers ('ABI'), the Financial Ombudsman Service ('FOS'), HM Treasury, the English Law Commission, Macmillan Cancer Support and Which? were present by invitation.

The meeting was chaired by Lord Borrie who asked David Hertzell, Law Commissioner at the English Law Commission, Peter Hinchliffe, a Lead Ombudsman at the FOS, and Peter Tyldesley to speak. These short addresses were followed by general discussion. Although the meeting took place before publication of the Law Commissions' report, David Hertzell was able to confirm that a draft Bill had been produced and was just 10 clauses in length.[6] With the exception of some hesitation expressed by the ABI, the meeting was firmly in favour of reform. As recorded in the minutes APPG-CATS resolved to push for change:

> 'Austin Mitchell MP concluded the meeting by saying that the Group would send a copy of the Minutes to the Minister with the hope that the 10 clause Bill could be included in the forthcoming Queen's Speech.'[7]

Campaigning

7F.3 TSI's campaign was led by David Sanders, then TSI Lead Officer for Civil Law and former TSI Chairman, and Jessica Tangye, then our Policy Officer. Suzanne Kuyser, our Director of Communications, Irja Howie and Lizi Piggins were also heavily involved.

As recorded by Macmillan Cancer Support in Chapter 7B, TSI was a member of an informal action group[8] of consumer groups and charities. We

---

5 See Appendix 9.
6 The Bill was ultimately enacted with 12 sections – see Appendix 14.
7 See Appendix 9.
8 The other members being Age Concern, the British Heart Foundation, Consumer Focus, Macmillan Cancer Support, the Multiple Sclerosis Society, Peter Tyldesley, UNLOCK and Which?.

signed a joint letter to the *Financial Times*,[9] and submitted joint position statements to the All Party Parliamentary Group on Insurance and Financial Services, the Special Public Bill Committee in the House of Lords and the Public Bill Committee in the House of Commons. Our support for the Bill was mentioned by Mark Hoban MP – then Financial Secretary to the Treasury – when the latter Committee sat on 22 February 2012.

TSI also ran an individual campaign. The meeting of APPG-CATS attracted some attention and shortly afterwards Paul Ramsden was interviewed on You & Yours on BBC Radio 4.[10] In October 2009 we published a policy brief: 'Consumer Insurance Law'.[11] Over the course of two years we also issued a series of five press releases: 'Fairness for Consumers', 'Consumers Paying the Price for Antiquated Insurance Law', 'Victory for Consumers is One Step Closer in Campaign for Law Reform', 'Campaign progress' and 'Change to archaic law overcomes first hurdle'.[12] We were delighted when the last of these releases led Andrew Penam and Nick Sommerlad, the *Daily Mirror*'s Investigations Team, to devote their entire blog for that day to the issue of consumer insurance law reform.[13] David Sanders was also quoted on the website of a leading insurance aggregator – confused.com[14] – and in Solicitors Journal.[15]

Special Public Bill Committee

7F.4 Perhaps most crucially, TSI became involved when the Consumer Insurance (Disclosure and Representations) Bill was under consideration in the House of Lords. Eight amendments were tabled. We were particularly concerned by Amendment 1 which was tabled by Lord Hodgson and read:

> 'It is the duty of the insurer to make it clear whether they comply with industry codes of practice.'

Whilst undoubtedly well-meaning, there were three difficulties with this proposed provision:

- Its application is unclear – which codes, and issued by whom? Would it be limited to those documents described as codes, or would it extend to statements, agreements, guidance and the like? The Association of

9 Appendix 8.
10 BBC Radio 4, You & Yours, 11 June 2009.
11 http://www.tradingstandards.gov.uk/policy/consumerinsurancelaw.cfm (as of 21 January 2013).
12 Issued May 2009, 4 June 2009, 14 December 2009, December 2010 and 17 May 2011 respectively.
13 http://blogs.mirror.co.uk/investigations/2011/05/hope-for-consumers-penalised-b.html (as of 21 January 2013).
14 Chris Torney, 'Ministers bid to stop insurers rejecting claims', 20 May 2011. http://www.confused.com/insurance/articles/ministers-bid-to-stop-insurers-rejecting-claims (as of 21 January 2013).
15 Peter J Tyldesley, 'Pearls of Wisdom', Solicitors Journal, SJ 155/27 12 July 2011.

British Insurers alone issues a plethora of codes.[16] Many have nothing to do with consumers. Others may have no connection with the types of insurance offered by the insurer in question or with the policy at hand.

- What would be the consequences of an insurer breaching this provision? If an insurer failed to make a representation that would potentially be a breach of statutory duty, but the Act would need to make it clear whether this gives private law rights to any consumer affected. Should an insurer misrepresent that it complies with the codes then the consumer might conceivably have the right to avoid the policy – but this would be of little value; what the consumer would presumably want is for the policy to remain in force and the insurer to act in accordance with the code.
- This uncertainty could act as a disincentive for insurers to create or maintain codes.

TSI was also conscious that the stakes were high. The Bill had been introduced through the Special Procedure described in Chapter 2.[17] A clear commitment regarding this procedure was given by the House of Lords Procedure Committee in 2008:

> 'If in the course of proceedings on the bill it becomes clear, for example during debate on second reading, that it does after all contain controversial provisions, the new procedures will be halted and it will then be for the Government business managers to decide whether or not to proceed with the bill under the normal procedures applying to any other public bill.'

If carried, an ill-advised amendment could lead the ABI to withdraw its support for the Bill, leading it to become regarded as controversial. The Bill would then be removed from the procedure. Given the pressure on Parliamentary time it was possible that it would be lost in its entirety.

Whilst recognising that Amendment 1 was well intended, David Sander wrote to the Committee suggesting that it was undesirable. Peter Tyldesley did likewise. Their comments were acknowledged in good humour by Lord Hodgson when the Committee met on 10 November 2011:

> 'I am sure the Minister will say, because he will also have received a copy of this letter, that we got a real savaging from Mr David Sanders, the principal trading standards officer from the Vale of Glamorgan. Rowing in behind him to give us an equally big beating is Peter Tyldesley. They have pointed out that this will add uncertainty to the law. That is the essence of their case.'

---

16 See Appendix 13.
17 See Section 2.56.

After discussion within the Committee, Amendment 1 was withdrawn.[18]

What next?

7F.5 TSI understands that the Consumer Insurance (Disclosure and Representations) Act 2012 is likely to be brought into force on 6 April 2013. It will address the worst flaws in consumer insurance law. However, other weaknesses remain. The Law Commissions' review of insurance law continues until the end of the year and is expected to result in a final report on additional issues of concern to consumers – insurable interest, warranties, post-contractual good faith, damages for late payment of claims and others. TSI very much hopes that this will lead to further improvements in this vital area of law.

[18] See Appendix 12 for a full transcript.

Chapter 8 Insurance Law Reform: Where Next?

Tamara Goriely
Tamara Goriely manages the commercial and common law team at the Law Commission and has been involved in the insurance contract law review since its inception in 2006. She is a qualified barrister who has worked for a variety of organisations including a law centre and the National Consumer Council. From 1996 to 2002 she was a senior research fellow at the Institute of Advanced Legal Studies, carrying out empirical research into the lawyers and the courts, including studies of the Woolf reforms.

Introduction

8.1 The Consumer Insurance (Disclosure and Representations) Act 2012 is only one part of a much wider review of insurance contract law. The Law Commission and Scottish Law Commission set up their joint review in 2006 – and it is scheduled to continue until December 2013. Since 2006, the review has produced nine issues papers and three more substantial consultation papers.

The first consultation paper, in July 2007, looked not only at the duty of disclosure in consumer insurance, but also at the duty of disclosure in business insurance and at the law of warranties.[1] The response showed a consensus for reform in consumer insurance, but little agreement on how to proceed in business insurance. The Law Commissions said that they would give priority to consumer insurance law reform and return to the issue of business insurance at a later date.

The second consultation paper, in December 2011, looked at four further issues: damages for late payment, remedies for fraud, insurable interests; and policies and premiums in marine insurance.[2]

---

1 'Insurance Contract Law: Misrepresentation, Non-Disclosure and Breach of Warranty by the Insured' (2007) Law Commission Consultation Paper No 182; Scottish Law Commission Discussion Paper No 134 ('the 2007 Consultation Paper').

2 'Insurance Contract Law: Post Contract Duties and other Issues' (2011) Law Commission Consultation Paper No 201; Scottish Law Commission Discussion Paper No 152 ('the 2011 Consultation Paper').

After the successful passage of the Consumer Insurance Bill, the Law Commissions then returned to the issues of disclosure in business in insurance and warranties, publishing a third consultation paper in June 2012.[3] The hope was that, with less radical proposals, a sufficient consensus could be found to permit another Law Commission Bill to proceed through the special procedure.

The Law Commissions have agreed to publish a final report and draft Bill by the end of 2013. The schedule would then allow a second insurance law Bill to be passed in the 2014/15 session, before the date set for the next general election in May 2015.

8.2 There are six potential subjects to be dealt with in that Bill. Some affect only business insurance, while some affect all insurance contracts (both for consumers and businesses). The six topics are:

- Disclosure in business insurance;
- Warranties;
- Section 17 and remedies for fraud;
- Damages for late payment;
- Insurable interest;
- Policies and premiums in marine insurance.

This chapter outlines each issue in turn. It sets out the nature of the problem and briefly summarises the solutions proposed by the Law Commissions in their consultation papers. It is important to stress, however, that the Law Commissions have not yet made any final recommendations. They will need to consider the consultation responses carefully. Reforms can only be included in the Bill if they are sufficiently uncontroversial to be suitable for the special procedure, and if resources can be found for the necessary drafting.

The duty of disclosure in business insurance

8.3 Section 18 of the Marine Insurance Act 1906 places an onerous duty on a business policyholder. Under section 18(1) a policyholder must disclose 'every material circumstance' which it knows or ought to know 'in the ordinary course of business'. Under section 18(2), a material circumstance is defined widely as 'every circumstance which would influence the judgment of a prudent insurer in fixing the premium, or determining whether he will take the risk'. The statute does not require the insurer to ask questions or

---

3 'Insurance Contract Law: The Business Insured's Duty of Disclosure and the Law of Warranties' (2012) Law Commission Consultation Paper No 204; Scottish Law Commission Discussion Paper No 155 ('the 2012 Consultation Paper').

indicate what it wishes to know. Instead, the policyholder must work out what a hypothetical prudent underwriter would consider relevant.

Problems

The duty is poorly understood

8.4 There is growing evidence that the duty of disclosure does not work well in the business market. Research shows that even professional risk managers may fail to understand the duty. A survey by the Mactavish Group found that 87% of buyers were unaware of how onerous the duty was. Furthermore, 65% demonstrated this ignorance by failing to review the information used to place their risks with insurers.[4]

The words of the statute are not necessarily complex. Rather the problem is that the concept is counter-intuitive. Despite continual warnings, few policyholders believe that the law really expects them to second-guess what the insurer wants to know. And even if insurance buyers are familiar with the words of section 18, they may have little idea of how to meet the duty. Companies are much more complex than they were in 1906, with knowledge spread through hundreds, if not thousands, of employees. It is unclear which knowledge is relevant to the insurer, or what a company 'ought to know'.

8.5 This leads to widespread failure to provide material information. The Mactavish Group reviewed over 100 market submissions, concluding that 'the same weaknesses and limitations seem to crop up in almost all cases'. They found many examples of material omissions, including:

- *cursory discussion of the end use to which products are put.* For example, companies failed to mention that apparently innocuous components may be used for risky medical, space or nuclear applications.
- *inadequate information about the firm's dependency on particular sources.* For example, a large UK retailer failed to mention that it had reduced the number of its suppliers and closed distribution centres.
- *failure to mention non-core activities.* For example, a manufacturing company failed to mention that it undertook sensitive contract testing work for third parties.

Most business insurance transactions involve a broker, who has a duty to assist with the presentation of the risk to insurers. The problem, however, is that broker fees have fallen sharply. The Mactavish Group estimated that in

---

4 Mactavish 'Corporate Risk & Insurance – The Case for Placement Reform', The Mactavish Protocols (2011). The Mactavish Group is a research and consultancy business specialising in risk and insurance.

2010 fees in the mid to large corporate sector were 25–30% lower than in 2007. Consultees confirmed that brokers now have less time to investigate companies' activities and prepare presentations. There was said to be 'widespread de-skilling' across the industry, with fewer site visits and surveys.

It is a problem for medium and large companies

8.6 When the Law Commissions started their review, there was an assumption that the problems caused by section 18 were greatest for small businesses, who had fewer resources to understand the law. In fact, consultees thought that the problems were greater for medium and large businesses. Small businesses are generally asked questions, which makes disclosure less onerous. The Mactavish Group commented that the most serious problems were experienced by mid-sized companies, with a turnover between £50 million and £5 billion. These companies are expected to present a risk to the insurer, but often struggle to distinguish relevant information from amongst the unlimited number of 'facts' known to one or more of their employees.

The risk managers' association Airmic represents the UK's largest companies, and even Airmic members report problems over the law of non-disclosure. In 2010, almost a third (31%) said that insurers had raised non-disclosure issues against them in the last five years. Of these, only around half reported that the claim had been resolved satisfactorily.

There was a high level of litigation: 5% of all Airmic members in the survey had been involved in litigation on the issue of non-disclosure in the last five years. This is reflected in the high number of reported cases. The Law Commission identified 41 reported judgments on section 18 from January 2002 to January 2012.[5]

Airmic notes that for large, complex international companies, 'identification, collection and collation of all material information' can be a very difficult task.[6] It is particularly difficult to know whether information known only to some employees should be taken as known by the company as a whole.

The law encourages 'underwriting at claims stage'

8.7 The law gives the impression that insurers may play a passive role, which can lead to 'underwriting at claims stage'. In other words, an insurer may accept a poor presentation and ask questions only once a claim arises. The words of section 18 suggest that if the insurer then discovers material circumstances which it was not told about, it may exercise its right to refuse

---

5 The figure includes 26 English High Court cases, 12 Court of Appeal cases and 3 Scottish Court of Session cases.

6 Airmic, 'Disclosure of Material Facts and Information in Business Insurance' (2011).

the claim. The courts have used the doctrine of 'waiver' to protect policyholders against this practice, but the case law may not be sufficiently clear or well-known.

The Mactavish Group noted that after many years of a soft insurance market,[7] insurers have grown to accept lower standards in submission. The problems come when soft markets start to turn hard. If insurers discover that they have asked too few questions and underpriced the risk, they may raise issues of non-disclosure when a claim is made. This could have serious consequences for businesses. It may mean delays in settlement, protracted negotiations about the size of the settlement, or even, in some cases, outright refusal of the claim.

The remedy is too harsh

8.8 Under the current law, the only remedy for non-disclosure is avoidance: the insurer may treat the policy as if it does not exist and refuse all claims.

It is an 'all or nothing' remedy. A policyholder who fails to mention a minor issue loses all benefit from the policy, even if the insurer would only have added a small amount to the premium had it known the true facts. This over-protects the insurer against the loss it might have suffered had the claim been paid, and it fails to act as a sufficient incentive for insurers to ask appropriate questions.

We have been told that insurers routinely ignore the law. They only avoid if they suspect fraud, and otherwise apply proportional remedies (or sometimes ask only for the premium increase). Avoidance is still a powerful weapon, however, which is open to misuse.

Proposals for reform

8.9 In 2007 the Law Commissions proposed that the test of materiality should be changed from one based on a prudent underwriter to one based on 'a reasonable insured'. The court should ask what 'a reasonable insured in the circumstances would think was relevant to the insurer'.[8] In June 2012, the Law Commissions announced that they were not proceeding with this proposal. Many consultees argued that any test based on what a reasonable insured thought an insurer would want to know was inherently uncertain.[9]

---

7 A soft market is where the availability of insurance outstrips demand, leading to lower premiums or more extensive cover.

8 2007 Consultation Paper, para 5.83.

9 2012 Consultation Paper, paras 4.60 to 4.71.

It was particularly unclear what the reasonable insured test meant for brokers. Brokers are meant to advise clients about what they should disclose. But should a reasonable broker advise the policyholder to disclose information which the broker thinks the insurer wants to know – or should the broker only tell the policyholder to mention facts which a reasonable policyholder would consider relevant? The former approach, it was suggested, involved little change from the current law. The latter approach, on the other hand, involved a hall of mirrors, in which the policyholder looked to the broker to find out what to do, while the broker looked back to find out what the policyholder already thought.

The proposals set out in 2012 are two-fold: to introduce proportionate remedies and to clarify the extent of the duty.

Compensatory remedies

8.10 The Commissions thought that automatic avoidance should only be available where the policyholder has acted dishonestly. In other cases, they propose a new system of proportionate remedies, based on the consumer reforms. The aim would be to put the insurer into the position it would have been in had full and accurate information been provided.

For example, where the insurer would have charged a greater premium, the claim should be reduced proportionately. Where the insurer would have accepted the risk but included another contract term, the contract should be treated as if it included that term. It is only where the insurer would have declined the risk altogether that the policy would be avoided, the claim refused and the premiums returned.

A fair presentation of the risk

8.11 The second change is evolutionary. The 2012 Consultation Paper draws out best practices from the current case law and proposes to include these principles within the statute itself in order to provide more guidance and certainty to policyholders and insurers.

In particular, the consultation paper proposes that an insured should disclose every material circumstance which is required to provide a fair presentation of the risk. This includes:

- any unusual or special circumstances which increase the risk;
- any particular concerns about the risk which led to the insurance being placed;
- standard information which market participants generally understand should be disclosed. This would enable the court to have regard to established protocols about what a presentation should include.

If the presentation of the risk suggests potential problems, the onus should then be on the insurer to ask further questions. Again, this principle is found in the existing case law,[10] but is not prominent or well-known.

The paper also proposes further guidance on what a corporate policyholder 'knows' or 'ought to know'. Where a business policyholder is a corporate entity, 'knowledge' would include information known both to 'the directing mind and will of the organisation' and to the persons who arranged the insurance on behalf of the organisation. In addition, a business policyholder would be under a duty to disclose information that would have been discovered by reasonable enquiries, which are proportionate to the type of insurance and to the size, nature and complexity of the business. This is designed to encourage the industry to develop protocols about the procedures a business should follow.

Contracting out

8.12 For business insurance, the new remedies would be subject to the parties' freedom of contract. The Law Commissions do not expect that contracting out of the default regime would be routine, but suggest that in some specialist markets the parties may wish to retain avoidance as the remedy for non-disclosure and misrepresentation.

Thus the parties to a business insurance contract would be entitled to contract out of the proportionate remedies regime. This would be subject to the safeguard that a term purporting to contract out of the default regime is to be written in clear unambiguous language and be brought to the attention of the other party.

Warranties

What is a warranty?

8.13 There is considerable uncertainty over the word 'warranty'. In general contract law, 'warranties' are relatively minor contractual terms. By contrast, an insurance warranty is a particularly important contractual term which, if breached, may have harsh consequences for the policyholder.

Section 33(1) of the Marine Insurance Act 1906 provides a potentially wide definition. It includes terms by which the policyholder undertakes to do or not to do some particular thing, or that some condition will be fulfilled (referred to as 'promissory warranties'). It also includes terms whereby the

---

10 *See WISE (Underwriting Agency) Ltd v Grupo Nacional Provincial SA* [2004] EWCA Civ 962; [2004] 2 All ER 613; *Cohen v Standard Marine Insurance Co* (1925) Comm Cas 139; and *Garnat Trading and Shipping (Singapore) Pte Ltd v Baominh Insurance Corporation* [2010] EWHC 2578 (Comm); [2011] 1 Lloyd's Rep 589. These cases are discussed in the 2012 Consultation Paper from paras 5.38 to 5.43.

policyholder 'affirms or negatives the existence of a particular state of facts' (referred to as 'warranties of past or present fact').

Identifying whether terms in insurance contracts are warranties is not easy. Merely calling a term a 'warranty' is not enough. The courts have held that some terms are warranties even though the word is not used; while in other cases a term called a warranty may not be a 'true warranty' in law. This uncertainty over what a warranty is has bedevilled attempts at reform.

Problems with the current law

8.14 The current law of warranties set out in the 1906 Act appears unfair and unprincipled. There are four main problems:

- Under section 33(3) of the 1906 Act, a warranty 'must be exactly complied with, whether it be material to the risk or not'. This means that an insurer may refuse a claim for a trivial mistake which has no bearing on the risk.
- Under section 34(2), once a warranty has been broken, the policyholder cannot use the defence that the breach has been remedied. For example, if a policyholder is late in checking the alarm, it is irrelevant that when the loss arises, the alarm has been checked and found to be working.
- The breach of a warranty discharges the insurer from all liability under the contract, not just for liability for the type of risk in question. Thus a failure to install the right sort of burglar alarm would discharge the insurer from paying a claim for flood damage.
- Basis of the contract clauses allow an insurer to convert a statement into a warranty using obscure words that most policyholders do not understand. For example, if a policyholder signs a statement on the proposal form that the answers form 'the basis of the contract', and then makes a mistake, the insurer is discharged from all liability under the contract, no matter how innocent, trivial or irrelevant the mistake.[11]

Moderating harsh law through strict interpretation

8.15 For many years, the courts have attempted to moderate the harshness of the law. A warranty may be construed strictly against the party who has put it forward.[12] Alternatively, a term which appears to be a warranty may be

---

[11] *Dawsons Ltd v Bonnin* [1922] 2 AC 413; 1922 SC (HL) 156.

[12] *Provincial Insurance Company Ltd v Morgan & Foxton* [1933] AC 240. For discussion see the 2012 Consultation Paper, paras 12.44 to 12.59.

construed as some other type of term, such as a 'suspensive condition', which only applies for the duration of the breach.[13]

This approach has allowed the courts to do justice in individual cases, and may discourage insurers from taking purely technical points. While this has its advantages, it also introduces complexity and uncertainty into the law.

Proposals for reform

8.16 The 2012 Consultation Paper made three main proposals to reform the law of warranties:

- *To abolish basis of the contract clauses.* Insurers may still use warranties of past or present fact, but they should be included specifically in the contract. The Consumer Insurance (Disclosure and Representations) Act 2012, section 6 prevents insurers using basis of the contract clauses in consumer insurance contracts, and a similar provision would apply to business insurance.
- *To treat warranties as suspensive conditions.* A breach of warranty would suspend the insurer's liability, rather than discharge it. Where the breach is remedied before the loss, the insurer must pay the claim.
- *To introduce special rules for terms designed to reduce the risk of a particular type of loss, or the risk of loss at a particular time or in a particular location.* For these terms, a breach would suspend liability in respect only of that type of loss (or a loss at that time or in that place). Thus, for example, the breach of a warranty to install a burglar alarm would suspend liability for loss caused by an intruder but not for flood loss.

8.17 In consumer insurance, the proposed consequences of breach of warranty could not be excluded by a contract term. In business insurance, the parties would be able to contract out of these provisions, provided they did so in clear, unambiguous terms and the term was brought to the attention of the other party.

An illustration

8.18 The effect of these proposals can be illustrated with an example.

A couple insure a small yacht. The policy includes three warranties:

- A 'premium payment' warranty, requiring payment by 1 June;
- A 'lock warranty' requiring the hatch to be secured by a special type of padlock; and

[13] *Kler Knitwear v Lombard General Insurance Co Ltd* [2000] Lloyd's Rep IR 47.

- A 'pleasure use only' warranty, forbidding the yacht to be used for commercial gain.

The policyholders breach all three warranties. They fail to pay until 15 June; they install the wrong type of padlock; and they use the yacht for paid fishing trips. On 1 July the policyholders are using the yacht to transport paying customers when it is hit by a sudden hurricane and sinks.

The effect of each breach would be as follows:

- Under the current law, breach of a premium payment warranty discharges the insurer from liability, which is not restored if the insurer later accepts payment.[14] Under the proposals, however, the payment on 15 June would remedy the breach and the insurer's liability would be restored. The insurer would not be permitted to reject the claim solely on this basis.
- The lock warranty is aimed at a specific type of loss: loss by theft. Under the proposals, it would not suspend the insurer's liability for other types of loss, such as loss in a storm. This would not be a good reason to refuse the claim.
- The pleasure use only warranty relates to the contract generally, and suspends the insurer's liability for all losses until such time as it is remedied. Clearly in this case it has not been remedied, and the insurer may reject the claim on this basis. It does not matter whether the breach caused the loss. The 2012 Consultation Paper argues that this would also apply where the yacht is damaged while berthed overnight, applying the case of *Murray v Scottish Automobile*, as this is ancillary to the forbidden activity.[15]

Section 17 and remedies for fraud

8.19 Section 17 of the Marine Insurance Act 1906 imposes duties of good faith on both parties. Sections 18 to 20 of the 1906 Act are specific examples of that principle in relation to non-disclosure and misrepresentation, but section 17 also extends more widely. The duty applies to both the insurer and the policyholder, both before and after the contract has been formed.

The problem is that section 17 provides only one remedy: avoidance of the contract. This remedy has been widely criticised. Where the policyholder is

14 See the 2012 Consultation Paper, Part 12 at para 12.33.
15 1929 SLT 114. See the 2012 Consultation Paper, paras 15.18 to 15.19.

at fault, it can be overly harsh. Where the insurer is at fault, it is often useless. A policyholder with a claim wants the claim paid, not their premium returned.

Section 17 causes particular problems for the law of fraudulent claims. Since the nineteenth century, the courts have held that a person who fraudulently exaggerates a claim forfeits the whole claim to which the fraud relates, but other claims are unaffected.[16] There is a mismatch between this common law rule and section 17. If an insurer avoids the contract, the result is that the policyholder would be required to repay all claims which had been paid under the policy, including genuine and legitimate claims finalised and paid before the fraud arose. In practice, the courts have been reluctant to allow insurers to recoup valid claims which arose before the fraud took place, but this has left some incoherence in the law.[17]

Proposals on remedies for fraud

8.20 In the second consultation paper, published in December 2011, the Law Commissions proposed to remove the remedy of avoidance from section 17. Instead, the remedies for fraud would be set out on the face of the legislation. The legislation would clarify that:

- A policyholder who commits a fraud *forfeits the whole claim to which the fraud relates.* Any interim payments made in respect of the claim must be repaid. This is the current law, which would be preserved.
- The policyholder *would also forfeit any claim which arises after the date of the fraud.* The law on this point is uncertain, although current market practice appears to be to refuse subsequent claims.
- The fraud w*ould not affect any previous valid claim* where the loss arises before the fraud takes place, whether or not the claim has been paid. In theory, section 17 appears to give insurers a right to recoup previous claims, but in practice the courts do not permit it. It is an unprincipled and impractical remedy, which introduces confusion into the law.

Many insurance contracts use express 'fraud clauses' to extend the insurer's remedies for fraud. In consumer insurance, the Law Commissions propose that any term which purports to give the insurer greater rights in relation to

---

16 *Agapitos v Agnew ('The Aegeon (No 1)')* [2002] EWCA Civ 247 and *Axa General Insurance Ltd v Gottlieb* [2005] EWCA Civ 112. These cases are discussed in Issues Paper 7, Part 4.

17 Lord Justice Aikens, 'The post-contract duty of good faith in insurance contracts: is there a problem that needs a solution?', speech to BILA 8 February 2010. The issue has generated considerable academic comment: see D Rhidian Thomas, 'Fraudulent insurance claims: definition, consequences and limitations' (2009) Lloyd's Maritime and Commercial Law Quarterly 485 at 515; and James Davey, 'Unpicking the fraudulent claims jurisdiction in insurance contract law: sympathy for the devil?' (2006) Lloyd's Maritime and Commercial Law Quarterly 223. See also J P Lowry, 'Redrawing the parameters of good faith in insurance contracts' in C O'Cinneide and J Holder, *Current Legal Problems 2007: Volume 60,* pp 338–407.

fraudulent claims should be of no effect.[18] In commercial contracts, an express fraud clause would be upheld, but only if it is written in clear unambiguous terms and specifically brought to the attention of the other party.

The 2012 Consultation Paper confirms the Law Commissions' intention to reform section 17. They propose to retain good faith as an interpretative principle, but breach of the duty would not, in itself, give either a policyholder or an insurer a cause of action. Instead, any remedies which are required, such as remedies for non-disclosure, misrepresentation or fraudulent claims, would be specified directly in the legislation.

Damages for late payment

8.21 One particular problem with English law is that damages are not available against an insurer who unreasonably delays or refuses payment of a claim. If a policyholder suffers further loss from the insurer's wrongful actions, no remedy is available except statutory interest.

The case of *Sprung v Royal Insurance (UK) Ltd* illustrates the problem.[19]

> Mr Sprung ran a small business. When vandals broke in and damaged his factory, he submitted a claim to his insurer but his claim was rejected. In difficult economic conditions, Mr Sprung was unable to finance the repairs himself. Six months later, he was out of business.
>
> Mr Sprung started proceedings against his insurers. Four years later, the court found that his claim was valid, and should have been paid. Mr Sprung was awarded an indemnity for his lost plant and machinery, plus simple interest and costs. The judge also found that as a result of the insurer's failure, Mr Sprung had suffered a further loss of £75,000.
>
> Mr Sprung was not, however, entitled to claim this further loss. The Court of Appeal, with 'undisguised reluctance', considered itself bound by the rule that there could be no award of damages for late payment. Lord Justice Beldam called for reform of the law.[20]

This is out of step with normal contract principles. The normal position in contract law is that where one party suffers loss because the other party has failed to meet its contractual obligations, the innocent party may claim damages for loss suffered. The victim must prove that they suffered actual

18 See the 2011 Consultation Paper, paras 8.24 to 8.30.
19 [1999] 1 Lloyd's Rep IR 111.
20 *Ibid*, at 119. See the 2011 Consultation Paper, paras 2.14 to 2.18.

financial loss; that the loss was foreseeable at the time the contract was made; and that they have taken reasonable steps to mitigate it.[21]

English law is also out of step with the law in Scotland and other Commonwealth countries. It appears unfair and unprincipled, which has the potential to reduce confidence in English law in the international marketplace.

Proposals for reform

8.22 The Law Commissions published proposals to reform the law in this area in their December 2011 Consultation Paper.

A duty to pay valid claims within a reasonable time

8.23 They proposed that an insurer should be under a duty to pay valid claims within a reasonable time. An insurer who unreasonably delays or wrongfully repudiates a claim should be liable to pay damages according to normal contract law principles – that is for proven and foreseeable losses.

The paper proposes that the definition of a reasonable time should be flexible, taking into account market practice, the type of the insurance, and the size, location and complexity of the claim.

Excluding the duty

8.24 In consumer insurance, insurers would not be entitled to exclude liability for failing to pay valid claims within a reasonable time. The Financial Ombudsman Service already recognises such a duty, and this appears to be accepted by the industry.[22]

8.25 For business insurance, the Law Commissions advance a more complex solution. They propose that an insurer would be able to use a contract term to limit or exclude its liability to pay damages for late payment, provided that the insurer has made an honest error in good faith. Thus insurers would not be allowed to exclude liability for losses brought about by their own bad faith. No policyholder who is properly advised would agree to that, which would be inimical to the nature of an insurance contract. If, for example, an insurer reasonably but mistakenly decides that a claim is disallowed under the policy, it should be able to rely on its exclusion clause. But if claims handlers delayed or rejected a claim they knew to be valid to secure a bonus payment, then the exclusion should not apply.[23]

---

[21] For further discussion, see the 2011 Consultation Paper, paras 2.6 to 2.13.
[22] See the 2011 Consultation Paper, paras 5.20 to 5.25.
[23] See the 2011 Consultation Paper, paras 5.26 to 5.33.

Insurable interest

8.26 Insurance differs from any other risk-transfer contract, such as gambling, because it is used to compensate for loss. For insurance to be valid, the insured must possess an 'insurable interest'.

The requirement may be imposed by a mix of contract, statute and the common law, but for some types of insurance the source of the requirement is unclear. The English law of insurable interest has been described as 'a confusing and illogical mess'.[24] Scots law is more straightforward,[25] but still contains anachronisms and anomalies.

Insurance is conventionally divided into two categories, although the distinction is not clear cut. 'Indemnity insurance' indemnifies the policyholder against actual loss, and includes buildings, goods and liability insurance. By contrast, life insurance (together with critical illness or personal accident insurance) pays out on the occurrence of a defined event. Here, the term 'life insurance' is used to include this entire second category.

Indemnity insurance

8.27 Issues Paper 4 asked whether the doctrine of insurable interest had a role to play in indemnity insurance. Most respondents thought that it did, arguing that it fulfilled four functions:

- It is a hallmark of insurance, distinguishing insurance from gambling.
- It enforces market discipline, ensuring efficient underwriting procedures.
- It forms a barrier against invalid claims.
- It helps to define both insurance, and where insurance is located, for tax and regulatory purposes.[26]

8.28 The Law Commissions therefore propose to retain the doctrine, but to re-state it in a clearer form. At present, it is based on a bewildering array of common law and statute. The proposals would:

- provide a clear statutory basis for the requirement of insurable interest;
- repeal two outdated statutes: the Marine Insurance Act 1788 and the Marine Insurance (Gambling Policies) Act 1909;
- clarify that the insured must have an insurable interest at the time of loss;

---

[24] Robert Merkin, *Reforming Insurance Law: is there a case for reverse transportation?*, p 78.

[25] In Scotland, the requirement for insurable interest is imposed by common law: see Bell's *Principles*, s 457.

[26] See the 2011 Consultation Paper, paras 12.2 to 12.35.

- provide that a policy is void unless there is a real probability that a party would acquire some form of insurable interest at some stage.[27]

Life insurance: problems with the current law

8.29 For life insurance the law is unduly restrictive. People may insure their own life and that of their spouse[28] for an unlimited amount. This is said to be based on 'natural affection'. But the class is limited: one cannot insure the life of a cohabitant, a child or parent on this basis.

Alternatively, policies may be based on the fact that the insured will suffer financial loss on another's death, but this is restricted to 'a pecuniary loss recognised by law'. It requires a legal right to payment rather than just a reasonable expectation of loss.

The courts have taken a strict approach: a father's expectation that his son would care for him or maintain him was held not to constitute an insurable interest in the son's life.[29] Similarly, a case from 1904 found that burial insurance was invalid because a son had no legal obligation to bury his mother.[30]

8.30 Under section 3 of the Life Assurance Act 1774, any recovery is limited to the value of the insurable interest at the time of the contract. Again, this has been interpreted strictly: thus 'key employee' insurance is limited to the costs of the notice period and replacement,[31] and may not include other loss to the employer on the employee's death.

It is common for life insurance policies to be written which go beyond those permitted under the current case law. Insurers frequently write 'key employee' insurance for sums which exceed the notice period. Furthermore, travel insurance often includes a fixed sum on the death or injury of a child. As noted in a leading textbook, 'insurance practice is becoming increasingly impatient' with the rigidity of the current law.[32]

Life insurance: proposals

8.31 The Law Commissions propose a new statutory requirement for insurable interest to replace the outdated Life Assurance Act 1774. This would provide that without an insurable interest, a policy is void.[33]

---

27 See the 2011 Consultation Paper, paras 12.36 to 12.59.

28 The term 'spouse' refers to a husband, wife or civil partner.

29 *Halford v Kymer* (1830) 10 B&C 724.

30 *Harse v Pearl Life Assurance Co Ltd* [1904] 1 KB 558. For an account of the case law, see the 2011 Consultation Paper, paras 11.70 to 11.93.

31 *Simcock v Scottish Imperial Insurance Co* (1902) 10 SLT 286.

32 *MacGillivray on Insurance Law*, (11th ed, 2008), at para 1–049.

33 See the 2011 Consultation Paper, paras 13.111 to 13.116.

The main proposal is to widen the test of economic dependency. At present, the law requires that the life insured has a legal obligation towards the proposer. This would be replaced with a factual test instead: it should be sufficient that there is a real probability that the proposer will retain an economic benefit on the preservation of the life insured, or incur an economic loss on the death. This would enable people to insure the lives of family members where they are dependent on them and would suffer a loss if they died.

8.32 In addition, the Law Commissions thought there was a case for specifying that some family members have an automatic right to insure another's life. They propose that:

- Parents should be entitled to take out insurance on the life of a child under 18. They asked if there should be a cap on the amount (possibly of around £30,000).
- Cohabitants should be entitled to insure each other's lives without evidence of economic loss if they have lived in the same household as husband and wife or as civil partners for the whole of five years before the policy is taken out.[34]

Policies and premiums in marine insurance

8.33 In 2006, the Law Commissions were asked to consider three provisions of the Marine Insurance Act 1906 which apply only to marine insurance, but which appeared outdated and problematic. These are: the requirement for a formal marine policy in section 22; the broker's liability for premiums in section 53(1); and the broker's lien in section 53(2).

The requirement for a formal marine policy

8.34 Under section 22 of the Marine Insurance Act 1906, a contract for marine insurance is inadmissible in evidence unless 'embodied in a marine policy'. This introduces a technicality with potentially drastic consequences. It means that, without a marine policy, the insured cannot prove the existence of a contract, and therefore cannot establish its right to make a claim.

The requirement dates from 1795, when stamp duty was imposed on marine insurance. It was a way of preventing tax evasion. As this form of stamp duty was repealed in 1970, the rationale behind the requirement has now disappeared.

---

[34] See the 2011 Consultation Paper, paras 13.87 to 13.103.

Section 22 appears to have little effect in practice, but it is difficult to defend its continued existence. It seems wrong to have a law which is widely ignored and difficult to justify to an international audience.

The 2011 Consultation Paper proposed to repeal section 22 and other related provisions. Although it is clearly desirable to put contract terms in writing, this should be a matter for the industry rather than a legal requirement. In any event, it would be wrong to penalise the insured for the insurer's failure.

The broker's liability for premiums

8.35 Section 53(1) of the Marine Insurance Act 1906 states that 'where a marine policy is effected on behalf of an assured by a broker, the broker is directly responsible to the insurer for the premium'. In other words, the broker is primarily liable to pay the premium, not the policyholder. In Issues Paper 8, the Law Commissions described this provision as anomalous, counter-intuitive and uncertain. It is widely misunderstood, as it needs to be read in the light of its common law background.

Where the policyholder is insolvent

8.36 Section 53(1) makes the broker liable to pay the premium to the insurer, even if the insured refuses to pay or becomes insolvent. Insurers told us that they do occasionally invoke section 53(1) against brokers. Although they usually relied on other methods of securing payment, they thought that section 53(1) provided insurers with a 'useful additional protection'.[35]

From the broker's point of view, however, it imposes a liability from which it is too difficult to escape. Although in theory the parties may contract out of the section, it is not easy. The section affects three parties; the insurer, the insured and the broker. To exclude its effects fully one would need three separate contracts, or one contract with three parties. Furthermore, the case law suggests that only a very clearly worded clause would suffice.[36]

Where the broker is insolvent

8.37 There may be more to section 53(1) than meets the eye. It codifies nineteenth century case law which underlines that a marine policyholder is not liable to pay premiums to the insurer. Instead, the insurer claimed the premium from the broker, and the broker had a separate claim against the policyholder. The broker received the money not as an agent but as a principal, in its own right.

---

[35] See the 2011 Consultation Paper, para 18.11, quoting the International Underwriting Association.

[36] *Universo Insurance Co of Milan v Merchants Marine Insurance Co Ltd* [1897] 2 QB 93. See the 2011 Consultation Paper, paras 18.72 to 18.76.

There is uncertainty about how far this is still the law. If it is, it may undermine statutory protection when a broker becomes insolvent. The Client Assets Sourcebook (CASS) rules in the FSA handbook are based on the idea that the broker holds the premium as an agent, either for the insurer or the insured. If the broker is paid as principal, then these rules would not apply. The Law Commissions point out that if a marine broker were to become insolvent, insurers could face unexpected risks.

Proposals for reform

8.38 The Law Commissions proposed that section 53(1) should be re-enacted in a clearer and simpler form. The policyholder should be liable to pay the premium to the insurer, and should pay the broker as agent. Any liability assumed by the broker should be in addition to the policyholder's liability, not a substitute.

The issue of whether the broker is liable to pay the premium to the insurer should be a matter of agreement between broker and insurer. The law should be reformed to make it easy to contract both in or out of any such liability, through a simple term in any contract between the broker and the insurer.

The controversial issue was the default rule. Should brokers be liable for paying premiums unless they contract out of liability, or only if they contract in? The 2011 Consultation Paper proposed that marine brokers should be liable to pay the premium to the insurer unless they contracted out. This preserves the current market practice, and was popular with insurers. It was not popular with marine brokers, who wished to see an opt-in rule.

The broker's lien

8.39 Section 53(2) provides the broker with a lien over a marine policy for unpaid premiums and charges. It permits the broker to retain not only the policy document but also any policy proceeds to discharge the policyholder's unpaid debts.

There is a problem with this section: it probably only applies where the broker has a paper policy document in its possession. As paper policies are rarely used, it may give brokers little protection.[37] The Law Commissions propose to replace section 53(2) with a new section which does not require a policy document.

---

[37] See the 2011 Consultation Paper, paras 20.2 to 20.25.

Appendix 1 Does the insurance industry need an Ombudsman?

Memorandum of 26 September 1975, written by Mike Harris of Guardian Royal Exchange

Background

1. Theoretically, the best protection for the consumer lies in the existence of a competitive market combined with the right to sue in order to enforce, if necessary, fulfilment of a contract. The first of these features is useful to a policyholder at renewal time only to prevent recurrence of unsatisfactory treatment and the second, is expensive. Do we need some alternative?

   (The background against which to consider this question is well set by quoting from the preamble to the recent British Insurance Law Colloquium -

   'Consensus ad idem is obviously a most desirable state for contracting parties. According to English legal text books it is an integral part of a contract, but in reality because of the unequal positions of the insurers and the insured it often seems sadly lacking in insurance contracts. The doctrine of uberrima fides adds further to the inequality and to the burdens of the consumer.

   But, in practice, is the consumer really prejudiced?

   The fact that insurers tend to act ethically clouds the principles and it is these that we will be examining at this our third Colloquium. The issues involved appear similar in many participating countries but the approach to them varies considerably. In some states the consumer is "protected" by strict control of insurers, which extends to the physical appearance of the policy document, whereas in others there is not even a legally prescribed solvency margin.'

2. The legal system in this country is in some respects weighted in favour of the insurer but a long tradition of fair dealing and a willingness to see commonsense solutions achieved a broadly acceptable position. However, our society is altering and both insurers and insured have themselves changed their characteristics. Everything is now organised in larger units whether it be industry, Central Government, Local Government or the insurance companies themselves. There is less personal

contact with our customers, whether in arranging their business or collecting their premiums, sophisticated costing systems have made us less tolerant of individual solutions to individual problems and the traditional quality of our staff has been considerably diluted in an attempt to reduce costs. The consumer wants the economic benefits from the operation of large units while resenting the concomitant disappearance of personal relationships and despairing of finding someone from whom he can obtain a sensible answer. The policyholder himself has changed because the wider dispersal of wealth through the social classes and the statutory requirement to insure certain motor risks have considerably extended the range of our customers. In addition to these changes we must accept the fact that because of the easy accessibility of the U.K. market to new insurers (in contrast to the situation prevailing almost everywhere else in the world) new companies become established which are not imbued with the traditional ethos of the older companies.

3. It could be argued that with the Government taking steps to establish a compensation fund to protect insurance policyholders from loss no further steps need be taken vis-a-vis our customers. In my view, the insurance industry is still suffering in the public estimation from the collapse of the Vehicle & General when policyholders found out the hard way that the B.I.A. was the trade protection organisation and not a medium for guaranteeing the contracts of its members. Now that the Government has made it clear that a compensation fund is necessary and has appeared to be pushing an unwilling industry in that direction the case for us to set up some form of complaints service seems to be correspondingly more urgent. It is important for the industry to show it has nothing to hide in permitting an independent monitoring of its actions and by taking the initiative with our consumers we should strengthen their feeling that a free market is in their best interest.

Objectives

4.

(a) To improve the standing of insurance companies with the insuring public.

(b) To fill a vacuum which is imperfectly filled at present and may eventually be filled from some less sympathetic source.

Existing channels for complaints

5. The D.o.T. receives between 300/400 a year. It has no standing in this matter other than to ensure that scheduled rates have been increased only in accordance with its authorisation. Department officials say that

the majority of the complaints made to them have little to justify them. The Director of Fair Trading receives about 2,000 complaints a year which are said to relate principally to door-to-door selling of unit-linked life contracts. The B.I.A. gets a number of complaints on which it normally takes no position but transmits the complaint to the company concerned. In addition, there are various consumer sections in the press, radio and television where complainants can publicise their grievance. Most of these channels would seek information from the company concerned before publicising the complaint but, in some cases, they would pronounce on the apparent merits of the complaint. I would surmise that the greatest volume of complaints is that reaching the insurers themselves and dealt with via normal administrative procedures.

Principal sources of complaint

6. I suggest that these are likely to be as follows:-

(a) Policyholders complaining that a claim has been refused or that less than generous treatment has been accorded to their claim.

(b) Complaints about NCD entitlement or failure to pursue uninsured claims against a Third Party often linked with a complaint that a Third Party has, in the Policyholder's view, been improperly or too generously indemnified.

(c) Complaints from Policyholders that their cover is different from that which they thought they were buying. This being brought to their notice by either a claim, a desire to surrender or, possibly, a wish to seek a house-purchase loan.

(d) Complaints against intermediaries and, much more rarely against insurance staff often related to (c) above.

(e) Complaints from Third Parties on liability or quantum.

How an Ombudsman service should be organised

7. As I see it, the organisation of a complaints service can do nothing to compensate for the failure of a customer to read or understand the cover he was buying at outset, or to compensate for the disappointment he may feel when the cover turns out to be different from that he thought he was buying. Any complaints service should be rooted firmly in the contract which exists between the parties and to complaints arising out of failure to fulfil that contract. From all the evidence of other countries which have established an Insurance Ombudsman its principal value lies in being seen to offer an independent and unbiased view on the facts of any case. It is irrelevant that in a majority of cases

the same view would probably be offered by the insurer, what is important is the clear independence of the spokesman. With these points in mind I think one could establish the following tentative guidelines for its operation –

(a) It should concern itself with points referred by individuals only, not corporate bodies.

(b) It should consider only complaints arising out of the insurance contract from the policyholder thus excluding Third Parties.

(c) It should probably cover both long term and short term contracts.

(d) It should not consider complaints against intermediaries.

(e) It should have no power to take decisions but should confine itself to investigating the facts on both sides and stating a view on those facts.

8. My justification for these guidelines would be as follows:

(a) Corporate and commercial policyholders are more equal parties in the insurance contracts than individuals and normally have the benefit of professional advice. A similar view is taken by the Office of Fair Trading which only deals with individual complaints.

(b) Third Party settlements are almost invariably compromises based on an assessment of balance of probability as to liability and a degree of negotiation to recognise the imponderables in the claim. There is a very difficult area of motor insurance complaints where a Third Party is 100% in the right but because the policyholder has refused to seek indemnity under his policy the insurer cannot indemnify the Third Party. This does much to bring insurers into disrepute, but can only be changed by legislation not by an Ombudsman.

(c) Because most life policies are very simple documents and therefore few disputes are likely to arise out of the contract there could be a case for excluding long term contracts altogether from the scope of the service. The main point of including them is to extend the educational scope of the service in perhaps explaining to complainants such matters as the difference between premiums paid and the quoted surrender value.

(d) Much depends here on whether the Department of Trade pursues the question of registration of intermediaries. If all were registered with possibly a compensation fund or compulsory professional negligence cover there would be a clear case for referring such complaints to the registration body. As it is I feel such complaints should be directed to the corporate body should the intermediary belong to one of the recognised associations, or else to the

Director of Fair Trading. I do not think that such complaints should be considered by the service unless the company is in some way involved, or possibly if the company concerned has benefited from the alleged error of the agent.

(e) It is self-evident that no insurer would wish to abrogate its management role in favour of an outsider. One accepts, however, that any insurer would be willing to act if the facts disclosed a case for doing so.

9. If something like the foregoing guidelines proved acceptable other interested bodies should be contacted and told of what was in contemplation. The D.O.T. and the Office of Fair Trading would, I think, welcome the establishment of such a service and would probably be willing to channel the relevant complaints from those that they themselves receive. Lloyd's, I think, would show no interest; the brokers' Association would probably accept that they should develop their own channels for complaints against intermediaries particularly as they tend in general to favour the transaction of business only via registered intermediaries.

10. I now turn to the probable reaction of the insurance company market. I would expect to find some support amongst the larger insurance companies for some kind of Ombudsman service but the response from some of the smaller companies could well prove negative. I had originally thought that one could make a start without universal support and that those companies who wished to participate would mention in their normal advertising that they were sponsor companies of the Insurance Customer Service Bureau, or whatever name one chose to adopt. On reflection, I am inclined to think that it is unrealistic to expect to run the service on the basis of only partial market support since the very companies likely to sponsor the service are the ones least likely to be the subject of a volume of complaints. To get full market support I think we should probably have to approach the matter under the auspices of the B.I.A., accepting the consequent apparent lack of independence as compared with a completely separate organisation. Perhaps the only way in which we could preserve the independence for the Ombudsman, which is so vital if the service is to command public acceptance, would be for the B.I.A. to approach the Consumers' Association, tell them what we had in mind, ask them to organise the service in our joint names and invite them to pay half the cost, the other half being paid by insurers.

11. I envisage that people wishing to make a complaint should pay a registration fee of, say, £5 in order to discourage the most frivolous complaints and make some contribution towards running costs. This is the pattern in some other countries. A variant would be to charge a larger fee and make it returnable should the complaint prove to be

partly or fully justified. (The National House Builders' Registration Council charge a fee of £40 before investigating a complaint against a builder which is returnable if the complaint is upheld but they, of course, have to provide for expensive professional fees for the investigation.)

12. The complaint service would require a fairly modest organisation because one would not on the evidence of the figures quoted from other European countries expect any very considerable volume of complaints. The main expense would probably be that of publicising the service which could be partly undertaken by the Consumers' Association, partly perhaps via the Department of Trade (in Norway much of the expenses of advertising is carried by their equivalent of the Central Office of Information) but possibly mainly through companies referring to the service in their normal advertising, just as they mention membership of B.I.A.

Disadvantages

13.

(a) Expenses coupled with the fact that the companies who inevitably will be the major contributors towards the insurance components of the expense are the ones whose practices are least likely to give rise to complaints.

(b) The fact that on the narrow guidelines suggested above many complaints would not be entertained. This could possibly argue the case for extending the scope of the service but this could only be done if it commanded general acceptance in the insurance market.

Advantages

14.

(a) The service should help convince Policyholders that the 'fine print' image of insurers was out of date.

(b) It will bring some justified complaints to light which might otherwise go unredressed.

(c) It might give early warning of companies that were in trading difficulties.

(d) It might reduce the number of Policyholders looking for a new insurer at renewal.

(e) The service would assist insurers to ensure that their customers got the benefits for which they have paid.

Appendix 2 Statement of General Insurance Practice[1]

Original version 1977 (replaced 1986)

This Statement is restricted to non-life insurances of policyholders resident in the UK and insured in their private capacity only.

1. *Proposal forms*

(a) The declaration at the foot of the proposal form should be restricted to completion according to the proposer's knowledge and belief.

(b) If not included in the declaration, prominently displayed on the proposal form should be a Statement: -

  (i) drawing the attention of the proposer to the consequences of the failure to disclose all material facts, explained as those facts an insurer would regard as likely to influence the acceptance and assessment of the proposal;

  (ii) warning that if the proposer is in any doubt about facts considered material, he should disclose them.

(c) Those matters which insurers have found generally to be material will be the subject of clear questions in proposal forms.

(d) So far as is practicable, insurers will avoid asking questions which would require expert knowledge beyond that which the proposer could reasonably be expected to possess or obtain or which would require a value judgment on the part of the proposer.

(e) Unless the prospectus or the proposal form contain full details of the standard cover offered, and whether or not it contains an outline of that cover, the proposal form shall include a statement that a copy of the policy form is available on request.

(f) Unless the completed form or a copy of it has been sent to a policy holder, a copy will be made available when an insurer raises an issue under the proposal form.

---

[1] Reproduced by kind permission of the Association of British Insurers.

2. *Claims*

(a) Under the conditions regarding notification of a claim, the policyholder shall not be asked to do more than report a claim and subsequent developments as soon as reasonably possible except in the case of legal processes and claims which a third party requires the policyholder to notify within a fixed time, where immediate advice may be required.

(b) Except where fraud, deception or negligence is involved, an insurer will not unreasonably repudiate liability to indemnify a policyholder: -

(i) on the grounds of non-disclosure or misrepresentation of a material fact where knowledge of the fact would not materially have influenced the insurer's judgment in the acceptance or assessment of the insurance;

(ii) on the grounds of a breach of warranty or condition where the circumstances of the loss are unconnected with breach.

The previous paragraph 2(b) does not apply to Marine and Aviation policies.

3. *Renewals*

Renewal notices should contain a warning about the duty of disclosure including the necessity to advise changes affecting the policy which have occurred since the policy inception or last renewal date, whichever was the later.

4. *Commencement*

Any changes to insurance documents will be made as and when they need to be reprinted, but the Statement will apply in the meantime.

5. *EEC*

This Statement will need reconsideration when the EEC Contract Law Directive is taken into English/Scots Law.

Revised version 1986 (withdrawn 2005)

The following Statement of normal insurance practice applies to general insurances of policyholders resident in the UK and insured in their private capacity only.

1. *Proposal forms*

(a) The declaration at the foot of the proposal form should be restricted to completion according to the proposer's knowledge and belief.

(b) Neither the proposal form nor the policy shall contain any provision converting the statements as to past or present fact in the proposal form into warranties. But insurers may require specific warranties about matters which are material to the risk.

(c) If not included in the declaration, prominently displayed on the proposal form should be a statement:-

- (i) drawing the attention of the proposer to the consequences of the failure to disclose all material facts, explained as those facts an insurer would regard as likely to influence the acceptance and assessment of the proposal;
- (ii) warning that if the proposer is in any doubt about facts considered material, he should disclose them.

(d) Those matters which insurers have found generally to be material will be the subject of clear questions in proposals forms.

(e) So far as is practicable, insurers will avoid asking questions which would require expert knowledge beyond that which the proposer could reasonably be expected to possess or obtain or which would require a value judgement on the part of the proposer.

(f) Unless the prospectus or the proposal form contains full details of the standard cover offered, and whether or not it contains an outline of that cover, the proposal form shall include a prominent statement that a specimen copy of the policy form is available on request.

(g) Proposal forms shall contain a prominent warning that the proposer should keep a record (including copies of letters) of all information supplied to the insurer for the purpose of entering into the contract.

(h) The proposal form shall contain a prominent statement that a copy of the completed form:-

- (i) is automatically provided for retention at the time of completion; or
- (ii) will be supplied as part of the insurer's normal practice; or

(iii) will be supplied on request within a period of three months after its completion.

An insurer shall not raise an issue under the proposal form, unless the policyholder is provided with a copy of the completed form.

2. *Claims*

(a) Under the conditions regarding notification of a claim, the policyholder shall not be asked to do more than report a claim and subsequent developments as soon as reasonably possible except in the case of legal processes and claims which a third party requires the policyholder to notify within a fixed time where immediate advice may be required.

(b) An insurer will not repudiate liability to indemnify a policyholder:-

(i) on grounds of non-disclosure of a material fact which a policyholder could not reasonably be expected to have disclosed;

(ii) on grounds of misrepresentation unless it is a deliberate or negligent misrepresentation of a material fact;

(iii) on grounds of a breach of warranty or condition where the circumstances of the loss are unconnected with the breach unless fraud is involved.

Paragraph 2 (b) above does not apply to Marine and Aviation policies.

(c) Liability under the policy having been established and the amount payable by the insurer agreed, payment will be made without avoidable delay.

3. *Renewals*

(a) Renewal notices shall contain a warning about the duty of disclosure including the necessity to advise changes affecting the policy which have occurred since the policy inception or last renewal date, whichever was the later.

(b) Renewal notices shall contain a warning that the proposer should keep a record (including copies of letters) of all information supplied to the insurer for the purpose of renewal of the contract.

4. *Commencement*

Any changes to insurance documents will be made as and when they need to be reprinted, but the Statement will apply in the meantime.

5. Policy documents

Insurers will continue to develop clearer and more explicit proposal forms and policy documents whilst bearing in mind the legal nature of insurance contracts.

6. Disputes

The provisions of the Statement shall be taken into account in arbitration and any other referral procedures which may apply in the event of disputes between policyholders and insurers relating to matters dealt with in the Statement.

Appendix 3 Statement of Long-Term Insurance Practice[1]

Original version 1977 (replaced 1986)

This statement relates to long-term insurance effected by individuals resident in the UK in a private capacity. Although the statement is not mandatory, it has been recognised by members of the LOA and ASLO as an indication of insurance practice, it being understood that there will sometimes be exceptional circumstances where the statement would be inappropriate.

Industrial life assurance policyholders are already protected by the Industrial Assurance Acts 1923 to 1968 and regulations issued thereunder, to an extent not provided for ordinary branch policyholders. The statement will; therefore, be modified in its application to industrial assurance business in discussion with the Industrial Assurance Commissioner.

Life assurance is either very largely or else entirely a mutual enterprise and the aim of the industry in recent years has been to reduce to a minimum the formalities – and therefore the expense to the policyholder – involved in issuing a new life policy subject only to the need to protect the general body of policyholders from the effects of non-disclosure by a small minority of proposers.

1. Claims

(a) An insurer will not unreasonably reject a claim. (However, fraud or deception will, and negligence or non-disclosure or misrepresentation of a material fact may, result in adjustment or constitute grounds for rejection). In particular, an insurer will not reject a claim on grounds of non-disclosure or misrepresentation of a matter that was outside the knowledge of the proposer.

(b) Under any conditions regarding a time limit for notification of a claim, the claimant will not be asked to do more than report a claim and subsequent developments as soon as reasonably possible.

[1] Reproduced by kind permission of the Association of British Insurers.

2. *Proposal forms*

(a) If the proposal form calls for the disclosure of material facts a statement should be included in the declaration, or prominently displayed elsewhere on the form or in the document of which it forms part: -

(i) drawing attention to the consequences of failure to disclose all material facts and explaining that these are facts that an insurer would regard as likely to influence the assessment and acceptance of a proposal;

(ii) warning that if the signatory is in any doubt about whether certain facts are material, these facts should be disclosed.

(b) Those matters which insurers have commonly found to be material should be the subject of clear questions in proposal forms.

(c) Insurers should avoid asking questions which would require knowledge beyond that which the signatory could reasonably be expected to possess.

(d) The proposal form or a supporting document should include a statement that a copy of the policy form or of the policy conditions is available on request.

(e) A copy of the proposal should be made available to the policyholder when an insurer raises an issue under that proposal – information not relevant to that issue being deleted where necessary to preserve confidentiality.

3. *Policies and accompanying documents*

Life assurance policies or accompanying documents should indicate: -

(a) the circumstances in which interest would accrue after the assurance has matured;

and

(b) whether or not there are rights to surrender values in the contract and, if so, what those rights are.

(Note: The appropriate sales literature should endeavour to impress on proposers that whole life or endowment assurance is intended to be a long-term contract and that surrender values, especially in the early years, are frequently less than the total premiums paid.)

4. *Commencement*

Any changes to insurance documents will be made as and when they need to be reprinted but the statement will apply in the meantime.

Revised version 1986 (partly replaced by ICOB 7.36 of the FSA Handbook in 2005, with the residual provisions incorporated in the Application Form Design for Life and Health Protection Insurances as from 2006)

The following Statement of normal insurance practice applies to policies of long-term insurance effected in the UK in a private capacity by individuals resident in the UK. Nothing in this statement should be interpreted as conflicting with or overriding the rules of LAUTRO in respect of long-term insurance policies which are treated as investments for the purposes of the Financial Services Act 1986.

Proposal forms

(a) If the proposal form calls for the disclosure of material facts a statement should be included in the declaration, or prominently displayed elsewhere on the form or in the document of which it forms part:-

  (i) drawing attention to the consequences of failure to disclose all material facts and explaining that these are facts that an insurer would regard as likely to influence the assessment and acceptance of a proposal;

  (ii) warning that if the signatory is in any doubt about whether certain facts are material, these facts should be disclosed.

(b) Neither the proposal nor the policy shall contain any provision converting the statements as to past or present fact in the proposal form into warranties except where the warranty relates to a statement of fact concerning the life to be assured under a life of another policy. Insurers, may, however, require specific warranties about matters which are material to the risk.

(c) Those matters which insurers have commonly found to be material should be the subject of clear questions in proposal forms,

(d) Insurers should avoid asking questions which would require knowledge beyond that which the signatory could reasonably be expected to possess.

(e) The proposal form or a supporting document should include a statement that a copy of the policy form or of the policy conditions is available on request

(f) The proposal form or a supporting document should include a statement that a copy of the completed proposal form is available on request

Policies and accompanying documents

(a) Insurers will continue to develop clearer and more explicit proposal forms and policy documents whilst bearing in mind the legal nature of insurance contracts.

(b) Life assurance policies or accompanying documents should indicate:-

(i) the circumstances in which interest would accrue after the assurance has matured; and

(ii) whether or not there are rights to surrender values in the contract and, if so, what those rights are.

(Note: The appropriate sales literature should endeavour to impress on proposers that a whole life or endowment assurance is intended to be a long-term contract and that surrender values, especially in the early years, are frequently less than the total premiums paid.)

Claims

(a) An insurer will not unreasonably reject a claim. In particular, an insurer will not reject a claim or invalidate a policy on grounds of non-disclosure or misrepresentation of a fact unless:

(i) it is a material fact; and

(ii) it is a fact within the knowledge of the proposer; and

(iii) it is a fact which the proposer could reasonably be expected to disclose.

(It should be noted that fraud or deception will, and reckless or negligent non-disclosure or misrepresentation of a material fact may, constitute grounds for rejection of a claim.)

(b) Except where fraud is involved, an insurer will not reject a claim or invalidate a policy on grounds of a breach of warranty unless the circumstances of the claim are connected with the breach and unless:

(i) the warranty relates to a statement of fact concerning the life to be assured under a life of another policy and that statement would have constituted grounds for rejection of a claim by the insurer under 3 (a) above if it had been made by the life to be assured under an own life policy or

(ii) the warranty was created in relation to specific matters material to the risk and it was drawn to the proposer's attention at or before the making of the contract.

(c) Under any conditions regarding a time limit for notification of a claim, the claimant will not be asked to do more than report a claim and subsequent developments as soon as reasonably possible.

(d) Payment of claims will be made without avoidable delay once the insured event has been proved and the entitlement of the claimant to receive payment has been established.

(e) When the payment of a claim is delayed more than two months, the insurer will pay interest on the cash sum due, or make an equivalent adjustment to the sum, unless the amount of such interest would be trivial. The two month period will run from the date of the happening of the insured event (i.e. death or maturity) or, in the case of a unit linked policy, from the date on which the unit linking ceased, if later. Interest will be calculated at a relevant market rate from the end of the two month period until the actual date of payment.

Disputes

The provisions of the Statement shall be taken into account in arbitration and any other referral procedures which may apply in the event of disputes between policyholders and insurers relating to matters dealt with in the Statement.

Commencement

Any changes to insurance documents will be made as and when they need to be reprinted, but the Statement will apply in the meantime.

<u>Note Regarding Industrial Assurance Policyholders</u>

Policies effected by industrial assurance policyholders are included amongst the policies to which the above Statement of Long-Term Insurance Practice applies. Those policyholders also enjoy the additional protection conferred upon them by the Industrial Assurance Acts 1923 to 1969 and Regulations issued thereunder. These Acts give the Industrial Assurance Commissioner wide powers to cover inter alia the following aspects:-

(a) Completion of proposal forms.

(b) Issue and maintenance of Premium Receipt Books.

(c) Notification in Premium Receipt Books of certain statutory rights of a policyholder including rights to:-

(i) an arrears notice before forfeiture,

(ii) free policies and surrender values for certain categories of policies,

(iii) relief from forfeiture of benefit under a policy on health grounds unless the proposer has made an untrue statement of knowledge and belief as to the assured's health.

(iv) reference to the Commissioner as arbitrator in disputes between the policyholder and the company or society.

The offices transacting industrial assurance business have further agreed that any premium (or deposit) paid on completion of the proposal form will be returned to the proposer if, on issue, the policy document is rejected by him or her.

Appendix 4 Insurance: Conduct of Business Sourcebook

ICOBS 8.1 Insurers: general

ICOBS 8.1.1

06/01/2008

An *insurer* must:

(1) handle claims promptly and fairly;

(2) provide reasonable guidance to help a *policyholder* make a claim and appropriate information on its progress;

(3) not unreasonably reject a claim (including by terminating or avoiding a *policy*); and

(4) settle claims promptly once settlement terms are agreed.

ICOBS 8.1.2

06/01/2008

A rejection of a *consumer policyholder's* claim is unreasonable, except where there is evidence of fraud, if it is for:

(1) non-disclosure of a fact material to the risk which the *policyholder* could not reasonably be expected to have disclosed; or

(2) non-negligent misrepresentation of a fact material to the risk; or

(3) breach of warranty or condition unless the circumstances of the claim are connected to the breach and unless (for a *pure protection contract*):

   (a) under a 'life of another' contract, the warranty relates to a statement of fact concerning the life to be assured and, if the statement had been made by the life to be assured under an 'own life' contract, the *insurer* could have rejected the claim under this *rule*; or

(b) the warranty is material to the risk and was drawn to the *customer's* attention before the conclusion of the contract.

Appendix 5 Conduct of Business Sourcebook

COBS 17.1.1

01/11/2007

When an *insurer* or *managing agent* receives a claim under a *long-term care insurance contract*, it must respond promptly by providing the *policyholder*, or the *person* acting on the *policyholder's* behalf, with:

(1) a claim form (if it requires one to be completed);

(2) a summary of its claims handling procedure; and

(3) appropriate information about the medical criteria that must be met, and any waiting periods that apply, under the terms of the *policy*.

Responding to a claim

COBS 17.1.2

01/11/2007

As soon as reasonably practicable after receipt of a claim, the *insurer* or *managing agent* must tell the *policyholder*, or the *person* acting on the *policyholder's* behalf:

(1) (for each part of the claim it accepts), whether the claim will be settled by paying the *policyholder*, providing goods or services to the *policyholder* or paying another *person* to provide those goods or services; and

(2) (for each part of the claim it rejects), why the claim has been rejected and whether any future rights to claim exist.

Rejecting a claim

COBS 17.1.3

01/11/2007

An *insurer* and a *managing agent* must not:

(1) unreasonably reject a claim; or

(2) except where there is evidence of fraud, reject a claim for:

   (a) non-disclosure of a fact material to the risk which the *policyholder* could not reasonably have been expected to disclose; or

   (b) misrepresentation of a fact material to the risk, unless the misrepresentation is negligent; or

   (c) breach of warranty, unless the circumstances of the claim are connected to the breach, the warranty is material to the risk and was drawn to the *policyholder's* attention before the conclusion of the contract.

Appendix 6 Application Form Design for Life and Health Protection Insurances

Guidance from the Association of British Insurers February 2006[1]

Table of contents

Introduction

1.1 The design and wording of proposal forms must meet the needs and circumstances of all interested parties, including applicants, insurers, and

[1] Reproduced by kind permission of the Association of British Insurers.

salespersons. With the wide ranging coverage now offered in the Life and Health Insurance protection market, it is vital that proposal form design keeps contemporary with such developments to ensure their success.

1.2 The reliability of the information that can be obtained from a proposal form in order to accurately assess risk is paramount. In addition, there are also commercial and legislative considerations that need inclusion, as well as those related to a variety of other published material from the ABI.

1.3 This document has been produced drawing on the experiences of many technicians in the industry and takes into account comments from the Financial Ombudsman's Service.

1.4 This guidance highlights best practice to improve the design of proposal forms. Common examples of good and bad structure and content of proposal forms are outlined. This guidance does not cover group policies.

1.5 In order to allow flexibility and to preserve competition between Insurers, the recommendations are not in any way prescriptive to ABI members, other than where existing legislation or Statements of Best Practice are applicable.

Concerns in connection with non-disclosure

2.1 The main reason for the production of this guidance is the continuing problems associated with non-disclosure that each year result in:

a. applicants purchasing policies which do not pay out when they expect them to;

b. unnecessary claims disputes;

c. un-priced for claims putting premiums up;

d. fraudulent claims.

2.2 One of the reasons people fail to disclose can be because of inadequacies in proposal form design. Potentially the rewards of reducing non-disclosure seen in the industry are very significant. In particular:

a. minimising disadvantage to diligent customers;

b. insurers can assess larger volumes of business, without the necessity to obtain costly medical evidence;

c. applications can be processed more quickly and efficiently with better take up rates and less risk of early cancellation;

d. reduced reputational risks arising from costly claims disputes;

e. claims pay out when expected – more satisfied customers;

f. ultimately, cost savings can benefit the consumer in the form of reduced premiums.

2.3 Although not all non-disclosure arises because of faults in proposal forms, insurers should do as much as they can to ensure that the questions they ask are clear and unambiguous. Doing so assists the applicant in their understanding of what is being asked of them. Thus when completing a proposal form, they should have confidence they are giving all the necessary correct and relevant information. This will also reduce the burden on salespersons in explaining or interpreting how questions should be responded to.

Insurance contracts and material facts

3.1 Insurance contracts are founded on the principles of *Uberrima Fides* or 'utmost good faith'. This places an obligation on a person applying for insurance cover to advise the other party (the insurance company) of any matter that he or she believes will affect the likelihood of the insured event happening.

3.2 As mentioned in more detail below, the Statement of Long term Insurance Practice (SoLTIP) and FSA rules require companies to ask questions about matters which have commonly been found to be material. A material fact can be regarded as any fact that may affect the risk of the insured event happening. Such material facts may have an effect on the price for the insurance cover.

3.3 Issues that are commonly material, include:

- Age and sex of the applicant;
- Lifestyle issues (smoking, alcohol consumption, use of drugs);
- Occupation;
- Participation in hazardous sports or activities;
- Residence overseas in the past or in the future;
- Personal medical history;
- Current medical condition;
- Family medical history.

The Statement of Long Term Insurance Practice (SoLTIP)

4.1 SoLTIP was issued by the ABI and derives from insurance companies earlier exemption to contract law. Insurance contracts are, however, now covered by the Unfair Terms in Consumer Contracts Regulations 1999. Nevertheless SoLTIP still stands and is used by the FOS in adjudicating claims disputes. From 2005 part of it was incorporated into the FSA rules. **The full Statement is attached at Annex A. Only the highlighted section has been moved into the FSA rules (1 ICOB 7 para 7.3.6)** The SoLTIP wording relevant to application forms is:

a if the proposal form asks for the disclosure of material facts, a statement should be included in the declaration or prominently displayed elsewhere on the form or in the document of which it forms part: -

i. drawing attention to the consequences of failure to disclose all material facts and explaining that these are facts that an insurer would regard as likely to influence the assessment and acceptance of a proposal;

ii. warning that if a signatory is in any doubt about whether certain facts are material, these facts should be disclosed.

b neither the proposal form nor the policy shall contain any provision converting the statements as to past or present fact in the proposal form into warranties except where the warranty relates to a statement of fact concerning the life to be assured under a life of another policy. Insurers, may, however, require specific warranties about matters, which are material to the risk.

c those matters, which insurers have commonly found to be material, should be the subject of clear questions in proposal forms.

d insurers should avoid asking questions, which would require knowledge beyond that which the signatory could reasonably be expected to possess.

e the proposal form or a supporting document should include a statement that a copy of the policy form or of the policy conditions is available on request.

Note: To expand upon the provisions as outlined above, questions should be designed to encourage applicants to disclose as much relevant information as possible and should not ask the applicant to judge whether something is relevant or irrelevant. If some condition is considered minor and not relevant, it should be specified (e.g. influenza). An exhaustive list of conditions does not need to be included.

4.2 There is additional law which can impact on application forms, in particular, the Data Protection Act, the Access to Medical Records Act, the Disability Discrimination Act, the Gender Recognition Act 2004, and the Privacy and Electronic Communication Regulations 2003. Annex B summarises some of the most relevant aspects. In addition insurers should take account of the Genetics moratorium and Code of Practice, and the Statement of Best Practice on HIV. Companies should also seek their own independent legal advice if necessary.

Practical implications

Clearly defining sections and headings

5.1 The different sections contained within the proposal form should be clearly identifiable with use of appropriate headings using distinctive title headings. Such as *Plan/Policy/Benefit Details, Cover Required, Mortgage/Loan Details (where applicable) etc.*

5.2 Usually there should be a clear distinction between personal and medical details with questions about each category asked together, rather than being integrated. This makes it easier for the applicant to complete these important sections. Questions relating to these sections, should be divided up (not necessarily in this order) as follows:

a. **Personal Details** – including name, title, address, sex, date of birth, marital status, contact details and occupational details. In addition, questions relating to hazardous pastimes and pursuits, aviation, existing or other proposed health protection insurance cover, previous adverse terms (i.e. if they have received adverse terms or have been refused acceptance), residence and travel.

b. **Medical Questions** – doctor's details, smoking and drinking habits, height and weight details, personal medical history, family medical history.

5.3 Whilst some of these questions might overlap somewhat between what is personal and medical information e.g. doctors details, smoking and drinking habits etc, it is important that the personal medical history questions are very obviously separated from other sections where at all possible. This helps to draw attention to this vital part of the proposal form and should assist in the consistency of the responses given.

5.4 Where appropriate, sufficient space should be provided for the applicant to answer each of the questions appropriately.

Clarity of the questions asked

6.1 **Easy to Understand**

Questions should be asked with particular attention to 'plain English', making them easy to understand and unambiguous. Where possible the use of technical medical terminology should be avoided e.g. use the term 'high blood pressure' rather than hypertension.

6.2 **Highlighting important text**

Important words or phrases should be highlighted in some way such as underlining or making the relevant text bold.

6.3 **Long questions**

Long questions with multiple parts that include a wide variety of different medical conditions or other factors should be avoided.

Example

'Have you ever suffered from heart attack, cancer, stroke, kidney disease etc ...'

6.4 **Judgemental questions**

Questions should avoid asking the applicant to make any judgement on the severity of medical conditions or symptoms i.e. being minor or serious. Rather this information should be gained through the appropriate questions being asked.

6.5 **Wide-ranging 'trawling' type questions**

Questions should be avoided that are so wide ranging that it would be difficult for practically anyone to truthfully answer them negatively.

Examples

'Have you ever suffered with back pain?.'

'Have you ever seen a doctor?'

6.6 **Unreasonable time period (sometimes referred to as 'memory test' questions)**

Questions that begin with the prefix of 'Have you ever had etc.' should only be used when referring to very serious conditions where the life assured can reasonably be expected to remember them. Therefore, this type of question could be used for conditions such as 'cancer' or 'heart attack'. However, it is not useful when enquiring about 'stomach complaints' or 'back pains', where to truthfully answer these questions would be virtually impossible and result in much useless disclosure from an underwriting perspective.

An appropriate period of time could be applied to the other conditions which are likely to be of underwriting significance when recent but become less so with the passage of time.

6.7 **Grouping questions together**

Questions should ideally put related conditions together, such as disorders of the heart, conditions related to cancer risks and so on. A reply should be sought following each individual question, rather than having one response area relating to a number of different questions.

6.8 **Specificity and order of medical conditions and symptoms**

Questions should be specific and concise. Where this is achieved, the order in which they are asked is likely to be less relevant than when long questions are asked.

6.9 **Other separate questions**

In addition to specific questions relating to medical conditions and symptoms, there should be separate questions such as:

- Any treatment currently being taken by the applicant;
- Any current symptoms for which the applicant might seek medical attention.

Family history questions

7.1 Applicants are often only asked questions about first degree relatives because there is less likelihood that they will have knowledge about remoter relatives, unless this has been specifically drawn to their attention because of a potentially inherited disease. Application forms should be clear about what is relevant information concerning the relationship of the relatives, the conditions themselves and the age of onset of the condition in the family member. Firms may wish to consider including a 'don't know' option in this section.

Additional information about disclosures

8.1 Where a disclosure has been made, it is advisable that as much relevant information as possible is obtained. This may be achieved by asking the applicant to complete a further section within the proposal form, or by completing an appropriate questionnaire, or by requesting a GP Report (GPR) or a medical examination, or any combination of these. This helps to improve disclosure (and reduce contested claims) by enabling the collection of all relevant information before the contract is agreed. In some cases this may also have the advantage of underwriters being able to accept higher volumes of business from the proposal form and reducing the need to obtain unnecessary medical evidence.

8.2 When asking for additional information, it is important that further questions are carefully worded to request specific detail where the applicant is asked to elaborate on their disclosures and expected to know what type of information is required.

8.3 Additional questionnaires should repeat the warning about the consequences of non-disclosure.

8.4 Applicants should be advised to consult their doctor if they are not confident they will remember to disclose all health details that may be relevant.

Declarations and warnings

9.1 **Prominent and easy to understand text**

Warnings should be shown prominently, for example in bold text, with greater emphasis over any other notes that might be included. Plain English should be used, avoiding jargon at all times.

9.2 **Consistency of approach**

All warnings should be consistent across all new business related documentation, including proposal forms, acceptance letters, Key Features Documents and marketing literature.

9.3 **Completion of proposal forms**

Warnings should state that the applicant is advised to complete the proposal forms themselves. Where this is not possible, warnings should state that the applicant is advised not to sign the proposal form until they have read and agree that the answers given to the questions are accurate and complete. They should also be asked to state who completed the form

9.4 Firms may wish to consider providing customers with a copy of their completed and signed application form.

9.5 **Confirmation schedules**

Warnings should be repeated in confirmation schedules that applicants are sent before going on risk.

9.6 **Detailing the consequences of non-disclosure**

The consequences of failure to disclose material facts should be as explicit as possible. Companies are free to decide on wordings. A common example is:

> 'FAILURE TO DISCLOSE RELEVANT INFORMATION MAY RESULT IN NON PAYMENT OF A CLAIM AND ALL COVER UNDER THE POLICY BEING CANCELLED'

In addition, firms may wish to advise customers that they will not automatically write to their doctor and that it is the customer's responsibility to complete their application form correctly. An example is:

> 'PLEASE DO NOT ASSUME THAT WE WILL WRITE TO YOUR DOCTOR, IT REMAINS YOUR RESPONSIBILITY TO COMPLETE THE APPLICATION FORM PROPERLY'

Alternatively, companies may wish to add an additional warning at the point when the applicant gives consent to approach their GP. An example is:

> 'YOU CANNOT ASSUME THAT YOUR DOCTOR WILL PROVIDE THE INFORMATION WE NEED. IT REMAINS YOUR RESPONSIBILITY TO COMPLETE THE APPLICATION FORM PROPERLY'

9.7 The first warning could be repeated, for example on the first page of the documentation and again at the top of each and every page where personal or medical questions are asked.

9.8 **Opportunity to disclose medical details to a Chief Medical Officer/Underwriter**

All applicants should be given the opportunity to provide answers to medical questions in private, directly to the insurer's Chief Medical Officer. This should also be highlighted or in bold print. Individuals may also be given the option of returning such information to the Chief Underwriter. Confidentiality rules should be mentioned, particularly in the latter situation.

Continuing duty to disclose

Application forms

10.1 Insurers should tell applicants that they must advise the insurer, in writing, of any changes in their circumstances which happen before the policy commences (or beyond if appropriate e.g. if you change your occupation, move abroad) that now make any of the answers on the proposal form wrong or incomplete. Please advise of any changes to the following:

- Personal health;
- Family history;
- Occupation;
- Travel or Residence;
- Hazardous pastimes;

- Alcohol consumption;
- Smoking habit
- Use of recreational drugs (e.g. cocaine, heroin)

10.2 Warnings under this section should be shown as a list (rather than free text) to add clarity, as well as including a statement that disclosures to any of the questions, medical or otherwise, are of equal importance.

Acceptance letters and policy documents confirming cover

10.3 It is advisable that acceptance letters and policy documents, remind applicants of their continuing duty to disclose until the policy starts. Warnings about the consequences of non-disclosure and the continuing duty to disclose should be included and prominent.

10.4 Other ways of re-enforcing the continuing obligation to disclose include:

a. repeating the list of changes that need to be reported as in 10.1

b. specifically asking about the key changes that the insurer is most interested in – for example any visits to a doctor

c. reminding applicants of what they disclosed on their application form

d. issuing a copy of the application form

e. issuing reminders at regular intervals

10.5 For joint life applications, the applicants should be made aware that the contract does not commence until both lives have been underwritten and accepted. As a result the continuing duty of disclosure continues until both applicants have been approved and the policy has reached commencement date.

Electronic and telephone applications

11.1 Separate discussions have been held with the FOS on electronic and tele-underwriting processes and are outside the scope of this consultation.

Post issue verification

12.1 When companies choose to obtain medical evidence shortly after completion to monitor accuracy and completeness of disclosure and/or to confirm smoker status they should consider including a statement within the documentation or the section headed 'Important Notes' which describes the practice to the applicant and details (again) the consequences of failure to disclose.

12.2 Insurer's should tell applicants when such a report is requested/required.

12.3 Post issue verification allows insurers to monitor the clarity of questions asked, non-disclosure, and prevent disputes at the point of claim.

Annex A

(Highlighted section moves to ICOB 7.3.6 from 2005 with some small amendments to the wording. The rest of the Statement remains ABI guidance)

Statement of Long-Term Insurance Practice

The following Statement of normal insurance practice applies to policies of long-term insurance effected in the UK in a private capacity by individuals resident in the UK. Nothing in this statement should be interpreted as conflicting with or overriding the rules of LAUTRO in respect of long-term insurance policies which are treated as investments for the purposes of the Financial Services Act 1986.

1. Proposal forms

a. If the proposal form calls for the disclosure of material facts a statement should be included in the declaration, or prominently displayed elsewhere on the form or in the document of which it forms part:-

   i. drawing attention to the consequences of failure to disclose all material facts and explaining that these are facts that an insurer would regard as likely to influence the assessment and acceptance of a proposal;

   ii. warning that if the signatory is in any doubt about whether certain facts are material, these facts should be disclosed.

b. Neither the proposal nor the policy shall contain any provision converting the statements as to past or present fact in the proposal form into warranties except where the warranty relates to a statement of fact concerning the life to be assured under a life of another policy. Insurers, may, however, require specific warranties about matters which are material to the risk.

c. Those matters which insurers have commonly found to be material should be the subject to clear questions in proposal forms.

d. Insurers should avoid asking questions which would require knowledge beyond that which the signatory could reasonably be expected to possess.

e. The proposal form or a supporting document should include a statement that a copy of the policy form or of the policy conditions is available on request.

2. Policies and accompanying documents

a. Insurers will continue to develop clearer and more explicit proposal forms and policy documents whilst bearing in mind the legal nature of insurance contracts.

b. Life assurance policies or accompanying documents should indicate:-

   i. the circumstances in which interest would accrue after the assurance has matured;

   and

   ii. whether or not there are rights to surrender values in the contract and, if so, what those rights are.

(Note: The appropriate sales literature should endeavour to impress on proposers that a whole life or endowment assurance is intended to be a long-term contract and that surrender values, especially in the early years, are frequently less than the total premiums paid.)

3. Claims

a. An insurer will not unreasonably reject a claim. In particular, an insurer will not reject a claim or invalidate a policy on grounds of non-disclosure or misrepresentation of a fact unless:

   i. it is a material fact; and

   ii. it is a fact within the knowledge of the proposer; and

   iii. it is a fact which the proposer could reasonably be expected to disclose.

   (It should be noted that fraud or deception will, and reckless or negligent non-disclosure or misrepresentation of a material fact may, constitute grounds for rejection of a claim.)

b. Except where fraud is involved, an insurer will not reject a claim or invalidate a policy on grounds of a breach of warranty unless the circumstances of the claim are connected with the breach and unless:

   i. the warranty relates to a statement of fact concerning the life to be assured under a life of another policy and that statement would have constituted grounds for rejection of

a claim by the insurer under 3(a) above if it had been made by the life to be assured under an own life policy or

ii. the warranty was created in relation to specific matters material to the risk and it was drawn to the proposer's attention at or before the making of the contract.

c. Under any conditions regarding a time limit for notification of a claim, the claimant will not be asked to do more than report a claim and subsequent developments as soon as reasonably possible.

d. Payment of claims will be made without avoidable delay once the insured event has been proved and the entitlement of the claimant to receive payment has been established.

e. When the payment of a claim is delayed more than two months, the insurer will pay interest on the cash sum due, or make an equivalent adjustment to the sum, unless the amount of such interest would be trivial. The two month period will run from the date of the happening of the insured event (ie death or maturity) or, in the case of a unit linked policy, from the date on which the unit linking ceased, if later. Interest will be calculated at a relevant market rate from the end of the two month period until the actual date of payment.

4. Disputes

The provisions of the Statement shall be taken into account in arbitration and any other referral procedures which may apply in the event of disputes between policyholders and insurers relating to matters dealt with in the Statement.

5. Commencement

Any changes to insurance documents will be made as and when they need to be reprinted, but the Statement will apply in the meantime.

Note Regarding Industrial Assurance Policyholders

Policies effected by industrial assurance policyholders are included amongst the policies to which the above Statement of Long-Term Insurance Practice applies. Those policyholders also enjoy the additional protection conferred upon them by the Industrial Assurance Acts 1923 to 1969 and Regulations issued thereunder. These Acts give the Industrial Assurance Commissioner wide powers to cover inter alia the following aspects:-

a. Completion of proposal forms.

b. Issue and maintenance of Premium Receipt Books.

c. Notification in Premium Receipt Books of certain statutory rights of a policyholder including rights to:-

   i. an arrears notice before forfeiture,

   ii. free policies and surrender values for certain categories of policies,

   iii. relief from forfeiture of benefit under a policy on health grounds unless the proposer has made an untrue statement of knowledge and belief as to the assured's health,

   iv. reference to the Commissioner as arbitrator in disputes between the policyholder and the company or society.

   The offices transacting industrial assurance business have further agreed that any premium (or deposit) paid on completion of the proposal form will be returned to the proposer if, on issue, the policy document is rejected by him or her.

Annex B

Summary of Additional Law of Relevance to Application Forms

Data Protection Act 1998

The Data Protection Act applies to forms that ask for any form of Personal Data if that data is held in an automated or relevant filing system. Personal data is data that relates to any living individual. All personal insurance applications are expected to fall within the scope of this Act as they ask for Personal Data and will be held in a filing system, which is accessible in a way that can identify data relating to the individual.

Forms and the way they are used must, therefore, comply with the Principles of the Act.

Also some personal data is further defined as Sensitive Personal Data and this has special requirements under the Act.

Sensitive Personal Data is defined as information about

1. The racial or ethnic origin of the data subject
2. Their political opinions
3. Their religious beliefs or other beliefs of a similar nature
4. Whether they are a member of a trade union
5. Their physical or mental health or condition
6. Their sexual life
7. The commission or alleged commission by them of any offence

8. Any proceedings for any offence committed or alleged to have been committed by them, the disposal of such proceedings or the sentence of any court in such proceedings.

Forms for insurance ask for such sensitive data to be disclosed and the specific requirements of the Act relating to Sensitive Data must be followed.

Personal data will be required for the performance of the insurance contract. This fulfils the requirement for lawful processing of data. In addition consent will be obtained in the form and as sensitive data is processed explicit consent is necessary. To demonstrate explicit consent a signed consent from the data subject should fulfil the requirement for processing such data.

The concept of fairness of collecting and processing of data is part of the scope of the Act. To ensure that a person is aware of why questions are asked on application forms details should be given about how the data will be used and any third parties that may also process personal data. The second principle refers to 'specified' purposes.

The primary purpose of the data that will be collected should be specified in application forms. This will generally be to underwrite, set-up and administer an insurance contract.

If data may be given to third parties the possibility of this must be mentioned and an explanation given about how details of any third parties, who are given data, can be identified. Third parties will include:

- Reassurance companies
- Third party administrators who may be involved in any part of the set-up or administration.

Care is required with other third parties that may be involved (GPs) and data from application forms should not be given to them unless it is reasonable to presume they are already in possession of the data. The medical history of the subject is data that can be expected to be in their possession but not necessarily data on sexual health or family history.

Data collected must be relevant to the purpose for which it will be used. Forms should ask questions about matters which are relevant to the insurance risk but any data which is not relevant or not needed to administer the contract should not be asked for.

Other aspects of the Data Protection Act relevant to application forms are

- Retention policy for data. The DPA does not state how long companies need to hold records. This is determined by the FSA. An explanation on a company's data retention can be given in the application form
- Right to prevent processing for the purposes of marketing. The process for an opt-out from marketing material can be given.

- Right in respect of automated decision taking. There is a right to ensure that no decision that significantly affects the person is based only by automatic means
- The application of the Privacy and Electronic Communications Regulations

The Data Protection Act also brings an obligation to hold data securely. A reference to the Confidentiality Policy of the Company will demonstrate that there are appropriate measures for data security.

Collection of data in application forms that involve third parties may inadvertently cause breaches of security. Providing a means for relevant data to be forwarded securely to those who require access to such data will remove this potential difficulty.

Access to personal data is also allowed under the Data Protection Act by a subject access request. When access is required to data that includes medical data there is an exemption in respect of data that may be harmful to the individual or others.

Access to Medical Reports Act 1988

A statement of the rights provided by this Act must be given to the applicant before a medical report can be obtained from the doctor.

This essential provision of this Act is to allow an individual to have access to any medical report about him or her that has been prepared by a doctor who has given the individual care. However the issue of concern to insurers is the effect of the Act on doctors' reports obtained by insurers to assess insurance applications.

Before a report can be requested by an insurer from a doctor the applicant must have consented to the report being obtained. The right to refuse to give consent is also provided by the Act, although this may result in an insurer refusing to process an application.

When consent is given the applicant should indicate whether or not he/she requires access to the report.

If access is required the applicant must be notified if a report is requested from the doctor. The doctor who has prepared the report will not release the report until the applicant has seen it or until 21 days have elapsed. If there is anything in the report with which the applicant disagrees he or she can ask to have the report amended or attach a statement of their own if the doctor refuses.

If access is not required, the applicant does not need to be informed if a report is requested.

The applicant also has the right to have access to this report for up to six months after it has been completed.

Appendix 7 Non-Disclosure and Treating Customers Fairly

Managing Claims For Individual and Group Life, Critical Illness and Income Protection Insurance Products

A Code of Practice from the Association of British Insurers, January 2009[1]
(An updated version of this Code is anticipated in April 2013)

1 Scope

1.1 This ABI code covers the continuing fair treatment of claims for UK individual and group life, critical illness, income protection and other long-term protection insurance contracts in the light of evolving industry practice, FSA regulations and the treating customers fairly (TCF) regime and experience. It covers individual policies and individually underwritten benefits within group schemes, but does not apply to any non-disclosure by scheme owners.

1.2 For the purposes of this ABI code, any reference to non-disclosure includes both the omission and misrepresentation of material information that the insurer has asked for.

1.3 This code covers the fair treatment of non-disclosure occurring during the application process and discovered at the point of claim.

1.4 This code replaces previous guidance issued by ABI dealing with non-disclosure discovered at the point of claim.

1.5 ABI believes that this code goes beyond the current legal position in many aspects. However, insurers should note that it does not purport in any way to replace the Law.

---

1 Reproduced by kind permission of the Association of British Insurers.

2 The three categories of non-disclosure and associated outcomes

2.1 The three high level categories of non-disclosure and outcomes are set out in the table below.

Category	Explanation	Outcome
Innocent	• The customer has acted honestly and reasonably in all of the circumstances, including the customer's individual circumstances but only where these were known to the insurer. • In the circumstances, a reasonable person would have considered that the information was not relevant to the insurer. • The non-disclosure would have resulted in a different underwriting outcome.	Pay the claim in full
Negligent	• Applies where the non-disclosure resulted from insufficient care – the failure to exercise reasonable care. This includes anything from an understandable oversight or an inadvertent mistake to serious negligence. In the circumstances, a reasonable person would have known that the information given was incorrect and was relevant to the insurer. • The non-disclosure would have resulted in a different underwriting outcome.	Apply a proportionate remedy
Deliberate or without any care	• Only applies where the non-disclosure was deliberate or without any care. • In the circumstances, on the balance of probabilities, the customer knew, or must have known, that the information given was both incorrect and relevant to the insurer, or the customer acted without any care as to whether it was either correct or relevant to the insurer. • The non-disclosure would have resulted in a different underwriting outcome.	Avoid the policy (decline the claim and cancel the policy from inception)

2.2 The overall principle is that the severe remedy of avoiding a policy from outset should be confined to the most serious cases of non-disclosure. See section 8 below.

3 Assessing claims

3.1 Customers cannot be expected to provide information that they are unaware of. In these circumstances, there is no lack of utmost good faith and therefore no non-disclosure.

3.2 In assessing claims, insurers should consider all of the circumstances, including:

3.2.1 How clear and concise the relevant questions were. Where the insurer has asked a clear question, there will be a presumption that the customer realised that it would be relevant to the insurer. Insurers can expect customers to answer clear questions carefully, accurately and to the best of their knowledge and belief. However, not much weight should be given to 'catch all' or 'memory test questions'.

3.2.2 The sales process and its effect on the customer – for example:

3.2.2.1 Whether or not an intermediary was involved (see 3.4 below).

3.2.2.2 Whether or not the customer had the opportunity to check their answers.

3.2.3 The warnings given and whether these were adequately prominent.

3.3 As far as possible, insurers should always try to understand the reasons for non-disclosure. Where possible, insurers should ask the customer (or the potential beneficiary) about the reasons why the information was incomplete or incorrect before making any judgement about the category of nondisclosure.

Intermediated sales

3.4 Insurers should always try to establish the facts and credibility of allegations that non-disclosure arose as a consequence of failures during the sales process and their effect on the customer, paying special regard to those parts of the process for which the insurer, or those acting for the insurer, is responsible. In particular, where the allegations are supported by credible evidence:

3.4.1 If the intermediary was acting on behalf of the insurer, and information was properly disclosed to that intermediary, then the insurer cannot claim that the information was not disclosed to it.

3.4.2 Whether an intermediary was acting as an insurer's agent in a transaction will depend on the facts and circumstances in each case.

3.4.3 The insurer will always benefit from being able to provide an audit trail – regardless of whether the sale was intermediated – to show that clear questions were asked and understood, and that the customer had the opportunity to check and confirm the accuracy of their answers.

3.4.4 If the intermediary was clearly acting on behalf of the customer, for example, an independent financial adviser, the intermediary (as opposed to the insurer) should be accountable for any non-disclosure resulting directly from the intermediary's action or omission.

Collecting medical information

3.5 Insurers are fully entitled to ask for any medical or other information needed to properly assess a claim.

3.6 However, insurers should have a legitimate reason for requesting medical information at the point of claim and should apply the principles set out in the joint BMA/ABI guidance, 'Medical Information and Insurance', on gathering medical information at the point of claim.

3.7 Accordingly, insurers should only ask for medical information beyond that needed to assess whether the insured event has occurred, or to case manage a disability claim, to the extent that the circumstances of the claim reasonably prompt the insurer to believe that there might have been non-disclosure by the customer. In particular, insurers should:

3.7.1 Keep an audit trail of the reasons for requesting medical records (the Financial Ombudsman Service, FOS, will be concerned at the use of medical evidence clearly obtained without an appropriate reason).

3.7.2 Note that an early claim is not a reason by itself (although it may be a relevant supporting factor).

3.7.3 Carefully consider the time period for which it is appropriate to request information and the relevant areas that should be investigated.

3.7.4 Ensure that claims investigations are consistent with the timely collation of evidence and the need to make claims decisions promptly.

See Annex, example cases 1 to 5 – asking for appropriate medical information

4 A proportionate remedy

4.1 A proportionate remedy means that, as far as possible, the insurer will seek to put the customer back to the same position as an identical customer who had accurately disclosed the omitted information and who paid the same premium for the same type of policy.

4.2 The outcome will therefore depend on what the underwriting decision would have been if the omitted information had been accurately disclosed at the time the customer took out the policy, as follows:

4.2.1 **The premium would have been rated** – the insurer will work out how much cover the total premium paid by the customer would have bought, and pay that amount.

See Annex, example case 6 – applying a proportionate remedy where the premium would have been rated

4.2.2 **An exclusion would have been applied to the cover** – in this case, the insurer will assess the claim as though the exclusion had been applied when the cover started. If the exclusion applies to the claim, no payment will be made. If the exclusion does not apply to the claim, a payment will be made (note: the amount paid may still be less than the full sum assured in cases where a premium rating would also have applied as above).

4.2.3 **The term would have been restricted** – in this case, the claim will be paid only if it arose within the restricted term (note: the amount paid may still be less than the full sum assured in cases where a premium rating would also have applied as above).

4.2.4 **The application would have been declined** – in this case, had the information been disclosed, there would have been no policy at all so the claim will result in no payment. However, the premiums will be returned.

4.2.5 **The underwriting decision would have been deferred** – In cases where the underwriting decision would have been deferred, or where the decision to defer the cover would have been made. As far as possible, insurers should try to determine what the ultimate underwriting decision would have been (that is, at the end of the deferred period or when the investigation was complete) and apply the appropriate remedy as above. If it is not possible to work out whether the insurer would have offered any cover, or if the deferral decision would have required the customer to re-apply at a future date, then this should be treated as a decline in 4.2.4 above.

See Annex, example cases 7 to 9 – deferred decisions

4.3 Important considerations:

4.3.1 In applying a proportionate remedy, in principle, no customer should be better off than any other customer who had disclosed all the requested information.

4.3.2 For the purpose of determining the appropriate amount to pay when a higher premium would have applied, proportionality applies at the policy level, for example where the policy covers more than one person or multiple types of benefit.

See Annex, example case 10 – applying a proportionate remedy to a multi-benefit policy

For a joint life policy see Annex, example case 6 – applying a proportionate remedy where the premium would have been rated

5 Non-disclosure and inducement

5.1 For the purposes of this section, 1.2 above and for the rest of this code, material information means that, if it had been disclosed, the omitted information would have induced the insurer at the time the cover started to have applied a different underwriting outcome. For example:

5.1.1 A higher premium would have applied to the policy for the same sum assured;

5.1.2 A lower sum assured would have applied to the policy for the same premium;

5.1.3 Part of the cover would have been excluded for the relevant life assured;

5.1.4 The term of the policy would have been restricted;

5.1.5 The application would have been deferred, for example, pending the outcome of a medical investigation; or

5.1.6 The application would have been declined.

6 Menu and multi-benefit policies – severable benefits and non-disclosure that is deliberate or without any care

6.3 Insurers may not decline a claim as a result of non-disclosure if the omitted information was material only to a severable benefit which is not the subject of the claim.

6.2 For this purpose, for combinations of critical illness and/or income protection and/or life cover benefits in a single policy, the severable benefit types are limited to Total Permanent Disability and Waiver of Premium Benefit.

See Annex, example case 11 – a claim with non-disclosure that relates only to a severable benefit

6.3 When considering non-disclosure, insurers should take into account the risk warnings given and whether these were adequately prominent – see section 3.2.3 above.

7 Notes on innocent non-disclosure or misrepresentation

7.1 Typical characteristics:

7.1.1 The question was not clear enough – any ambiguous wording should be construed in favour of the customer.

7.1.2 The question did not apply clearly to the facts in question.

7.1.3 It was reasonable for the customer to have overlooked the omitted information – for example, a minor childhood ailment.

7.2 It is irrelevant whether or not there is a link between the non-disclosure and the cause of the claim.

8 Notes on non-disclosure that is deliberate or without any care

8.1 The overall principle is that the severe remedy of avoiding a policy from outset should be confined to the most serious cases of non-disclosure.

8.2 The insurer has the initial burden of establishing whether any case falls into this category on the balance of probabilities. Accordingly, insurers need clear evidence to show this applies.

8.3 This category does not apply where:

8.3.1 Having investigated the matter, the customer has a credible explanation supported by the facts for having omitted information and/or there are other credible mitigating circumstances.

8.3.2 The degree of materiality associated with the non-disclosure is relatively low and, in cases where a premium rating would have applied, the underlying risk premium rating resulting from the non-disclosed information in aggregate would not have been more than +50% (or £1/mil) for the applicable life assured.

8.4 Typical characteristics:

8.4.1 **Deliberate** – in the circumstances, the customer knew, or must have known, that the representation they made in answer to a question was incorrect, and knew, or must have known, that the information was relevant to the insurer (that is, they intended to omit the information).

8.4.2 **Without any care** – it is clear that the customer had a complete disregard for the question or the accuracy of the answer when completing the application and must have understood that the information was relevant to the insurer.

8.4.3 **Medical information** – in cases where the omitted information was about the customer's medical history or family medical history (as opposed to, for example, about occupation, time spent abroad, the use of tobacco products, alcohol or drugs) insurers should take into account that in some circumstances consumers may not have a full understanding of their medical history. Accordingly, this category is more likely to apply in the following situations:

8.4.3.1 The omitted information is widely known by consumers to be important to the risk of a claim being made (for example, cancer, heart disease, diabetes or, for income protection, periods of time off work as a result of incapacity).

8.4.3.2 The omitted information concerns recent or ongoing treatment, specialist consultations and/or medical investigations about matters that a reasonable consumer would have understood to be important to their health.

8.4.3.3 The customer has specialist knowledge – for example, someone in the medical profession or relevant parts of the insurance industry.

See Annex, example cases 12 & 13 – non-disclosure of medical information

8.4.4 **Lifestyle information** – since lifestyle information is usually more familiar and easier for customers to understand, it follows that customers will need to give a particularly credible and convincing explanation for clearly evidenced non-disclosure not to be classified as deliberate or without any care.

See Annex, example cases 14 & 15 – where smoking is not disclosed

8.4.5 **Continuing duty of disclosure** – insurers will need to have a particularly robust case for classifying non-disclosure occurring after the application was completed as deliberate or without any care (that is, when the non-disclosure results from a change of health or other circumstances after the application was completed but before the cover starts).

8.5 **Returning premiums** – when avoiding a policy, insurers will normally return the premiums paid. Insurer will only keep the premiums in cases where there is clear evidence of fraud, or if the nondisclosure has been proved fraudulent in a court of law.

9 Notes on negligent non-disclosure or misrepresentation

9.1 Includes all cases between innocent and deliberate or without any care.

10 Notes on the application of this code for group schemes

10.1 This code only applies to non-disclosure by individual members of group schemes. It does not apply to any non-disclosure by employers, trustees or other group scheme owners.

10.2 Any non-disclosure by an individual group scheme member should not affect that member's entitlement to benefits up to the amount of any free cover limit applicable to that member at the time of joining the scheme.

10.3 Any non-disclosure by an individual scheme member should not affect any other scheme member's entitlement to receive benefits from the scheme.

Annex – Illustrative Examples

Case 1 – asking for appropriate medical information for a benign brain tumour claim

A 42 year old woman makes a critical illness insurance claim for a benign brain tumour after her policy has been in force for a year. The insurer's medical advice is that there is a reasonable likelihood that the woman experienced related symptoms before the policy started.

In addition to asking for all the details relating to the need to assess whether the benign brain tumour definition is met, the insurer asks her GP for a report that includes details of all consultations concerning neurological and related symptoms in the two years before the woman took out the policy. The insurer explains that it is interested in all relevant symptoms including loss of coordination or motor control, hemiparesis, numbness, speech difficulties, hearing loss, impairment of vision, intellectual impairment, headache, epilepsy, vomiting. The insurer makes it clear that it wants a copy of the original medical records, referral letters, etc that relate to any such consultations. This is so that it can get the most accurate picture of what underwriting terms, if any, it would have offered.

If the claim had been for cancer, depending on the site, the potential early symptoms might be too wide in scope for the insurer to list for the GP.

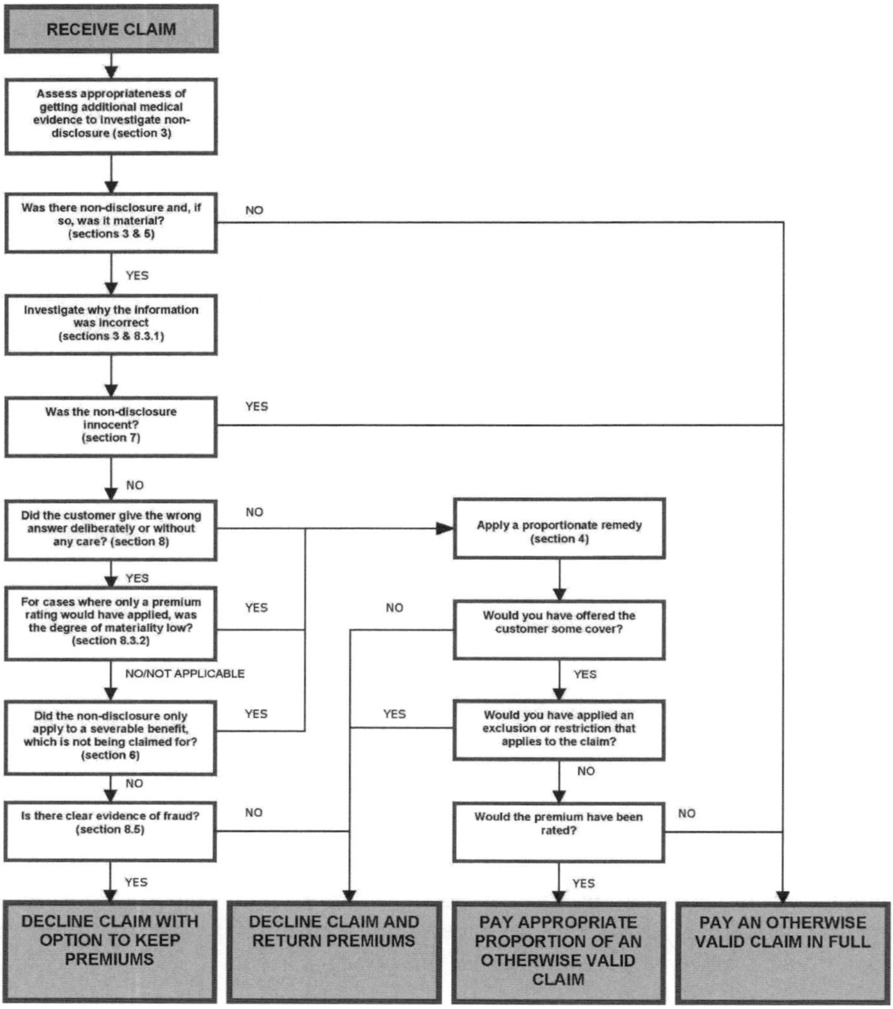

Therefore, it would be appropriate for the insurer to ask for a copy of the original medical records over a time period appropriate to the likely onset of the cancer.

Case 2 – asking for appropriate medical information in an accidental death claim

A man takes out life insurance and dies less than two years later. The information on the interim certificate of the fact of death leaves the insurer with reason to believe that the customer might have committed suicide, been the victim of an unlawful killing, suffered an accident with no contributory medical factor or suffered an accident with a contributory medical factor. The insurer is at first unable to get further credible information from the Coroner or other sources.

The insurer is keen to avoid delaying settlement of the claim. It wishes to avoid repeated requests for additional information or evidence; especially for evidence that the customer could reasonably say that the insurer was able to ask for earlier in its consideration of the claim.

In some of the potential scenarios, it is likely that the customer would have experienced undisclosed symptoms of a contributing medical condition before the policy started. However, this could involve a wide range of relevant medical conditions or symptoms. In these circumstances, it is therefore reasonable for the insurer to request from the GP sight of the medical records over a time period appropriate to the medical conditions that it has reason to believe may have existed.

Before receiving this medical information, and before the Inquest has been held, the Coroner is able to inform the insurer that there is no evidence to suggest anything other than that the customer was the innocent victim of a road traffic collision and the customer had no contributory medical condition. The insurer should pay the claim and inform the GP that it no longer needs sight of the medical information.

Case 3 – asking for appropriate medical information in an accidental death claim with an underlying medical cause

A man takes out life insurance and dies less than a year later. The circumstances of his death are such that the insurer believes that he has died in a road traffic collision. The Coroner and post-mortem indicate that the man suffered a heart attack at the wheel of his car.

The insurer therefore has reason to believe that not all questions about the customer's cardiovascular history, and related factors such as family history, weight and smoking history were correctly answered. This includes coronary heart disease, congenital and valvular heart disease, cardiac arrhythmias, hypertension and other circulatory disorders, and their related symptoms, tests and treatment. The insurer writes accordingly to the GP.

The information received from the GP shows that the customer did not disclose a history of angina, related treatment and a relevant family history. However, the information doesn't enable the insurer to determine whether the non-disclosure was deliberate or precisely what terms it might have offered if there had been full disclosure at outset. Accordingly, the insurer asks the doctor for further clarification of the matters that were not disclosed.

Case 4 – asking for appropriate additional medical information for an income protection claim

A 40 year old woman makes a claim for chronic fatigue syndrome under her income protection policy which she took out six years ago. The insurer asks her GP and her Consultant Neurologist for the full medical reports on her current condition.

The GP report confirms that she is currently incapacitated. The Consultant's report suggests that a neurological investigation revealed no adverse findings. However, this report also refers to episodes of anxiety and depression when she was in her late 20's and early 30's. These episodes were not disclosed when she took out the policy, despite being the subject of clear questions in the application.

The insurer therefore asks the GP for a copy of her medical records since the age of 25. These records show recurrent episodes of depression, irritable bowel syndrome, stress at work, reports of being tired all the time, treatment with fluoxetine and prozac, as well as time off work for depression in the year before she took out the policy.

Accordingly, the insurer asks her why she did not disclose this information as the next first step in assessing her claim.

Case 5 – asking for appropriate medical information for a death claim caused by liver failure

A man dies of liver failure three years after taking out life insurance. The circumstances are such that the insurer has reason to suspect that the claim might be related to a history of heavy alcohol consumption or drug use that started before the policy was taken out, but was not disclosed.

Accordingly, the insurer asks the customer's GP for information, including a copy of the original medical records, relating to the use of alcohol and drugs in the period before the policy started, together with details of any history of liver disorder such as hepatitis or cirrhosis, or of any metabolic disorder. The insurer also asks for details of any consultations and treatment regarding the customer's mental health. The time period asked about is appropriate to the development of the conditions that the insurer has reason to be concerned about.

Case 6 – applying a proportionate remedy where the premium would have been rated

When assessing a man's critical illness claim, an insurer finds that he had incorrectly answered a question about his medical history when he took out the policy, jointly with his wife, several years before. They paid a premium of £50 a month for joint cover of £100,000. The insurer assesses the nondisclosure in accordance with this code and concludes that he had been negligent.

If he had given the correct information, using the premium rates that applied when the policy was taken out, the insurer works out that the premium of £50 a month would only have bought joint cover of £75,000.

As the claim is otherwise valid and a proportionate remedy is appropriate, the insurer pays out £75,000.

Case 7 – where the underwriting decision would have been deferred pending an investigation

A man takes out critical illness insurance and subsequently claims for cancer. In assessing the claim, the insurer discovers that when he took out the policy he failed to disclose that he was waiting for the results of a test for the malignancy of a mole. The insurer assesses the non-disclosure in accordance with this code and concludes that he had been negligent.

If the insurer had known about this, it would have deferred the underwriting decision until the result of the test was known. However, on this occasion the test showed that the mole was perfectly normal with no signs of malignancy. In these circumstances, the insurer would have accepted the application on standard terms. Accordingly, in applying a proportionate remedy, the insurer pays the claim in full.

Case 8 – where the underwriting decision would have been deferred subject to a fresh application at an unspecified time in the future

A woman takes out life insurance and subsequently dies of a heart attack. In assessing the claim, the insurer discovers that she failed to disclose that, shortly before she took out the policy, she had made a failed suicide attempt after a significant life event and she was taking treatment for depression. The insurer assesses the non-disclosure in accordance with this code and concludes that she had been negligent.

If the insurer had known this, it would have deferred the underwriting decision indefinitely, but would have been prepared to consider a new application for life insurance when she has been free from treatment for at least a year.

In these circumstances, the insurer would not have offered any cover at all at the time of her application, nor in the foreseeable future. Accordingly, the insurer applies a proportionate remedy meaning that it declines the claim, cancels the policy from inception and returns her premiums in full.

Case 9 – where the insurer would have asked for specific tests

A man takes out life insurance and subsequently dies in the early years of the policy. In assessing the claim, the insurer discovers that he failed to disclose GP consultations six months before he took out the policy. At these consultations he reported alcohol-related symptoms, including early morning tremors and a jaundiced appearance. However, there is no evidence that shows the amount of alcohol he was consuming in the period immediately before he took out the policy, nor can the insurer establish with certainty that he was advised to stop or reduce his drinking on medical grounds. The insurer assesses the non-disclosure in accordance with this code and concludes that he had been negligent. If the insurer had known about these GP consultations, it would have deferred the underwriting decision until he had taken a liver function test.

Depending on what the outcome of the liver function test would have been (if one had been performed) the underwriting decision might have been any of the following:

- Application accepted at normal rates.
- Application accepted with a higher premium (where the amount of the extra premium would have depended on the actual test result).
- Application declined.

In a case where his medical history while the policy was in-force is consistent with continuing excessive alcohol consumption (for example, death from liver cirrhosis), the insurer concludes that the most likely result of the liver function test would have meant that using the underwriting guidelines applicable at that time they would not have offered insurance when he applied for the policy. In these circumstances, the insurer would have declined his application and, accordingly, in applying a proportionate remedy the insurer declines the claim.

However, in a case where there is evidence of only moderate alcohol consumption after the initial GP consultations, the insurer might conclude on the balance of probabilities that the test result would have allowed the insurer to accept the case on rated terms. Accordingly, in these circumstances, in applying a proportionate remedy the insurer will apply their expert judgement as to the terms that are most likely to have been offered and makes the appropriate payment.

Case 10 – applying a proportionate remedy to a multi-benefit policy

A man takes out a multi-benefit policy with £100,000 critical illness insurance (CI) and £1000 a month income protection (IP). The premium he pays is £80 a month. When he took out the policy he incorrectly answered a specific question about his occupation.

Some time later, he makes an otherwise valid critical illness claim for testicular cancer. After a review of the circumstances of the non-disclosure, the insurer concludes that the misrepresentation was negligent and applies a proportionate remedy.

Using the premium rates that would have applied at the time the policy was taken out, the insurer works out that, if he had correctly disclosed his occupation, the premium for the whole policy would have been £100 a month. By applying the same proportion to all benefits, a premium of £80 a month would have provided £80,000 CI and £800 a month IP. As the CI claim is otherwise valid, the insurer pays out £80,000.

Under the terms of the policy, cover for CI ends with the payment of a claim, and the premium for this part of the cover stops. However, as IP is a continuing benefit, the insurer reduces the ongoing IP cover to £800 a month and notifies the customer.

Case 11 – a claim with non-disclosure that relates only to a severable benefit

A woman takes out a policy for critical illness insurance (CI) with total permanent disability (TPD) benefit where cover for one of the benefits continues after a successful claim on the other. When she took out the policy she knowingly answered a specific question incorrectly, deliberately concealing an ongoing history of serious back problems. She then makes an otherwise valid CI claim for breast cancer.

The insurer does not decline the claim because the outcome of the underwriting would only have changed the terms offered for TPD, and not for the main CI benefit being claimed for.

If the back problems had been disclosed, the insurer would have issued the policy at standard premium rates but with an exclusion for back problems for TPD. As this exclusion does not apply to breast cancer, the insurer pays the CI claim in full.

However, as there was deliberate non-disclosure relating to TPD, the insurer avoids the remaining TPD benefit.

Case 12 – finding out why medical information was not disclosed

A man aged 42 takes out a critical illness (CI) policy for £100,000 for a premium of £40 a month. Some time later he makes a claim for a heart attack. In assessing the claim, the insurer finds that when he took out the policy he had for several years been taking tablets daily to control hypertension. However, he incorrectly answered a clear question about high blood pressure and a clear question about ongoing treatment. He answered the remaining questions in the application correctly. If he had disclosed his high blood pressure and treatment, the insurer would have charged a premium of £80 a month.

The insurer asks him why he wrongly answered the questions. He explains that he did not consider himself to have had high blood pressure as his pills were effectively controlling it. Further, his doctor had told him that the treatment was 'routine' and that his condition was very common for a man of his age and that it was 'nothing to worry about'. He did not therefore consider this to be relevant.

The insurer decides that his explanation for the incorrect answer is credible because it fits his medical records and the other circumstances of the case. However, the representation was incorrect and the omission was material.

Taking into account all the circumstances, the insurer gives him the benefit of the doubt. That is, on the balance of probabilities, although he must have known about his condition and treatment, the insurer cannot say that he must have known that his condition was relevant to the insurer or that he acted with complete disregard to the truth of his answers. Accordingly, the insurer does not classify the nondisclosure as deliberate or without any care.

Given the questions asked, the insurer concludes that a reasonable person ought to have known that the representation given was relevant to the insurer. In the circumstances, the customer's answer to the question about ongoing treatment was not reasonable. Accordingly, the insurer treats his misrepresentation as negligent having concluded that it was not innocent.

Using the premium rates that applied when the policy started, the insurer works out that a premium of £40 a month would have provided cover of £48,500. As a proportionate remedy applies and the claim is otherwise valid, the insurer pays out £48,500.

Case 13 – where non-disclosure of medical information is deliberate or without any care

A man aged 47 takes out critical illness insurance for £100,000. Two years later he makes a claim for a heart attack.

In assessing the claim, the insurer finds out that when he took out the policy, for a continuous period of three years he had been taking a combination of three types of medication for hypertension. His medical records show that, despite the treatment, his blood pressure had been significantly raised during this period and that he had been to see his doctor at regular intervals to monitor his blood pressure and renew his prescription for treatment. However, he wrongly answered two clear questions in the application about high blood pressure and ongoing treatment. If he had disclosed his high blood pressure and treatment, using the underwriting manual applicable when he took out the policy, the insurer would have applied a risk premium rating of +100%.

The insurer asks him why his answers to the questions were incorrect. He explains that, because he had been taking treatment for many years, he did not consider his condition or the treatment to be important, and that his blood pressure was controlled by the treatment.

However, contrary to his explanation, the evidence in his medical records shows that his GP had repeatedly warned him about his uncontrolled high blood pressure. Therefore, the insurer concludes that:

- he must have known that his answers were incorrect; and
- he must have known they were relevant to the insurer.

If he had correctly disclosed his condition and treatment, the underwriting outcome would have been a risk premium rating of more than +50%. Accordingly, the insurer classifies the non-disclosure as deliberate or without any care. The insurer therefore avoids the policy and refunds the premiums.

Case 14 – where smoking is negligently not disclosed

A woman takes out a combined (accelerated) life and critical illness insurance policy and declares that she is a non-smoker. Following an otherwise valid claim for cancer, the insurer finds that her medical records show that she was a smoker six months before she took out the policy, and she was also a smoker at the time of the claim.

The insurer asks her why she declared herself to be a non-smoker. She explained that her reason for buying the policy was because she was starting a family. She said she had given up smoking since finding out she was pregnant which was when she took out the policy. The evidence supports this. Her adviser, an employee of the insurer, filled in her application on-line. She recalls that her adviser had only asked her if she was a smoker and not whether she had used tobacco within the preceding 12 months as asked in the application. She accepted that she should have been more careful in checking the copy of the completed application sent to her to review.

In the circumstances, the insurer accepts her explanation as credible given the evidence of the pregnancy as mitigating circumstances and does not avoid the policy. It therefore treats the nondisclosure as negligent (as opposed to deliberate or without any care) and applies a proportionate remedy. Based on the smoker rates that applied when she took out the policy, the insurer works out how much cover her premium would have provided and pays that amount.

If she had not been asked to check the application, as she answered the question asked by the adviser (acting on behalf of the insurer) to the best of her knowledge and belief, there would have been no nondisclosure and the claim should be paid in full.

Case 15 – where smoking is deliberately not disclosed

A man applies for critical illness insurance and declares that he is a non-smoker. Following a claim for cancer, the insurer finds that his medical records show that he was a heavy smoker three months before he took out the policy and also after the start of the policy.

The insurer asks why he had declared himself to be a non-smoker but he fails to offer any plausible mitigating explanation. In the circumstances, the insurer concludes that either:

- he must have known that he was a smoker and, given the question in the application, must have known that this was relevant; or
- he showed no care at all in answering the question about whether he had smoked.

Accordingly, on the balance of probabilities, the insurer concludes that the non-disclosure was deliberate or without any care. The insurer therefore avoids the policy and refunds the premiums.

Appendix 8 Campaign Letters

Daily Telegraph
Saturday 5 September 2009
Unfair insurance deals

SIR—We urge that the Queen's Speech should confirm the intention of her Government to reform consumer insurance law.

A joint report on the topic will be published by the English and Scottish Law Commissions this year. Reform is overdue and has been advocated by previous official reports and leading judges.

Insurance law is derived largely from commercial cases and can produce injustice when applied to consumer contracts. Reports published by the Financial Ombudsman Service provide disturbing examples.

The better insurers do not rely on their strict legal rights, but follow guidance from the Ombudsman on what is fair and reasonable. The Law Commissions are in essence expected to recommend that this best practice should be given legal force.

This is a straightforward piece of law reform. The Law Commissions have been working towards their proposals for three years, have consulted widely and issued some impressive interim papers. A short draft Bill will be included in their report.

We hope the proposals will attract all-party support and rapidly pass into law.

Professor John Birds
University of Manchester

Professor Malcolm Clarke
St John's College, Cambridge

Professor Richard Lewis
Cardiff University

Professor John Lowry
University College, London

Professor Andrew McGee
University of Manchester

Consumer Insurance Law

Professor Robert Merkin
University of Southampton

Professor Philip Rawlings
University College, London

Maggie Hemsworth
University of Plymouth

Ray Hodgin
University of Birmingham

Peter Tyldesley
University of Manchester

Financial Times
2/3 October 2010
Insurance law from Georgian times needs update

Sir, Insurance law needs change. Its current inadequacies are well illustrated by your report ("Consumer groups urge insurers to back law reform", FT Money, September 25) of the woman denied a critical illness payout for leukaemia following a failure to declare unrelated ear infections.

The same harsh rules apply to all other types of consumer insurance, including motor and household. We therefore urge the government to implement the Law Commissions' proposals for reform.

The present law was developed to govern face-to-face commercial insurance deals in the coffee houses of Georgian London.

It requires consumers to volunteer any facts an insurer would regard as relevant – an unreasonable obligation in a modern mass-market internet world.

If a consumer fails to make full disclosure the insurer may later be entitled to cancel the policy from outset and reject any claim – even if the consumer acted honestly and reasonably and there is no connection between the fact concerned and the loss.

Commendably many insurers do not rely on their legal rights. Instead they follow best practice set out in ombudsman's guidance.

We believe the law should be brought into line with best practice, giving consumers the certainty of legally enforceable rights, and benefiting insurers by increasing confidence in their products and professionalism.

Laurence Baxter, Head of Policy and Research, Chartered Insurance Institute

Lola Bello, Senior Policy Advocate, Consumer Focus

Professor John Birds, University of Manchester

Beatrice Brooke, Policy Manager, British Heart Foundation

Peter Hinchliffe, Former Lead Ombudsman for Insurance

Mike Hobday, Head of Campaigns, Policy and Public Affairs, Macmillan Cancer Support

Martin Lewis, MoneySavingExpert.com

Professor Robert Merkin, Deputy President, British Insurance Law Association

Helen McCallum, Director of Policy, Advocacy and Communications, Which?

Michelle Mitchell, Charity Director, Age UK

David Sanders, Lead Officer for Civil Law and Former Chairman, Trading Standards Institute

Christopher Stacey, Unlock, the National Association of Reformed Offenders

Peter J. Staddon, Head of Technical Services, British Insurance Brokers' Association

Peter J. Tyldesley, Senior Lecturer, University of Bedfordshire

Laura Weir, Head of Policy and Campaigns, MS Society

The Times
Tuesday 5 October 2010
Update archaic insurance law

Sir, Students of insurance law must sometimes wonder whether they have strayed into a history lecture. Carter v Boehm 1766, the Life Assurance Act 1774 and the Marine Insurance Act 1788 – which applies only to non-marine insurance – are but elements of a delightful hotchpotch of archaic law. Regrettably much of this law has the potential to inflict serious injustice, particularly where consumers are concerned (Laura Whateley, Troubleshooter, Oct 2).

When purchasing insurance, for example, consumers are obliged to volunteer all facts that a prudent insurer would regard as material. Failure to do so may later entitle the insurer to cancel the policy and reject any claim. Requiring a prospective policyholder to look into the mind of an insurer made sense at a time when merchants were coming together to share risk, contracting on equal terms in Edward Lloyd's coffee house. It is absurd to apply the same rule to modern mass-market consumer policies, often purchased over the internet without the benefit of advice and with no knowledge of insurance law or practice.

The better insurers do not rely on their strict legal rights. Instead they follow guidance from the Financial Ombudsman Service, which tellingly declines to enforce the duty of disclosure. A glance through cases reported by the Ombudsman, however, confirms that some insurers continue to rely on bad law.

Unsurprisingly consumers will lose confidence in insurance if equitable treatment is seen to be at the discretion of the insurer. The solution is law reform, giving consumers fair rights and protecting the reputation of insurers. A consumer insurance law reform bill was published by the Law Commission in 2009. It should be implemented without delay, even if the lives of students and lecturers become a little duller.

PETER J. TYLDESLEY
Senior Lecturer in Insurance Law
University of Bedfordshire

The Times
Thursday 7 October 2010
Unfair insurers

Sir, Consumer insurance law is out of date, unclear and unfair (letter, Oct 5). It allows insurers to reject claims for spurious reasons. Consumers have no legal guarantee against the possibility of an insurance company rejecting a claim for non-disclosure, even when the undisclosed matter has no bearing whatsoever on the claim. This uncertainty prevents many people from taking out the protection they need, and can also leave individuals unexpectedly being refused an insurance payout at a time when they are most vulnerable.

The law should be brought into line with best practice as soon as possible, to give vulnerable consumers the protection they need.

PETER VICARY-SMITH
Chief Executive, Which?

The Times
Tuesday 12 October 2010
Health insurance in need of reform

Sir, Macmillan Cancer Support has experience of the best and worst of insurance practice (letters, Oct 5 and 7). There is no doubt that insurance is an invaluable product which can allay financial concerns for patients and their families after a diagnosis of cancer. Most insurers act professionally and abide both by guidance from the Ombudsman and by a voluntary code published by the Association of British Insurers. However, in a minority of cases, the unwarranted rejection of a claim inflicts further stress at what is already a difficult time.

Macmillan recently supported an ovarian cancer patient whose claim under a critical illness policy was rejected for what the insurer alleged was deliberate non-disclosure. After investigation, the Ombudsman found against the insurer, instructing it to pay out £46,000. Payment was eventually received more than 13 months after the claim was made. How much more useful those funds would have been had the claim been settled promptly and fairly.

The Ombudsman is able to assist because she makes decisions on a "fair and reasonable" basis, meaning that the anachronistic rules of insurance law can be ignored. This is not a complete solution. There is a range of restrictions on the Ombudsman, most notably a limit on awards of £100,000.

Anyone turning to the courts as an alternative – for reasons of speed, or because their claim is caught by a restriction – will face the full harshness of antiquated law.

No one developing a life-changing condition should be told that although they prudently provided for just such a situation their insurance has been rendered valueless on a legal technicality.

MIKE HOBDAY
Head of Campaigns
Policy and Public Affairs
Macmillan Cancer Support

Appendix 9

Briefing Note for Members attending the All Party Parliamentary Group for Consumer Affairs and Trading Standards (CATS)

19 May 2009 (5–6pm) in Committee Room 7, House of Commons

Insurance law reform
Fairer treatment for consumers will bring increased confidence in the insurance industry

In a joint report, to be published later this year, the English and Scottish Law Commissions are expected to recommend that many of the archaic laws presently governing consumer insurance contracts should be replaced. Proposed new rules will broadly follow the approach taken by the Financial Ombudsman Service and reflect best practice within the insurance industry. The report will cover some of the major areas of insurance law including misrepresentation, non-disclosure and breach of warranty.

Existing law provides insurers with remedies which, in many cases, are wholly disproportionate. If an insurer is induced to issue a policy by a consumer's misrepresentation or non-disclosure of a relevant fact it may later, on becoming aware of the true position, withdraw cover retrospectively and reject any claims. And a breach of warranty terminates cover immediately – even if the breach is swiftly remedied.

The Commissions have cited a range of cases reported by the Financial Ombudsman Service or heard in the courts as illustrating the potential lack of fairness in the law. For example, this misrepresentation case was referred to the Ombudsman:

> 'Mrs C made a claim under a critical illness policy after she was diagnosed as suffering from leukaemia. The insurer rejected the claim because when completing the application form her husband had inadvertently omitted to mention that she had suffered from unrelated ear infections and resultant loss of hearing.'

It is anticipated that the Commissions' recommendations will largely follow the line taken in a consultation paper they issued in 2007:

- Misrepresentation – consumers will be expected to act honestly and reasonably. Hence deliberate or reckless misrepresentation will still entitle the insurer to withdraw cover from outset and reject any claim.

  In contrast, if the consumer has been honest and careful, the policy will remain in force and any claim will be met. If the misrepresentation is negligent the remedy will be based on what the insurer would have done had it known the true facts. For example, in the case of Mrs C, this would mean an exclusion relating to hearing loss would be added to the policy but the leukaemia claim would be paid in full.
- Non-disclosure – the duty on consumers to volunteer information will be abolished. Consumers' rights will no longer be dependent on their ability accurately to look into the mind of a prudent insurer to establish what should be disclosed.
- Warranties – a breach of warranty will not lead to the rejection of a consumer's claim unless there is a causal connection between the breach and the loss that has occurred.

These issues will be discussed at the CATS meeting on 19 May.

Notes for Editors

1. **The Law Commissions** are statutory independent bodies created by the Law Commissions Act 1965 to keep the law under review and to recommend reform where it is needed.
2. **Misrepresentation and non-disclosure**

   A consumer applying for insurance is obliged to disclose all material facts – that is, facts which would have an effect, whether decisive or not, on the mind of a prudent insurer in assessing the risk. If the misrepresentation or non-disclosure of a material fact induces an insurer to issue a policy, it may on becoming aware of the true position avoid the contract – that is, withdraw the cover from outset – and decline to pay any claims.

The main criticisms of these rules are:

- The law on non-disclosure dates from the decision of Lord Mansfield in *Carter v Boehm 1766.* Law which seemed appropriate for face-to-face transactions in the coffee houses of Georgian London is unsurprisingly not fit for purpose when applied to modern consumer contracts purchased by telephone or internet.
- The test of materiality requires the applicant for insurance to look into the mind of a prudent insurer. Most consumers do not have the knowledge or expertise to do so.
- There is no requirement of a causal connection between the misrepresentation or non-disclosure and any claim that has occurred. An insurer may avoid the policy and decline to pay a claim even where the misrepresentation or non-disclosure had no direct bearing on the loss.
- The conduct or state of mind of the consumer is irrelevant. Even if a misrepresentation or non-disclosure was entirely understandable and innocent, the policy may be avoided.
- Avoidance is an all-or-nothing remedy. Where a policy is avoided, the consumer foregoes the right to have claims paid and may be required to return any payments already received. The avoidance will itself need to be disclosed on subsequent applications for insurance, which may make it difficult to obtain cover in the future.
- The law does not require the insurer to ask the consumer any questions. If questions are asked, a duty of disclosure still exists in respect of any matters which the questions do not cover.

3. **Warranties** are terms of an insurance policy which are akin to promises. If a warranty is breached cover ceases immediately and any claim for a subsequent loss can be rejected. Even if a breach is rapidly remedied cover does not recommence.

   Basis of the contract clauses turn all the answers a consumer gives on an application form into warranties. The effect is that if a wrong answer is given there is a breach of warranty and cover never commences.

For further information please contact Paul Allen, Ex Sec CATS, on 01273 475877 or at pallen@dircon.co.uk or Peter Tyldesley, Solicitor and lecturer in insurance law, on 07973 210210 or at peter.tyldesley@manchester.ac.uk

All Party Parliamentary Group for Consumer Affairs and Trading Standards

Thirty-Second Meeting 19 May 2009, 5–6pm

Committee Room 7, House of Commons

1. Present: Austin Mitchell MP, APPG Chairman

    Michael Foster MP, APPG Secretary

    John Penrose MP

    Baroness Crawley, Incoming President TSI

    Lord Borrie of Abbotts Morton, Vice President TSI

    David Hertzell, Law Commission Commissioner

    Peter Hinchliffe, Lead Ombudsman Financial Ombudsman Service

    Peter Tyldesley, Solicitor and Lecturer in Insurance Law

    Heather Miller, Head of General Insurance Policy, HM Treasury

    Tamara Goriely, Law Commission

    Ben Davies, Parliamentary Researcher to John Penrose

    Paul Allen, Vice President TSI

    Paul Ramsden, Deputy Chief Executive TSI

    Vera Cottrell, WHICH?

    Shradha Patel, Association of British Insurers

    Steve Munro & Dan Ellacott, NACO Services Limited

    Mike Hobday, Head of Campaigns Macmillan Cancer Support

    Joanne Milligan, Senior Public Affairs Advocate Consumer Focus

    Natalie Yelton, Public Affairs Advocate Consumer Focus

    Clive Grenyer, Constitutional Lawyer

    Suzanne Kuyser, Policy and Communications Manager TSI

    Irja Howie, Press Officer TSI

    Jessica Tangye, Policy Officer TSI

2. Apologies: Baroness Miller of Hendon

    Rt. Honourable Francis Maude MP

    Baroness Dean of Thornton-Le-Flyde

Lord Bowness

Lord Janner

Ian Pearson MP

Nick Harvey MP

Michael Fallon MP

Linda Gilroy MP

Norman Baker MP

Richard Thomas; Information Commissioner

Ron Gainsford Chief Executive TSI

Noel Hunter Chairman of The Board TSI

Peter Denard Chairman TSI

3. No matters arising

4. 'Fairness needed for insurance contracts'

4.1 The Chairman introduced the subject to the Group and then invited David Hertzell, Law Commission Commissioner to address the meeting. Mr Hertzell gave a brief history of the basic insurance law going back to the Marine Insurance Act of 1906 and the Law Commission's proposals to bring the law up to date. He concluded, in answer to questions 'This is not a radical agenda, we are trying to codify best practice. There are no huge costs attached. We will try to move quickly to have our final report and a draft Bill available by the autumn.' (A copy of Mr Hertzell's speaking notes is available on request)

4.2 The Chairman then invited Peter Hinchliffe, Lead Ombudsman for the Financial Ombudsman Service (FOS) to address the meeting. Mr Hinchliffe told the Group that 2 years ago the FOS received 15,000 complaints; Last year the figure was 50,000. The FOC is required to take account of the law but can depart from it and deal with complaints on a fair and reasonable basis. Mr Hinchliffe said that the questions asked of consumers by insurance companies are not always reasonable. Questions like 'have you ever suffered from stress? Have you ever had pins and needles?' The only answer to such questions is 'Yes'. He went on to say 'What can we expect from the consumer – a reasonable, diligent, honest person? The consumer should answer specific questions honestly and reasonably.' (A copy of Mr Hinchliffe's speaking notes is available on request).

4.3 Lord Borrie QC responded, and in the absence of the Chairman, who was called away by the division bell, took the Chair. Lord Borrie drew attention to the changes in insurance practices during the past 100 years. He went on to say 'Today consumers do not necessarily go looking for insurance, it comes with goods and services such as electrical goods, mortgages etc. It can no longer be assumed that the buyer/consumer knows about the risks involved, whereas the retailer or insurer does. There is an imbalance between the insurer and the insured.' Lord Borrie continued 'The current situation is not satisfactory whereby everything is dependent on goodwill because there is a risk that the insurance companies might decide to stand by the law rather than the Ombudsman. The Ombudsman has done a good job but the law needs to more accurately reflect the fair and reasonable approach of the Ombudsman.'

4.4 Lord Borrie invited Peter Tyldesley, Solicitor and lecturer in insurance law to address the meeting. Mr Tyldesley expressed support for the FOS and the approach it took but pointed out that it was unsatisfactory that consumers may have to complain to obtain fair treatment. He also drew attention to the fact that the Ombudsman cannot help with certain types of case – for example there is a limit on awards of £100,000 which dates back to 1981 and where there is an evidential dispute the FOS may refer consumers to the courts. Mr Tyldesley stressed that for many insurers the proposed reforms held no fear – they already follow the FOS approach. The Association of British Insurers had a difficult task in representing a wide range of insurers with different standards, but its press release of 17 July 2007 was unfortunate. The Law Commissions were not proposing more law, but better law. (A copy of Mr Tyldesley's Briefing Note is available on request.)

4.5 Lord Borrie invited contributions from others and Baroness Crawley and Michael Foster MP both supported the reforms outlined by the Law Commission. Speakers representing HM Treasury, WHICH, Macmillian Cancer Support and the Trading Standards Institute, did likewise. The Insurance Industry representative, Shradha Patel, from ABI was more cautious. She said 'By updating the law we will be locked into a legal framework that we will be unable to update and adapt to ongoing changes. There is consumer protection currently in place. We don't think the regulations proposed provide any more clarity or protection to the consumer. We would look to see some real evidence of the proposed Bill providing these things.'

4.6 Austin Mitchell MP concluded the meeting by saying that the Group would send a copy of the Minutes to the Minister with the hope that the 10 clause Bill could be included in the forthcoming Queen's Speech.

5. The Chairman announced that the next meeting would be jointly with Consumer Focus and would take place on 9th June 2009. Mr Mitchell closed the meeting, with thanks to the speakers and to the many contributors, at 6pm.

Appendix 10 Bill Stages — Consumer Insurance (Disclosure and Representations) Act 2010–12

Dates for all stages of the passage of the Bill

House of Lords

1st reading:	16 May 2011
Second reading committee:	13 June 2011
2nd reading:	15 June 2011
Committee stage:	11 October 2011
Committee stage:	19 October 2011
Report stage:	20 December 2011
3rd reading:	17 January 2012

House of Commons

1st reading:	17 January 2012
Second reading committee:	31 January 2012
2nd reading:	6 February 2012
Committee debate: 1st sitting:	22 February 2012
Report stage:	6 March 2012
3rd reading:	6 March 2012

Royal Assent:	8 March 2012

Appendix 11 Minutes of Evidence Taken Before the Special Public Bill Committee on the Consumer Insurance (Disclosure and Representations) Bill

Tuesday 11 October 2011

Present

Lord Borrie
Lord De Mauley
Lord Eatwell
Lord Goodhart
Lord Lloyd of Berwick (Chairman)
Baroness Kramer
Baroness O'Cathain
Lord Sassoon

Examination of Witnesses (Questions 1–25)

Witnesses: LORD SASSOON, Commercial Secretary to the Treasury, and MR DAVID HERTZELL, Law Commissioner, were examined.

Q1 The Chairman: We welcome the Minister, Lord Sassoon, who is a member of the Committee, and Mr Hertzell, from the Law Commission. It would be helpful if Lord Sassoon started the ball rolling.

Lord Sassoon: Thank you. Before the recess, we had very useful and detailed discussions on the Bill, but of course that was nearly four months ago, so I hope that the Committee might find it useful if I briefly summarise some of the key points from the discussion to date and address some of the issues raised then and subsequently.

As I said at Second Reading, this is a limited and targeted Bill which applies only to consumer insurance contracts. It does not apply to insurance contracts solely or mainly covering business, including micro-businesses.

This has been subject to extensive consultation, and Mr Hertzell can talk a little more about that process in a moment. It builds that approach on a broad consensus of support from industry, consumer groups and regulators. The Bill essentially updates the law on consumer insurance contracts, aligning the statute with modern best practice.

This Bill has a narrowly defined scope. Its effect is to place the onus on the insurer to ask the questions and on the consumer to answer them honestly and carefully. This shifts the burden between the insurer and consumer more in the consumer's favour. This is entirely appropriate, as current legislation is considerably tilted in favour of insurers. In aligning the law with the existing code of best practice, the Bill is deregulatory. The current mismatch between the law and layers of regulation is complex and confusing for both industry and consumers. In future, this law will be taken into account by the Financial Ombudsman when deciding cases as required by FSA rules. Those complaints about claims above the FOS's limit or otherwise not resolved by the ombudsman could be addressed in the courts. However, the Bill will not lead to consumers being driven to the courts any earlier than now.

I thank again the noble Lord, Lord Eatwell, and my noble friends Lord Higgins, Lord Hodgson, Lord Goodhart, Lady Kramer and Lady Noakes for their contributions to the discussion so far. In those discussions, a few consistent themes have emerged and it might be helpful if I addressed them now.

There was some discussion on the specific meaning of 'consumer' in the Bill. I believe that the FSA will be writing to the Committee, if it has not already, on that point. Clause 1 defines a consumer as an individual who is wholly or mainly for non-business purposes. It is worth mentioning that the Law Commissioners were concerned to ensure consistency with other legislation and regulation. The definition was the result of extensive discussion with stakeholders and represents a careful balance and consideration of opinions, not least that of the FSA itself.

A number of noble Lords asked about the use of questions under the Bill. In particular, the noble Lord, Lord Eatwell, asked whether the Bill permitted insurers to ask catch-all questions and how it affected whether insurers might pose questions that could be viewed by society as unacceptable. The Bill does not prohibit insurers from asking catch-all questions. However, use of such questions could conceivably expose an insurer to adverse FOS judgments or FSA action. This is because under Clause 3(1), if a consumer acted reasonably in providing an incomplete answer, the insurer would still be obliged to honour the contract.

On unacceptable questions, as I said at Second Reading, this issue is dealt with elsewhere. It is not part of the scope of the Bill to discuss questions of discrimination or equalities legislation – nor do I believe it should be. That said, there are of course existing obligations not to discriminate on grounds of race or gender under the Equality Act, with which insurers will still have to comply. Additionally, under the terms of the 2008 ABI code of practice on genetic testing, with the exception of Huntington's disease, ABI members have agreed not to ask consumers to have genetic tests or disclose the result of predictive tests.

The final area where there has been some discussion to date has been on the Bill's implementation. A number of noble Lords have been understandably concerned to ensure that the Government's plan in this respect fits well with other regulatory initiatives – for example, the FSA's retail distribution review and the insurance mediation directive. In so far as this Bill simply moves the letter of the law towards existing best practice, we do not believe that the implementation burdens will be at all large. However, I am happy to reconfirm that we will be mindful of the burdens of implementation on the industry. There will be at least a year after the Act's passage to bring it into force, and we will continue to consult extensively with industry representatives, including the British Bankers' Association, the ABI and others, on the best implementation date.

That concludes all I wanted to say at the opening. I have attempted to pick up some of the key themes from our discussions so far, but it may be helpful if I hand over to Mr David Hertzell, the Law Commissioner, to make some opening remarks himself.

Q2 The Chairman: We are very grateful to you, Lord Sassoon. Thank you. I welcome Mr Hertzell to this meeting. We have all read the very useful summary of the report. Some of us have actually dipped into the report itself, which is a pretty massive document. We have also all read the Government's response to the further consultation that they conducted and the amendments, few in number, that were made to the Bill as a result of the consultation. You were probably aware of that document. Having said what we are aware of or should be aware of, perhaps we could now ask you to give us a general picture of what the Bill is doing.

David Hertzell: Thank you, my Lord. In view of that statement, I will keep things as brief as I can. I am grateful for this opportunity to give evidence to the Committee and to participate in the first Bill to be introduced since the procedure for uncontroversial Law Commission Bills was made permanent last year.

As Lord Sassoon said, this Bill has been widely consulted on. We first consulted in 2007 and had 105 responses from across the industry, including from consumer groups and intermediaries, many of which were representing quite large bodies of members; there were association responses on behalf of several. The Treasury consulted again in 2010 with some of the key stakeholders who had participated in those discussions. There have been an awful lot of informal meetings and discussions to try to thrash out the correct response here. I think it is fair to say that the Bill enjoys wide support from all interested parties, including both insurers and consumer groups. It remains uncontroversial in all senses.

The Bill seeks to reform the Marine Insurance Act 1906 as it applies to consumer policies alone. The Act was drafted 105 years ago. It is a piece of commercial legislation, drafted long before consumers existed to any significant extent. It requires the purchaser of insurance to disclose anything that a prudent underwriter might consider relevant when considering whether or not to write the policy. Consumers often buy by internet or on the phone; these days they do not very often buy with the support of any form of intermediary. They are very unlikely to know what a prudent underwriter would consider relevant and, even if they did, it is quite hard, given the mechanisms by which insurance is sold to consumers, to give that information if they are not asked a direct question. The problem is that, under the law, if the consumer fails to make full disclosure, the insurer can avoid the policy and refuse to pay any claims.

It is fair to say that concerns about the Marine Insurance Act have been raised on several occasions over the past 50 years or so, and this is the third time that the Law Commission has looked at it since 1957. As Lord Sassoon said, this is a targeted and limited measure that will apply only to consumers and deal only with the issue of what a consumer must tell an insurer before entering a contract or varying an insurance contract. We are doing work on other aspects of insurance, post-contract and in relation to business, beyond this Bill.

To be fair to insurers, they have long recognised that the Marine Insurance Act is inappropriate for consumers. To mitigate the harshness of the Act, we have various industry codes, the Financial Services Authority rules and the Financial Ombudsman Service. These all aim to deal with the problem that one is seeking to apply commercial marine law to a consumer, in a consumer context, when the law simply was not drafted with that in mind. The problem also is that the various mechanisms by which the harshness of the Marine Insurance Act is sought to be ameliorated are overlapping and inconsistent and add to industry cost and consumer confusion.

In reality, the ombudsman deals with most consumer disputes; such disputes do not generally go into the courts. There has been, and is, a steady stream of complaints to the ombudsman in circumstances where it appears that neither the consumer nor the insurers were clear about their rights. We believe that removing this confusion should increase consumer confidence and protect vulnerable groups such as older consumers and those with serious but latent illnesses, which are the subject of a lot of complaints to the ombudsman. We hope that it also reduces uncertainty for insurers, because all the rules applicable to this particular part of the insurance contract will now be in one place. The Bill seeks to codify current best practice, and part of the consultation we undertook was to pursue that. Doing that should reduce the possibility of unintended consequences. It also provides a framework for the FSA and the ombudsman, both of which support the Bill.

The Bill has been drafted to provide high-level overarching principles. It sets out a framework to deal with the problems but does not seek to lay down guidance. We do not deal with, for example, underwriting processes and practices in any particular detail. We were conscious that it is 105 years since the Act was passed and we hope that this Bill might last, if not quite so long, then for a reasonable period of time in future. Our view was that trying to lay down detailed guidance covering every eventuality, particularly those that might relate to scientific and information technology matters, would quickly become out of date and the Bill would become ossified, so we tried to set out principles rather than detailed practices. On the reasonable assumption that detailed rules – for example, around inappropriate questions – should come via guidance from the insurance industry, from targeted legislation such as the Equality Act or, as appropriate, from the FSA.

I will run through the key features of the Bill so that we have them in mind. The key thing is that the Bill abolishes the consumer's duty to volunteer information. The Marine Insurance Act imposes a duty on the consumer to tell the insurer anything that could influence the judgment of the prudent insurer. If the consumer fails to disclose that information, the policy may be treated as void. That is being abolished by this Bill; instead, the consumer must take reasonable care to answer the insurer's questions fully and accurately. If the consumer chooses to volunteer information, they must take reasonable care to ensure that that information is not misleading.

Lord Borrie: Excuse me, Lord Chairman, I am having a little difficulty in hearing Mr Hertzell at the moment. That may be my fault, but would he please speak up?

David Hertzell: I will do. Sorry. It is already accepted good practice that insurers should ask questions about what they want to know. The ombudsman refuses to allow insurers to avoid consumer policies for non-disclosure where no questions have been asked. The Bill also sets out the insurer's remedies where they have been induced by misrepresentation to enter into an insurance contract, and the remedy will depend upon the consumer's state of mind. If the misrepresentation was honest and reasonable – the sort of representation that anyone could make in the circumstances – the insurer must pay that claim. As I said, though, there is an obligation on consumers to answer the questions that they are asked by insurers honestly and reasonably and to ensure that their replies are accurate and complete.

The consumer is expected to exercise the standard of care of a reasonable consumer, taking into account a range of factors listed in the Bill such as the types of insurance policy and the clarity of the insurance questions.

Q3 Lord Eatwell: I am sorry, but could you repeat what you just said?

David Hertzell: Yes. Taking into account a range of factors—

Lord Eatwell: No, before that, about the consumer.

David Hertzell: The consumer is expected to exercise the standard of care of a reasonable consumer, taking into account a range of factors – and I quoted a couple that are listed in the Bill, including the type of insurance policy and the clarity of the question that they were asked. If the misrepresentation was careless, the insurer will have a compensatory remedy based on what the insurer would have done had the consumer taken care to answer the question accurately. For example, if the insurer would have charged more, it will have to pay only a proportion of the claim. If the misrepresentation was deliberate or reckless, the insurer may treat the policy as if it never existed and may decline all claims. It would also be entitled to retain the premiums. It is fair to say that this approach is supported by the ombudsman. It is reflected in the 2009 ABI code on group life, critical illness and income protection, so it is familiar to the industry in a consumer context.

We are abolishing the basis of the contract clauses in the Bill. Under current law, an insurer may add a declaration to a proposal form or policy in which they state that the consumer warrants the accuracy of all the answers that they give. That means that if some of that information is inaccurate, whether or not it was relevant to the claim or the loss, the insurer is discharged from all liability – even if the insurer was not induced to enter the contract by that statement. It is a very harsh remedy. It was recognised by the Statement of General Insurance Practice in 1986 that these clauses should be barred for consumers as they were not thought to treat consumers fairly.

We also deal with group insurance. Typically, a group scheme is where an employer takes out insurance on behalf of the employees. The problem is that the employer is the contracting party and therefore, under the obligation to disclose information, but the information is in the knowledge of the individual employees who are protected by the policy. This is a very important sector to individuals – about 40 per cent of life cover comes through such group schemes – but the law is quite underdeveloped. We have tried to bring it into line with good practice so that, where a misrepresentation is made by a group member, the consequences of that fall on the group member in line with the Bill but do not affect the rest of the members. That is pretty well the approach applied by the industry now.

We are trying to deal with the position of intermediaries. If there is an intermediary between the proposer and the insurer, it is not unusual for consumers sometimes to blame intermediaries for the failure to transmit information. The central question is who should bear the risk. Should the insurer pay the claim and then recover from the intermediary, or may the insurer refuse to pay the consumer's claim, leaving the consumer to proceed against the intermediary? It is a question of whose agent the intermediary was when they were acting, and we are trying to set out some guidance to establish that.

This Bill is being prepared in the context of a significant part of the UK economy. Consumer insurance is worth about £40 billion a year to the economy. The FOS receives around 1,000 complaints a year about misrepresentation and non-disclosure, and around half of those complaints are upheld. In the overall context, that is an extremely good record, although, as Lord Sassoon has said, this uphold rate is lower than one might expect if the rules were clear. One would expect the insurers to know what the rules were and the uphold rate to be much higher. By 'uphold rate' I mean the claims that are upheld in favour of the insurer. It is also worth bearing in mind that even though the overall number of such disputes going to the ombudsman is relatively small, it affects consumers at a time when they are particularly vulnerable and not in a position necessarily to take on a dispute about whether their claim should be paid.

Looking forward, it is possible that insurance may play a greater role in providing welfare and security – for example, in the funding of long-term care – and it is difficult to see how the current hotchpotch of different rules and fairly antiquated legislation gives us a firm foundation to do that. We sought to codify the current best practice and put the rules into one place so that both parties know what their rights are.

Lord Justice Rix summarised the problem rather neatly in his keynote address to the insurance law conference in 2007 when he said that 'in a country that prides itself on its adherence to the rule of law, the opening up of a gap between the law as applied in the courts and the self-regulation that applies as a matter of discretion to the relations between the insurance industry and its consumers might be said to be an unsatisfactory state of affairs'. This Bill aims to correct that.

The Chairman: Mr Hertzell, the Committee is very grateful to you for that very clear explanation of what the Bill is doing and why it is needed. I think that we will need at some point to go through the clauses one by one to make sure that the points you covered are dealt with by Members of the Committee and we have your answers to them. First, I want to ask Members of the Committee whether they have any general questions, either to the Minister or to Mr Hertzell, as to the approach that the Bill adopts.

Q4 Lord Eatwell: I have a general question for Mr Hertzell. The Marine Insurance Act basically shifted risk on to the consumer. The risk is now being re-shifted from the consumer to the insurance industry. Is that right?

David Hertzell: The Marine Insurance Act sought to place an obligation on the proposer to volunteer information and we are taking that obligation off the consumer. To that extent you are correct.

Lord Eatwell: So greater risk is being imposed on the insurance industry.

David Hertzell: In practice no, because the rules that we are codifying are the rules that apply in practice now anyway. What we are describing here is what the ombudsman would apply to an insurer. So that is the practical consequence of this shift.

Lord Eatwell: That would not seem to agree with Mr Tyldesley's article in which he points out that that the Financial Ombudsman Service has a limit of £100,000 and therefore claims in excess of that must be shifted on. This must be a shift.

David Hertzell: Yes, if claims are over £150,000 from January this year, and if they involve evidence, or dispute of that evidence, then the ombudsman does not hear them. Whether or not the insurance industry complies with the decisions of the ombudsman is of course an open question. I cannot answer that. Generally, I think it does, but I do not know whether that is the case on every occasion.

Lord Eatwell: I find this very puzzling. Risk is ending up somewhere. As I understand it from your answer, the risk has been mitigated for the consumer in the past and shifted towards the industry by custom and practice.

David Hertzell: Yes.

Lord Eatwell: But if that were so we would not have all these scandalous cases.

David Hertzell: If it were effectively so. The problem we have, to which I have alluded, is that you have four separate sets of rules being applied here. You have the underlying law, you have the industry guidance, you have ombudsman discretion and – that is three, isn't it? There is another one. It is very difficult for insurers in the claims departments on every occasion to be clear as to what they should look at. The problem becomes particularly acute when you have a new risk being introduced into the market, which is why with critical illness we saw a big series of disputes. When people are unclear about the pedigree and experience of the particular class of risk, they tend to look at the rules and tend to look around. They then have these different places in which they can find different rules, which are all inconsistent among themselves. That leads to disputes. It is the lack of clarity that leads to the problem.

Lord Eatwell: Thank you.

Q5 Baroness Kramer: Obviously, nobody wants to come back with new pieces of legislation every time you turn around so it is important that this piece of legislation anticipates, if you like, new areas of insurance and potential issues that they might raise. You pointed out that long-term care is likely to be a very large piece of the industry. I wanted to press you slightly on this issue, which is crystallised a little in genetic testing. There is an Association of British Insurers code, but that code is not a legal obligation on insurers, is it? It plays such a significant role. Anecdotally, many of us will have met people who have been told that if they get genetic testing that, for example, demonstrates the breast cancer gene, it would be virtually impossible to get life insurance as a consequence. That is not in keeping with the ABI code, but the code is in no way captured in law through this document, is it?

David Hertzell: No, it is not.

Baroness Kramer: Do we carry on then having this same problem, which is that there is a convention that a large number of insurers observe and that there is a piece of legislation that is meant to have cleaned up that difference but has not caught it? Would it be sensible to try to capture that within this document?

David Hertzell: There are two bits to that. If it is an ABI code, it is binding on ABI members as a condition of their membership of the ABI. That covers most insurers. To that extent it is binding. But you are right that it is not enforced through this particular Bill. We gave some thought to whether or not we should make industry codes of guidance part of the legislation. We were persuaded not to in the end on the basis that the purpose is different. First, the ABI was reluctant to become a kind of second-string legislator on the basis that if it put forward a code it would be binding through this Bill on all its members – and possibly on other insurers, too. The purpose of guidance is a little different, in the sense that it is written more fluidly; it is written purposefully rather than legalistically. The ABI was concerned that it might have to draft things in a fashion that it did not want to do. The feeling was that, as the system was working reasonably effectively, it should be left alone and that we should not seek to introduce rules, regulations and guidance that were written for different purposes into the law.

Q6 Baroness Kramer: Would there be value in linking, for example, these codes and practices with the reasonableness test? They would not become statute, in a sense, but if the behaviour of the insured was in line with that industry code then they would at least have been deemed to have behaved reasonably. Is that worth considering?

David Hertzell: I think that in practice it would be very unlikely that a court would ignore the industry code if there was flagrant breach of it. There is more of a sort of technical concern about introducing industry codes into legislation.

Baroness Kramer: But is there any value in trying to do the link to a reasonableness test, which is slightly different? The reason why I say that is, again, that we are in a dynamic situation, and unless you constantly keep changing these things, there has in some way to be a mechanism to capture that dynamism.

David Hertzell: You are right that there has to be a mechanism to capture the dynamism because things change considerably – you mentioned IT and genetics in particular. The view of the consultees was that generally they would prefer to keep control of that a little bit loose because they were unsure perhaps of where it was going to develop, and they were concerned about linking guidance too closely to legislation. We reflected that consensus in what we have done.

The Chairman: Are there any other general questions before we move on to the details?

Q7 Baroness O'Cathain: Further to Baroness Kramer's point about catch-alls and the need for these things to be relevant, when you said during your very good explanation that the current legislation was originally introduced in 1906, I immediately thought of that book from the 1970s about the accelerating pace of change. Things have changed and changed utterly, and there is a still greater acceleration in the pace of change than there was in 1906 or whatever. After we finish our work on this Bill, the provisions that we are considering will almost certainly not be current in the year 2106. Is there any precedent – I am not a lawyer, as is patently obvious – whereby the Bill could include a time clause that would require issues such as genetics, IT, or going to the moon or whatever to be looked at again at some point? Would that give some comfort to people that the Government will look at this from time to time to ensure that neither the consumer nor the industry is disadvantaged by rigidity in the legislation? I know that you can always amend legislation, but is there a precedent for a provision saying that we ought to have a look at this again in 25 years?

David Hertzell: Yes, there is. We have sought to do that in one provision in the Bill, where it talks about the way in which insurance is sold and the role of intermediaries. Schedule 2 includes a power for the Treasury to review the particular circumstances that are listed and to update those as necessary. That is a reflection of the fact that, to date, changes in information technology have had had a big impact on how insurance is sold and, I suspect, may have an even bigger impact in the future.

The Chairman: Paragraph 4 of Schedule 2 is the relevant provision.

Baroness O'Cathain: Would that cover my point?

The Chairman: Does the Minister want to respond?

Lord Sassoon: Yes, I think that Baroness O'Cathain's core point has been addressed.

Q8 Lord Eatwell: I want to start with a question of a general sort. Baroness Kramer raised the issue of the link to the ABI codes and catch-all questions. I was a little shocked when the Minister said in his introduction that catch-all questions are not excluded, which seems to be slightly at variance with what he wrote to me last June. I examined his letter carefully, which refers to the ABI guidance on this question. The notion of reasonableness and protection provided under Clause 3(1) is based on ABI codes rather than on any legislation. Therefore, the exclusion of catch-all questions simply relies on the ABI code. Is that correct?

David Hertzell: I am not sure that it is. I think that insurers can ask a catch-all question if they want to, but they would need to overcome two hurdles. First, the answer that they got would be judged according to what a reasonable consumer would have said in response. If the question was a completely useless question along the lines of 'Have you ever been ill?', one would need to interpret whatever random answer one got accordingly. Secondly, insurers always have to show that the information with which they were provided had some relevance to their decision to take the risk on the terms that they took it.

Lord Eatwell: Is there any information relative to the contract that you think should be relevant? That would be a catch-all question.

David Hertzell: You would get a completely random set of hopeless answers, and you would have to show that something in the answer that you received induced you to enter into the contract. For very unspecific questions, you have two quite significant hurdles to jump.

Q9 The Chairman: If there are no further general questions, perhaps we should we just go through the Bill clause by clause to ensure that any problems have been covered. On Clause 1, the definition of 'consumer insurance contract' does not cover small businesses. What is the reason for that?

David Hertzell: Small businesses are part of the second part of our review of insurance laws. We will publish a consultation on small businesses at, I think, the beginning of next year.

The Chairman: Are there any other questions on Clause 1?

Q10 Lord Borrie: I have been worried, although I am not sure that I should continue to be, about the opening lines of Clause 1, which state that a consumer insurance contract is one between 'an individual who enters into the contract wholly or mainly for purposes unrelated to the individual's trade, business or profession'. There may be quite a lot of uncertainty in individual cases where someone in business – in a small business, in all likelihood – takes out that insurance to cover things that are his own private belongings as well as those of his trade. How do you then interpret 'wholly or mainly'? The definition seems wide open and could lead to quite a lot of uncertainty.

David Hertzell: I agree. One needs to look at the purpose of the insurance contract that is being taken out, which at the end of the day is, I am afraid, fact specific. Therefore, we were unable to come up with anything that was more precise than that. What we have in mind is business extensions on car policies, dual-use computers and so on, where the main use of the item is for the consumer but people send the odd e-mail from the computer or make the occasional business trip in the car. At the end of the day, it is a question of fact whether the purpose of the insurance policy was mainly for business or mainly for the consumer. That will always have a degree of uncertainty attached to it.

Lord Borrie: In so far as there will be a difficulty in interpreting the 'wholly or mainly' point, does that not go back to the Lord Chairman's initial point that there may be disadvantages in dealing wholly and exclusively with consumer insurance contracts now and small business men – as well as big business men – later?

David Hertzell: There may be, but logistically we could not manage to do it all in one.

Q11 Lord Borrie: I believe that Mr Hertzell – he can tell me if I am wrong – is also dealing in the Law Commission with sale of goods legislation, where problems of a similar kind will arise. Similar problems have arisen when the issue has been debated in the Law Commission and elsewhere in previous decades. Does that make any difference to his thinking about how we deal with insurance matters in Clause 1 or to the idea that we should deal with other matters later?

David Hertzell: This is actually a fascinating topic in its own right. The market has evolved a separate set of rules to deal with consumers – those who are wholly or mainly consumers, if I may use that definition – and businesses. I think that that has happened because the economics of these two areas is actually quite different. Ultimately, consumer insurance is written on a portfolio basis, with the underwriting of a huge pool of individual risks. With advances in IT and with experience, people have a pretty clear idea of what the loss outcome will be on a portfolio of consumer risks; they do not really need to ask anything, other than to find out the individual idiosyncrasies so that they can allocate costs in the risk pool between one consumer and another. That is quite a different mechanism of risk transfer from that of business insurance, which is much more specific around the particular business – the risk pools are very much smaller so the allocation of risk is much more constrained, and the volatility in the pool is much greater because of the variety of risks involved. You can see why the rules have evolved to reflect the underlying activity. We felt that, although this division is not wholly satisfactory, it reflects the way in which the market has developed. In a way, we were influenced by the evolution of practice as much as by our own desire not to try to cover everything in one go – let alone the logistics of trying to do that.

Q12 Lord Eatwell: Could I follow up on Clause 1? I am interested in 'wholly or mainly' as well and I was intrigued that Mr Hertzell said that the term had developed in the industry because, as I understand it, this is the first time that the term has ever been used in insurance law.

David Hertzell: That is true. It is reflected in the way that the ombudsman deals with consumer issue rights and in the practice of the FSA, although not in the way that it writes things.

Lord Eatwell: So are we really waiting for the courts to define the use of this term in the context of insurance?

David Hertzell: I think that it will be fact specific on the individual claim.

Lord Eatwell: I see, so the individual is exposed in that respect. There are some complicated borderline cases, some of which we discussed in Committee. I would like to go back to the case that I raised there of a ballet dancer whose body is actually their tool – an expression of their art and the basis of their employment. If they take out general health insurance, is that consumer insurance or is it associated with their business or profession?

David Hertzell: You would need to look at the purpose of the policy. To take a ballet dancer, for example, if that dancer took out holiday insurance and bought a standard policy, there would be a disablement clause in it for a fixed sum of money and that, in my view, would be consumer insurance, because you are part of the overall pool of people taking a holiday in that particular destination, so it works like that. But if the ballet dancer specifically went out to insure themselves for the tools of their trade, as it were, you would be looking at a completely different kind of product, because they would be looking at income protection and there would need to be an assessment of how long their career might last. A whole series of factors would be brought in, which makes it a much more complicated piece of underwriting. For many significant performers – I think that we discussed David Beckham last time – this would be handled by their management on a purely commercial basis, rather than by them as individuals, so the risks that one is discussing are inherently different depending on the purpose and the person whose policy it is.

Lord Eatwell: Then is insuring this going to be on the basis of percentage of use, or something like that?

David Hertzell: That would be a very crude measure of doing it, but I guess that one could use that.

Lord Eatwell: For the purpose of the record, 'this' was a BlackBerry.

The Chairman: Let us move on to Clause 2, which of course is the core of the Bill, abolishing the rules relating to nondisclosure in the case of consumer insurance but leaving them alive in relation to commercial insurance and modifying to that extent the doctrine of uberrimae fidei. I have no questions on Clause 2, but does anybody else have one?

Q13 Baroness Kramer: It is just a small question on this in subsection (3): 'A failure by the consumer to comply with the insurer's request to confirm or amend particulars previously given'. Given the propensity of insurance companies to lose current addresses, revert to former addresses et cetera, I am wondering whether there is any mechanism or way to be slightly clearer on who has the responsibility for making sure that communications have taken place – in other words, that the request has been received.

David Hertzell: I understand the problem. This is a difficult area because retention of business is popular with insurers and consumers are slightly lazy, as I think we all are, so we are probably quite happy with this kind of automatic renewal process. Legally, it is a new contract and therefore, if they do not ask you any questions, either because they are incompetent and do not send the thing to the right address or because they choose not to, they would not be able to rely upon—

Baroness Kramer: But it is quite hard to demonstrate that this request went to the wrong address, if you see what I mean. I realise that this is getting into minutiae, but I can see a whole host of endless narks over this and I presume that that happens already.

David Hertzell: I fear that that is right.

Q14 Baroness O'Cathain: Is there then a way of overcoming it? I would have thought that the onus on the consumer is to make sure that they are insured. If it therefore went astray and the consumer did not get it, they would not be insured, would they? Surely you have to say, 'Yes, I agree about this.' I have one on my desk at the moment for a car and that is an automatic thing – I have not looked at the small print, which I never do – but I would still have thought that I would just ring them up or send my cheque off, or whatever.

David Hertzell: Yes. I suppose what we have done to support consumers here is that, technically, under the law at the moment you would have a duty to disclose things – whatever they might want to know – whether or not you were asked that on renewal.

Baroness O'Cathain: They say it.

David Hertzell: And they say it, even though that does not actually apply any longer with the ombudsman. What we have done here is to say that they have to ask you a question on renewal, which you have to answer honestly and reasonably because it is a new contract. By taking away the onus on you to disclose things, we are making the job slightly more consumer-friendly than it currently is.

Q15 Baroness Kramer: I hate to be picky but this does not talk about renewal. This is a request for information at some point during the life of a contract; that is all I was trying to point out. I do not think that this is a major issue, but I am constantly getting letters for the people who used to live in my property because, for some reason, the insurers managed to lose the new address.

Lord Sassoon: Lord Chairman, may I ask Mr Hertzell a question which may or may not help to clarify this? If the insurer has written to the wrong address to ask a question, I am not clear – but maybe Mr Hertzell can clarify this – whether that actually constitutes a valid request by the insurer. If they have been incompetent enough to write to another address, I assume that it is does not. It may have other consequences, but in terms of Clause 2(3), if the insurer is incompetent and sends a request to the wrong address, the consumer has not had a request and is under no obligation to answer it. In the particular case here, I think that the consumer is actually covered.

Baroness O'Cathain: But is the consumer insured? Say that there was a debit on your bank account, because you normally paid that way, and you still did not—

David Hertzell: I think that is a slightly different question. What you are asking there is whether the automatic renewal process has effectively taken place because you have moved and have not told them or they have the wrong address, or whatever. I guess that it has, in effect. If they continue to take the money and send out the policy to the wrong address, it is effectively renewed.

Q16 Lord Eatwell: Could I ask about renewal? I am puzzled about it because The Law of Insurance Contracts, Clarke, fourth edition, says 'the renewal of existing insurance is the conclusion of a new contract of insurance for a further period of time on the same risk and on broadly the same terms as before but perhaps with slight changes concerning, for example, the premium'. This does not seem to refer to slight changes. It refers to the request to provide further supplementary information, or whatever, and the failure to do so. What is the relationship of this to the law as set out in The Law of Insurance Contracts?

David Hertzell: I think that Malcolm Clarke is describing a general position, in that a renewal is a new contract and, de facto, they may well decide to change some of the terms and the premium may go up or down, but that is a description of the position under the current law. We are not seeking to alter that. We are saying here that it is a new contract if you renew insurance, automatically or otherwise, and the obligations that you have to answer any questions that you are asked honestly and reasonably would come into being. But if you are not asked any questions, then nothing can be relied on.

The Chairman: I think that we should move on to Clause 3, on reasonable care. Does anybody have any questions on that?

Q17 Lord Eatwell: I was very struck by the sentence that I asked you to repeat in your introduction. The consumer is expected to exercise 'reasonable care', taking into account 'the type of… insurance'. What does that mean?

David Hertzell: One has to look at what the consumer did in the overall context. Some forms of insurance would be very simple and the means by which they are sold very simple. At one time you could put a card into a machine at an airport to buy a travel policy and hardly any questions were asked. On the other hand, a consumer may be taking out something far more complicated, such as a critical illness policy, where there might be much greater sums at stake. One would therefore expect a greater degree of care to be taken, simply because the logistics of the way in which the insurance product has been sold do not allow you to do so, on the one hand, and allow you to do so on the other hand.

Lord Eatwell: Should that be made clear in some sense?

David Hertzell: Perhaps in the Explanatory Notes, because again it is a question of principle against detail.

Q18 Lord Eatwell: Perhaps I could move on to misrepresentation. These days, a lot of statistical analysis is done on risks and their nature. Some of the correlations are not particularly obvious to consumers. A consumer may therefore be asked a question, the relevance of which is completely obscure to them – yet if you are a statistician, you know where it comes from. There is no clear obligation on the insurer to clarify the relevance of a question, is there?

David Hertzell: No. There is in fact a presumption that if they ask a question, it is relevant. The consumer has the obligation to answer the question honestly and reasonably, even if it seems a bit odd to them, but the insurer still has to show that the question – or the answer that they have given – induced them to enter the contract. What happens sometimes is that they may ask marketing information, so if you renew your car policy they ask lots of stuff about your car. Then they ask, 'When are you renewing your household cover?' The assumption would be that that was relevant – because that is the presumption – but the insurer would not be able to show that anything you have told them there led them to take the car policy on the terms that they did, so that requirement of inducement remains.

Q19 Lord Eatwell: Thank you. The other general question of that type is that while issues of discrimination are clearly for other legislation, there are racial and gender issues associated with insurance. Clearly, gender issues are there because you are always asked if you are a man or a woman even in a driving contract – women are much safer drivers. Can you ask general questions on race and gender where they have an underlying relevance to a consumer's insurance? As you will have seen, the case that I put in my speech was that of black people and sickle cell anaemia.

David Hertzell: Yes you can. You can ask any question that is pertinent to the risk that one is allowed to ask, if it is not prevented by other rules and regulations. As we know, the Europeans are currently looking at the gender issue, which is very relevant to all of this.

The Chairman: Anything else on Clause 3?

Q20 Baroness Kramer: If I may, very quickly: to go back to my more general point under reasonable care, did you consider putting in under subsection (2) – 'The following ... examples of things which may need to be taken into account' – the equivalent of a paragraph (e) that might read something like 'terms laid out in relevant industry codes of conduct', or something along those lines?

David Hertzell: We did consider that, but we still had the same concern about introducing codes as legislation.

Q21 The Chairman: I have an unimportant question on Clause 4. I notice that you use the phrase 'a remedy against a consumer'. I have always thought of nondisclosure or misrepresentation as giving rise to a defence on the part of the insurer. After all, the plaintiff is always the consumer, is he not? 'Remedy' seems to be a rather odd word to use in relation to the defendant.

David Hertzell: I suppose that it follows from using misrepresentation and looking for the damages that one might have were one to be subject to that and lose as a consequence of it, so 'remedy' is derived from that rather than from the defendant as such. I think that is parliamentary counsel drafting.

The Chairman: It struck me as being an odd word but I am sure that it is quite clear what it actually means. Is there anything else on Clause 4?

Q22 Lord Borrie: The definition of 'Qualifying misrepresentations' includes Clause 4(1)(b) – 'the insurer shows that without the misrepresentation, that insurer would not have entered into the contract … or would have done so only on different terms' – so it is that particular insurer and not necessarily a reasonable or prudent insurer. It strikes me as a little strange that we should have this subjective phrase brought in here, when one of the basic reasons that the Law Commission has adduced and repeated today for getting rid of the duty of disclosure is, to use Peter Tyldesley's phrase, that you are supposed to peer into the mind of a prudent insurer. Here, you have to peer into the mind of your particular insurer, who may – unlike other insurers, or not unlike them – refuse to provide insurance, or only want it on different terms compared with the average, usual or normal insurer.

David Hertzell: You are absolutely right.

Lord Borrie: Should we go forward with the two words 'that insurer' that are so relevant in Clause 4(1)(b)?

David Hertzell: We were being quite specific about that because we were seeking to put into law the Pan Atlantic case and subsequent cases, which are about the subjective 'that insurer'. We did not feel that it caused too much of a problem because we have the presumption that the questions being asked were relevant – they were therefore relevant to 'that insurer', not to a prudent underwriter as such – and then there is the need to show that the questions were in fact relevant to the insurer's decision to take the risk. We have taken out, on the one hand, the need to disclose something to an objective standard to a prudent underwriter but reintroduced two subjective tests about this particular contract by taking out that objective prudent underwriter requirement. That is because we did not want to put any constraints on the market, so that if the insurers want to sell a particular product and have a particular desire to know certain things, we should not test that against an objective standard that is no longer required because we have the need to apply reasonableness to the consumer's disclosure.

The Chairman: I must say that I thought it quite important to leave it as 'that insurer', so that the insurer has to go into the box and say why he would not have insured, had it not been for the misrepresentation. I am trying to see whether that is perhaps what Pan Atlantic decided. I cannot remember now.

David Hertzell: Pretty well.

The Chairman: We should certainly think about that when we come to the detail. Is there anything on Clause 5?

Q23 Lord Goodhart: I have put down a couple of amendments to this. I am afraid that these are entirely pedantic and would have no effect whatsoever on the substance of the Bill, but it seemed to me that they would make the language a little simpler and easier to understand.

The Chairman: Thank you very much. Is that a point on which you wish to comment?

Lord Sassoon: Only to say that I am grateful to Lord Goodhart for saying that his amendment does not make any change of substance to the Bill, which confirms the advice that I had from my officials. We will have a look to see which of the alternatives is clearer. The initial analysis of officials is that the amendment makes things a little less clear because it could bring into doubt the Bill's split between a deliberate or reckless and a careless misrepresentation. I think we agree that there is no intention to change the substance here, but these two amendments possibly cause other difficulties.

Lord Goodhart: I do not think that they do, but I will obviously not press them if they are not going to be acceptable.

Lord Sassoon: We are certainly looking at it very carefully.

The Chairman: Clause 6 is the basis of contract clause. Are there any questions on that? I would have thought it is a very good thing that we are getting rid of it.

Q24 Lord Eatwell: I have a question on that. Mr Hertzell said that this abolishes warranties. In his letter to me, which I referred to earlier, the Minister said, 'Warranties are rarely if ever used in consumer insurance contracts and do not present a problem beyond that posed by the basis of contract clauses'. It seems that warranties will survive but in some peculiar place in the ether that is relevant to consumer law.

David Hertzell: I am sorry if I gave you the impression that we were abolishing them. That is not quite right. What we are abolishing is the ability of the insurer to take down all the information you provide them with at renewal and convert that into a warranty, because a warranty has stricter outcomes.

Lord Eatwell: Or is it any information that you have provided?

David Hertzell: Any information, yes. So that is what we are getting rid of. Warranties are the subject of another piece of work that we are doing with businesses. The other issue is of post-contract matters.

Lord Eatwell: But are they abolished for consumers?

David Hertzell: They still exist for consumers, other than being introduced through this mechanism, although they are not a problem in consumer insurance.

Lord Eatwell: All right – I will leave it.

The Chairman: Clause 7 on group insurance seems fairly straightforward; you explained it very well earlier. Are there any questions on that? Clause 8 is on insurance on the life of another, which I think is again fairly straightforward. Clause 9, on agencies, might be more controversial because it involves Schedule 2 and how one decides whether an agent is acting for the insurer or the assured. It seems to me at the moment that it reaches the right sort of balance on that. Are there any questions on Schedule 2?

Q25 Lord Borrie: Will there be a problem with certain no doubt unscrupulous insurers saying that so-and-so is your agent when he is in fact their agent, and that being written into the contract?

The Chairman: I am not sure whether I quite follow that.

Lord Borrie: It is if the insurer purports to say that such and such is the agent of the insured when that is not so. You might get a signature saying that he is when that is not really the case, if you look at it more closely.

David Hertzell: Yes, we were concerned about that. In fact, that was suggested to us as a possible solution here. Our concern was that it may not reflect the actual circumstances of what was occurring. I think we tried to set out overriding principles that would decide who was acting for whom, regardless of what they have actually signed.

Lord Borrie: I am happy if you can go behind the signature.

Lord Eatwell: I think that this is a very difficult one, which we ought to come back to. It is not at all clear to me how an agent is defined as acting for the consumer in a particular way, when the objective of the agent is to sell insurance but that agent may not be acting for anybody specific on the industry side.

David Hertzell: If one looks at commercial insurance, the agent is often acting for themselves in reality – if one was being commercial about it.

Lord Eatwell: Acting for themselves?

David Hertzell: Or acting for either party, to take a commercial view. But this is a very complicated area and what we have tried to do is to set out some broad principles, which will assist with consumer issues.

Lord Eatwell: When filtered through the agent, all these issues of misrepresentation, misleading questions and so on and so forth could expose the consumer.

The Chairman: Presumably, if this ever became a question that mattered and had to be decided by a court, the court would look at all the things you have in Schedule 2 – and, indeed, at the point made by Lord Borrie – and reach a conclusion as to whether the agent in question was the agent of the insured or the insurers.

David Hertzell: Yes.

The Chairman: But all this is doing is providing a certain background to what would have to be decided.

David Hertzell: A framework, yes.

The Chairman: I think that that perhaps completes the main provisions of the Bill. I wonder whether there are any further general questions that anybody would like to ask at this stage and, if not, whether the Minister would like to add anything.

Lord Sassoon: Thank you, no.

The Chairman: We are deeply indebted to you, Mr Hertzell, if I may say so, for all the help that you have given us today. Thank you very much indeed.

Appendix 12 Extract from the Special Public Bill Committee on the Consumer Insurance (Disclosure and Representations) Bill

Thursday, 10 November 2011 Committee Stage

Members present:

Lord Borrie
Lord Davies of Stamford
Lord Eatwell
Lord Goodhart
Lord Hodgson of Astley Abbotts
Lord Lloyd of Berwick
Baroness O'Cathain Lord Sassoon
Also present: Baroness Rawlings

Clause 2: Disclosure and representations before contract or variation

Amendment 1 Moved by Lord Hodgson of Astley Abbotts

> **1:** Clause 2, page 1, line 22, at end insert—
>
> '( ) It is the duty of the insurer to make it clear whether they comply with industry codes of practice.'

Lord Hodgson of Astley Abbotts: My Lords, since the backgrounds to Amendments 1 and 1A are vaguely similar, I shall take a moment to explain them so that I can be briefer on the second amendment. Before doing so, since we are starting the next stage of proceedings on this Bill, I should declare an interest. I am chairman of a company that is called an IFA network firm. That is, it provides compliance services to independent financial advisers. In this, it provides insurance to individual consumers, which falls within the purview of the Bill. It provides insurance for people's lives, homes, as part of their mortgage requirements and so on. It will have particular resonance when we come to Amendment 8. I may refer to it again then.

My first amendment would add a further subsection to Clause 2, which is headed 'Disclosure and representations before contract or variation'. Here I seek to add a further requirement about disclosure, which will provide additional information to the consumer. As I understand it, the purpose of the Bill is, in non-legal terms, to achieve greater equality of arms between what are predominantly large, well sourced and, at times, bureaucratic companies and the man or woman in the street who is taking out insurance. This is to be achieved by changing the legal background because the Marine Insurance Act 1906 confusingly applies not only to marine insurance but to all forms of insurance, including consumer insurance; and by some operational background changes. Some of these are statutory, through the Financial Services Authority, and some are – one might say – quasi-statutory, through the Financial Ombudsman and the Financial Services Compensation Scheme. They are also partly self-regulatory, through the use of industry codes. These three threads provide a tangled mixture of redress for the consumer.

If we were debating a conventional Bill, we would ask the Minister to bring forward some draft regulations – statutory instruments – for the Committee to get some idea of the practical implications of the architecture and structure of the Bill that we were being asked to approve. In essence, I would argue that the industry codes or detailed regulations are equivalent to the statutory instruments. However, the Bill as drafted does not even mention the existence of the possibility of codes. I have raised this before and Mr David Hertzell and his team have been extremely courteous. They gave me a lot of time when I went to see them. Nothing that I say should reflect on the time that I was given and the courtesy that I was shown.

However, as we look through the transcript of the evidence sessions, we find ourselves flirting with the importance of these codes. On page 6 of the evidence session of Tuesday 11 October, Mr Hertzell says:

> 'The Bill has been drafted to provide high-level overarching principles. It sets out a framework to deal with the problems but does not need to lay down guidance'.

He goes on to say that guidance should come via the insurance industry and, on page 8, says:

> 'It is reflected in the 2009 ABI code on group life, critical illness and income protection'.

He also quotes Lord Justice Rix, who, when speaking to an insurance law conference in 2007, said that, 'in a country that prides itself on its adherence to the rule of law, the opening up of a gap between the law as applied in the courts and the self-regulation that applies as a matter of discretion to the relations between the insurance industry and its consumers might be said to be an unsatisfactory state of affairs'.

It seems that what we are doing here is opening up that gap by proposing to have these overarching principles with no reference to the underlying codes that will provide much of the day-to-day guidance and show the practical implications of this.

This is clearly not an open-and-shut case; I understand that. Clearly, the ABI has said several times – including in a letter sent out today – that it does not want to be bound by this. However, my amendment does not bind anyone to anything. It just says:

> 'It is the duty of the insurer to make it clear whether they comply with industry codes of practice'.

It does not say that they must comply, merely that they must let the consumer know whether they do or not. That would enable the insured party to say, 'Look, I see this. What does this mean? What are the codes? What protection do they provide? What further do I have to do to be protected by them?'

I am sure the Minister will say, because he will also have received a copy of this letter, that we got a real savaging from Mr David Sanders, the principal trading standards officer from the Vale of Glamorgan. Rowing in behind him to give us an equally big beating is Peter Tyldesley. They have pointed out that this will add uncertainty to the law. That is the essence of their case. That may be but I submit to the Committee that without some cross-referencing, there is a risk that the statute law we are now setting out – which is very broad in principle – will become out of date and confusing. It will be left behind by events, as the Marine Insurance Act was, and the codes will become more and more important. In conclusion, without in any way binding anyone, we should make reference to the codes in the Bill and give the consumer a piece of information that he may or may not choose to use. I beg to move.

Lord Borrie: May I propose something? Do I need the Chairman's permission? I cannot remember whether I do on these occasions. The microphone was not very good for the previous speaker; it whistles and so on.

The Chairman of Committees: If the noble Lord, Lord Borrie, could carry on, we will try to sort this out with the sound engineer.

Lord Borrie: I want to oppose the amendment moved by the noble Lord, Lord Hodgson, for this reason: during the long period when consumers and their organisations understood that the law was very unsatisfactory, reliance on industry codes, especially that of the ABI, was extremely useful. Many disputes were settled informally on the basis of codes of practice. If they went to the ombudsman, they were settled on the basis of best practice, which included reference to the ABI codes. However, when the Bill is passed we will be in a completely different situation, in which the consumer will have the benefit of law. No longer will he be required by the old duty of uberrimae fideii – the duty of disclosure. He also has the benefit of a range of remedies if there is a so-called qualifying misrepresentation. The world of the insurance consumer will be much improved if the Bill passes.

However, would the Bill benefit by having, as the noble Lord, Lord Hodgson, suggests, just a reference to industry codes of practice? It is not surprising that the ABI referred to this as nebulous and undefined. There is no definition of industry codes of practice, nor does the noble Lord, Lord Hodgson, propose one. A reference to industry codes of practice is nebulous because, whereas some are in existence at the moment, others might emerge, and who knows which one will be thought appropriate and be activated by this amendment, if it is agreed to?

My own view, which I expressed at an earlier stage of the Bill, is that it would not be helpful to have this amendment. It would damage the clarity of the law as laid down in the Bill as it stands. Of course, industry codes of practice are what the phrase implies: they are industry codes of practice and they are proposed, and imposed, by the industry. Just because they have been very good to the consumer over the years in the way that I have described, that does not mean that that will always be the case. The Bill, once enacted, is surely intended to last for some considerable time. It would be terrible if we had to come back to it and, because of some reference to industry codes of practice, had to amend it so that it did not apply to this or that code of practice. Therefore, I am not inclined to support the amendment.

Lord Lloyd of Berwick: I express my complete agreement with the noble Lord, Lord Borrie. The Bill was based on the codes, as has been pointed out by the noble Lord, but it was also intended to replace the codes. If we reintroduce the codes in this way, it seems to me that we will reintroduce uncertainty, the elimination of which was the whole object of the Bill. To take one example of that, according to the ABI letter which we have just had, there are apparently – this is entirely news to me – 70 codes to which there might be reference. Clearly, we would want to identify which codes they were. Therefore, this will not work.

Lord Eatwell: My Lords, just to show what a bipartisan Committee this is, I am going to be more sympathetic to the noble Lord, Lord Hodgson. The problem that we face is that Mr Hertzell told us that the codes were fundamental to the way that the Bill was drawn up. I quote from his evidence:

> 'Our view was that, in trying to lay down detailed guidance covering every eventuality, particularly those that might relate to scientific and information technology matters, it would quickly become out of date and the Bill would become ossified, so we tried to set out principles rather than detailed practices on the reasonable assumption that detailed rules – for example, around inappropriate questions – should either come via guidance in the insurance industry, from target legislation such as the Equality Act or, as appropriate, from the FSA'.

So we have been told in evidence that the fact that industry guidance would be available was a component in the design of the Bill. Therefore, I am very sympathetic to the intention behind the amendment of the noble Lord, Lord Hodgson, particularly given that the noble Baroness, Lady Kramer, who cannot be here this afternoon, was very concerned about this, as we can see from the evidence proceedings. We had extensive discussion about the role that codes and the ombudsman's activities played in the development of fair practice within the insurance industry.

I was puzzling over the various ways in which we might be able to incorporate some reference to the codes of practice without turning them into quasi-legislation while retaining the flexibility which Mr Hertzell claims was fundamental background to the way in which the Bill was drafted. Therefore, I think that we should be more sympathetic to the intention behind the amendments of the noble Lord, Lord Hodgson, even if we are not happy with the precise formulation.

Lord Goodhart: My Lords, to begin with, I take the view that Amendment 1A is not appropriate to these proceedings. It seems to me that Amendment 1 would not be seriously damaging to the Bill but my view is that it is not really necessary here. However, I should say that my noble friend Lady Kramer, who is unable to be here today, asked me to pass on to the Committee her view that the industry codes of practice should be included. As I said, my view is a definite 'no' to Amendment 1A, and I am not prepared to go forward in support of Amendment 1.

The Commercial Secretary to the Treasury (Lord Sassoon): My Lords, just to be clear, I do not think that Amendment 1 is grouped with Amendment 1A, so, if that is correct, I shall address my remarks just to Amendment 1. I am sure that we will move on to Amendment 1A afterwards.

I, too, am sympathetic to the intentions behind the amendment of my noble friend Lord Hodgson of Astley Abbotts because it is clear that industry codes have an important role to play. They are taken account of, among other places, in false determinations, but they occupy a rather anomalous position, which is both a strength and a weakness. So far as I am aware, they are not directly linked into any financial services legislation that I have been able to turn up. The fact that they are not officially endorsed by the FSA but are seen by the FSA when they are worked up means that they are in an unusual position. However, that is also a strength because it means that they can be adapted flexibly over time, and we should not underestimate the effect of their being endorsed by a powerful body such as the ABI.

To step back for a moment, I buy some of the arguments in the ABI's recent letter on this point but I certainly do not buy into all the arguments that it makes. However, it is worth stressing that the strength of the ABI opposition to this is relevant to the way that we are handling this Bill. Of course, we are going through the special procedure which is applicable to Law Commission Bills, and this means that the Bill has to remain non-controversial. This is a very important point that we should discuss, but I stress as a general point that, as we go through the Bill, we have to be cognisant of the fact that, if we move into what the usual channels might deem to be controversial territory, we will be putting the passage of the Bill at risk under this procedure. I do not know what would happen then, but the Bill would have to come back in some other form. I think that every amendment that we are discussing this afternoon raises an important topic. I assure the Committee that I am not going to resist every single one of them but I make the general point that we need to be careful about the nature of the Bill.

Turning to the specifics of the amendment, what we have not previously discussed in this Committee is that the Law Commission gave very careful consideration to a reference to industry codes in the Bill and specifically consulted on that. This is discussed in paragraphs 10.29 to 10.43 of its 2009 report and it suggested a draft clause, which read:

> 'The insurer may not take advantage of any remedy provided for under this Schedule if, or to the extent that, it would be unreasonable to do so according to written guidance generally recognised by insurers providing the type of insurance in question'.

There was a consultation very directly to this point and detailed consideration was given by the Law Commission. Following the consultation, its recommendation was that it was not included in the Bill. It was concerned that the clause would discourage the industry from agreeing codes, which would also be a consequence of any amendments along the lines of the one suggested.

I do not want to labour the point about self-regulation, or undermine the nature or the practical points made by noble Lord, Lord Borrie, about how the definition would be and how it would link to which particular codes out of the many that the ABI has. I certainly will look, as a practical matter, at whether it would be possible for the codes themselves to reference the fact that an insured party should be aware of the existence of the code, which would at least go some way to close the loop. But I do not know whether that is possible or practical.

I certainly do not buy into the argument of having another line somewhere in the detail along the lines of 'We are FSA-regulated'. I do not see why it would be burdensome necessarily to have a confirmation online or in the written material that refers back to the industry code. I do not know whether anything will be possible but I say to my noble friend and the Committee that I will continue to look at non-legislative ways of handling what is a substantive point.

However, one important point is to be made in respect of the specific reason, which was originally brought up by my noble friend Lady Kramer, in relation to genetic testing. It is important and relevant to explain to the Committee what else is in place to help consumers in this specific area. The *Concordat and Moratorium on Genetics and Insurance* is in place between the Government and the insurance industry. It is working well and is perhaps an exemplar of how self-regulation can work in an area such as this. It was explicitly recognised by your Lordships' House in its 2009 inquiry report on genomic medicine.

The Government believe that compliance with this code is very important. We are working to strengthen how it is enforced. A new form of the agreement is being developed, which will see the ABI commit to publish a list of firms which have confirmed compliance on its website and to provide annual reports to the Government on the number of complaints received about the operation of the concordat and moratorium.

On the specific point, I do not know whether it was behind my noble friend specifically bringing forward this amendment, but I know that in relation to my noble friend Lady Kramer's concerns, there is a specific backstop to which the Government and the industry are party and which we will continue to operate. Of course, as this law develops over the next decades we will have the ability to backstop the Bill, or the law as it may become, in this way.

My final point is that during consultation on this Bill, which supported the inclusion of a provision on codes, there was concern about how the clause was to be drafted so as to ensure that only codes which benefited the consumer at the time of entry into the contract were included. Again it comes very much to the point made by the noble Lord, Lord Borrie, that a wholesale reference to industry codes would not be able to ensure that only elements in favour of consumers should be included. On the basis of what I have said, I ask my noble friend to withdraw his amendment.

Lord Hodgson of Astley Abbotts: I am grateful to my noble friend and all other noble Lords who have participated in this debate. Perhaps I may respond to the points made, first, by the noble Lord, Lord Borrie. I agree that the Bill improves the situation. I am just trying to make the situation still better with this amendment. I think he indicated that I was making the Bill worse, which I am not. I am trying to make the Bill better. He made a point about it being from the industry, which I understand. The industry is providing the insurance. I am trying to get into the Bill something that tells the consumer, 'This is an industry code. These are the people from whom you are getting your insurance. You need to find out about what it implies and what it requires'. That is important. I do not mind the fact that it may be one-sided so long as the person knows from whence it comes.

The noble and learned Lord, Lord Lloyd of Berwick, said that we are replacing the codes. That is not what the evidence said. Mr Hertzell said:

> 'The Bill has been drafted to provide high-level overarching principles. It sets out a framework to deal with the problems but does not need to lay down guidance'.

The consumer will be forced back to the code for his protection in the future. These are five principles, but we do not get any further into the detail, which of course is where it affects individuals. I am grateful to the noble Lord, Lord Eatwell. I am not in any way wedded to the wording I used. This was to try to get the issue on the table and I suspected that I had not managed to draft this in a parliamentary way.

I am grateful for the Minister's reassurance that he will do what he can to build awareness of codes along the lines of the concordat on genetic testing. It is very important that we should try to do that. I accept entirely his argument that more clauses and more paper are unlikely to benefit the consumer. It may well confuse him more. I refute the idea that doing this will discourage the industry from agreeing new codes. That is just an attempt to avoid having to accept this because new codes will be produced whether this is in here or not.

The Minister referred to the uncontroversial nature of our proceedings. The uncontroversial part is whether it is drawn on political lines. That is the problem with Law Commission Bills. It is not that we disagree about them. The noble Lord, Lord Eatwell, and I are on different sides of the political spectrum. It is uncontroversial in terms of politics but not uncontroversial in terms of impact and effect. That having been said, I sense that noble Lords would not support this amendment if I pushed to test the opinion of the Committee. I beg leave to withdraw the amendment.

Amendment 1 withdrawn.

Amendment 2 Moved by Lord Eatwell

> **2:** Clause 2, page 2, line 6, at end insert—
>
> '( ) Subsection (3) applies only when the insurer has made clear to the consumer that such renewal of an insurance contract constitutes a new

contract, and that questions asked at renewal constitute the set of questions relevant to the new contract.'

Lord Eatwell: My Lords, one issue that became clear during the taking of evidence and the earlier discussions we had on this Bill was that most consumers do not realise that the renewal of an insurance contract is in fact a new contract and that therefore the posing and answering of questions, whether at an initial proposal or at a renewal, have equivalent status. The purpose of my amendment is simply to ensure that consumers are well aware at the time of a renewal that they are entering into a new contract and that therefore the questions asked at renewal constitute the entire set of questions relevant to the new contract.

In the drafting, an erroneous word 'such' entered the second line which, if I were allowed a manuscript amendment, I would withdraw, since sometimes a request to confirm or amend particulars may not have anything to do with renewal. I want to focus simply on the issue of renewal and to incorporate this clause into the Bill to ensure that there is clarity about the status of questions and the stage at which questions are asked. I beg to move.

Lord Davies of Stamford: My Lords, I intervene very briefly in support of the amendment proposed by my noble friend Lord Eatwell. It seems entirely reasonable that an ordinary consumer buying a consumer insurance product from an insurance company and then renewing that product in subsequent years or subsequent periods would assume that the declarations made at the outset were still valid and still recorded by his or her insurance company. It seems to me that even if that assumption is wrong, a lot of the responsibility for that mistake lies in the hands of the insurance company, which should keep good records of its clients or, if it is not prepared to do that, should at least ask one of the relevant questions – and we provided for insurance companies to take responsibility for asking the right questions – or should make it clear in the application form that it is a new contract and therefore the assured has to begin ab initio to think of what might be relevant or declarable. To void a contract on the grounds of non-declaration when a declaration has previously been made by the customer to the insurance company, perhaps several times, over several years or for several periods, would be quite unreasonable and unfair, and quite contrary to the purposes of this Bill.

Lord Hodgson of Astley Abbotts: I have some sympathy with this amendment too. I do not think I have ever realised that when I renew my motor car insurance once a year, I am entering into a new contract. I have just assumed that it is an extension of what I have done before. Although this may not be relevant in terms of the way the forms are completed, I suspect that everybody thinks that motor car insurance just rolls on from year to year and that an existing contract just goes on. I think that is what one would assume, and with household insurance likewise. There are a series of policies that we individually undertake, and we would be under the misapprehension that they are just a continuation of an existing contract. I think there is a substantive point here which I support.

Baroness O'Cathain: I, too, support this amendment. It was quite a revelation to me to realise that insurance contracts do not just roll on. I never for one moment thought that they were new contracts, particularly on motor cars. If you add or subtract something – household items, pictures or something – you would be aware of that, and you would make a statement to that effect to the insurer, but a motor car is a motor car. If you have insured it for three or four years, you keep on insuring it. I think this is a very good point.

Lord Goodhart: I, too, was persuaded by the noble Lord, Lord Eatwell. I am happy to support this amendment.

Lord Lloyd of Berwick: I, too, have been persuaded. All I would say at the moment is that I cannot see any harm in the amendment proposed. As to whether it is strictly necessary, well, it may not matter, but I cannot see any harm, and unless the Minister can persuade me that there is some harm, I will be supporting the amendment.

Lord Sassoon: My Lords, let me try to persuade the noble and learned Lord, Lord Lloyd of Berwick, on a technical legal matter such as this. I am not sure that I am up to it, but I will try.

There is an important point here. I, too, would not have the faintest idea whether a renewal of any of my insurance policies was or was not a new contract. This is an important question, but as a consumer, where would I be if I did know or was told that I was entering into a new contact as opposed to a continuation of the old contract? What would flow from that? What am I supposed to do about it?

There is a technical issue here but, as I will attempt to persuade the Committee, it has already been considered by the FSA, the commissioners and others, and the position is that rather than confusing consumers by drawing their attention to this point, we need to make sure that they are protected through the way that this Bill will operate in relation to this very simple but important question of misrepresentation that we are trying to address. The point is very much recognised, but let me try to take the Committee through the logic of the position, which is to end up saying that we do not believe that this amendment is necessary or appropriate.

The amendment would have two effects. The first is that insurers would be required to make consumers aware that renewal constitutes a new contract, and the second is that the questions they ask at renewal would have to constitute the set of questions relevant to the new contact. It may be easiest if I take the second effect of the amendment first and suggest that it is already achieved by the existing provisions of the Bill. Let me set out to the Committee how it is already covered.

First, in order to have any remedy, the insurer must ask a question. If it fails to do so or chooses not to do so, there can be no misrepresentation by the consumer. It follows that any questions insurers ask are the relevant questions for the new contract. Secondly, consumers must take reasonable care to answer any questions they are asked. However, a failure to respond, for example, may be considered reasonable if the insurer's questions were unclear or if the consumer did not receive the insurer's letter – a point that was raised in previous discussions in this Committee. In these circumstances, the insurer may not have a remedy. Clause 3 sets out examples of matters that should be taken into account when deciding whether the consumer has acted reasonably. These include in Clause 3(2)(b) how clear and specific the insurer's questions were. Thirdly, even if the consumer has made a misrepresentation, Clause 4(1)(b) means that the insurer has to show that the misrepresentation caused it to provide the insurance on the terms it did or at all. The questions an insurer asks at renewal will need to be relevant to a new contract, otherwise an insurer will not have a remedy. I suggest that that deals with the second effect of this amendment. If we turn back to the concerns that have been raised in discussion—

Lord Davies of Stamford: I am grateful to the Minister for giving way. What I think he is saying is that essentially he agrees in principle with the idea behind the amendment tabled by my noble friend Lord Eatwell, but that its purpose is equally well met by the general provisions of the Bill, that the insurer has to ask the right questions and so forth. I put it to him that that is not the same thing. To say that the remedy is in the general provisions is nothing like as good as providing a specific remedy. In the case of a dispute, the assured would have to argue that the general provisions adequately cover his or her case. If you put in a specific provision we can cover the point much more effectively, and instead of using the subjunctive, which the noble Lord has just used in saying that the assured 'may' have a remedy, the assured then would have a remedy. There is a great difference between those two positions.

Lord Sassoon: My Lords, perhaps I may move on to the second part of my response to the discussion, which may help the noble Lord, Lord Davies of Stamford. I want to establish first of all that the Government firmly believe, as indeed must the Law Commission have believed, that there was complete protection for consumers at renewal in relation to questions asked, just as there is protection clearly relevant to any contract being entered into for the first time. However, I want to come on to the specific concern about consumers being in a position where they may not understand the precise legal nature of a renewal and the fact that it is a new contract. A number of us have agreed as we have spoken that we ourselves would not understand that point. Having considered it, I certainly agree that most consumers are unlikely to take the point or, indeed, as I said in my introduction, are unlikely to understand the significance of being told that a renewal is a new contract. We must make sure that we protect them in the circumstances of both a totally new contract and of a renewal, and I would suggest that that is what the purpose of the Bill must be rather than doing anything that might unnecessarily confuse consumers in consideration of the nature of the contract they are entering into at any stage.

The critical point here is that the understanding consumers need to have of their position at renewal is already regulated by the FSA. In this respect, the insurer's obligation under FSA rules is to ask clear questions as outlined above, which I believe addresses the concern. Of course, the conduct of the insurer when renewing a contract of insurance is itself subject to regulation by the FSA and there is existing FSA guidance for firms on explaining to customers what they must disclose and the consequences of any failure to make such disclosure. In addition to that general requirement, the FSA also requires that on renewal of a contract, firms should

> 'take reasonable steps to ensure that a customer is given appropriate information about a policy in good time and in a comprehensible form so that the customer can make an informed decision about the arrangements proposed'.

The FSA requires that all communications with customers, including renewal documents, be clear, fair and not misleading. So I believe that it is unnecessary for this clause to require insurers to make it clear that a renewal is a new contract. They are already required to disclose anything that is relevant and, as I have explained, if they fail to ask questions, there is no obligation on the prospectively insured party to answer them.

I shall address the specific question that came up in previous discussions. Under the provisions of the Bill, a failure to respond to an insurer's request because a letter was lost in the post or delivered to the wrong address is capable of not being a misrepresentation. There may always be circumstances where communications between the insurer and the policyholder break down, and one of the benefits to consumers under this Bill is that in such circumstances it is open to the policyholder to argue that failure to confirm or amend particulars because this has occurred may be considered reasonable in all the circumstances.

In conclusion, requiring that insurers make it clear that a renewal is a new contract is unnecessary because insurers would not be able to refuse a claim unless the duties around disclosure were made clear to the consumer. Existing regulation also addresses some of the concerns expressed by the Committee, and the other consequences of this amendment are covered by existing provisions. I suggest that the amendment is unnecessary and risks confusing consumers, and therefore I request the noble Lord to withdraw it.

Lord Lloyd of Berwick: Does the noble Lord happen to know whether this particular point was considered at all by the Law Commission or, indeed, in the further consultation carried out by the Government?

Lord Sassoon: My Lords, I have to say that I am not immediately aware of whether the commission did consider it, although I am sure that it would have considered everything relevant – and this is highly relevant. In fact, I can confirm that it did explicitly consider this point.

Lord Eatwell: My Lords, I am enormously grateful for the support I have received around the Committee for the amendment, but I regret to say that I am rather unconvinced by the Minister's arguments against it. For his second argument on the issue of confusion, clarification and so on, he quoted the FSA rules. He said that those rules provide the assurance that everybody will be clear that a renewal of insurance is a new contract. But he himself admitted that he did not know this. Indeed, virtually everyone in the Committee has admitted that the existence of the FSA rules had not provided them with this piece of information and that they did not know it. So I am afraid that the idea that there is existing protection for the consumer either in FSA rules or elsewhere is demonstrated by the opinion poll taken around this Committee to be false.

Lord Sassoon: It may be helpful if I intervene, and I am grateful to the noble Lord for giving way. I think the implication he reads into my absolute confirmation that neither I nor other Members of the Committee understand or know whether a renewal constitutes a new contract or not means that perhaps he is taking a different conclusion from it than the one I was seeking to draw, which is this. We should expect consumers not to understand or, even if they are told, not to be able to assess the implications of knowing that fact, and therefore I was trying to suggest that the construction of the Bill and the FSA regulations taken together is precisely to protect the consumer and ensure that he is held harmless, if you like, against a background where we cannot and should not expect consumers either to know that a renewal is a new contract or what the legal consequences of that knowledge would be.

Lord Eatwell: I am grateful to the noble Lord because I think he has just defeated the first part of his own argument. His first argument referred to whether sufficient protections are already in the Bill with respect to the questions which on renewal a consumer might answer or not answer. The problem here is that the potential for the catch-all question of whether circumstances have changed is very high. If that question were to be asked and the reasonable consumer, not realising that this was a new contract, did not feel that they had to answer all of the points they had made already, they might be disadvantaged.

The Bill gives consumers significantly more rights than they had before. We are all delighted by that and pleased by the construction of the Bill, but it imposes responsibilities on consumers with respect to the answers that they give to questions and we ought to provide a firm foundation on which the consumers can exercise that responsibility. I am very taken with the argument by the noble and learned Lord, Lord Lloyd, that this would do no harm. If it would do no harm and clarify the issue of renewal, I believe it would be worth while. I am also persuaded by my noble friend Lord Davies, who referred to the need to argue this case with respect to the clauses in the Bill, rather than have a clear right specified as I have proposed. Given the arguments made, in which I regret that the Minister did not manage to convince me, and the support which I have heard around the Committee, I beg to test the opinion of the Committee.

The Chairman of Committees: Because of the change in its wording, theoretically I should read the amendment out. In fact, I shall just say that, with the exception in line 2 of the removal of 'such', the question is that Amendment 2 be agreed to.

Noble Lords: Content.

Lord Sassoon: Not content.

The Chairman of Committees: My Lords, in that case we have to go to a Division and as not all Members are present, we have to allow for a pause of eight minutes while those who are not present are able to reach this Room. However, I know that two Members of the Committee are not here at all – I am looking at my Clerk for guidance here – and that there is therefore only one Member of the Committee, the noble Baroness, Lady Wheeler, who is not here in the Room and whose whereabouts I do not know. Is it possible to go to a vote, and only if that is within one vote would we have to go to the eight minutes? Perhaps I am being too revolutionary. I understand that there is no guidance to do that in the *Companion* but if both Front Benches agree to do so, it could be the will of the Committee. Would the Committee agree that that is the procedure?

Lord Lloyd of Berwick: Is the question not whether if there are other amendments which need to be voted on, we can in some kind of way vote on them all together?

The Chairman of Committees: No, my Lords, we cannot do that. All I am trying to do is to avoid us having to wait eight minutes, so perhaps the Committee could then go to the vote. I explained how it was going to be. The Clerk is going to go around the Committee and take one of these options: content, not-content or abstain.

Division on Amendment 2

Contents 7; Not-Contents 1.

Amendment 2 agreed.

Division No. 1

CONTENTS

Borrie, L. Davies of Stamford, L. Eatwell, L. Goodhart, L. Hodgson of Astley Abbots, L. Lloyd of Berwick, L. O'Cathain, B.

NOT-CONTENTS

Sassoon, L.

Clause 2, as amended, agreed.

Appendix 13 Association of British Insurers Conditions of Membership and Other Arrangements March 2007

Membership of the Association is open to all Companies or bodies of persons authorised by the appropriate supervisory authority to transact insurance business of any class in the United Kingdom, including EEA companies trading under the Single Licence. The Association has around 400 companies in membership. Between them, they provide 91% of domestic insurance services sold in the UK. ABI member companies account for almost 20% of investments in the London Stock Market.

This document relates to the compulsory and voluntary arrangements that are conditions of ABI membership. An arrangement is any agreement or undertaking between members that the ABI is a party to, facilitates or administers. Arrangements include, but are not limited to, statements and codes of practice, memoranda of understanding, undertakings, model wordings terms of business, guidance and other agreements.

Compulsory Arrangements applicable to all Members

- **Constitution** – the Association is governed by its Constitution. It lays the framework for the entire organisation of the ABI – The Board, Councils and Management Committees – and sets out details of membership, resignation, general meetings and related matters. The Constitution states that members must comply with the Constitution, must not bring the industry or the Association into disrepute, must abide by the codes of conduct and statements of practice which are affirmed by the Board, and must pay subscriptions (see below). Please visit the Member Relations' pages of our website (www.abi.org.uk) for a full copy of the Constitution.
- **Subscriptions** – the Constitution gives the Board Members power to determine the annual subscription. The Board shall give notice to every

Member of the total amount of any levy and of the amount payable by that Member, and every Member shall pay such levy within 14 days of the giving of such notice.

The Board shall also have power from time to time to determine the amount of levy required to be paid by Members and the proportions thereof to be paid by each Member or prospective Member to meet the expenses (including estimated future expenses) of the Association or to meet any deficit in any financial year as shown in the audited accounts submitted to the Annual General Meeting.

- **Pension Scheme Deficit Levy**

  The Board has decided that the Pension Scheme deficit ('the scheme deficit') should be paid off over 10 years (including 2005) from increased subscriptions.

  To ensure that all members of the ABI share equally in the funding of the scheme deficit the Board has determined, in accordance with Article 10 of the Constitution, that members are to pay a levy ('the Pension Scheme Deficit Levy') covering the full amount of their share of the scheme deficit with payments to be made in annual instalments until that deficit is fully paid off.

  Any member paying all their instalments of the Pension Scheme Deficit Levy in the period from 2006 to the date the scheme deficit is fully paid off will be deemed to have paid the full amount of their share of that deficit. However, pursuant to Article 13 of the Constitution, any member leaving the ABI before the scheme deficit is fully paid off is required to pay all their outstanding annual instalments of the Pension Scheme Deficit Levy.

- **Arbitration Clause Agreement** – requires insurers not to insist on the enforcement of arbitration clauses in standard forms of policy if the insured prefers to have questions of liability determined by the Court. It does not apply to reinsurance, marine, aviation or credit insurance. It dates from 1956.

- **Genetic Testing Concordat, Moratorium and Code of Practice** – regulates the use of predictive genetic test results in respect of all relevant classes of insurance. Members providing relevant insurance must nominate a Genetics Underwriter for compliance and contact purposes. Insurers cannot use any tests unless they are approved by the Government's Genetics and Insurance Committee as clinically accurate and actuarially relevant. Even if a test is approved insurers cannot use it except for high value policies above the financial limits set out in the Moratorium. The Code was first published on 1 January 1998 and last revised in August 1999.The Moratorium was agreed with the Government in October 2001. In March 2005, ABI and the Government entered into a Concordat and Moratorium on Genetics and insurance.

This provides a single high-level policy agreement on the use of genetic test results in insurance underwriting practices.

Voluntary Arrangements applicable to Members transacting both Life and General Insurance Business

- **Statement of Recommended Practice (SORP) on Accounting for Insurance Business** – aims to narrow the range of accounting practices in order to enhance the usefulness of insurers' financial statements and to provide guidance on certain provisions of the Companies Act 1985 which require further clarification, or are insufficient to ensure a uniform interpretation. It was originally introduced in 1986 and last revised on 21 December 2006.
- **Supplementary Reporting for Long-Term Insurance Business (the achieved profits method)** – guidance aimed at listed life insurers as an alternative method of determining shareholder profits from life insurance business to be disclosed as supplementary information. It was introduced in December 2001.
- **An Insurers' Guide to the Disability Discrimination Act 1995** – sets out best practices and procedures to enable insurers to interpret and apply legislation correctly and consistently. It was published in September 2001 and revised in January 2003.
- **Data Protection Guidance – A Practitioner's Handbook** – joint financial services trade association guidance to ensure that firms receive consistent advice and guidance and adopt a common interpretation of the legislation. It was published in October 2000. ABI began working on bespoke guidance for the insurance sector in mid-2005. Guidance has been published on **'Subject Access Requests', 'Fair Obtaining'** and **'Lawful Processing'**. Guidance on the **'Instruction and Use of Private Investigators and Tracing Agents'** will be published during Spring 2007.
- **Insurance Policies and Unfair Contract Terms** – guidance for Members on the major issues covered by the Unfair Contract Terms Regulations including the meaning of 'consumer', the implications of the requirement of 'utmost good faith' and 'plain intelligible language'. It was published in 1996 and revised in December 2000. Further advice on the regulations and reviewable premiums was issued in 2006.
- **Industry Process Guide for FOS Issues with Wider Implications** – joint financial services industry protocol setting out a framework for the appointment of industry experts who will prepare presentations to better inform the Ombudsman's decisions where an issue with wider implications arises.

- **A Guide to the ICA Process for Insurers** – provides advice to companies in developing their ICA submission. It describes a variety of established approaches companies currently use to meet the ICA requirements, as well as emerging thinking in the industry on how to prepare the ICA. The Guide complements the FSA's ICA rules and guidance with advice on the approaches that firms may wish to use in meeting the FSA's requirements. Firms are not bound to follow this advice and there may be circumstances where it is appropriate to adopt different techniques. First published February 2007.

Applicable to Members Transacting General Insurance Business

- **Credit Hire Protocol** – non-binding protocol between motor insurers and credit hire organisations that is also known as the General Terms of Business Agreement. It provides a mechanism for the settlement of claims relating to the hire charges for replacement vehicles offered by credit hire organisations to innocent drivers involved in accidents, the cost of which is recoverable from the at fault driver's insurer. It was introduced on 1 September 1999 and revised in July 2005.
- **Memorandum of Understanding (Subrogated Motor Claims – Courtesy Cars)** – streamlines the subrogation claims process by standardising the treatment of claims in respect of courtesy cars. It dates from December 1996.
- **Memorandum of Understanding (Subrogated Motor Claims)** – streamlines the subrogation claims process, in particular the administration of inspections, so controlling repairs costs whilst at the same time maintaining quality and customer service standards. It was introduced in February 1997.
- **Statement on 'Inevitable Accident'** – this Statement, which was introduced during the 1960s, applies to all Members of the Motor Conference. It deals with the unexpected death of the driver at the wheel, causing injury to another party.
- **Motor Insurers' Notification Scheme** – MoU between the Motor Conference and Hire Purchase Information Ltd to ensure that the proceeds of an insurance payout go to the owner of the vehicle. Insurers submit details of intended total loss claims. It was originally introduced in the 1930s and became automated in 1987.
- **Recommendation on Treatment of Loss of No Claims Discount Claims to Motor Insurers' Bureau** – recommendation to the Motor Conference that insurers should not disallow no claims discounts in certain circumstances where a policyholder had successfully pursued a claim against the MIB. It was introduced on 21 December 1995.

- **Declined Cases Agreement** – applies to members of the Motor Conference who undertake not to decline cover to existing customers or to anyone who has not held a policy within the previous three years, unless this will be contrary to the public interest. It was introduced in the 1930s.
- **Recommendations for Handling Loss of Use Claims** – recommendations to the Motor Conference to minimise delays in settlement of loss of use claims. It is also known as the Forbearance Recommendation. It was introduced in 1981.
- **Road Traffic Act 1988 'Use' Agreement** – this Agreement, sometimes known as the 'Cork Bays Agreement', discourages insurers from using the Cork Bays and Moran decisions to avoid RTA Liability. It was introduced on 1 July 1999.
- **Third EU Motor Directive Market Agreement** – ensures that policyholders are not left unwittingly without insurance cover. It was introduced on 30 July 1996.
- **Code of Practice for the Disposal of Motor Vehicle Salvage** – commonly known as the 'Salvage Code'. This sets down standards for the disposal of Motor Vehicle Salvage to apply to Motor Conference Members as well as Motor Vehicle Salvage Agents. It was introduced in February 1998. A revised version, reflecting changes in associated statutory and related regulatory requirements, was published in March 2007.
- **Dual Indemnity Agreement** – sets down clear no claims discount rules where dual Insurance is held, thereby speeding up and making more equitable the claims settlement process. It was introduced in September 1991.
- **The Car Sharing Undertaking** – by this undertaking, given by the Motor Conference to the Government, insurers agree not to regard the receipt of contributions as part of a car sharing arrangement for social or other similar purposes as constituting the carrying of passengers for hire or reward. It came into force on 30 August 1978.
- **Treasury Undertaking** – this undertaking, given by the Motor Conference to the Treasury, clarifies the extent of cover under a private car policy when a mileage allowance is received for travel on-business. Similar undertakings have been agreed with a wide range of bodies. It dates back to the 1940s.
- **Trade Association Health and Safety Risk Assessment Initiative** – aims to improve the knowledge of good health and safety practice amongst trade associations and insurers. It was introduced in September 2003.

- **Statement of Recommended Good Practice for Minimum Notice Renewal –** gives employers a minimum period of notice for renewal of employers' liability insurance and package insurance which contains an employers' liability element. It was introduced in August 2003.

- **The Rehabilitation Code** – this code of best practice on rehabilitation, early intervention and medical treatment in personal injury claims was introduced in 1999.

- **Model Pollution Wordings** – clarifies the extent of cover provided under public liability policies in respect of pollution. It was introduced in 1990.

- **Guidelines for Apportioning and Handling Employers' Liability Mesothelioma Claims** – this Agreement, also known as the 'Fairchild Agreement', was introduced in October 2003.

- **Lister V Romford Ice Agreement** – EL Insurers agree not to institute a claim against an employee or an insured employer in respect of death or injury to a fellow employee unless there is evidence of collusion or wilful misconduct. It was introduced in 1959.

- **Code of Practice for Tracing Employers' Liability Insurance Policies** – facilitates the tracing of insurance policies taken out by employers in the past and ensures that insurers keep future records for a period of 60 years. It was introduced in October 1999.

- **Employers' Liability Claims Experience Form** – any Liability Insurer may request that a broker uses this standardised pro-forma in providing the claims history of a customer. The current version dates from 2001.

- **Model E-Commerce Wordings** – suggested wordings to clarify the extent of cover provided in respect of e-commerce risks. They were introduced in 2001.

- **Model Y2K Wordings** – suggested wordings to clarify the extent of cover provided in respect of Y2K Risks. They were introduced in August 1999.

- **Model 'Driving Other Cars' Wordings** – suggested wordings to prevent unintended use of insurance cover to secure recovery of an uninsured vehicle that has been seized by the police. They were introduced in January 2007.

- **Broker Reporting Mandates** – recommended procedures agreed with BIBA to be observed by Members when approached by a reporting broker or other intermediary for certain general classes of business. They were introduced in 1993 and revised in 1996.

- **The Personal Effects Contribution Agreement** – sets out the criteria for deciding whether the contribution will be made either by a household or travel insurer when both policies are held. It was originally introduced in 1981 and revised in January 1999 and January 2005.
- **Terms of Business Agreements (between Brokers and Insurers)** – provides guidance on possible indicative high level principles to which insurers and intermediaries should have regard when developing TOBA. They were introduced on 26 May 2004.
- **ABI/BBA Banks Agreement** – agreement to notify subscribing banks with an interest in a mortgage property of any change or cancellation of cover of a property and also to keep a policy in force for the bank's benefit if asked to do so. This was introduced in April 1992.
- **Recommended Practices** – Wordings and Procedures relating to Material Damage and Business Interruption Commercial and Industrial Insurance – also known as the 'Blue Book'. This contains details of standard policy wordings to assist insurers in developing policies and to improve the comparability of cover available for consumers. It was published in October 1986.
- **The Combe Down Stone Mines Subsidence Agreement** – facilitates continued provision of insurance cover in respect of properties affected by historical stone mine workings until such time as remedial strengthening works have been finished. It was introduced in December 1999.
- **Dual Insurance –** guidance note which sets out the procedure to follow where there are two household policies in place and one of the policies has been effected or renewed in error. It was issued in October 1999.
- **Joint Code of Practice on the Protection from Fire of Construction Sites and Buildings Undergoing Renovation** – facilitates the prevention of fires on construction sites outlining measures on safe working practices. It was introduced in January 2005.
- **ABI Statement of Principles on the Provision of Flooding Insurance** – provides a framework within which insurers can deliver the industry's stated intention to continue to make available flood insurance to as many domestic and small business customers as possible. It was introduced on 1 January 2003.
- **The Domestic Subsidence Agreement** – sets out the way that insurers deal with subsidence, heave and landslip claims when the homeowner changes insurer. It was originally introduced in October 1993 and revised in January 2000.

- **Domestic Subsidence Tree Root Claims Agreement** – sets out the way that insurers deal with tree root damage claims. It was introduced in June 1997.
- **The ABI Theft/Impact Claims Agreement** – agreement to deal with a theft or attempted theft that gives rise to a claim for damages for a building under both a theft policy and the impact extension of a material damage policy. It was introduced in June 1995.
- **The ABI/British Tunnelling Society Joint Code of Practice for Risk Management of Tunnel Works in the UK** – aims to secure best practice for the minimisation and management of risks associated with the design of tunnel works. It was introduced in September 2003 and revised in May 2005.
- **Guidance on Continuation of Cover following a Subsidence Claim** – relates to policies covering domestic properties owned and occupied in a personal capacity where subsidence, heave or landslip has caused damage to insured property. Following the claim, it is good practice to work with a policyholder to identify action that could be taken to manage ongoing risks and maintain cover wherever possible. It was introduced on 1 January 2005.
- **Contract Certainty Code of Good Practice** – joint code which sets out the standards to which members of the ABI, BIBA and the IIB should adhere in order to achieve contract certainty. The purpose is to make clear to policyholders, intermediaries and insurers the totality of coverage when general insurance policies are incepted and renewed. It is supplemented by guidance notes and a checklist and applies to all contracts incepted or renewed on or after 1 October 2005.
- **Model Payment Protection Insurance (PPI) Refund Wording** – suggested wording to explain to customers that their refund when cancelling their PPI policy may not be pro-rata and to indicate the level of refunds they can expect to receive through the use of a table and/or example.
- **ABI, ACPO, CILA Protocol for responding to emergencies** – sets out procedures for ABI and insurers to receive information from the Police and emergency services following a disaster.

Voluntary Arrangements Applicable to Life and Health Insurers and Pension Providers

- **Customer Impact Scheme** – a concerted commitment by the pensions, protection and investment industry to drive up customers' experience and be openly held to account for its performance. It includes a series of good practice guides covering **'Clear language and layout'; 'Handling customer claims'; 'Reporting against**

customer commitments'; **'Yearly statements'**; **'Complaints handling'** and **'Responsibilities of providers and advisers'**. Further guides will be developed during 2007.

- **Endowment Mortgage Policy Review Code of Practice –** aims to ensure that all investors with mortgage endowment policies bought with the intent to pay-off all or part of a mortgage and who are still paying premiums, are kept regularly informed of the progress of such life policies in meeting this intention. It was originally introduced in October 1999 and revised in May 2004.
- **Statement of Long-Term Insurance Practice** – applies to life insurance for policyholders resident in the UK and insured in their private capacity only. It covers what level of information the proposer can be expected to disclose on any proposal forms and how that disclosure of information affects claims and renewals. It was introduced in January 1986. Whilst much of the Statement has been superceded by the FSA ICOB rules, the Statement has been incorporated into the **ABI Guidance on Application Form Design for Life and Health Protection Insurance** published in February 2006. This aims to ensure that all relevant information is disclosed at the application stage.
- **The Statement of Best Practice for the Selling of Private Medical Insurance** – aims to ensure that the particular information needs of individual customers are met so that that they can make an informed choice when buying a PMI Policy. It was introduced on 14 January 2005 and revised in July 2006. The revised Statement should be implemented at the very latest by 31 December 2007.
- **Statement of Best Practice for Critical Illness Cover** – aims to protect consumers and aid understanding and comparison of critical illness policies through having a common format for describing cover at point of sale, the use of common generic terms and model wordings and exclusions that meet minimum standards. It originally dates from April 1999, was revised in August 2004 and April 2006. The revised Statement should be implemented by April 2007.
- **Statement of Best Practice for Income Protection Insurance** – covers clarity, use of key features requirements and gives guidance on certain policy terms and conditions. It was introduced in August 1999 and revised in August 2003.
- **ABI Statement of Practice – Underwriting Life Insurance for HIV/Aids** – aims to enable insurers to assess accurately applications for long-term insurance where HIV may be an issue in such a way that avoids intrusive or inappropriate questioning. It was introduced in July 1994 and revised in October 2004.
- **ABI/BMA Joint Guidelines on Medical Information and Insurance** – sets out best practice and practical advice on the use of medical

information and insurance. It is primarily designed for general practitioners and other doctors who are asked to provide medical information to insurance companies. It was published in December 2002 and will be reviewed during 2007.

- **ABI/BMA Fees Agreement** – sets out the agreed fees for GP reports, supplementary reports and medical examinations as well as agreed standards for the quality of such reports. It was introduced in 2002 and revised in July 2006.
- **Industry Standard General Practitioners Report Form and Informed Consent – wording agreed by the ABI and BMA** of the standard GPR form and covering letter for obtaining medical information on insurance protection products and the informed consent wording on the insurance application.
- **The Pensions Maturities Statement of Good Practice –** describes minimum standards in timing and terminology recommended to apply to the handling of pensions on maturity, from issue of the claims notification to purchase of annuity or drawdown. It was originally introduced in August 2002 and revised in December 2005.
- **The Pension Transfers Statement of Good Practice** – describes the minimum standards for the smooth transfer of pension arrangements between providers, in order to ensure a quick, clear and smooth pension transfer process for consumers, financial advisers and pension providers. It was originally introduced in January and revised in June 2006.
- **Resource Pack for Financial Promotions** – ABI resource pack aimed to improve customers' experience of the industry. It contains a risk assessment; good practice on processes and measures and guidance for with-profits and structured products promotional literature.
- **Guide for Ensuring Balance in Financial Promotions for Equity Release Products** – outlines information firms should consider when designing equity release promotions to ensure a balanced picture of the product is given. It was introduced in September 2006.
- **Guide on Provider-Adviser Responsibilities in relation to Financial Promotions** – joint guidance with AIFA intended to help firms and advisers understand their responsibilities and mechanisms they may need to consider. It was introduced in September 2006.
- **Guidance on Basic Advice** – aims to raise confidence in basic advice on stakeholder products to foster a shared understanding of standards expected of advisers and help break down barriers to entry. It was introduced in October 2005.
- **Guide of Good Practice for Unit Linked Funds –** establishes standards that the ABI believes all companies managing unit linked

funds should aspire to and work towards and to provide specific guidance for firms looking to understand what TCF means in the context of unit linked fund governance. The guidance will inform the FSA's approach to supervision of unit linked life offices.

- **Markets Statistics Exchange (MSE)** – statistical scheme which facilitates the exchange of information amongst life insurers which shows trends in particular sectors of the market. It was introduced in 1989.

Appendix 14 Consumer Insurance (Disclosure and Representations) Act 2012 [with Explanatory Notes]

An Act to make provision about disclosure and representations in connection with consumer insurance contracts.
[8th March 2012]

BE IT ENACTED by the Queen's most Excellent Majesty, by and with the advice and consent of the Lords Spiritual and Temporal, and Commons, in this present Parliament assembled, and by the authority of the same, as follows:—

Main definitions

1 Main definitions

In this Act—

'consumer insurance contract' means a contract of insurance between—

(a) an individual who enters into the contract wholly or mainly for purposes unrelated to the individual's trade, business or profession, and

(b) a person who carries on the business of insurance and who becomes a party to the contract by way of that business (whether or not in accordance with permission for the purposes of the Financial Services and Markets Act 2000);

'consumer' means the individual who enters into a consumer insurance contract, or proposes to do so;

'insurer' means the person who is, or would become, the other party to a consumer insurance contract.

Pre-contract and pre-variation information

2 Disclosure and representations before contract or variation

(1) This section makes provision about disclosure and representations by a consumer to an insurer before a consumer insurance contract is entered into or varied.

(2) It is the duty of the consumer to take reasonable care not to make a misrepresentation to the insurer.

(3) A failure by the consumer to comply with the insurer's request to confirm or amend particulars previously given is capable of being a misrepresentation for the purposes of this Act (whether or not it could be apart from this subsection).

(4) The duty set out in subsection (2) replaces any duty relating to disclosure or representations by a consumer to an insurer which existed in the same circumstances before this Act applied.

(5) Accordingly—

(a) any rule of law to the effect that a consumer insurance contract is one of the utmost good faith is modified to the extent required by the provisions of this Act, and

(b) the application of section 17 of the Marine Insurance Act 1906 (contracts of marine insurance are of utmost good faith), in relation to a contract of marine insurance which is a consumer insurance contract, is subject to the provisions of this Act.

3 Reasonable care

(1) Whether or not a consumer has taken reasonable care not to make a misrepresentation is to be determined in the light of all the relevant circumstances.

(2) The following are examples of things which may need to be taken into account in making a determination under subsection (1)—

(a) the type of consumer insurance contract in question, and its target market,

(b) any relevant explanatory material or publicity produced or authorised by the insurer,

(c) how clear, and how specific, the insurer's questions were,

(d) in the case of a failure to respond to the insurer's questions in connection with the renewal or variation of a consumer insurance contract, how clearly the insurer communicated the importance of answering those questions (or the possible consequences of failing to do so),

(e) whether or not an agent was acting for the consumer.

(3) The standard of care required is that of a reasonable consumer: but this is subject to subsections (4) and (5).

(4) If the insurer was, or ought to have been, aware of any particular characteristics or circumstances of the actual consumer, those are to be taken into account.

(5) A misrepresentation made dishonestly is always to be taken as showing lack of reasonable care.

Qualifying misrepresentations

4 Qualifying misrepresentations: definition and remedies

(1) An insurer has a remedy against a consumer for a misrepresentation made by the consumer before a consumer insurance contract was entered into or varied only if—

(a) the consumer made the misrepresentation in breach of the duty set out in section 2(2), and

(b) the insurer shows that without the misrepresentation, that insurer would not have entered into the contract (or agreed to the variation) at all, or would have done so only on different terms.

(2) A misrepresentation for which the insurer has a remedy against the consumer is referred to in this Act as a 'qualifying misrepresentation'.

(3) The only such remedies available are set out in Schedule 1.

5 Qualifying misrepresentations: classification and presumptions

(1) For the purposes of this Act, a qualifying misrepresentation (see section 4(2)) is either—

(a) deliberate or reckless, or

(b) careless.

(2) A qualifying misrepresentation is deliberate or reckless if the consumer—

(a) knew that it was untrue or misleading, or did not care whether or not it was untrue or misleading, and

(b) knew that the matter to which the misrepresentation related was relevant to the insurer, or did not care whether or not it was relevant to the insurer.

(3) A qualifying misrepresentation is careless if it is not deliberate or reckless.

(4) It is for the insurer to show that a qualifying misrepresentation was deliberate or reckless.

(5) But it is to be presumed, unless the contrary is shown—

(a) that the consumer had the knowledge of a reasonable consumer, and

(b) that the consumer knew that a matter about which the insurer asked a clear and specific question was relevant to the insurer.

Specific issues

6 Warranties and representations

(1) This section applies to representations made by a consumer—

(a) in connection with a proposed consumer insurance contract, or

(b) in connection with a proposed variation to a consumer insurance contract.

(2) Such a representation is not capable of being converted into a warranty by means of any provision of the consumer insurance contract (or of the terms of the variation), or of any other contract (and whether by declaring the representation to form the basis of the contract or otherwise).

7 Group insurance

(1) This section applies where—

(a) a contract of insurance is entered into by a person ('A') in order to provide cover for another person ('C'), or is varied or extended so as to do so,

(b) C is not a party to the contract,

(c) so far as the cover for C is concerned, the contract would have been a consumer insurance contract if entered into by C rather than by A, and

(d) C provided information directly or indirectly to the insurer before the contract was entered into, or before it was varied or extended to provide cover for C.

(2) So far as the cover for C is concerned—

(a) sections 2 and 3 apply in relation to disclosure and representations by C to the insurer as if C were proposing to enter into a consumer insurance contract for the relevant cover with the insurer, and

(b) subject to subsections (3) to (5) and the modifications in relation to the insurer's remedies set out in Part 3 of Schedule 1, the remainder of this Act applies in relation to the cover for C as if C had entered into a consumer insurance contract for that cover with the insurer.

(3) Section 4(1)(b) applies as if it read as follows—

'(b)the insurer shows that without the misrepresentation, that insurer would not have agreed to provide cover for C at all, or would have done so only on different terms.'

(4) If there is more than one C, a breach on the part of one of them of the duty imposed (by virtue of subsection (2)(a)) by section 2(2) does not affect the contract so far as it relates to the others.

(5) Nothing in this section affects any duty owed by A to the insurer, or any remedy which the insurer may have against A for breach of such a duty.

8 Insurance on life of another

(1) This section applies in relation to a consumer insurance contract for life insurance on the life of an individual ('L') who is not a party to the contract.

(2) If this section applies—

(a) information provided to the insurer by L is to be treated for the purposes of this Act as if it were provided by the person who is the party to the contract, but

(b) in relation to such information, if anything turns on the state of mind, knowledge, circumstances or characteristics of the individual providing the information, it is to be determined by reference to L and not the party to the contract.

9 Agents

Schedule 2 applies for determining, for the purposes of this Act only, whether an agent through whom a consumer insurance contract is effected is the agent of the consumer or of the insurer.

10 Contracting out

(1) A term of a consumer insurance contract, or of any other contract, which would put the consumer in a worse position as respects the matters mentioned in subsection (2) than the consumer would be in by virtue of the provisions of this Act is to that extent of no effect.

(2) The matters are—

(a) disclosure and representations by the consumer to the insurer before the contract is entered into or varied, and

(b) any remedies for qualifying misrepresentations (see section 4(2)).

(3) This section does not apply in relation to a contract for the settlement of a claim arising under a consumer insurance contract.

Final provision

11 Consequential provision

(1) Any rule of law to the same effect as the following is abolished in relation to consumer insurance contracts—

(a) section 18 of the Marine Insurance Act 1906 (disclosure by assured),

(b) section 19 of that Act (disclosure by agent effecting insurance),

(c) section 20 of that Act (representations pending negotiation of contract).

(2) The Marine Insurance Act 1906 is amended as follows—

(a) in section 18, at the end add—

> '(6) This section does not apply in relation to a contract of marine insurance if it is a consumer insurance contract within the meaning of the Consumer Insurance (Disclosure and Representations) Act 2012.';

(b) in section 19, the existing text becomes subsection (1), and after that add—

> '(2)This section does not apply in relation to a contract of marine insurance if it is a consumer insurance contract within the meaning of the Consumer Insurance (Disclosure and Representations) Act 2012.';

(c) in section 20, at the end add—

> '(8)This section does not apply in relation to a contract of marine insurance if it is a consumer insurance contract

within the meaning of the Consumer Insurance (Disclosure and Representations) Act 2012.'.

(3) In section 152 of the Road Traffic Act 1988 (exceptions to duty of insurers to satisfy judgment against persons insured against third-party risks), in subsection (2)—

(a) in paragraph (a), after 'avoid it' insert 'either under the Consumer Insurance (Disclosure and Representations) Act 2012 or, if that Act does not apply,';

(b) in paragraph (b), after 'policy or security' insert 'under that Act or', and for 'it' substitute 'the policy or security'.

(4) In Article 98A of the Road Traffic (Northern Ireland) Order 1981 (S.I. 1981/154 (N.I.)) (exceptions to duty of insurers to satisfy judgment against persons insured against third-party risks), in paragraph (2)—

(a) in sub-paragraph (a), after 'avoid it' insert 'either under the Consumer Insurance (Disclosure and Representations) Act 2012 or, if that Act does not apply,';

(b) in sub-paragraph (b), after 'policy or security' insert 'under that Act or', and for 'it' substitute 'the policy or security'.

12 Short title, commencement, application and extent

(1) This Act may be cited as the Consumer Insurance (Disclosure and Representations) Act 2012.

(2) Section 1 and this section come into force on the day on which this Act is passed, but otherwise this Act comes into force on such day as the Treasury may by order made by statutory instrument appoint.

(3) An order under subsection (2) may not appoint a day sooner than the end of the period of 1 year beginning with the day on which this Act is passed.

(4) This Act applies only in relation to consumer insurance contracts entered into, and variations to consumer insurance contracts agreed, after the Act comes into force.

In the case of group insurance (see section 7), that includes the provision of cover for C by means of an insurance contract entered into by A after the Act comes into force, or varied or extended so as to do so after the Act comes into force.

(5) Nothing in this Act affects the circumstances in which a person is bound by the acts or omissions of that person's agent.

(6) Apart from the provisions listed in subsection (7), this Act extends to England and Wales, Scotland and Northern Ireland.

(7) In section 11—

(a) subsection (3) extends to England and Wales and Scotland only;

(b) subsection (4) extends to Northern Ireland only.

SCHEDULES

SCHEDULE 1

Section 4(3).

INSURERS' REMEDIES FOR QUALIFYING MISREPRESENTATIONS

Part 1

CONTRACTS

General

1 This Part of this Schedule applies in relation to qualifying misrepresentations made in connection with consumer insurance contracts (for variations to them, see Part 2).

Deliberate or reckless misrepresentations

2 If a qualifying misrepresentation was deliberate or reckless, the insurer—

(a) may avoid the contract and refuse all claims, and

(b) need not return any of the premiums paid, except to the extent (if any) that it would be unfair to the consumer to retain them.

Careless misrepresentations – claims

3 If the qualifying misrepresentation was careless, paragraphs 4 to 8 apply in relation to any claim.

4 The insurer's remedies are based on what it would have done if the consumer had complied with the duty set out in section 2(2), and paragraphs 5 to 8 are to be read accordingly.

5 If the insurer would not have entered into the consumer insurance contract on any terms, the insurer may avoid the contract and refuse all claims, but must return the premiums paid.

6 If the insurer would have entered into the consumer insurance contract, but on different terms (excluding terms relating to the premium), the contract is to be treated as if it had been entered into on those different terms if the insurer so requires.

7 In addition, if the insurer would have entered into the consumer insurance contract (whether the terms relating to matters other than the premium would have been the same or different), but would have charged a higher premium, the insurer may reduce proportionately the amount to be paid on a claim.

8 'Reduce proportionately' means that the insurer need pay on the claim only X% of what it would otherwise have been under an obligation to pay under the terms of the contract (or, if applicable, under the different terms provided for by virtue of paragraph 6), where—

Careless misrepresentations – treatment of contract for the future

9

(1) This paragraph—

(a) applies if the qualifying misrepresentation was careless, but

(b) does not relate to any outstanding claim.

(2) Paragraphs 5 and 6 (as read with paragraph 4) apply as they apply where a claim has been made.

(3) Paragraph 7 (as read with paragraph 4) applies in relation to a claim yet to be made as it applies in relation to a claim which has been made.

(4) If by virtue of sub-paragraph (2) or (3), the insurer would have either (or both) of the rights conferred by paragraph 6 or 7, the insurer may—

(a) give notice to that effect to the consumer, or

(b) terminate the contract by giving reasonable notice to the consumer.

(5) But the insurer may not terminate a contract under sub-paragraph (4)(b) if it is wholly or mainly one of life insurance.

(6) If the insurer gives notice to the consumer under sub-paragraph (4)(a), the consumer may terminate the contract by giving reasonable notice to the insurer.

(7) If either party terminates the contract under this paragraph, the insurer must refund any premiums paid for the terminated cover in respect of the balance of the contract term.

(8) Termination of the contract under this paragraph does not affect the treatment of any claim arising under the contract in the period before termination.

(9) Nothing in this paragraph affects any contractual right to terminate the contract.

Part 2

VARIATIONS

10 This Part of this Schedule applies in relation to qualifying misrepresentations made in connection with variations to consumer insurance contracts.

11 If the subject-matter of a variation can reasonably be treated separately from the subject-matter of the rest of the contract, Part 1 of this Schedule applies (with any necessary modifications) in relation to the variation as it applies in relation to a contract.

12 Otherwise, Part 1 applies (with any necessary modifications) as if the qualifying misrepresentation had been made in relation to the whole contract (for this purpose treated as including the variation) rather than merely in relation to the variation.

Part 3

MODIFICATIONS FOR GROUP INSURANCE

13 Part 1 is to be read subject to the following modifications in relation to cover provided for C under a group insurance contract as mentioned in section 7 (and in this Part 'A' and 'C' mean the same as in that section).

14 References to the consumer insurance contract (however described) are to that part of the contract which provides for cover for C.

15 References to claims and premiums are to claims and premiums in relation to that cover.

16 The reference to the consumer is to be read—

(a) in paragraph 2(b), as a reference to whoever paid the premiums, or the part of them that related to the cover for C,

(b) in paragraph 9(4) and (6), as a reference to A.

Part 4

SUPPLEMENTARY

17 Section 84 of the Marine Insurance Act 1906 (return of premium for failure of consideration) is to be read subject to the provisions of this Schedule in relation to contracts of marine insurance which are consumer insurance contracts.

SCHEDULE 2

Section 9.

RULES FOR DETERMINING STATUS OF AGENTS

1 This Schedule sets out rules for determining, for the purposes of this Act only, whether an agent through whom a consumer insurance contract is effected is acting as the agent of the consumer or of the insurer.

2 The agent is to be taken as the insurer's agent in each of the following cases—

(a) when the agent does something in the agent's capacity as the appointed representative of the insurer for the purposes of the Financial Services and Markets Act 2000 (see section 39 of that Act),

(b) when the agent collects information from the consumer, if the insurer had given the agent express authority to do so as the insurer's agent,

(c) when the agent enters into the contract as the insurer's agent, if the insurer had given the agent express authority to do so.

3

(1) In any other case, it is to be presumed that the agent is acting as the consumer's agent unless, in the light of all the relevant circumstances, it appears that the agent is acting as the insurer's agent.

(2) Some factors which may be relevant are set out below.

(3) Examples of factors which may tend to confirm that the agent is acting for the consumer are—

(a) the agent undertakes to give impartial advice to the consumer,

(b) the agent undertakes to conduct a fair analysis of the market,

(c) the consumer pays the agent a fee.

(4) Examples of factors which may tend to show that the agent is acting for the insurer are—

(a) the agent places insurance of the type in question with only one of the insurers who provide insurance of that type,

(b) the agent is under a contractual obligation which has the effect of restricting the number of insurers with whom the agent places insurance of the type in question,

(c) the insurer provides insurance of the type in question through only a small proportion of the agents who deal in that type of insurance,

(d) the insurer permits the agent to use the insurer's name in providing the agent's services,

(e) the insurance in question is marketed under the name of the agent,

(f) the insurer asks the agent to solicit the consumer's custom.

4

(1) If it appears to the Treasury that the list of factors in sub-paragraph (3) or (4) of paragraph 3 has become outdated, the Treasury may by order made by statutory instrument bring the list up to date by amending the sub-paragraph so as to add, omit or alter any factor.

(2) A statutory instrument containing an order under sub-paragraph (1) may not be made unless a draft of the instrument has been laid before and approved by a resolution of each House of Parliament.

These notes refer to the Consumer Insurance (Disclosure and Representations) Bill [HL] as brought from the House of Lords on 17 January 2012 [Bill 274]

EXPLANATORY NOTES

Introduction

1. These explanatory notes relate to the Consumer Insurance (Disclosure and Representations) Bill as brought from the House of Lords on 17 January 2012. They have been prepared by HM Treasury in order to assist the reader of the Bill and to help inform debate on it. They do not form part of the Bill and have not been endorsed by Parliament.

2. These notes need to be read in conjunction with the Bill. They are not, and are not meant to be, a comprehensive description of the Bill. So where a clause or part of a clause does not seem to require any explanation or comment, none is given.

Territorial extent and application

3. The Bill extends to the whole of the United Kingdom apart from clause 11(3) which does not extend to Northern Ireland and clause 11(4) which extends only to Northern Ireland: clause 11(3) amends legislation which extends only to Great Britain and clause 11(4) amends the equivalent legislation in Northern Ireland.

4. This Bill does not contain any provisions falling within the terms of the Sewel Convention. Because the Sewel Convention provides that Westminster will not normally legislate with regard to devolved matters in Scotland without the consent of the Scottish Parliament, if there are amendments relating to such matters which trigger the Convention, the consent of the Scottish Parliament will be sought for them. In relation to Northern Ireland this Bill only covers matters that are reserved to Westminster. If there are amendments relating to a matter that has been transferred the consent of the Northern Ireland Assembly will be sought for them. The Bill does not deal with provisions within the legislative competence of the National Assembly for Wales. If there are amendments which fall within the legislative competence of the National Assembly its consent will be sought for them.

Background

5. The Bill gives effect, with minor modifications, to the recommendations set out in the Law Commission and the Scottish Law Commission's 2009 joint report 'Consumer Insurance Law: Pre-Contract Disclosure and Misrepresentation' (Law Com No. 319; Scot Law Com No. 219).

6. British insurance law developed during the 18th and 19th centuries, and was partly codified by the Marine Insurance Act 1906 ('the 1906 Act'). Although strictly the 1906 Act only applies to marine insurance, the courts have consistently held that it applies to all forms of insurance, including consumer insurance, on the grounds that it codifies the common law.

7. The 1906 Act requires that the insured person must disclose every matter that would be material to the insurer's decision to insure. Failure to do this permits the insurer to avoid the contract and refuse all claims under it, even where the insured person is not aware of what the insurer would consider material.

8. To ameliorate the effects of the existing statute law a series of guides and codes have been produced by regulators (the Financial Services Authority and the Financial Ombudsman Service have both produced guidance) and industry (the Association of British Insurers has produced a code of conduct). The 1906 Act specifies one set of rules, FSA Rules set out different standards and the FOS reaches decisions on a third and separate set of principles.

9. The purpose of the Bill is to update the law relating to pre-contractual disclosure and misrepresentations and simplify the existing legal framework by removing layers of case law, guidance and voluntary codes which currently set the standards expected in this area.

Summary

Abolishing the consumer's duty to volunteer information

10. The Bill replaces the duty to volunteer material information with a duty on consumers to take reasonable care not to make a misrepresentation during pre-contractual negotiations. If a consumer breaches this duty and this misrepresentation induces the insurer to enter the contract, the insurer will have a remedy. The nature of the insurer's remedy depends on the nature of the consumer's misrepresentation. If a consumer makes a deliberate or reckless misrepresentation, the Bill permits the insurer to treat the contract as if it never existed and refuse all claims. If, when answering questions posed by an insurer, a consumer answers carelessly, the Bill provides that the insurer may have a remedy according to whether it would have entered into the contract on different terms. If it would not have entered into the contract at all it may refuse all claims but it must return the premiums paid. If it would have entered into the contract on different terms, the contract may be taken to include those different terms. If the premium would have been higher this may have consequences for the amount of any claim. If the consumer acts with reasonable care, the insurer must pay the claim in full.

Group insurance

11. The Bill makes provision for a situation where a member of a group insurance policy makes a misrepresentation. Where this happens the misrepresentation will only have consequences for the cover of that member and not for the policy as a whole.

Life insurance on the life of another

12. The Bill also makes provision in relation to insurance taken out by a consumer on another person's life. Currently, the person whose life is being insured does not normally owe a duty of care when providing information, because they are not a party to the contract. The Bill changes this so that when answering questions posed by the insurance company, the person whose life is being insured has a duty to take reasonable care not to make a misrepresentation. If that individual makes a misrepresentation, the insurer will have the same remedies they would have had if the consumer taking out the policy made the misrepresentation.

Intermediaries

13. The Bill expressly preserves normal agency law, which states that a party is responsible for the actions of their own agent. The Bill sets out a framework for deciding whether, for the purposes of the Bill, the intermediary acts as an agent for the insurer or for the consumer.

Consequential Amendments

14. The Bill disapplies sections 18, 19 and 20 of the 1906 Act in respect of consumer insurance contracts, as defined in the Bill. The Bill also makes section 17 of the 1906 Act subject to the provisions of the Bill. In addition, the Bill disapplies any common law rule to the same effect as these sections.

15. Section 152(2) of the Road Traffic Act 1988 and Article 98A of the Road Traffic (Northern Ireland) Order 1981 (S.I. 1982/154 (N.I.)) are amended by the Bill because they relate to insurance companies avoiding motor insurance contracts where the insured has made a non-disclosure or misrepresentation.

16. The scheme of the Bill is best thought of as a series of questions which the insurer, court or ombudsman must ask before deciding to reject all or part of the claim.

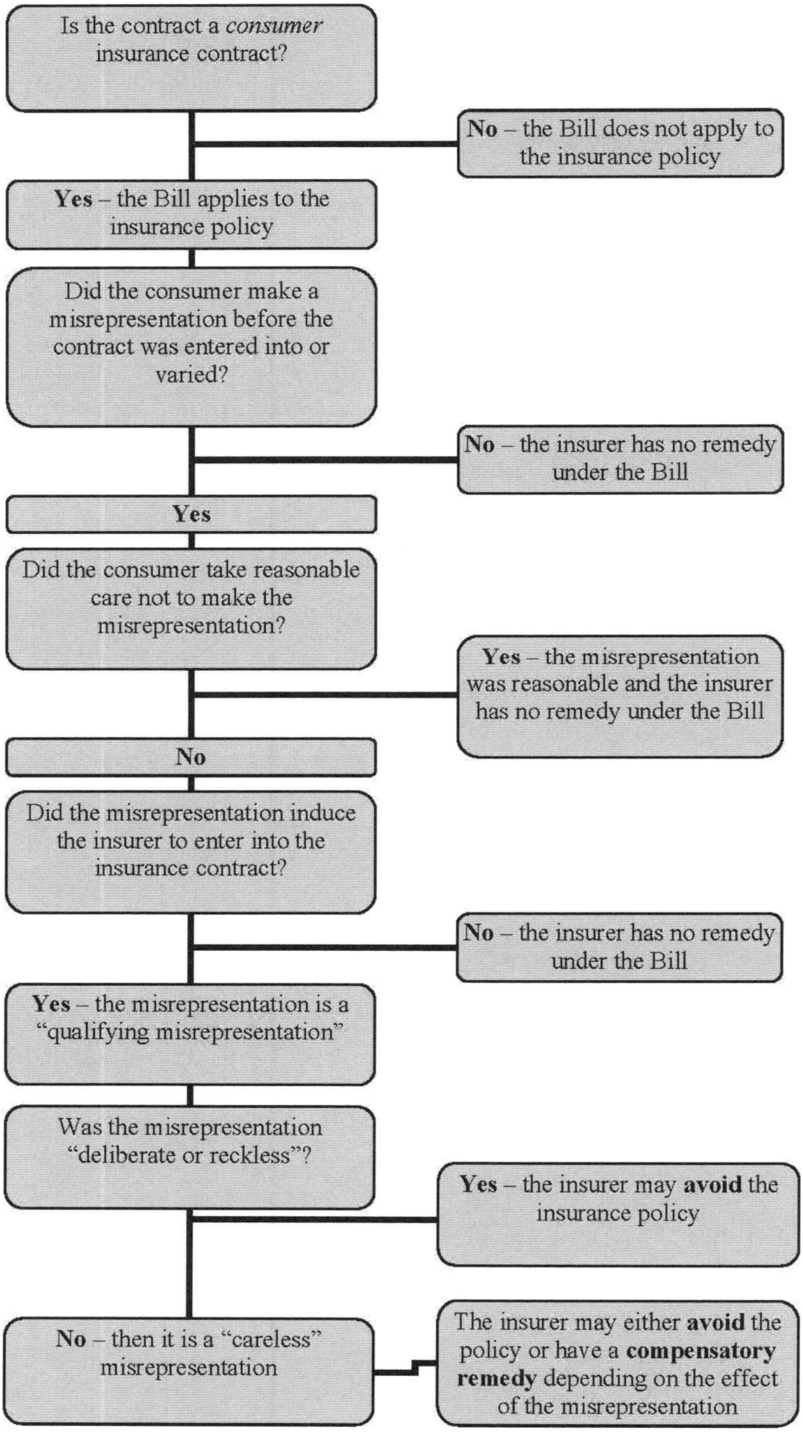
Is the contract a *consumer* insurance contract?
No – the Bill does not apply to the insurance policy
Yes – the Bill applies to the insurance policy
Did the consumer make a misrepresentation before the contract was entered into or varied?
No – the insurer has no remedy under the Bill
Yes
Did the consumer take reasonable care not to make the misrepresentation?
Yes – the misrepresentation was reasonable and the insurer has no remedy under the Bill
No
Did the misrepresentation induce the insurer to enter into the insurance contract?
No – the insurer has no remedy under the Bill
Yes – the misrepresentation is a "qualifying misrepresentation"
Was the misrepresentation "deliberate or reckless"?
Yes – the insurer may **avoid** the insurance policy
No – then it is a "careless" misrepresentation
The insurer may either **avoid** the policy or have a **compensatory remedy** depending on the effect of the misrepresentation

Commentary on clauses

Clause 1: Main definitions

17. Clause 1 defines the terms 'consumer insurance contract', 'consumer' and 'insurer'. The Bill defines a consumer insurance contract based on the status of the persons who enter into the contract. The contract must be between a consumer and an insurer.

18. A consumer is defined as an 'individual' who is acting wholly or mainly for non-business purposes. Thus the consumer must be a natural person, rather than a legal person (such as a company or corporation). The definition expressly provides for mixed use contracts. Where a policy covers some non-business and some business use, the main purpose of the insurance needs to be considered. For example, insurance would be considered to be 'consumer insurance' if private vehicle insurance covers a limited amount of business use, or if home contents insurance covers some business equipment.

19. The 'business of insurance' is not defined in the Bill. The majority of those who carry on insurance business are required to have permission to carry on business from the Financial Services Authority (FSA) (in accordance with the Financial Services and Markets Act 2000). The definition of insurance for purposes of FSA regulation is set out in an Order,[1] and generally follows the common law, as established by case law. However, the Order includes some contracts which may not be insurance at common law (such as pension management contracts) and excludes some contracts which may be insurance, such as funeral plans. For the purposes of the Bill, the definition of insurance follows the common law definition. It includes all consumer insurance contracts, even those which are specifically excluded from FSA regulation.

20. However, a person does not need to have such permission before they are an 'insurer' for the purposes of the definition in clause 1 of the Bill. On the other hand, the insurer must be acting in the course of business: the Bill does not apply to purely private arrangements made between two individuals.

Clause 2: Disclosure and representations before contract or variation

21. Clause 2 abolishes the duty of disclosure in consumer insurance contracts and replaces it with the duty 'to take reasonable care not to make a misrepresentation'. This removes the consumer's duty to volunteer information to the insurer. Instead, consumers are required to answer insurers'

[1] The Financial Services and Markets Act (Regulated Activities) Order 2001, S.I. 2001/544.

questions honestly and to take reasonable care that their replies are accurate and complete. If consumers do provide insurers with information which was not asked for, they must do so honestly and carefully.

22. Subsection (1) stipulates that the consumer's duty arises during pre-contractual negotiations when entering into a new insurance contract or varying an existing contract. There is no explicit reference to renewals, as in law these are regarded as new contracts. However, renewals are covered by the duty.

23. Subsection (2) contains the duty on the consumer to take reasonable care not to make a misrepresentation to the insurer. There is a considerable body of case law defining a misrepresentation which is relevant to this provision. In particular, even though it is literally true, a statement may amount to a misrepresentation because it is incomplete.[2]

24. Subsection (3) confirms that a failure to reply is capable of being a misrepresentation for the purposes of the Bill. For example if the consumer gives particulars by telephone and later fails to respond to a written request to amend them if incorrect or incomplete, the failure may constitute a misrepresentation. This may be a significant issue on renewal, where a consumer may be asked to confirm or amend the information previously given. Whether such a failure is a misrepresentation will depend on the facts.

25. Subsection (4) states that the duty in subsection (2) replaces the current duty of disclosure, which is found in section 18 of the 1906 Act. The duty in section 18 derives from the duty of utmost good faith, which is set out in section 17 of the 1906 Act. Clause 2(5) modifies the duty of utmost good faith so that a consumer is no longer required to volunteer information to the insurer.

26. The Marine Insurance Act 1906 applies directly to marine insurance but it has also been held to be an authoritative statement of common law principles to be applied to other non-marine insurance contracts. Therefore, clause 2(5) works in two ways. Subsection (5)(a) applies to any common law rule to the same effect as section 17. Subsection (5)(b) then applies to any consumer insurance contracts which are also marine insurance (such as insurance on private yachts).

27. However, section 17 is wider than just the pre-contractual duty to disclose and also imposes duties on the parties after the contract has been formed. The Bill does not affect these post-contractual duties such as the duty not to make a fraudulent claim.

---

[2] See *Winter v Irish Life Assurance plc* [1995] 2 Lloyd's Rep 274.

Clause 3: Reasonable care

28. Subsection (1) states that when deciding whether a consumer has taken reasonable care not to make a misrepresentation, all relevant circumstances are to be taken into account. Subsection (2) lists examples of factors that may need to be taken into account when making a judgment as to whether reasonable care was taken. These include the type of insurance in question, any relevant explanatory material and how clear and specific the question was. This list is indicative and non-exhaustive: additional factors may be taken into account when suitable. Where a consumer contract is renewed or varied the consumer may, in some circumstances, make a misrepresentation by failing to respond to the insurer's questions (see clause 2(3)). Subsection (2)(d) indicates that how clearly the insurer communicated the importance of answering its questions is a factor that may be taken into account in deciding whether the consumer failed to take reasonable care. So for example an insurer may, before renewing a consumer insurance contract, ask the consumer whether particulars previously given have changed. This does not mean that the consumer would necessarily have to respond if the facts have not changed – in some cases (such as motor insurance) insurers may ask the consumer to respond only if the consumer's circumstances have changed.

29. The list of factors in subsection (2) is indicative and non-exhaustive: additional factors may be taken into account when relevant.

30. Under subsection (3) the test when looking at whether the consumer has taken reasonable care, is objective; that of the reasonable consumer. This test does not usually take into account any particular characteristics of the actual consumer, such as their age, knowledge of English or level of understanding. The notion of 'reasonableness' is a commonly used concept in English law to provide an objective but flexible standard against which any individual's conduct can be measured. The reasonable consumer denotes an average consumer with no special skills or knowledge taking into account the examples in subsection (2).

31. An exception to the application of that test is contained in subsection (4). Where an insurer knew about, or should have known about a consumer's particular characteristics or circumstances, those are to be taken into account. The Association of British Insurers' Code of Practice,[3] states that insurers should pay the claim in full where:

> The consumer has acted honestly and reasonably in all of the circumstances, including the customer's individual circumstances but only where these were known to the insurer.

---

[3] ABI Code of Practice, 'Managing Claims for Individual and Group Life, Critical Illness and Income Protection Insurance Products' (January 2009).

Subsection (4) reflects this but goes further in adding 'ought to have been aware'. This is not intended to impose onerous duties on inquiry on the insurer but is intended to catch characteristics and circumstances they should have noticed, but failed to do so.

32. Subsection (5) states that acting dishonestly is always a breach of the duty. This is also an exception to the 'objective' standard in subsection (3).

Clause 4: Qualifying misrepresentations: definition and remedies

33. Clause 4 sets out the circumstances in which an insurer will be entitled to a remedy for a misrepresentation. Two conditions must be met.

34. Firstly, under subsection (1) the consumer must have made a misrepresentation in breach of the duty set out in clause 2(2) to take reasonable care not to make a misrepresentation.

35. Secondly, the insurer must establish on the balance of probabilities that, had it known the true facts, it would not have entered into the contract or agreed the variation in exactly the terms agreed. This reflects the current law on inducement as developed following the House of Lords decision in *Pan Atlantic Insurance Co Ltd v Pine Top Insurance Co Ltd.*[4]

36. Under the current law (set out in section 20(2) of the 1906 Act) a misrepresentation only provides the insurer with a remedy if the misrepresentation would influence the judgement of a hypothetical prudent underwriter. This test is not preserved by the Bill. The Bill provides instead that the insurer which is a party to the contract must show that it relied on the misrepresentation, regardless of whether any hypothetical insurer would have done so.

37. Under subsections (2) and (3), if the conditions in subsection (1) are met, the misrepresentation is termed a 'qualifying misrepresentation' and attracts the appropriate remedy set out in Schedule 1.

Clause 5: Qualifying misrepresentations: classification and presumptions

38. Subsection (1) provides for qualifying misrepresentations to be classified under the Act as either (i) deliberate or reckless or (ii) careless.

39. A consumer acts deliberately if they act with knowledge. As established in the case of *Derry v Peek*,[5] a consumer acts recklessly if they act without care and regard for the truth of an answer. This can be distinguished from

---

4 [1995] 1 AC 501.
5 (1889) LR 14 App Cas. 337.

making a statement which one genuinely believes to be true but without sufficient care to check the facts. This would potentially be a careless misrepresentation.

40. In this context 'careless' is being used in a special sense. Subsection (3) makes clear that a qualifying misrepresentation is 'careless' if it is not 'deliberate or reckless'.

41. Under subsection (4), the onus is on the insurer to show that a misrepresentation was deliberate or reckless. There are, however, two presumptions set out in subsection (5). Where the presumptions apply, the burden of proof is reversed.

42. The effect of the presumptions may be illustrated by an example, in which a consumer fails to mention a heart attack in response to a clear and specific question. As most reasonable people would normally know that they had suffered a heart attack, the insurer does not need to prove that the consumer acted deliberately or recklessly. Instead it is up to the consumer to show that he or she did not know about the heart attack, or did not understand the question. Thus the consumer might explain that they had confused a minor heart attack with another condition, or might provide other evidence of lack of understanding.

Clause 6: Warranties and representations

43. This clause abolishes 'basis of contract' clauses. Under the current law, insurers may include a declaration on an insurance proposal form or policy stating that the consumer warrants the accuracy of the answers or that the answers form the basis of the contract. This effectively turns the consumer's representation into a warranty. The insurer is therefore discharged from liability for all claims if a misrepresentation was made, even if the misrepresentation was immaterial and did not induce the insurer to enter the contract.

44. It would remain possible for insurers to include specific warranties in the contract of insurance. To be valid, such a warranty would need to be fair within the meaning of the Unfair Terms in Consumer Contracts Regulations 1999.

Clause 7: Group insurance

45. Subsection (1) provides a definition of group schemes to which this clause applies. It is a wide definition and can include insurance policies such as employment schemes, block building policies taken out by landlords for tenants and building insurance taken out by freeholders for long leaseholders.

46. In order to meet the test set out in subsection (1)(a) the policy entered into by a person ('A') should offer a direct benefit to a third party ('C'). The policy should do more than simply cover A's liability towards C, and must provide some additional cover for C.

47. By subsection (1)(c), the contract must meet the definition of consumer insurance, if C had taken out the cover directly. In other words, C must be an individual who is acting for purposes wholly or mainly unrelated to their trade, business or profession.

48. By subsection (1)(d), C must have provided the insurer, directly or indirectly, with information before the insurer becomes liable for the insurance cover that C benefits from.

49. Where a group member makes a misrepresentation, the scheme under the Bill applies. Subsections (2) and (3) provide that an insurer has a remedy if the individual (C) acted without reasonable care when answering questions posed by the insurer and these representations induced the insurer to provide a particular level of cover for C.

50. When a member of the covered group makes a misrepresentation, subsection (4) stipulates that this only affects the cover of that individual (not the policy as a whole).

51. Subsection (5) provides that nothing in this clause affects duties and remedies in respect of A. Of particular relevance is that the majority of policyholders will be businesses and therefore governed by the law applicable to business insurance. Their duties under the law of business insurance, such as the duty of disclosure, are unaffected by the Bill.

Clause 8: Insurance on the life of another

52. When a consumer takes out insurance on the life of another, the person whose life is being insured ('L') may be required to answer questions posed by the insurer. This is information that an insurer may rely upon, but the duty under clause 2(2) to take reasonable care not to make a misrepresentation would not apply, as L is not a party to the contract. Subsection (2)(a) provides that in consumer insurance contracts taken out on the life of another, the representations made by L will be treated as if they were made by the consumer taking out the insurance. In effect, L owes the insurer a duty to take reasonable care when answering their questions.

53. By subsection (2)(b), when the state of mind of the provider of the information is in question, it is the state of mind of L that is relevant and not that of the individual taking out insurance on L's life.

54. The result of this clause is that an insurer has a remedy against the consumer if either the consumer or L fails to take reasonable care when answering the insurer's questions.

Clause 9: Agents

55. This clause stipulates that the factors contained in Schedule 2 apply when determining whether an 'agent' is acting as the agent for the insurer or for the consumer. The term agent can cover a variety of job titles such as insurance brokers, insurance consultants, intermediaries and others.

56. Under normal agency law, a person is responsible for the actions of their own agent. This rule is specifically preserved in clause 12(5) and has the following consequences.

57. If the agent acts for the insurer, any wrongdoing by the agent is the responsibility of the insurer and the insurer will have to pay any claim accordingly.

58. If the agent is acting for the consumer, the agent's knowledge is considered to be that of the consumer. If an agent acts deliberately or recklessly an insurer may be entitled to avoid a policy even if the consumer themselves had acted honestly and reasonably. If the agent acts carelessly then the insurer has the same proportionate remedies (set out in Schedule 1) that it would have had against a careless consumer.

59. Schedule 2 is only to be applied when determining for whom an agent acts for the purposes of this Bill. It applies only to consumer insurance.

Clause 10: Contracting out

60. Subsection (1) prevents insurers from contracting out of the provisions of the Bill to the detriment of the consumer. A term in a consumer insurance contract or a term in another contract is void to the extent that it would put the consumer in a worse position than provided for in the Bill.

61. Subsection (2) stipulates that this clause only covers matters that are within the scope of the Bill. Therefore this clause has no effect on terms in insurance contracts requiring disclosure after the contract has been agreed.

62. Subsection (3) provides that this clause does not apply to contracts for the settlement of a claim. Without this subsection, it might be possible to argue that a contract settling a claim for less than the claim was worth would be a contract which put the consumer in a worse position than provided for in the Bill.

Clause 11: Consequential provision

63. This clause abolishes certain existing rules in relation to consumer insurance contracts.

64. Sections 18, 19 and 20 of the 1906 Act require the insured and the insured's agent to act with utmost good faith before entering into an insurance contract, by disclosing material information and not making a misrepresentation. The sections apply to consumer insurance in two ways. First, they embody the common law rules which apply to all insurance, including consumer insurance. This is because the 1906 Act has been taken to state the common law position in relation to pre-contract information and disclosure in non-marine insurance. Secondly, they apply directly to marine insurance, including any marine insurance taken out by consumers (for example, to cover pleasure boats).

65. The subsection therefore acts in two ways. Subsection (1) abolishes any common law rules having the same effect of sections 18, 19 or 20 of the 1906 Act on consumer insurance contracts. Subsection (2) disapplies sections 18, 19 and 20 of the 1906 Act specifically in relation to consumer marine insurance.

66. Subsection (3) amends section 152(2) of the Road Traffic Act 1988. The Road Traffic Act provides for a scheme of compulsory motor insurance by which motor insurers generally have an obligation to satisfy judgments obtained by third parties, even if the insured person had breached their insurance contract. There is however an exception in section 152(2) by which an insurer can obtain a declaration that it is entitled to avoid the policy because the insured made a non-disclosure or misrepresentation. The effect of this section is more limited than first appears. Under an agreement between the Motor Insurance Bureau and the government, insurers have undertaken to ensure that the third party is compensated whether the policy is avoided or not. Section 152(2) only has a practical effect where there are two or more possible insurers who might be obliged to pay the third party. For example, if one insurer is able to avoid the contract under this section, the other insurer is obliged to pay the full cost.

67. The amendments to section 152(2) made by this subsection provide that an insurer is only entitled to avoid a consumer insurance policy if they would be able to avoid the policy under the Bill.

68. Subsection (4) amends the equivalent provision for Northern Ireland.

Clause 12: Short title, commencement, application and extent

69. Subsections (2) and (3) provide for the operative provisions of the Bill to be brought into force by order, subject to there being an interval of at least one year after the Bill is passed.

70. Subsection (4) ensures that the Bill does not have a retrospective effect on contracts made before it comes into force. The Bill only applies to contracts made, and to variations (of earlier contracts) agreed, after commencement.

71. Subsection (5) provides that the existing principles of agency law shall continue to apply to consumer insurance contracts. Under existing agency law, a person is responsible for the actions of their own agent. This is discussed in the notes to clause 9.

72. Subsections (6) and (7) specify the territorial extent of the Bill, which is described in paragraph 3 above.

Schedule 1: Insurers' remedies for qualifying misrepresentations

Part 1: Contracts

73. The first part of this Schedule provides the remedies available to insurers when a consumer has made a qualifying misrepresentation before a consumer insurance contract was entered into. This would include a renewal.

Deliberate or reckless misrepresentations

74. Paragraph 2 specifies the remedies available where a consumer has made a deliberate or reckless misrepresentation. The insurer is entitled to avoid the contract and refuse all claims. The insurer may also retain premiums, unless it would be unfair to do so.

Careless misrepresentations – claims

75. Paragraphs 3 to 8 set out the remedies available when a consumer who has made a careless misrepresentation makes a claim. The remedies are based on what the insurer would have done had the consumer complied with their duty to take reasonable care not to make a misrepresentation.

76. By virtue of paragraph 5, if the insurer would not have entered into the contract, the insurer can avoid the contract and refuse to pay all claims. If the insurer chooses to avoid the contract, it must repay to the consumer all premiums paid.

77. Paragraphs 6 to 8 set out the position if the insurer would have entered a contract, but on different terms. If the terms would not relate to the premium, paragraph 6 provides that the insurer can treat the contract as having been entered into on those different terms. If, for example, the insurer would have included an exemption clause or imposed an excess, the claim would be treated as if the contract included that exemption clause or excess.

78. If the insurer would have charged a higher premium, paragraph 7 allows the insurer to reduce the claim proportionately. The formula for calculating the reduction is contained in paragraph 8. It stipulates, for example, that if an insurer only charged £1,000 but should have charged £1,500, the consumer would receive two thirds of the claim.

79. In some cases, both paragraphs 6 and 7 may apply: the consumer would obtain a proportionate settlement of the element of the claim that falls within the adjusted contract terms.

Careless misrepresentations – treatment of contract for the future

80. Paragraph 9 addresses the effect of a careless misrepresentation on the future of the contract.

81. If the insurer would not have entered into the contract at all, then paragraph 5 applies. The insurer may avoid the contract (and must return the premiums). This means that the contract no longer exists, and the insurer may refuse all past and future claims.

82. However, where the insurer would have contracted on different terms or for a higher premium (or both):

a) in non-life insurance, either side is entitled to terminate future cover on reasonable notice;

b) for life insurance, the insurer must continue the policy either on the existing terms or on amended terms.

83. In a non-life insurance contract, where an insurer discovers a careless misrepresentation (either in the context of an existing claim or otherwise), it has a choice: it may notify the consumer that it intends to treat the contract as subsisting on different terms (sub-paragraph (4)(a)); or it may terminate the contract (sub-paragraph (4)(b)). If it decides to terminate the contract, then it must give reasonable notice to the consumer, and refund the amount of the premium that relates to the balance of the contract term (sub-paragraph (7)). If an insurer simply does nothing, it is very likely to be found to have waived its rights, under the English law of waiver or the Scots law of personal bar.

84. If the consumer receives notice that the insurer intends to continue the contract on different terms, the consumer also has a choice: he or she may

agree to continue the contract on amended terms; or he or she may terminate the contract (sub-paragraph (6)). Again, the consumer must give reasonable notice, and is entitled to a refund of the part of the premium which relates to the future.

85. Where the contract is wholly or mainly life insurance, however, a careless misrepresentation does not give the insurer the option to terminate the contract. Instead, the contract will continue on the existing terms or on amended terms (sub-paragraph (5)). If the insurer would have charged more, the insurer may give the consumer the option to pay the additional premium. It is not, however, obliged to do this. It may prefer to continue the existing premium and pay only a proportion of the claim. However, the insurer must notify the consumer of the amended terms in accordance with sub-paragraph (4)(a). The consumer may then choose to continue the contract or to terminate it as described above.

Part 2: Variations

86. Where a qualifying misrepresentation is made before a variation is agreed, it is necessary to ascertain whether that variation can reasonably be treated separately from the rest of the contract. For example, a consumer insures a house and at a later date, extends the insurance to include a lock-up garage. It would be necessary to ascertain whether the lock-up garage could be treated separately from the rest of the contract.

87. If the variation can be treated separately, then the remedies contained in Part 1 of Schedule 1 apply only to the variation.

88. If, however, the variation cannot be treated separately, then the remedies in Part 1 of Schedule 1 are available in relation to the whole of the contract. In effect it will be treated as if the misrepresentation had been in relation to the whole contract.

Part 3: Modifications for group insurance

89. Under clause 7(4), where a member of a group scheme breaches the duty to take reasonable care not to misrepresent, this has consequences only for the cover of that individual, and not for the policy as a whole.

90. Part 3 therefore provides modifications to the remedies available to the insurer, so that where a group member has made a qualifying misrepresentation, the remedies only affect the group member's cover, and not the rest of the contract.

91. Paragraph 16(a) is included because, in group insurance schemes, the premiums can be paid by either the policyholder or the group members who are receiving the benefit of the cover. When deciding whether it would be

unfair to retain premiums (under paragraph 2(b) of the Schedule) an insurer should consider whether it would be fair on the person who paid the premiums, whether that be the policy holder or the group member.

92. Paragraph 16(b) stipulates that the right to terminate cover (under paragraph 9) belongs to the policyholder rather than the group member.

Part 4: Supplementary

93. Section 84 of the 1906 Act stipulates when an insurer has a duty to return premiums. Paragraph 17 of the Schedule provides that where the insurance policy is for marine insurance which is also consumer insurance, section 84 should be read in conjunction with Schedule 1. This is particularly relevant to section 84(3)(a), which states that where an insurer avoids an insurance contract from the outset, the premium is returnable unless there has been fraud or illegality. This must be read subject to paragraph 2 of Schedule 1 of this Bill, which allows the insurer to retain premiums in some cases for deliberate or reckless misrepresentations.

Schedule 2: Rules for determining status of agents

94. Schedule 2 provides rules to determine for whom an agent is acting where an intermediary assists a consumer in providing an insurance contract.

95. Under paragraph 2, the intermediary is always considered to act for the insurer in three cases:

a) Where the intermediary acts as an appointed representative under section 39 of the Financial Services and Markets Act 2000. Section 39(3) states that:

> 'The principal of an appointed representative is responsible, to the same extent as if he had expressly permitted it, for anything done or omitted by the representative in carrying on the business for which he has accepted responsibility.'

At present, the section only applies to regulatory matters under the 2000 Act, though it is often taken to apply more widely. Paragraph 2(a) extends the same principle to acts done by the intermediary in relation to collecting and transmitting pre-contract information.

b) Where the intermediary has been given express authority to collect information as the insurer's agent.

c) Where the intermediary has express authority to bind the insurer to the contract.

96. Paragraph 2 focuses on the intermediary's capacity at the time of the action in question. Thus paragraph 2(b) only determines the status of the

agent 'when the agent collects information from the consumer'. Similarly, paragraph 2(c) only applies 'when the agent enters into the contract'. Thus an intermediary may act for the consumer in advising on the choice of insurer, and for the insurer in binding the insurer to cover.

97. If none of the circumstances listed in paragraph 2 are met, paragraph 3(1) sets out a rebuttable presumption that the agent is acting for the consumer. The presumption can be rebutted if considering all the circumstances it is clear that the agent is acting for the insurer. Paragraph 3(3) contains some factors which help confirm the presumption that the agent is acting for the consumer. Paragraph 3(4) contains factors which tend to show that the agent is acting for the insurer. Even if there are some factors indicating a close relationship between the insurer and insured, these may be outweighed by specific factors indicating that the intermediary acts for the consumer.

98. Neither of the lists of factors in paragraph 3(3) or 3(4) is exhaustive, individual factors may not always be significant and any other relevant factors and sources should be considered such as those contained in industry guidance and the Financial Services Authority's Handbook.

99. Paragraph 4 contains a power, subject to affirmative resolution, which will enable the Treasury to add, omit or alter any factor. The Treasury may only exercise this power if either or both of the lists have become outdated, for example owing to developments in the market.

Financial effects and public service manpower

100. The implementation of the Bill will require some administrative activity by the Treasury, but the costs are expected to be insignificant.

101. The Bill is not expected to have any significant effect on the workload of the courts, but it may reduce some of the work of the Financial Ombusdman Service (which is a private body).

102. The Bill will not affect public service manpower.

Regulatory impact assessment

103. The Bill is a Law Commission Bill. It seeks to clarify the law in relation to pre-contractual disclosure in relation to consumer insurance contracts. The Treasury has carried out an impact assessment. This is available from the Insurance and Risk Team, HM Treasury, 3/19, 1 Horse Guards Road, SW1A 2HQ.

104. The Bill is essentially a codification of existing best practice. The behaviour of most insurers is not expected to change significantly as a result. The aim is to provide for clear, coherent and understandable law so that

insurers and consumers can fully understand their rights and obligations. It is expected that compliance will be simplified and consumers will benefit from clearer protection. This is expected to result in a net financial benefit to the insurance industry with the one off transitional training and documentation costs (c £1.25m) and ongoing annual increased legal costs (c £0.06m) offset by significantly fewer complaints to the Financial Ombudsman Service saving £0.7 per year.

European Convention on Human Rights

105. Section 19 of the Human Rights Act 1998 requires the Minister in charge of a Bill in either House to make a statement about the compatibility of the Bill with the Convention rights (as defined in section 1 of that Act).

106. The Financial Secretary to the Treasury has made the following statement under section 19(1)(a) of the Human Rights Act 1998:

> 'In my view the provisions of the Consumer Insurance (Disclosure and Representations) Bill are compatible with the Convention rights.'

107. The Bill modifies the existing strict duty of disclosure broadly in accordance with best practice and provides a framework for finding the appropriate remedy when there has been a qualifying misrepresentation. It only applies in relation to contracts made after the Bill comes into force and to variations (of earlier contracts) that are agreed after that time.

108. It is possible that the result of clauses 2, 3 and 11 (replacing a consumer's duty to volunteer material information with a duty to take reasonable care not to make a misrepresentation) will result in consumers being asked more, and more specific, questions about their circumstances. Under clause 8 the same result may apply in relation to an individual whose life is insured but who is not a party to the insurance contract as that clause provides for statements made by that individual to be treated as having been made by the party to the contract.To the extent that Article 8 (right to respect for private life) is engaged it is considered that the provisions are justified by the benefits to consumers of removing the current strict disclosure requirements (which can lead to hardship if misunderstood) and of providing clear rules imposing reasonable disclosure requirements.

109. Clause 4 and Schedule 1 specify rules relating to the remedies that an insurer may have when the consumer has made a misrepresentation. In some cases insurers will have a lesser remedy for a misrepresentation than exists in theory under the present law. If Article 1 of the First Protocol (protection of property) is engaged by these provisions they are thought to be justified as conditions provided for by law which are in the public or general interest. It is thought necessary, and in the interests of both consumers and insurers, to provide for a balanced, fair and proportionate sequence of remedies for

misrepresentation. Any adverse effect on insurers by altering the balance between insurers and consumers in relation to remedies for misrepresentation is thought to be fully justified to prevent hardship for consumers.

110. The provisions of the Bill broadly match the best practice expected of insurers and consumers by the Financial Ombudsman Service before the Bill comes into force, so it may be that any changes in the practice of insurers of the kind mentioned in paragraph 108 and any adverse effects on property rights mentioned in paragraph 109 will be extremely modest in practice.

Commencement dates

111. Under clause 12, clauses 1 and 12 will come into force on the day the Act is passed. However the remainder of the Bill will not come into force until an Order is made by the Treasury appointing the day on which it will come into force. This appointed day cannot be within the period of one year beginning with the day on which the Act is passed.

Index

[all references are to paragraph number]